Clojure Programming Cookbook

Handle every problem you come across in the world of Clojure
programming with this expert collection of recipes

Makoto Hashimoto
Nicolas Modrzyk

BIRMINGHAM - MUMBAI

Clojure Programming Cookbook

First published: October 2016

Production reference: 1211016

Published by Packt Publishing Ltd.
Livery Place
35 Livery Street
Birmingham
B3 2PB, UK.

ISBN 978-1-78588-503-7

www.packtpub.com

Credits

Authors

Makoto Hashimoto

Nicolas Modrzyk

Reviewers

Eduard Bondarenko

Dmitri Sotnikov

Commissioning Editor

Kartikey Pandey

Acquisition Editor

Kirk D'costa

Content Development Editor

Sachin Karnani

Technical Editor

Pranav Kukreti

Copy Editors

Safis Editing

Sameen Siddiqui

Project Coordinator

Ritika Manoj

Proofreader

Safis Editing

Indexer

Tejal Daruwale Soni

Graphics

Abhinash Sahu

Production Coordinator

Aparna Bhagat

About the Authors

Makoto Hashimoto is a technical enthusiast in Japan. He has been involved in a lot of projects as an IT architect and led them successfully with his technical leadership. Makoto loves programming, especially with functional programming languages. Thus, he became an enthusiast of Clojure since his first encounter with this language. Recently, he is often involved in projects of the big data domain, and he constantly thinks up new ways to use Clojure for this domain. He loves spending time with his family during weekends and apart from that he loves cooking, classical music, arts and sports.

Makoto has also written two books in Japanese. You can find them at `http://amzn.to/2e0jySv` and `http://amzn.to/2eg3gq8`.

> *To my coauthor, Nicolas, working with you has been a great honor for me. Many thanks for your valuable advices and encouragements.To my family, I would like to thank my family and friends for their constant encouragements and support. Without you, there is no way that I would have been able to complete this work.*

Nicolas Modrzyk has many years of experience in the field of IT and has spent many years in Asia. He loves making ideas a reality and the fact that this reality brings people from all around the planet together. He's been involved in many IT projects, helping customers reach their goal and in general trying to make IT easier to reach for everyone.

Nicolas fell into the Clojure soup 5 years ago; it helped him become more focused, and stop wasting time on the things that are not worth it. Clojure is more than just a fantastic programming language; it is a life full of adventure. Hopefully, this book takes you on the road to that adventure.

Nicolas has also written a book, *Oishii Clojure* (`http://gihyo.jp/book/2013/978-4-7741-5991-1`), in Japanese, with plenty of short Clojure recipes to enjoy the Clojure language and to make you want to try new things.

> *Thank you, Makoto, for reaching out and making this book a fantastic adventure! Also, I'm looking forward to our next one! To my daughters, Mei and Manon, I think about you always, even during those late nights spent working on the book. To my loving family and awesome friends, for their continuous support, even in those times when I only talk about Clojure.*

About the Reviewer

Eduard Bondarenko is a long-time Ruby and Clojure programmer. He got into Android development recently. He prefers concise and expressive code with some comments, and has tried many programming languages, such as Python, Erlang, Nodejs, Elm, Scala, and others. Eduard has reviewed a couple of Clojure books, and he liked all of them for their interesting and broad topics. Besides programming, he likes to spend time with his family, play soccer, and travel.

I want to thank my family for supporting my desire to work on the book, and the authors for the demonstration of different and extraordinary applications of Clojure.

www.PacktPub.com

eBooks, discount offers, and more

Did you know that Packt offers eBook versions of every book published, with PDF and ePub files available? You can upgrade to the eBook version at www.PacktPub.com and as a print book customer, you are entitled to a discount on the eBook copy. Get in touch with us at customercare@packtpub.com for more details.

At www.PacktPub.com, you can also read a collection of free technical articles, sign up for a range of free newsletters and receive exclusive discounts and offers on Packt books and eBooks.

https://www.packtpub.com/mapt

Get the most in-demand software skills with Mapt. Mapt gives you full access to all Packt books and video courses, as well as industry-leading tools to help you plan your personal development and advance your career.

Why subscribe?

- Fully searchable across every book published by Packt
- Copy and paste, print, and bookmark content
- On demand and accessible via a web browser

About the Reviewer

Eduard Bondarenko is a long-time Ruby and Clojure programmer. He got into Android development recently. He prefers concise and expressive code with some comments, and has tried many programming languages, such as Python, Erlang, Nodejs, Elm, Scala, and others. Eduard has reviewed a couple of Clojure books, and he liked all of them for their interesting and broad topics. Besides programming, he likes to spend time with his family, play soccer, and travel.

I want to thank my family for supporting my desire to work on the book, and the authors for the demonstration of different and extraordinary applications of Clojure.

www.PacktPub.com

eBooks, discount offers, and more

Did you know that Packt offers eBook versions of every book published, with PDF and ePub files available? You can upgrade to the eBook version at www.PacktPub.com and as a print book customer, you are entitled to a discount on the eBook copy. Get in touch with us at customercare@packtpub.com for more details.

At www.PacktPub.com, you can also read a collection of free technical articles, sign up for a range of free newsletters and receive exclusive discounts and offers on Packt books and eBooks.

https://www.packtpub.com/mapt

Get the most in-demand software skills with Mapt. Mapt gives you full access to all Packt books and video courses, as well as industry-leading tools to help you plan your personal development and advance your career.

Why subscribe?

- Fully searchable across every book published by Packt
- Copy and paste, print, and bookmark content
- On demand and accessible via a web browser

Table of Contents

Preface

This is a book designed to make you want to try things. It will take you back to the days when you had tons of energy and were ready to just start and make things happen.

Clojure is a one of a kind programming language, where the core is very important, and you can just write efficient code, based on strong building blocks.

With the upcoming release of Clojure 1.9, this language is ahead of other languages due to its simplicity and conciseness. So whether you are embarking on a weekend programming project with Raspberry Pi or getting ready to challenge the world with your new start-up, the tons of good recipes provided in this book are for you.

This book can mostly be read in any order, but make sure that you go through the first few recipes to review the basics of Clojure.

Make things happen and enjoy every piece of it.

What this book covers

Chapter 1, *Live Programming with Clojure*, helps you review how the Clojure basics work with different data types, how the code control flows, and also how to integrate third-party libraries. You probably know this already, but you simply cannot start a good cookbook without a strong base.

Chapter 2, *Interacting with Collections*, covers selecting, filtering, transforming, merging, joining, and how to become lazy. Laziness is one of the greatest Clojure feature, and we want to make sure that you will always be lazy enough.

Chapter 3, *Clojure Next*, introduces you to macros, advanced macros, transducers (what transducers are, anyway), and logic programming. It covers preprocessing and postprocessing of Clojure data as code features.

Chapter 4, *File Access and the Network*, covers StreamingQueues and real-time networking, which gives you the power to think about distributed systems and how to connect your IoT devices. It also covers files and how to manipulate files to help you with lightweight processing for interconnections.

Chapter 5, *Working with Other Languages*, introduces you to the basic Clojure tooling that allows you to easily integrate code written in other languages, such as Java, Scala, and .NET, all the way to Clojure on the JavaScript runtime, ClojureScript.

Chapter 6, *Concurrency and Parallelism*, helps you learn multiple ways of splitting jobs among Clojure processes, interacting with Scala-like actors, and to also sharing states between different instances. Of course, this chapter covers the simplest way of writing a parallel code in Clojure, core.async.

Chapter 7, *Advanced Tips*, helps you if you want to know how to perform not only pair programming but also shared real-time pair programming. You will also see how to hack the Clojure source code yourself.

Chapter 8, *Web Applications*, takes you through web applications, web services, or API endpoints or whatever you call them. You also learn how to use nice-looking widgets with Vaadin, how to write rest-like APIs with Liberator, and use Immutant, a set of server-side services at the finger of your Clojure code.

Chapter 9, *Testing*, not only helps you with validating your code but also with using random pattern testing for the cases you had not thought about. This chapter also introduces behavior-driven development in Clojure with some OpenCV validation, and finally, explains how to benchmark the speed of your code.

Chapter 10, *Deployment and DevOps*, covers dockerizing your Clojure code, making it run locally as it would in the Cloud, putting real-time monitoring in place for your critical services, and finally, your favorite Amazon tricks are also covered here.

What you need for this book

You need a bit of time, a computer, and a text editor. That's all this book requires. Of course, previous functional programming experience is a big plus, but having motivation and energy is pretty much all you need.

Who this book is for

This book is for people who want to make things happen. Follow along the lines of the zillions of code samples included in this book, and go ahead from there. Each example should make you want to try things around, and bring up some new ideas. This book should start by being just a cookbook, but by the end, will become your cookbook.

Sections

In this book, you will find several headings that appear frequently (Getting ready, How to do it, How it works, There's more, and See also).

To give clear instructions on how to complete a recipe, we use these sections as follows:

Getting ready

This section tells you what to expect in the recipe, and describes how to set up any software or any preliminary settings required for the recipe.

How to do it...

This section contains the steps required to follow the recipe.

How it works...

This section usually consists of a detailed explanation of what happened in the previous section.

There's more...

This section consists of additional information about the recipe in order to make the reader more knowledgeable about the recipe.

See also

This section provides helpful links to other useful information for the recipe.

Conventions

In this book, you will find a number of text styles that distinguish between different kinds of information. Here are some examples of these styles and an explanation of their meaning.

Code words in text, database table names, folder names, filenames, file extensions, pathnames, dummy URLs, user input, and Twitter handles are shown as follows: "However, declaring libraries in `project.clj` is much simpler than doing it in the `pom.xml` file of Maven."

A block of code is set as follows:

```
String str = "Hello ".concat("world !");
```

Any command-line input or output is written as follows:

```
$ mv lein ~/bin
```

New terms and **important words** are shown in bold. Words that you see on the screen, for example, in menus or dialog boxes, appear in the text like this: "Go to the **Data Buckets** tab and click on the **Create New Data Bucket** option."

 Warnings or important notes appear in a box like this.

 Tips and tricks appear like this.

Reader feedback

Feedback from our readers is always welcome. Let us know what you think about this book-what you liked or disliked. Reader feedback is important for us as it helps us develop titles that you will really get the most out of.

To send us general feedback, simply e-mail feedback@packtpub.com, and mention the book's title in the subject of your message.

If there is a topic that you have expertise in and you are interested in either writing or contributing to a book, see our author guide at www.packtpub.com/authors.

Customer support

Now that you are the proud owner of a Packt book, we have a number of things to help you to get the most from your purchase.

Downloading the example code

You can download the example code files for this book from your account at `http://www.packtpub.com`. If you purchased this book elsewhere, you can visit `http://www.packtpub.com/support` and register to have the files e-mailed directly to you.

You can download the code files by following these steps:

1. Log in or register to our website using your e-mail address and password.
2. Hover the mouse pointer on the **SUPPORT** tab at the top.
3. Click on **Code Downloads & Errata**.
4. Enter the name of the book in the **Search** box.
5. Select the book for which you're looking to download the code files.
6. Choose from the drop-down menu where you purchased this book from.
7. Click on **Code Download**.

You can also download the code files by clicking on the **Code Files** button on the book's webpage at the Packt Publishing website. This page can be accessed by entering the book's name in the **Search** box. Please note that you need to be logged in to your Packt account.

Once the file is downloaded, please make sure that you unzip or extract the folder using the latest version of:

- WinRAR / 7-Zip for Windows
- Zipeg / iZip / UnRarX for Mac
- 7-Zip / PeaZip for Linux

The code bundle for the book is also hosted on GitHub at `https://github.com/PacktPublishing/Clojure-Programming-Cookbook`. We also have other code bundles from our rich catalog of books and videos available at `https://github.com/PacktPublishing/`. Check them out!

Downloading the color images of this book

We also provide you with a PDF file that has color images of the screenshots/diagrams used in this book. The color images will help you better understand the changes in the output. You can download this file from `https://www.packtpub.com/sites/default/files/downloads/ClojureProgrammingCookbook_ColorImages.pdf`.

Errata

Although we have taken every care to ensure the accuracy of our content, mistakes do happen. If you find a mistake in one of our books-maybe a mistake in the text or the code-we would be grateful if you could report this to us. By doing so, you can save other readers from frustration and help us improve subsequent versions of this book. If you find any errata, please report them by visiting `http://www.packtpub.com/submit-errata`, selecting your book, clicking on the **Errata Submission Form** link, and entering the details of your errata. Once your errata are verified, your submission will be accepted and the errata will be uploaded to our website or added to any list of existing errata under the Errata section of that title.

To view the previously submitted errata, go to `https://www.packtpub.com/books/content/support` and enter the name of the book in the search field. The required information will appear under the **Errata** section.

Piracy

Piracy of copyrighted material on the Internet is an ongoing problem across all media. At Packt, we take the protection of our copyright and licenses very seriously. If you come across any illegal copies of our works in any form on the Internet, please provide us with the location address or website name immediately so that we can pursue a remedy.

Please contact us at `copyright@packtpub.com` with a link to the suspected pirated material.

We appreciate your help in protecting our authors and our ability to bring you valuable content.

Questions

If you have a problem with any aspect of this book, you can contact us at `questions@packtpub.com`, and we will do our best to address the problem.

Live Programming with Clojure

1

In this chapter, we will cover the following topics:

- REPL up!
- Working with primitive data types
- Using bindings of vars, conditions, loops, and error handling
- Using and defining functions
- Using third-party libraries
- Using namespaces

Introduction

Clojure is a blend of Lisp and Java. Clojure allows you to solve what you want quickly and keeps code simple. Once you learn Clojure, it's great fun to use it! Clojure provides the following fantastic features:

- Clojure is a dialect of Lisp and supports the functional programing style
- It runs on **Java Virtual Machine** (**JVM**) and can use Java's assets seamlessly
- It also supports immutability and concurrent programming

In this chapter, we will review how to set up a Clojure REPL environment and Clojures' basic structure, including primitive data types, programming flow controls, and functions. Then we will go over how to use third-party libraries and namespaces.

Let's take you to Clojure's fantastic world; we'll begin with *REPL up!*

REPL up!

REPL is the interpreter of Clojure, and it is an acronym of **Read Evaluate Print Loop**. Unlike other interpreter languages, such as Python or Ruby, Clojure REPL automatically compiles into Java's byte code after the reading expression. Then, REPL evaluates the expression and returns the result of the expression. This dynamic compilation feature of REPL makes Clojure code execution as fast as executing pre-compiled code.

Getting ready

Before you set up your Clojure environment, the **Java Development Kit (JDK)** is necessary. The JDK version should be 1.6 or later. Throughout the book, we will use JDK 1.8 to develop and test the code.

This is how the command-line result will look, once you type `java -version`:

```
$ java -version
java version "1.8.0 60"
Java(TM) SE Runtime Environment (build 1.8.0_60-b27)
Java HotSpot(TM) 64-Bit Server VM (build 25.60-b23, mixed mode)
$
```

How to do it...

Leiningen is a standard build tool for Clojure. It simplifies the Clojure development, including setting up your project, compiling and testing code, and creating libraries for deployment.

It's easy to set up a Clojure environment using Leiningen. There are only a few steps before you can enjoy Clojure in REPL!

Here are the steps we need to perform to run Clojure REPL:

1. Download and set up Leiningen from `http://leiningen.org/`.
2. Download the `lein` script (or on Windows, `lein.bat`).

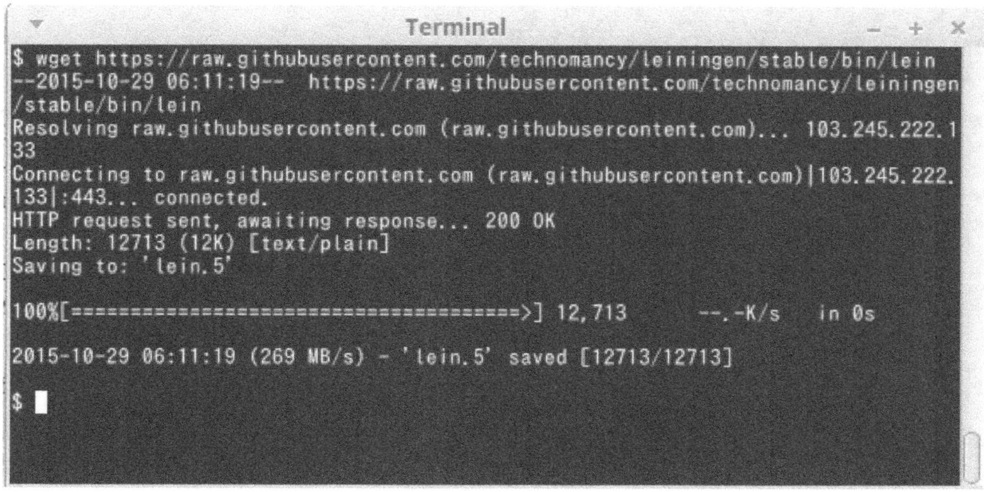

3. Place it on your `$PATH` where your shell can find it (for example, `~/bin`):

   `$ mv lein ~/bin`

4. Set it to be executable:

   `$ chmod a+x ~/bin/lein`

5. Run `lein`, and it will download the self-install package:

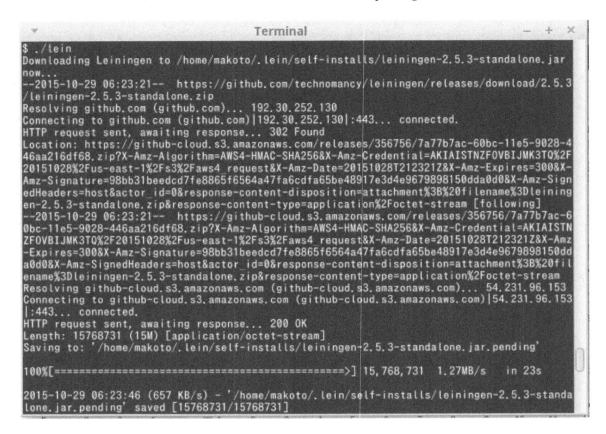

6. Create a new project and go there. Using Leiningen, you can create a project from a project template. This example creates a project called `living-clojure`:

```
$ lein new living-clojure
```

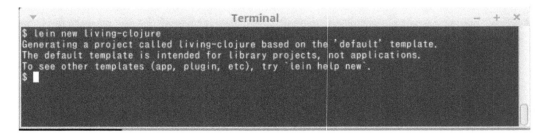

7. Run REPL and put Clojure code into it:

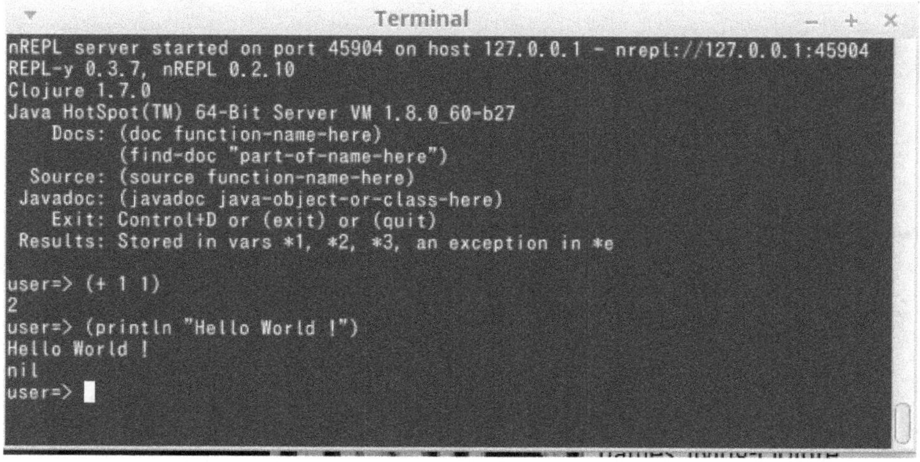

How it works...

Here is a very simple code to demonstrate how REPL works. This code simply loops forever with `read`, `eval`, and `println` functions:

```
user=> (defn simple-repl []
  #_=>    (try
  #_=>      (while true
  #_=>        (println (eval (read)))
  #_=>      )
  #_=>      (catch Exception e (println "exited.."))
  #_=>    )
  #_=>  )
#'user/simple-repl
user=> (simple-repl)
(+ 1 1)
2
(defn hello [s] (println "Hello world " s))
#'user/hello
(hello "Makoto")
Hello world  Makoto
nil
exited..
nil
user=>
```

You can exit `simple-repl` by entering ^D (*Ctrl + D*).

There's more...

Leiningen is a very powerful tool for Clojure developers. The lein new `living-clojure` command generates the following directory structure:

```
$ tree
|-- CHANGELOG.md
|-- LICENSE
|-- README.md
|-- dev-resources
|-- doc
|   `-- intro.md
|-- project.clj
|-- resources
|-- src
|   `-- living_clojure
|       `-- core.clj
|-- target
|   |-- classes
|   |   `-- META-INF
|   |       `-- maven
|   |           `-- living-clojure
|   |               `-- living-clojure
|   |                   `-- pom.properties
|   `-- stale
|       `-- extract-native.dependencies
`-- test
    `-- living_clojure
        `-- core_test.clj

14 directories, 9 files
$
```

Let's pick up `project.clj`, which defines the project:

```
(defproject living-clojure "0.1.0-SNAPSHOT"
  :description "FIXME: write description"
  :url "http://example.com/FIXME"
  :license {:name "Eclipse Public License"
            :url "http://www.eclipse.org/legal/epl-v10.html"}
  :dependencies [[org.clojure/clojure "1.8.0"]])
```

In `project.clj`, the `:dependencies` section declares the libraries used by your project.

Leiningen internally uses Maven to solve the dependencies of libraries. However, declaring libraries in project.clj is much simpler than doing it in the pom.xml file of Maven.

To use other libraries for your project, add them to the dependency section. We will review how to do this in a later recipe. In the preceding project.clj file, the Clojure library named org.clojure/clojure is declared and automatically downloads in the maven directory. This is the reason why you don't need to download and set up the Clojure library explicitly.

Without Leiningen, you have to do it in a more native way. Here are the steps:

1. Download clojure-1.8.0.jar.
2. Download clojure-1.8.0.jar using wget:

```
$ wget http://repo1.maven.org/maven2/org/clojure/clojure/1.8.0/
clojure-1.8.0.jar
```

```
Terminal                                                          - + x
$ wget http://repo1.maven.org/maven2/org/clojure/clojure/1.8.0/clojure-1.8.0.jar
--2016-10-16 17:01:53--  http://repo1.maven.org/maven2/org/clojure/clojure/1.8.0/clojure-1.8.0.jar
repo1.maven.org (repo1.maven.org) をDNSに問いあわせています... 151.101.24.209
repo1.maven.org (repo1.maven.org)|151.101.24.209|:80 に接続しています... 接続しました。
HTTP による接続要求を送信しました、応答を待っています... 200 OK
長さ: 3622815 (3.5M) [application/java-archive]
`clojure-1.8.0.jar' に保存中

100%[================================================================>] 3,622,815    287KB/s    時間 17s

2016-10-16 17:02:11 (206 KB/s) - `clojure-1.8.0.jar' へ保存完了 [3622815/3622815]

$
```

3. Run Clojure and test the Clojure code:

```
$ java -jar clojure-1.8.0.jar
Clojure 1.8.0
user=> (+ 1 1)
2
```

REPL supports the command-line editing feature, like Linux bash shell does, but the preceding way does not. Another difference is that REPL solves library dependency problems in `project.clj`, but using the native way, you can solve them by yourself.

See also

Please see related web sites as follows:

- TryClojure is a browser-based Clojure tool that provides a REPL environment. You don't need to set up your own environment: `http://www.tryclj.com/`
- The REPL and main entry points explain more details about REPL: `http://cloju re.org/repl_and_main`
- Please see the Leiningen web page: `http://leiningen.org/`
- If you are an emacian, use CIDER and Clojure-mode. You might be very comfortable with CIDER: `http://clojure-doc.org/articles/tutorials/emac s.html`
- If you are a `vi` user, try the fireplace plugin: `https://github.com/tpope/vim-fi replace`
- If you love IntelliJ/Idea, try to use cursive: `https://cursiveclojure.com/`
- If you are a traditional Eclipse user, use Counterclockwise: `http://doc.ccw-ide .org/documentation.html`
- Light table is very cool. It's worth trying: `http://lighttable.com/`

Working with primitive data types

In this recipe, we will review primitive data types that Clojure supports and a few functions that manipulate these types. Here, we will review the following:

- Using numbers
- Using strings and characters
- Using booleans and nil
- Using keywords and symbols

Getting ready

You only need REPL, as described in the previous recipe, and no additional libraries. Start REPL so that you can review the sample code of primitive types immediately in this recipe.

How to do it...

Let's start with numbers in Clojure data types.

Using numbers

The + function returns the sum of numbers. You can specify any number of numbers as arguments:

```
(+ 1 2)
;;=> 3
(+ 1 2 3)
;;=> 6
(+ 1.2 3.5)
;;=> 4.7
```

The − function subtracts the numbers. If a single argument is supplied, it returns the negation of the numbers:

```
(− 3 2)
;;=> 1
(− 1 2 3)
;;=> −4
(− 1)
;;=> −1
```

The * function returns the product of numbers:

```
(* 5 2)
;;=> 10
(* 1 2 3 4 5)
;;=> 120
```

The / function returns the numerator divided by all of the denominators. It is surprising for beginners of Clojure that if the numerator is not indivisible by the denominators, it returns a simple fraction. You can check the name of the class by the class function.

In the following example, `10` divided by `3` returns `10/3` and not `3.3333333…`

```
(/ 10 5)
;;=> 2
(/ 10 3)
;;=> 10/3
```

To obtain numerical figures after a decimal point, cast the result by a `float` or `double` function:

```
(float (/ 10 3))
;;=> 3.3333333
(double (/ 10 3))
;;=> 3.333333333333333
```

The `quot` function returns the quotient of dividing the numerator by the denominator, and the decimal point is suppressed. `rem` returns the remainder of dividing the numerator by the denominator:

```
(quot 10 3)
;;=> 3
(rem 10 3)
;;=> 1
```

Clojure supports big numbers, and they are Java's `BigDecimal`. The `bigdec` function casts any number to `BigDecimal`. The suffix `M` denotes `BigDecimal`. Though it can express very large numbers, it cannot express repeating decimals and causes an error:

```
(bigdec (/ 10 2))
;;=> 5M
(bigdec (/ 10 3))
;; ArithmeticException Non-terminating decimal expansion; no exact
representable decimal result.  ;; java.math.BigDecimal.divide
(BigDecimal.java:1690)
```

Clojure also provides large integers, `clojure.lang.BigInt`. It is equivalent to Java's `java.math.BigInteger`:

```
(= (bigint 10) 10N)
;;=> true
```

Using strings and characters

Clojure strings are Java's String(`java.lang.String`) enclosed by double quotes (" "):

```
"Hello world ! "
;;=> "Hello world ! "
```

Clojure has good interoperability with Java, and it's easy to call Java's member methods from Clojure. In the following example, the code calls the `concat` method in Java's String class:

```
(.concat "Hello " "world !")
;;=> "Hello world !"
```

The following syntax is how to call Java's member methods from Clojure:

```
(.method-name object arg1 arg2 ...)
```

The first argument is a dot (`.`) prefix followed by the method name, then the object and its arguments.

The equivalent Java code is as follows:

```
String str = "Hello ".concat("world !");
```

The `str` function is similar to the `concat` method, but it can take an arbitrary number of arguments:

```
(str "Hello " "world !" " Clojure")
;;=> "Hello world ! Clojure"
```

To examine the length of the string, use the `length` method or `count` function:

```
(.length "Hello world !")
;;=> 13
```

`clojure.string` is a built-in Clojure library to manipulate strings. Here, we show some functions in `clojure.string`:

```
(clojure.string/blank? "    ")
;;=> true
(clojure.string/trim "  Hello ")
;;=> "Hello"
(clojure.string/upper-case "clojure")
;;=> "CLOJURE"
(clojure.string/capitalize "clojure")
;;=> "Clojure"
(clojure.string/lower-case "REPL")
```

```
;;=> "repl"
```

Let's go to Clojure character type. Characters in Clojure are `java.lang.Character` and are preceded by a backslash (\):

```
\a
;;=> \a
```

The `int` function gets the integer value of a character. Meanwhile, `char` gets an integer value from a character:

```
(int \a)
;;=> 97
(char 97)
;;=> \a
```

The `seq` function returns a sequence of characters from a string, and `str` makes a string from characters:

```
(seq "Hello world!")
;;=> (\H \e \l \l \o \space \w \o \r \l \d \!)
(str \C \l \o \j \u \r \e)
;;=> "Clojure"
```

Using booleans and nil

Clojure's booleans are `java.lang.Boolean`, and their values are `true` and `false`:

```
true
;;=> true
false
;;=> false
(= 1 1)
;;=> true
(= 1 2)
;;=> false
(= "Hello" "Hello")
;;=> true
(= "Hello" "hello")
;;=> false
```

The `not` function returns `true` if an expression is logically false. It returns `false` otherwise:

```
(not true)
;;=> false
(not false)
;;=> true
```

```
(not= 1 2)
;;=> true
(not true)
;;=> false
```

The `true?` function returns `true` if the expression is true; otherwise, it returns `false`. The `false?` function returns `false` if the expression is true; otherwise, it returns `true`:

```
(true? (= 1 1))
;;=> true
(false? (= 1 1))
;;=> false
```

The `nil` function means nothing, or the absence of a value. The `nil` function in Clojure is almost equivalent to the `null` function in Java. `nil` is logically false in Clojure conditionals. `nil` is often used as a return value to indicate false:

```
(if nil true false)
;;=> false
```

`nil` is the return value used to indicate an empty sequence:

```
(seq [])
;;=> nil
```

`nil` is returned by default when a map collection looks up and can't find a given key:

```
(get {:a 1 :b 2} :c)
;;=> nil
```

Using symbols and keywords

The function `def` binds global symbols to their values. The next example shows the `def` binding the `pi` symbol to a value (`3.14159265359`):

```
(def pi 3.14159265359)
;;=> #'user/pi
pi
;;=> 3.14159265359
pi-not-bind
;;=> CompilerException java.lang.RuntimeException: Unable to resolve
symbol:
;;   pi-not-bind in this context, compiling:(/tmp/form-
init1426260352520034213.clj:1:7266)
```

Keywords are similar to symbols, but keywords evaluate to themselves:

```
:key1
;;=> :key1
```

Keywords are used to identify things, so they are often used in Clojure's map:

```
(def person {:name "John McCarthy" :country "USA"})
;;=>#'living-clojure.core/person
```

How it works...

Clojure primitive data types are mostly Java classes, but some data types are Clojure's own classes.

For numbers, Clojure's integers are `java.lang.Long` and floating point numbers are `java.lang.Double`. `bigInt` and ratios are `clojure.lang.BigInt` and `clojure.lang.Ratio` respectively:

```
(class 1)
;;=> java.lang.Long
(class 1.0)
;;=> java.lang.Double
(class (float 1.0))
;;=> java.lang.Float
(class 5.5M)
;;=> java.math.BigDecimal
(class 1N)
;;=> clojure.lang.BigInt
(class (/ 10 3))
;;=> clojure.lang.Ratio
```

Clojure's strings and characters are `java.lang.String` and `java.lang.Character` respectively:

```
(class "Hello world ! ")
;;=> java.lang.String
(class \a)
;;=> java.lang.Character
(class true)
```

Clojure's booleans are `java.lang.Boolean`:

```
(class true)
;;=> java.lang.Boolean
(class false)
```

```
;;=> java.lang.Boolean
```

Clojure's keywords and symbols are Clojure's own classes:

```
(class :key)
;;=> clojure.lang.Keyword
(class (quote a))
;;=> clojure.lang.Symbol
(class nil)
;;=> nil
```

There's more...

Clojure supports hexadecimal and octal notations:

```
0xff
;;=> 255
0400
;;=> 256
```

Clojure also supports flexible numeral bases. You can specify in any base with a radix from 2 to 36:

```
2r11111
;;=> 31
16rff
;;=> 255
8r11000
;;=> 4608
7r111
;;=>57
```

There are some specially named character literals, as follows:

- \space
- \tab
- \newline
- \return
- \formfeed
- \backspace

Unicode characters are represented by \uNNNN in Clojure, like in Java:

```
\u0031\u0032\u0061\u0062
;;=> \1
;;=> \2
;;=> \a
;;=> \b
```

Functions in Clojure are also symbols and bind to their functional definitions. The next example shows the value of +:

```
+
;;=> #object[clojure.core$_PLUS_ 0x3c2ace8a "clojure.core$_PLUS_@3c2ace8a"]
```

To evaluate symbol and return itself, use quote:

```
(quote pi-not-bind)
;;=> pi-not-bind
```

To use the math library in Clojure, try clojure.math.mumeric-tower. Here are the steps:

1. Add the following dependency to project.clj:

   ```
   [org.clojure/math.numeric-tower "0.0.4"]
   ```

2. You can use expt and sqrt in the library:

   ```
   (require '[clojure.math.numeric-tower :as math])
   (math/expt 2 10)
   ;;=> 1024
   (math/sqrt 10)
   ;;=> 3.1622776601683795
   ```

Using bindings of vars, conditions, loops, and error handling

In this recipe, we will review Clojure programming control structures related to vars and values, conditions, iterations, and loops. We will use the following special forms, macros, and functions:

- def and let
- if and if-not
- when and when-not

- `case` and `cond`
- `do` and `dotimes`
- `loop` and `recur`
- try… catch… throw

Getting ready

You only need REPL, as described in the first recipe in this chapter, and no additional libraries. Start REPL so that you can test the sample code immediately in this recipe.

How to do it…

Let's start with how to use `def` and `let` to bind vars.

def and let

`def` is a special form that binds symbols in the global scope in their namespace. `def` requires var and value:

```
(def var val)
```

This sample binds x to `100`:

```
(def x 100)
;;=> 100
```

Whereas `let` binds symbols in its local scope. You can put multiple expressions in a `let` clause. `let` evaluates them and returns the last expression:

```
(let [var-1 val-1 var-2 val-2 ...]
    expr-1
    expr-2
    ....
    )
```

In this example, let binds x to 3 and y to 2. Then, it evaluates two expressions consecutively and returns the second expression:

```
(let [x 3 y 2]
  (println "x = " x ", y = " y)
  (* x y)
  )
;;=> x =  3 , y =  2
;;=> 6
```

if and if-not

if takes three arguments; the third argument (else-expression) is optional:

```
(if condition then-expression else-expression)
```

In the next example, the code returns the absolute value of numbers:

```
(let [x 10]
  (if (> x 0)   x   (- x))
  )
;;=> 10
(let [x -10]
  (if (> x 0)   x   (- x))
  )
;;=> 10
```

If there's no third parameter and if the test results as false, it returns nil:

```
(let [x -10]
  (if (> x 0)   x))
;;=> nil
```

if-not is opposite to if. It returns then-expression if the test fails:

```
(if-not condition then-expression else-expression)
```

The example should return false:

```
(if-not true true false)
;;=> false
```

when and when-not

The when function is similar to if, but it evaluates one or more expressions if the condition is evaluated to true; otherwise, it is false:

```
(when condition expr-1 expr-2 ...)
```

The first expression prints out x = 10 and returns 100. The second one only returns nil:

```
(let [x 10]
  (when (> x 0)
    (println "x = " x)
    (* x x)))
;;=> x = 10
;;=> 100
(let [x -10]
  (when (> x 0)
    (println "x = " x)
    (* x x)))
;;=> nil
```

when-not is the opposite of when:

```
(when-not condition expr-1 expr-2 expr 3 ...)
```

The next code uses when-not and does the same thing as the preceding function:

```
(let [x 10]
  (when-not (<= x 0)
    (println "x = " x)
    (* x x)))
;;=>x = 10
;;=> 100
(let [x -10]
  (when-not (<= x 0)
    (println "x = " x)
    (* x x)))
;;=> nil
```

case and cond

`case` tests whether there is a matched value. If so, `case` evaluates the corresponding expression. If there is no matched value, it returns `otherwise-value`. If there is no `otherwise-value` specified, it returns `nil`:

```
(case condition
    value1  expr-1
    value2  expr-2
    otherwise-value
    )
```

In the first expression, the condition matches the value 2 and `"two"` is returned. The second expression returns a string, `"otherwise"`:

```
(let [x 2]
  (case x
    1 "one"
    2 "two"
    3 "three"
    "otherwise"
        ))
;;=> "two"
(let [x 4]
  (case x
    1 "one"
    2 "two"
    3 "three"
    "otherwise"
        ))
;;=> "otherwise"
```

`cond` is a macro and is similar to `case`. `cond` has been heavily used in the Lisp language. `cond` is more flexible than case.

`cond` takes a set of condition/expr pairs and evaluates each condition. If one of the conditions is true, `cond` evaluates the corresponding expression and returns it. Otherwise, it returns the expression of `:else`:

```
(cond
    condition-1 expr-1
    condition-2 expr-2
    ...
    :else expr-else
    )
```

The next sample code acts the same as the preceding one:

```
(let [x 10]
  (cond
    (= x 1) "one"
    (= x 1) "two"
    (= x 3) "three"
    :else "otherwise"
        )
  )
```

do and dotimes

do evaluates the expressions in order and returns the last:

```
(do expr-1 expr-2 ...)
```

In the next sample, do evaluates the first expression and prints x = 10, then it evaluates the second and returns 11:

```
(def x 10)
;;=> #'living-clojure.core/x
(do
  (println "x = " x)
  (+ x 1))
;;=> x = 10
;;=> 11
```

dotimes repeats the expression while var increments from 0 to (number-exp – 1):

```
(dotimes [var number-exp]
    expression
  )
```

This example prints the square of x where x is 0 to 4:

```
(dotimes [x 5]
  (println "square : " (* x x)))
;;=> square :  0
;;=> square :  1
;;=> square :  4
;;=> square :  9
;;=> square :  16
```

loop and recur

You may sometimes want to write a program that loops with a condition. Since Clojure is an immutable language, you cannot change a loop counter, unlike in imperative languages such as Java.

The combination of loop and recur is used in such a situation. Their forms are as follows:

```
(loop [var-1 val-1 var-2 val-2 ...]
  expr-1
  expr-2
  ...
  )
(recur expr-1 expr-2   ... )
```

The next very simple example shows how loop and recur work. In the loop, x is set to 1 and increased until it is smaller than 5:

```
(loop [x 1]
  (when (< x 5)
    (println "x = " x)
    (recur (inc x))
    ) )
;;=> x =  1
;;=> x =  2
;;=> x =  3
;;=> x =  4
;;=> nil
```

The next example calculates the sum of 1 to 10 using loop and recur:

```
(loop [x 1 ret 0]
  (if (> x 10)
    ret
    (recur (inc x) (+ ret x))
    )
)
;;=> 55
```

try... catch... throw

Clojure uses an error handler borrowed from Java:

```
(try exp-1 exp 2 ...
  (catch class-of-exception var exception
  (finally finally-expr)
  )
```

Inside `try`, there are one or more expressions. `finally` is optional. The following example emits an exception and returns a string generated in the `catch`:

```
(try
  (println "Let's test try ... catch ... finally")
      (nth "Clojure" 7)
  (catch Exception e
      (str "exception occured: " (.getMessage e)))
  (finally (println "test finished"))
  )
;;=> Let's test try ... catch ... finally
;;=> test finished
;;=> "exception occured: String index out of range: 7"
```

How it works...

Clojure's lexical scope hides the outside bindings of vars inside bindings of vars. The next example shows the scopes of a nested `let`. The inside `let` binds x to 10 and y to 10. Thus, inside `println` prints 100. Similarly, the outside `let` binds x to 3 and y to 2. Thus, it prints 6:

```
(let [x 3 y 2]
  (let [x 10 y 10]
    (println "inside : " (* x y))
    )
  (println "outside : " (* x y))
  )
;;=> inside :  100
;;=> outside :  6
;;=>  nil
```

Similarly, a local binding of a var hides the global binding of a var:

```
(def x 1)
;;=> #'living-clojure/x
;;=> 1
(println "global x = " x)
;;=> global x =  1
(let [x 10] (println "local x = " x))
;;=>local x =  10
(println "global x = " x)
;;=> global x =  1
```

The `when` is a macro using the `if` special form. You can see how the `when` is defined using `macroexpand`:

```
(macroexpand
  '(when (> x 0)
     (println "x = " x)
     (* x x)))
;;=> (if (> x 0) (do (println "x = " x) (* x x)))
```

`if-not` is also a macro using `if`:

```
(macroexpand '(if-not true true false))
;;=> (if (clojure.core/not true) true false)
```

Using and defining functions

In this recipe, we will review Clojure's function definitions:

- Defining simple functions
- Defining variadic functions
- Defining multiple arity functions
- Defining functions that specify arguments using a keyword
- Defining functions with a pre-condition and a post-condition

Getting ready

You only need REPL, as described in the first recipe in this chapter, and no additional libraries. Start REPL so that you can test the sample code immediately in this recipe.

How to do it...

Here, we will learn how to define functions using Clojure. Let's start with a simple function which returns `Hello world`:

Defining simple functions

Let's start with a minimum function definition. Here is a minimal syntax of `defn`:

```
(defn funtion-name [arg1 arg2 ...]
```

```
    expr-1
    expr-2
    ..
    expr-n
    )
```

defn is a special form. The first argument is a function name and is followed by a vector of one or more arguments, then one or more expressions. The last expression is returned to the caller.

Here, we define a very simple function. The hello function returns a Hello world string:

```
(defn hello [s]
  (str "Hello world " s " !"))
;;=> #'living-clojure.core/hello
(hello "Nico")
;;=> "Hello world Nico !"
(hello "Makoto")
;;=> "Hello world Makoto !"
```

The next sample defines a simple adder function:

```
(defn simple-adder [x y]
  (+ x y)
  )
;;=> #'living-clojure.core/simple-adder
(simple-adder  2 3)
;;=> 5
```

Defining variadic functions

A variadic function allows a variable number of arguments. The next example defines another adder. It may have an arbitrary number of arguments:

```
(defn advanced-adder [x & rest]
  (apply + (conj rest x))
  )
;;=> #'living-clojure.core/advanced-adder
(advanced-adder 1 2 3 4 5)
;;=> 15
```

Defining multiple arity functions

Here, we will introduce the multiple arity function. The following function defines a single argument function and a couple of argument functions with the same `defn`:

```
(defn multi-arity-hello
  ([] (hello "you"))
  ([name] (str "Hello World " name " !")))
;;=> #'living-clojure.core/multi-arty-hello
(multi-arity-hello)
;;=> Hello World you !
(multi-arity-hello "Nico")
  ;;=> Hello World Nico !
```

Defining functions that specify arguments using a keyword

Sometimes, specifying a keyword is useful, since it is not necessary to remember the order of arguments.

The next example shows how to define such a function. The options are `:product-name`, `:price`, and `:description`. The `:or` expression supplies default values if any values in keys are omitted:

```
(defn make-product-1
  [serial &
   {:keys [product-name price description]
    :or {product-name "" price nil description "no description !"}
    }
   ]
   {:serial-no serial :product-name product-name
    :price price :description description}
   )
;;=> #'living-clojure.core/make-product-1

(defn make-product-2
  [serial &
   {:keys [product-name price description]
    :or {:product-name "" :description "no description !"}
    }
   ]
   {:serial-no serial :product-name product-name
    :price price :description description}
   )
;;=> #'living-clojure.core/make-product-2
```

```
(make-product-1 "0000-0011")
;;=> {:serial-no "0000-0011", :product-name "", :price nil, :description
"no description !"}
(make-product-2 "0000-0011")
;;=> {:serial-no "0000-0011", :product-name nil, :price nil, :description
nil}
```

Defining functions with pre-condition and post-condition

Clojure can define functions with pre-condition and post-condition. In the following `defn`, `:pre` checks whether an argument is positive. `:post` checks whether the result is smaller than 10:

```
(require '[clojure.math.numeric-tower :as math])
;;=> nil
(math/sqrt -10)
;;=> NaN
(defn pre-and-post-sqrt [x]
  {:pre  [(pos? x)]
   :post [(< % 10)]}
  (math/sqrt x))
;;=> #'living-clojure.core/pre-and-post-sqrt
(pre-and-post-sqrt 10)
;;=> 3.1622776601683795
(pre-and-post-sqrt -10)
;;=> AssertionError Assert failed: (pos? x)  user/pre-and-post-sqrt (form-
init2377591389478394456.clj:1)
(pre-and-post-sqrt 120)
AssertionError Assert failed: (< % 10)  user/pre-and-post-sqrt (form-
init2377591389478394456.clj:1)
```

Moreover, in this recipe, we will show a more complicated function. The `make-triangle` function prints a triangle with a character. If this function is called without a `:char` argument, it prints a triangle made of asterisks. If it is called with a `:char` argument, it prints a triangle comprising characters specified by `:char`:

```
(defn make-triangle
  [no & {:keys [char] :or {char "*"}}]
  (loop [x 1]
    (when (<= x no)
      (dotimes
          [n (- no x)] (print " "))
      (dotimes
          [n
```

```
          (if (= x 1)
            1
            (dec (* x 2)))]
        (print char))
      (print "\n")
      (recur (inc x))
      )
   )
 )
(make-triangle 5)
;;=>     *
;;=>    ***
;;=>   *****
;;=>  *******
;;=> *********
;;=> nil
(make-triangle 6 :char "x")
;;=>      x
;;=>     xxx
;;=>    xxxxx
;;=>   xxxxxxx
;;=>  xxxxxxxxx
;;=> xxxxxxxxxxx
```

How it works...

We have already reviewed how to define functions and how to use them. You should understand how they work after reviewing the previous section.

To define functions using `defn` is the same as `vars` bind to functions by `fn` as follows:

```
(defn pow-py-defn [x] (* x x))
;;=> #'living-clojure/pow-py-defn
(def pow-by-def (fn [x] (* x x)))
;;=> #'living-clojure/pow-by-def
(pow-py-defn 10)
;;=> 100
(pow-by-def 10)
;;=> 100
```

There's more...

`clojure.repl` has some useful functions to use with other functions. To get a symbol in the specific namespace, use `clojure.repl/dir`:

```
(require 'clojure.string)
;;=> nil
(clojure.repl/dir clojure.string)
;;=> blank?
;;=> capitalize
;;=> escape
;;=> join
;;=> lower-case
;;=> re-quote-replacement
;;=> replace
;;=> replace-first
;;=> reverse
;;=> split
;;=> split-lines
;;=> trim
;;=> trim-newline
;;=> triml
;;=> trimr
;;=> upper-case
;;=> nil
```

To get the documentation of a function, use `clojure.repl/doc`:

```
(clojure.repl/doc clojure.string/trim)
-------------------------
;;=> clojure.string/trim
;;=> ([s])
;;=>    Removes whitespace from both ends of string.
;;=> nil
```

To get symbols that have a specific string, use `clojure.repl/apropos`:

```
(clojure.repl/apropos "defn")
;;=> (clojure.core/defn
;;=>   clojure.core/defn-
;;=>   deps.compliment.v0v2v4.compliment.sources.local-bindings/defn-like-
forms
;;=>   deps.compliment.v0v2v4.deps.defprecated.v0v1v2.defprecated.core/defn)
```

Using third-party libraries

So, you have found someone else's code that you would like to use, and you are trying to take their work and use it in your project, great! This is what this recipe is all about. There are a few ways to get the code closer to you.

Getting ready

This recipe will introduce you to the art of adding dependencies, packaged as JAR files, to your project and how to reference them, as well as using them from your Clojure code. We will go from downloading the file and starting Clojure REPL manually, to using dependency management tools. Lastly, we will also present how to add new dependencies at runtime, so you do not need to restart your live programming environment.

How to do it...

Each minor section in this recipe shows you how to add the dependency, using different ways in different scenarios.

Adding the JAR file manually to your classpath

Say we have found the following library, `clj-tuples`, and we want to add this to our REPL session. Most JARs for Clojure are available on either `mvnrepository.com` or `clojars.org`.

`clj-tuples` is on `clojars`, and since `clojars` is a regular Maven repository, we can navigate directly through the file. Download and save it (`https://clojars.org/repo/rui yun/tools.timer/1.0.1/tools.timer-1.0.1.jar`), and now let's start a Clojure REPL:

```
java -cp .:clj-tuple-0.2.2.jar:clojure-1.8.0-beta1.jar  clojure.main
```

And let's quickly have fun with our new library code...mmmmm, tuples:

```
user=> (use 'ruiyun.tools.timer)
; nil
user=> (run-task!
#(println "Say hello every 5 seconds.") :period 5000);
#object[java.util.Timer 0x45a4b042 "java.util.Timer@45a4b042"]
user=> Say hello every 5 seconds.
   user=> (cancel! *1)
```

Ok, great!

Using Leiningen and a project.clj file

So, that was fun, but maybe you have more than one person's code you want to steal, and also, you just noticed that some of the stolen code is also stealing code from somebody else's code…what do you do?

Leiningen is a command-line tool that will, among other things, help you maintain stolen code. This recipe will not look into installing Leiningen because there is documentation all around that does this, so we just want to make sure at this stage that you have a recent version:

```
NicolassMacBook:chapter01 niko$ lein version

Leiningen 2.5.1 on Java 1.8.0_45 Java HotSpot(TM) 64-Bit Server VM
```

To make Leiningen understand what we want, most of the time, we would give it a `project.clj` file with a DSL that looks mostly like a gigantic Clojure map. If we want to import the same dependency as we did previously, this is the way we would write it:

```
(defproject chapter01 "0.1.0"
  :dependencies
  [[org.clojure/clojure "1.8.0-beta1"]
   [clj-tuple "0.2.2"]])
```

At its root, declaring a dependency on a third-party library is done through this mini DSL, where a two element vector points to a name and a version:

```
[name "version"]
```

So here:

```
[clj-tuple "0.2.2"]
```

Dependencies are declared as Clojure vectors in the project map, with `:dependencies` as its key. We now have access to billions of libraries of somewhat different quality depending on the author, but anyway, it's done. Leiningen also uses `clojars` by default, so there's no need to define repository definitions yet. The same code as before works:

```
(use 'clj-tuple)
```

Viewing dependencies

Using the `project.clj` file, we can directly see what our code depends on, and in particular the version of things our code depends on. The `project.clj` file of `clj-tuple` is located at `https://github.com/Ruiyun/tools.timer/blob/master/project.clj` and the portion we are interested in is as follows:

```
(defproject clj-tuple "0.2.2"
  :description "Efficient small collections."
  :dependencies []
  ...)
```

This means that `clj-tuples` does not depend on anything else and is a well behaved self-contained library.

This is obviously not always the case, and while we are at it we can look at another library, named `puget`.

Puget has the following dependencies defined:

```
:dependencies
    [[fipp "0.6.2"]
    [mvxcvi/arrangement "1.0.0"]
    [org.clojure/clojure "1.8.0"]]
```

But the great thing is that we don't need to write all those dependency lines ourselves. Transitive dependencies are pulled properly by Leiningen, so our `project.clj` file will now look simply like this:

```
(defproject chapter01 "0.1.0"
  :dependencies [
              [org.clojure/clojure "1.8.0-beta1"]
              [clj-tuple "0.2.2"]
              [mvxcvi/puget "0.9.1"]]])
```

The first time we launch a new REPL we will notice all the dependencies being downloaded:

```
NicolassMacBook:chapter01 niko$ lein repl
Retrieving mvxcvi/puget/0.9.1/puget-0.9.1.pom from clojars
Retrieving fipp/fipp/0.6.2/fipp-0.6.2.pom from clojars
Retrieving org/clojure/core.rrb-vector/0.0.11/core.rrb-vector-0.0.11.pom
from central
Retrieving mvxcvi/arrangement/1.0.0/arrangement-1.0.0.pom from clojars
Retrieving org/clojure/core.rrb-vector/0.0.11/core.rrb-vector-0.0.11.jar
from central
Retrieving fipp/fipp/0.6.2/fipp-0.6.2.jar from clojars
```

```
Retrieving mvxcvi/arrangement/1.0.0/arrangement-1.0.0.jar from clojars
Retrieving mvxcvi/puget/0.9.1/puget-0.9.1.jar from clojars
```

This only applies the first time. The second time it occurs without extra messages, and you can now check for yourself that the library is there, and you get the expected colorized output, but not in this book:

```
user=> (require '[puget.printer :as puget])
nil
user=> (puget/pprint #{'x :a :z 3 1.0})
#{1.0 3 :a :z x}
nil
user=> (puget/cprint #{'x :a :z 3 1.0})
#{1.0 3 :a :z x}
```

one-off

Sometimes it is great to just try things out, and have a one-off REPL to try out the new dependencies. This is where we can use a Leiningen plugin named `try`.

Plugins for Leiningen can be installed globally on your machine with a file named `profiles.clj` located here:

$HOME/.lein/profiles.clj

The file is a simple map with user-defined settings; here, we just want to add a plugin, so we add it to the vector:

```
{:user {:plugins [ [lein-try "0.4.3"] ]}}
```

That's it. From anywhere on your computer you can now try dependencies. To make things new, we will look at a new useful dependency named `env`, which makes it easy to retrieve environment settings.

This is the usual Leiningen definition of `env`, and the following code would be used in `project.clj`, as seen before:

```
[adzerk/env "0.2.0"]
```

Here, we just type the following:

```
lein try adzerk/env
```

And we can see the dependencies coming along locally (provided you have an Internet connection):

```
Retrieving adzerk/env/0.2.0/env-0.2.0.pom from clojars
Retrieving adzerk/env/0.2.0/env-0.2.0.jar from clojars
```

And we can now use the `require` macro:

```
(require '[adzerk.env :as env])
```

And try it. `env` returns all the `env` variables available, whether through Java or Shell:

```
user=> (env/env)
; ...
```

If you have the chance to run the preceding command where `project.clj` was located, the dependencies from the project are also available, so we can combine dependencies:

```
user=> (require '[puget.printer :as puget])

user=> (puget/cprint (env/env))
{"Apple_PubSub_Socket_Render"
"/private/tmp/com.apple.launchd.jI7P2DRL6X/Render",
 "HOME" "/Users/niko",
 "JAVA_ARCH" "x86_64",
 "JAVA_CMD" "java",
 "JAVA_MAIN_CLASS_3927" "clojure.main",
 "JVM_OPTS" "",
 ...
```

Voila! Now we have combined a temporary dependency with our main project dependencies.

New dependencies at runtime

So far we have seen how to add dependencies offline, in the sense that we need to stop our REPL in order for the new dependencies to be handled properly. Now we will see how to add a dependency on the fly.

The dependency we will look at now is named `pomegranate` and it does just that, add dependencies on the fly.

In the same way we added a Leiningen plugin earlier on, we will add a global dependency to our runtimes by adding a dependency to the same `profiles.clj` file:

```
{:user
    {:dependencies
    [[com.cemerick/pomegranate "0.3.0"]] }}
```

Those dependencies will be ready to be loaded through all your Leiningen-based projects, so be careful not to add too many. With a new REPL loaded, we can now load `pomegranate`, and the only method we need is happily named `add-dependencies`:

```
(require '[cemerick.pomegranate :refer [add-dependencies]])
```

The newly required function takes a vector of coordinates using the same pattern we have seen so far, and a map of repositories, with a name for the key and a URL to a Maven-like repository for the value:

```
(add-dependencies
                :coordinates '[[active-quickcheck "0.3.0"]]
                :repositories  {"clojars" "http://clojars.org/repo"})
```

The first time this is called, the dependency and all the underlying will be downloaded and be ready for use. We took `active-quickcheck` as a sample, a library that can be used to generate random tests based on some given predicates. The library still needs to be required in the current namespace:

```
(use 'active.quickcheck)

; sample dependency test, we will not go in the details here
(quickcheck (property [a integer
                b integer]
        (= (+ a b) (+ b a))))
```

So we have pretty much seen all the different ways to add dependencies to our Clojure environment, whether through:

- Direct JAR file
- Leiningen's `project.clj`
- Leiningen's `profiles.clj`
- Leiningen's `try` plugin
- Using `pomegranate`

Using namespaces

Clojure organizes code via namespaces, or small units of code. Each namespace contains a set of define functions. One of the recurring questions is to figure out how to do the layout of your namespaces, and how to organize your different namespaces so they relate to each other in a clean way. This is what this recipe will go through.

Getting ready

This recipe does not require any special installation steps apart from a running REPL. Also, it is recommended to keep the Clojure namespaces page open so we can refer to it quickly.

How to do it...

We will go through the steps of creating a Clojure namespace, referencing code from other namespaces, as well as loading and reloading namespaces on demand. Lastly, we will go briefly through a few concepts of how to organize those namespaces properly.

Creating a new namespace

We start here by looking at how namespaces are created. While working in the REPL, making changes to or creating a namespace mostly resorts to using the `in-ns` function from `clojure.core`:

```
(in-ns 'hello)
```

And next time we define a var using `def`, we see it bound to that namespace:

```
hello=> (in-ns 'hello)
#object[clojure.lang.Namespace 0x3b5fad2d "hello"]
hello=> (def a 1)
#'hello/a
```

Great. Now, since the function resolves to var as well, we can define the function in our namespace. We need to give the full path to `fn` now to define the definition, so `clojure.core/fn`:

```
hello=> (def b (clojure.core/fn[c] (clojure.core/inc c)))
#'hello/b
hello=> (b 2)
3
```

Inspecting namespaces

Namespaces are regular objects, so on the JVM we can see their internals very easily. find-ns tells us what the object is, and on the JVM we then call .getMappings from the namespace object:

```
(find-ns 'hello)
; #object[clojure.lang.Namespace 0x3b5fad2d "hello"]
(.getMappings *1)
....
```

Namespaces are listed and retained statically in a static field of this class on the JVM so we can refer to things later.

While in-ns helps us define namespaces, we will actually use a higher-level function named ns:

```
helloagain=> (ns helloagain)
nil
helloagain=>
```

If you want to go and have a look, ns actually does quite a bit for us. The two main keywords that can be used are imports and refers.

Adding functions with :import and :refer

:import will import classes from the hosting virtual machine (JVM, JavascriptVM, and .NET VM for now). Say in Java we want to use the raw Random Java object directly, we will import it in the namespace with the following:

```
(ns helloagain (:import [java.util Random]))
(Random.)
; #object[java.util.Random 0x6337c201 "java.util.Random@6337c201"]
```

We can also check the imports defined in each namespace with ns-imports:

```
(ns-imports 'helloagain)
;...
```

By default, Clojure does some work for us, to make sure the basic Java objects are already available in each new namespace.

In the same way as we can import Java objects, we can go along and require other Clojure namespaces in the current namespace. This is done through the `:require` keyword in the namespace definition:

```
helloagain=>  (ns helloagain (:require [clojure.string :refer :all]))
WARNING: reverse already refers to: #'clojure.core/reverse in namespace:
helloagain, being replaced by: #'clojure.string/reverse
WARNING: replace already refers to: #'clojure.core/replace in namespace:
helloagain, being replaced by: #'clojure.string/replace
nil
helloagain=> (reverse "helloagain")
"niagaolleh"
```

The newly referred functions can be seen using `ns-refers`:

```
(ns-refers 'helloagain)
; ... (somewhere clojure.string ...)
```

Loading namespaces from files

Now, effectively, the `ns` calls will mostly be located at the top of each file. Let's say we want to keep the code we have now on this `helloagain` namespace; we will create a `helloagain.clj` file and copy the following content:

```
(ns helloagain
    (:import [java.util Random])
    (:require [clojure.string :refer :all]))

(println
    (clojure.string/reverse (str (.getName *ns*))))

(println (Random.))
```

The namespace and thus the file can be loaded through `require`. For this to work, we need to validate our classpath, so let's review the way we started the REPL earlier on:

```
java -cp .:clojure-1.8.0-beta1.jar clojure.main
```

The `.` makes the files in the current folder available on the classpath, so then `require` can look through the defined classpath and find the file `helloagain.clj` we have just defined:

```
user=> (require 'helloagain)
niagaolleh
nil
user=>
```

You will notice the code is executed when calling `require` on the command line. The ' is required because `helloagain` should not be evaluated, but instead kept as a symbol.

Reloading namespaces

Now, here's something slightly more complicated. We want to add a function to the `helloagain` namespace:

```
(defn only-one []
    (println "only one"))
```

We want to use this function in a different user namespace, so we can call the `ns` macro again to do this, or we can also use `require` directly. Supposing we have added the preceding function to our filename; simply calling `require` should do it for us:

```
user=> (require 'helloagain)
nil
user=>  (helloagain/only-one)
CompilerException java.lang.RuntimeException: No such var: helloagain/only-
one, compiling:(NO_SOURCE_PATH:4:2)
```

Or not. What happened there? The file was not reloaded from disk, and we just got a reference to the already created namespace. The `:reload` keyword gives us a chance to specify that we want to reload from disk:

```
(require 'helloagain :reload)
user=> (helloagain/only-one)
; only one
```

IDEs such as IntelliJ will actually, most of the time, reload the full current file from the buffer, and so the definition of the namespace can be updated.

When loading and reloading namespaces, state management becomes problematic, so we will focus on that a little bit later.

How to organize namespaces

There is great science and research being done on how to organize namespaces; even Albert Einstein had a biweekly meeting to make sure namespaces would be organized in a compatible way.

Here is a list that will help you focus on creating namespaces around coherent goals:

- Group architectural layers with different causes for concern
- Functional modules that have to define contracts to communicate with each other
- Define a public API on top of internal low-level functions

A public API namespace will have well defined contracts and extensive documentation, while low-level functions maybe be more tested but could be less well documented.

Some people have suggested grouping functions depending on the kind of data they are handling. This is also good when you do not have to deal with the relationships of those namespaces; for example, you defined a `User` namespace and a `ShoppingList` namespace, but then `Users` with many `ShoppingList` items make the relationship management between the two namespaces cumbersome. Only use this way of organization if the data handled is straightforward and simple.

Possibly the most interesting motivation to separate namespaces is the public API method.

There's more...

In the previous section, we saw that having a namespace for the public API of your library is important, so the following will describe, with the `potemkin` library as an example, how to extract just what you need from your code to present the API you want to present:

`tools.namespace, potemkin`

Namespace for public API

`potemkin` has a very interesting method, named `import-vars`, that allows something like a copy/paste of a function from a different namespace to a current one. If we remember the previous recipe, we can simply try the `potemkin` dependency as follows:

```
lein try potemkin "0.4.1"
```

Then we can select on-demand functions and clean up our public-facing namespace:

```
user=> (require 'potemkin)
(potemkin/import-vars [clojure.string reverse])
 (user/reverse "hello")
```

This makes selecting functions for our namespace clean, without any code, mostly documentation.

This also makes a case for versioning our namespace, in case some breaking changes are introduced but there is no need to make a completely new version of your code.

tools.namespace

Now, we saw just a few moments ago that we can force `:reload` on a namespace, but things get complicated when namespaces depend on each other, and you are not sure which one was reloaded and which one was not. This is where `tools.namespace` makes it easier for you to track all this for you. Let us start a REPL and try this out:

```
lein try org.clojure/tools.namespace "0.2.11"
```

As per the doc, the `refresh` function will scan all the directories on the classpath for Clojure source files, read their `ns` declarations, build a graph of their dependencies, and load them in dependency order. (You can change the directories it scans with `set-refresh-dirs`.)

So, at the REPL, the function we mostly need from `tools.namespace` is `refresh`:

```
(require '[clojure.tools.namespace.repl :refer [refresh]])
```

Now, supposing our file `helloagain.clj` is in the `src` folder so, `src/helloagain.clj`, and `lein` can find and load the file with `require`:

```
(require '[helloagain :refer :all])
user=> (only-one)
only one
```

We will quickly add a new function to our file:

```
(defn only-two []
   (println "only two"))
```

And call `refresh` to make sure we have the latest code:

```
user=> (refresh)
; :reloading (helloagain)
user> (helloagain/only-two)
; only two
```

And that is all. We have pulled the latest from our namespace code, and the required namespaces will be reloaded as needed.

What's next?

In this chapter, we have seen how to create namespaces and how to inspect them. We also looked at how to organize those namespaces, and how to make sure we always have the code we want at the place we want. We remembered that a public API is a key point for creating namespaces as well as organizing code into functional modules.

The next step is to look at the workflow for reloading a full application that has dependent components. Those components will require a workflow to manage their state and the now famous component library has been established as the way to go.

Maybe this could also be part of a future Clojure version, in which the need to break namespaces into something smaller than files will be handled.

Interacting with Collections

2

In this chapter, we will cover the following topics:

- Clojure collections and their basic functions
- Accessing and updating elements from collections
- Filtering elements from collections
- Transforming and sorting collections
- Merging and splitting collections
- How to become lazy

Introduction

Clojure belongs to the Lisp language family, and Lisp can handle collections in a very cool and efficient way. Clojure inherits rich and cool sets from Lisp. In this chapter, we will show basic and advanced recipes for manipulating collections.

Another advantage of manipulating collections in Clojure is to guarantee immutability. In the case of large or concurrent applications, mutability causes unintended behaviors resulting in serious bugs.

After reading this chapter, you'll be able to write Clojure code to handle collections with a lot of fun.

Clojure collections and their basic functions

There are four collection types in Clojure:

- Lists
- Vectors
- Maps
- Sets

In this recipe, we will describe what these types are and some basic functions for them.

Getting ready

You only need REPL described in the recipe *Repl up!* in `Chapter 1`, *Live Programming with Clojure,* and no additional libraries. Start REPL so that you can review the sample code in this recipe.

How to do it...

We will learn collection types in Clojure including lists, vectors, maps, and sets. We will learn how to create them and use basic functions for them.

Lists

Lists are commonly used in Lisp. Clojure also supports the list data type. Lists are internally implemented as a linked list. To create a list, begin with quote (') and then enclose elements with (). If you want to create an empty list, use '(), or (list):

```
'("A Study in Scarlet"
"The Sign of the Four"
"The Hound of the Baskervilles"
"The Valley of Fear")
;;=> ("A Study in Scarlet" "The Sign of the Four" "The Hound of the
Baskervilles" "The Valley of Fear")
'()
;;=> ()
(list)
;;=> ()
```

There are three basic functions, `car`, `cdr`, and `cons`, to manipulate lists in traditional Lisp. Instead of them, Clojure uses `first`, `rest`, and `conj`. Let's see how they work:

- `first` takes the head element from a list:

```
(first '(1 2 3 4 5))
;;=> 1
(first '())
;;=> nil
(first nil)
;;=> nil
```

- The `first` of an empty list or `nil` returns `nil`.

- `rest` returns a list after the first element:

```
(rest '(1 2 3 4 5))
;;=> (2 3 4 5)
(rest '())
;;=> ()
(rest nil)
;;=> ()
```

- The `rest` of an empty list or `nil` returns an empty list.

- `conj` adds elements at the beginning:

```
(conj '(2 3 4 5) 1)
;;=> (1 2 3 4 5)
```

- `conj` is a variadic function and can take multiple elements as its arguments:

```
```clj
(conj '("d" "e" "f") "c" "b" "a")
;;=> ("a" "b" "c" "d" "e" "f")
```

Vectors

A vector also represents a sequence of elements, like list, but it supports efficient access to its elements by index.
```

To create a vector, enclose its elements with `[]`. To create an empty vector, use `[]` or `(vector)`:

```
["A Study in Scarlet"
 "The Sign of the Four"
 "The Hound of the Baskervilles"
 "The Valley of Fear"]
;;=> ["A Study in Scarlet" "The Sign of the Four" "The Hound of the
Baskervilles" "The Valley of Fear"]
[]
;;=> []
(vector)
;;=> []
```

We can use `first`, `rest`, and `conj` with vectors. Let's begin with `first` and `rest`:

```
(first [1 2 3 4 5])
;;=> 1
(first [])
;;=> nil
(rest [1 2 3 4 5])
;;=> (2 3 4 5)
```

The `rest` of the vector looks like a returning list, but it is not list. It is `ChunkedSeq`:

```
(class (rest [1 2 3 4 5]))
;;=> clojure.lang.PersistentVector$ChunkedSeq
```

To add elements to a vector, use the `conj` function. `conj` appends elements to the vector:

```
(conj [1 2 3 4] 5)
;;=> [1 2 3 4 5]
```

Maps

Maps are associative lists, and they can be accessed efficiently with keys and return their values.

To create a map, enclose key-value pairs with `{}`:

```
{:name "Arthur Ignatius Conan Doyle"
 :born "22-May-1859"
 :died "7-July-1930"
 :occupation ["novelist" "short story writer" "poet" "physician"]
 :nationality "scotish"
 :citizenship "United Kingdom"
 :genre ["Detective fiction", "fantasy", "science fiction", "historical
```

```
novels", "non-fiction"]
 :notable-works ["Stories of Sherlock Holmes" "The Lost World"]
 :spouse ["Louisa Hawkins" "Jean Leckie"]
 :no-of-children 5
 }
;;=> {:genre ["Detective fiction" "fantasy" "science fiction" "historical
novels" "non-fiction"], :occupation ["novelist" "short story writer" "poet"
"physician"], :name "Arthur Ignatius Conan Doyle", :no-of-children 5,
:nationality "scotish", :died "7-July-1930", :spouse ["Louisa Hawkins"
"Jean Leckie"], :notable-works ["Stories of Sherlock Holmes" "The Lost
World"], :citizenship "United Kingdom", :born "22-May-1859"}
```

To create an empty map, use `{}` or `(hash-map)`:

```
{}
;;=> {}
(hash-map)
;;=> {}
```

We can use `first`, `rest`, and `conj` for maps, just as for lists or vectors:

```
(first {:a 1, :b 2, :c 3 :d 4 :e 5})
;;=> [:a 1]
(rest {:a 1, :b 2, :c 3 :d 4 :e 5})
;;=> ([:b 2] [:c 3] [:d 4] [:e 5])
(conj {:a 1, :b 2, :c 3 :d 4 } [:e 5])
;;=> {:a 1, :b 2, :c 3, :d 4, :e 5}
(conj {:a 1, :b 2, :c 3 :d 4 } [:d 5] [:e 6])
;;=> {:a 1, :b 2, :c 3, :d 5, :e 6}
(conj {:a 1, :b 2, :c 3 :d 4 } [:d 5])
;;=> {:a 1, :b 2, :c 3, :d 5}
```

Maps are often used as dictionaries. `get`, `dissoc`, and `assoc` are more commonly used with maps.

`get` looks up a map entry by its key and returns its value. If `get` cannot find the key in a collection, it returns `nil`.

If you don't want to obtain `nil` in such a case, specify the value you want when the key does not exist:

```
(get {:a 1, :b 2, :c 3 :d 4 :e 5} :c)
;;=> 3
(get {:a 1, :b 2, :c 3 :d 4 :e 5} :f)
;;=> nil
(get {:a 1, :b 2, :c 3 :d 4 :e 5} :f :not-found)
;;=> :not-found
```

`assoc` adds key-value pairs to maps. If there is already a key-value pair in the map, it replaces the value:

```
(assoc {:a 1, :b 2, :c 3 :d 4} :e 5)
;;=> {:a 1, :b 2, :c 3, :d 4, :e 5}
(assoc {:a 1, :b 2, :c 3 :d 4} :c 5)
;;=> {:a 1, :b 2, :c 5, :d 4}
```

`assoc` can use multiple key-value pairs as its arguments:

```
(assoc {:a 1, :b 2, :c 3 :d 4} :e 5 :f 6)
;;=> {:a 1, :b 2, :c 3, :d 4, :e 5, :f 6}
```

The `dissoc` removes key-value pairs from a map:

```
(dissoc {:a 1, :b 2, :c 3 :d 4} :c)
;;=> {:a 1, :b 2, :d 4}
(dissoc {:a 1, :b 2, :c 3 :d 4} :c)
;;=> {:a 1, :b 2, :d 4}
(dissoc {:a 1, :b 2, :c 3 :d 4} :e)
;;=> {:a 1, :b 2, :c 3, :d 4}
```

Sets

Sets maintain the uniqueness of their elements. To create a set, being with a hash (#) and then enclose elements with { }. If you want to create an empty set, use #{} or (hash-set):

```
#{"apple" "orange" "banana" "peach" "strawberry"}
;;=> #{"peach" "apple" "banana" "orange" "strawberry"}
#{}
;;=> #{}
(hash-set)
```

We can use `first`, `rest`, and `conj` for sets. Sets do not keep the order of elements as you input data, so `first` or `rest` may look different to what you expected:

```
(first #{:a :b :c :d :e})
;;=> :e
(rest #{:a :b :c :d :e})
;;=> (:c :b :d :a)
(conj #{:a :b :c :d} :e)
;;=> #{:e :c :b :d :a}
(conj #{:a :b :c :d :e} :e)
;;=> #{:e :c :b :d :a}
```

The `contains?` function examines whether the element exists in a set, whereas `disj` eliminates the element from the set:

```
(contains? #{:a :b :c :d :e} :c)
;=> true
(contains? #{:a :b :c :d :e} :f)
;;=> false
(disj #{:a :b :c :d :e} :c)
;;=> #{:e :b :d :a}
(disj #{:a :b :c :d :e} :c :d)
;;=> #{:e :b :a}
```

How it works...

All collection types in Clojure are persistent and immutable. A persistent data structure preserves the previous versions of itself when it is modified. Clojure has efficient implementation to create modified versions of collections so it doesn't simply copy the entire data structure, but shares the original data.

Clojure collections

All collection types implement the `clojure.lang.Seqable` interface and its `seq` method returns `clojure.lang.ISeq`. `ISeq` has the `cons`, `first`, `more`, and `next` functions:

```
public interface Seqable {
    ISeq seq();
}
public interface ISeq extends IPersistentCollection {
    Object first();
    ISeq next();
    ISeq more();
    ISeq cons(Object o);
}
```

`ISeq` implements `IPersistentCollection` and it has `count`, `cons`, `empty`, and `equiv`:

```
public interface IPersistentCollection
    extends Seqable {
    int count();
    IPersistentCollection cons(Object o);
    IPersistentCollection empty();
    boolean equiv(Object o);
    }
```

Differences between lists and vectors

Lists and sets represent sequences of elements, but there are some differences:

- Lists are `clojure.lang.PersistentList` and vectors are `clojure.lang.PersistentVector`.
- Lists are implemented as a linked list. Vectors are implemented using a tree structure, and each node has 32 elements.
- Vectors are efficient for index access. Index access for lists takes `O(n)`, whereas it takes `O(log32(n))` for vectors.
- That is why, with `conj`, the order of the results is different in lists and vectors. `conj` puts an element at the beginning of lists, but it puts an element at the end of vectors:

```
(conj '(2 3 4 5) 1)
;;=> (1 2 3 4 5)
(conj [1 2 3 4] 5)
;;=> [1 2 3 4 5]
```

The following code tests index access for a list and a vector. This test measures access to the last element in a collection consisting of 1 million elements. The test loops 100 times. Access to the list takes half a second, but access to the vector only takes 0.1 milliseconds:

```
(let [n 1000000 iter 100
      l (into () (repeat n "a"))
      v (into [] (repeat n "a"))
      ]
  (time (dotimes [_ iter](nth l (dec n) )))
  (time (dotimes [_ iter](nth v (dec n) )))
  )
"Elapsed time: 532.623841 msecs"
"Elapsed time: 0.167739 msecs"
```

Reversing the order of vectors is faster than reversing the order of lists:

```
(do
  (time (reverse (into '() (range 100000))))
  (time (reverse (into [] (range 100000))))
  nil
  )
"Elapsed time: 60.67435 msecs"
"Elapsed time: 26.431954 msecs"
nil
```

The reason is that `clojure.lang.PersistentVector` implements
`clojure.lang.Reversible` but `clojure.lang.PersistentList` does not.

Clojure is immutable

Since Clojure functions for collections are immutable, it does not modify the original
collection. It is different from Python or Ruby. In the following Python code, insert modifies
the original list:

```
l = [2, 3, 4, 5]
l.insert(0, 1)
l
#[1, 2, 3, 4, 5]
```

The next Ruby code also modifies the original list:

```
$ irb
irb(main):001:0> letters = Array.new([2,3,4])
=> [2, 3, 4]
irb(main):002:0> letters.insert(0, 1)
=> [1, 2, 3, 4]
```

But Clojure does not change the original data:

```
(def l '(2 3 4 5))
#'collection.core/l
(conj '(2 3 4 5) 1)
;;=> (1 2 3 4 5)
l
;;=> (2 3 4 5)
```

Using immutable data ensures that arguments are unmodified after returning from other
function calls. On the other hand, calling functions causes unexpected modification of
arguments, which causes bugs that are difficult to find.

There's more...

Here, we will show you some techniques for manipulating collections.

Converting collections between different types

`into` converts types in collections. The following code converts between a vector and a list:

```
(into [] '(1 2 3 4 5))
;;=> [1 2 3 4 5]
(into '() [1 2 3 4 5])
;;=> (5 4 3 2 1)
```

In the following code, `into` converts between a map and a vector:

```
(into {} [[:a 1][:b 2] [:c 3][:d 4][:e 5]])
;;=> {:a 1, :b 2, :c 3, :d 4, :e 5}
(into [] {:a 1 :b 2 :c 3 :d 4 :e 5})
;;=> [[:a 1] [:b 2] [:c 3] [:d 4] [:e 5]]
```

Finally, this `into` converts between a set and a vector:

```
(into [] #{:a :b :c :d :e})
;;=> [:e :c :b :d :a]
(into #{} [:a :b :c :d :e])
#{:e :c :b :d :a}
```

Using distinct

`distinct` is similar to `into` with sets. It eliminates duplicated elements:

```
(distinct ["apple" "orange" "melon" "grape" "orange" "pinapple"])
;;=> ("apple" "orange" "melon" "grape" "pinapple")
(into #{} ["apple" "orange" "melon" "grape" "orange" "pinapple"])
;;=> #{"apple" "pinapple" "orange" "grape" "melon"}
```

Unlike `set`, using `distinct` does not change the data type.

Accessing and updating elements from collections

In this recipe, we will teach you how to access elements and update elements in collections.

Getting ready

You only need REPL, as described in the recipe in Chapter 1, *Live Programming with Clojure*, and no additional libraries. Start REPL so that you can review the sample code in this recipe.

How to do it...

Let's start with accessing collections.

Accessing collections using the nth function

nth gets the nth element from collections. The second argument of nth starts from 0 and throws an exception if the second argument is larger than the number of elements minus 1:

```
(nth [1 2 3 4 5] 1)
;;=> 2
(nth '("a" "b" "c" "d" "e") 3)
;;=> "d"
(nth [1 2 3] 3)
;;=> IndexOutOfBoundsException    clojure.lang.PersistentVector.arrayFor
(PersistentVector.java:153)
```

If you would like to avoid such an exception, use the third argument as the return value:

```
(nth [1 2 3] 3 nil)
;;=> nil
```

Notice that nth does not work with maps and sets.

Accessing maps or sets using get

get accesses maps and sets using a key, and if there is a corresponding key in a map or set, it returns its value. If there is not the same key in a map or set, it returns nil or the third argument:

```
(get {:a 1 :b 2 :c 3 :d 4 :e 5} :c)
;;=> 3
(get {:a 1 :b 2 :c 3 :d 4 :e 5} :f)
;;=> nil
(get {:a 1 :b 2 :c 3 :d 4 :e 5} :f :not-found)
;;=> :not-found
```

```
(get #{:a :b :c} :c)
;;=> :c
(get #{:a :b :c} :d)
;;=> nil
(get #{:a :b :c} :d :not-found)
;;=> :not-found
```

Maps, sets, and keywords are functions to access collections

It is an idiomatic Clojure approach to use maps or sets as the first argument. The following code is the same as using `get`:

```
;;=> :not-found
```

Using keywords is also Clojure-idiomatic. This is the same as `get`:

```
(:c {:a 1 :b 2 :c 3 :d 4 :e 5})
;;=> 3
(:f {:a 1 :b 2 :c 3 :d 4 :e 5})
;;=> nil
(:f {:a 1 :b 2 :c 3 :d 4 :e 5} :not-found)
;;=> :not-found
```

`get` for maps returns the key if the key exists in the elements. It returns `nil` if there is no matching key:

```
(get #{:banana :apple :strawberry :orange :melon} :orange)
;;=> :orange
(get #{:banana :apple :strawberry :orange :melon} :grape)
;;=> nil
(get #{:banana :apple :strawberry :orange :melon} :grape :not-found)
;;=> :not-found
```

We can use a set or a keyword as the first argument, but there is a third argument in this set:

```
(#{:banana :apple :strawberry :orange :melon} :orange)
;;=> :orange
(#{:banana :apple :strawberry :orange :melon} :grape)
;;=> nil
(:orange #{:banana :apple :strawberry :orange :melon})
;;=> :orange
( :grape #{:banana :apple :strawberry :orange :melon})
;;=> nil
```

Accessing a collection using second, next, ffirst, and nfirst

`second` returns the second element from a collection:

```
(second [1 2 3 4 5])
;;=> 2
(second '())
;;=> nil
```

The behavior of `next` is almost the same as `rest`, but `next` returns `nil` when the result is empty:

```
(next [1])
;;=> nil
(rest [1])
;;=> ()
```

`ffirst` returns the first element of the first element:

```
(ffirst [[1 2 3] 4 [3 5 6]])
;;=> 1
(ffirst {:a 1 :b 2})
;;=> :a
```

This is equivalent to the following code:

```
(first (first [[1 2 3] 4 [3 5 6]]))
;;=> 1
(first (first {:a 1 :b 2}))
;;=> :a
```

`nfirst` returns the next element of the first element:

```
(nfirst [[1 2] [3 4][5 6]])
;;=> (2)
(nfirst {:a 1 :b 2})
;;=> (1)
```

Using update to update collections

`update` updates the matched value using the function specified by the third element:

```
(update {:a 1 :b 2 :c 3} :a inc)
;;=> {:a 2, :b 2, :c 3}
```

How it works...

Maps, sets, and vectors implement `clojure.lang.IFn`. Clojure functions such as +
implement `IFn`. This is the reason why maps and sets can be functions. `ifn?` tests whether
an argument implements `clojure.lang.IFn`:

```
(ifn? +)
;;=> true
(ifn? [])
;;=> true
(ifn? {})
;;=> true
(ifn? #{})
;;=> true
(ifn? :a)
;;=> true
(ifn? '())
;;=> false
(ifn? 1)
;;=> false
```

Vectors and maps are functions, but lists and integers are not functions.

There's more...

Here, we will teach you some functions that are useful for accessing and updating
collections.

Using get for vectors

Like with maps and sets, `get` works with vectors:

```
(get ["a" "b" "c" "d" "e"] 3)
;;=> "d"
(get ["a" "b" "c" "d" "e"] 5)
;;=> nil
(get ["a" "b" "c" "d" "e"] 5 :not-found)
;;=> :not-found
```

Vectors are also functions:

```
(["a" "b" "c" "d" "e"] 3)
;;=> "d"
(["a" "b" "c" "d" "e"] 5)
```

```
;;=> IndexOutOfBoundsException    clojure.lang.PersistentVector.arrayFor
(PersistentVector.java:153)
```

Using `get` for lists always returns `nil`. Never do that:

```
(get  '(1 2 3) 1)
;;=> nil
```

Using collections as keys in maps

Unlike Java, Python, and Ruby, Clojure can use collection types as keys. The next map type uses maps as keys and finds the value using a map key:

```
(def location
  {{:x 1 :y 1} "Nico" {:x 1 :y 2} "John" {:x 2 :y 1} "Makoto"
   {:x 2 :y 2} "Tony"}
  )
;;=> #'chapter03.core/location
(location {:x 2 :y 2} )
;;=> "Tony"
```

This is useful when the key is a spatial dimension.

Using get-in

`get-in` associates given keys in a vector with a collection and returns a value of the matched element. `get-in` takes the first argument as a collection and the second argument usually has multiple keys as vectors that you want to look up. We will go back to Conan-Doyle's biography and see how `get-in` works:

```
(def biography-of-konan-doyle
  {:name "Arthur Ignatius Conan Doyle"
   :born "22-May-1859"
   :died "7-July-1930"
   :occupation ["novelist" "short story writer" "poet" "physician"]
   :nationality "scotish"
   :citizenship "United Kingdom"
   :genre ["Detective fiction", "fantasy", "science fiction", "historical
novels", "non-fiction"]
   :notable-works ["Stories of Sherlock Holmes" "The Lost World"]
   :spouse ["Louisa Hawkins" "Jean Leckie"]
   :no-of-children 5
   }
  )(get-in biography-of-konan-doyle [:genre 2])
  ;;=> "science fiction"
```

In the preceding example, the second argument of get-in is [:genre 2]. get-in looks for :genre in the var of biography-of-konan-doyle and finds the value as follows:

```
["Detective fiction" "fantasy" "science fiction" "historical novels" "non-
fiction"]
```

Then it looks for the third element in the vector and returns "science fiction". The following code is the equivalent code and returns the same result:

```
(get (get biography-of-konan-doyle :genre) 2)
;;=> "science fiction"
```

Using assoc-in

assoc-in is similar to get-in. It returns a collection that replaces the matched value with the third argument. If there are no matched keys, assoc-in inserts a new value in a new location:

```
(assoc-in {:a {:b 1 :c 2} :d 3} [:a :c] 1)
;;=> {:a {:b 1, :c 1}, :d 3}
(assoc-in {:a {:b 1 :c 2} :d 3} [:a :d] 1)
;;=> {:a {:b 1, :c 2, :d 1}, :d 3}
```

Using update-in

update-in is similar to get-in, but it only updates existing data. It is also different in that the third argument for update-in is a function.

In the next sample, the first update-in expression increments the matched value. The second expression sets a constant value, 10, using the constantly function:

```
(update-in {:a {:b 1 :c 2} :d 3} [:a :c] inc)
;;=> {:a {:b 1, :c 3}, :d 3}
(update-in {:a {:b 1 :c 2} :d 3} [:a :c] (constantly 10))
;;=> {:a {:b 1, :c 10}, :d 3}
```

Filtering elements from collections

This section quickly shows how to select only some elements of a Clojure sequence.

Getting ready

The first parts of the recipe do not need any special preparation, but the final section needs the `core.async` library to be added to your `project.clj` file (or any other dependency management you are using):

```
:dependencies [
    [org.clojure/clojure "1.8.0"]
    [org.clojure/core.async "0.2.371"]]
```

How to do it...

There are four main functions to filter elements:

- `filter`
- `keep` and `keep-indexed`
- `remove`
- `take` and `take-while`

Let's go through a few simple examples.

Filtering multiples of three

The following code filters numbers that are multiples of three:

```
(filter
 #(= 0 (rem % 3))
 (range 1 10))
; (3 6 9)
```

Filtering items of a map

This filters keys that are in the map, which is used as a function here:

```
(filter
 {:b 2 :c 3}
 [:a :b])
; (:b)
```

Filtering non-nil values

This filters non-nil values:

```
(filter #(not (nil? %))
        '(nil 1 2 3))
```

Removing odd values from a sequence

Here, we generate five random even integers lower than 100. `remove` will indeed remove all the elements that are odd:

```
(take 5
      (remove
      odd?
      (repeatedly #(rand-int 100))))
; (56 54 86 62 52)
```

Using keep

`keep` first applies a function to each item of a collection, and then keeps all the non-nil values :

```
(keep
even?
(range 10  20))
; (true false true false true false true false true false)
```

Using keep-indexed

`keep-indexed` is similar to `keep`, but allows you to put a condition on the index along with the item itself. In the following example, we keep items when the index is even, and then we return the item along a minor transformation. Just like `keep`, `keep-indexed` only keeps non-nil values from the function passed as the first parameter:

```
(defn mien [ index item ]
  (if (even? index)
    (inc item)
    nil)
  )

(keep-indexed
 mien
```

```
(range 10 20))
```

There's more...

Filtering is a very useful Clojure function, that can be used in many different coding situations.

Filter as a transducer

The `filter` function can also be used as a transducer when no argument is given. We will see that in the next chapter, but here is a quick reminder of how you use this feature.

In the following examples, both `filter` and `map` are used to create a transducer:

```
(transduce
(filter even?)  conj (range 5))
; [0 2 4]

(transduce
(map inc)
conj
(range 5))
```

Filtering with core.async

As of recent times, the `filter` function can be used directly with the channels from the `core.async` library. This makes it very interesting to apply filtering directly at the stream level. This is also done through transducers, as seen here.

We require the library:

```
(require '[clojure.core.async :as async])
```

We create the channel and how to filter odd values that come through it:

```
(def c (async/chan 1 (filter  odd?)))
; We put an infinite lazy sequence on the channel
(async/onto-chan c (range))
; We then retrieve values ...
(async/<!! c) ; => 1
(async/<!! c) ; => 3
(async/<!! c) ; => 5
```

As planned, only odd values are popping up from the channel. Good job! It's now up to you to imagine new uses for those transducers. In this section, we have seen how to use a set of functions to filter elements from sequences and lazy sequences. We also previewed how those generic filtering functions can be used as transducers, and even Clojure's `core.async` channels. We will also review those last concepts in the coming chapters!

Transforming and sorting collections

In this section, we will review different ways of getting sorted. All you ever wanted to know about sorting Clojure collections will be in this recipe.

As usual, Clojure offers practical ways of using the same functions in generic situations so as to refine your sorting to the particular needs.

In almost all cases, the sorted collection is a new instance of the input, but we will also look at corner cases when using Clojure/Java interop, where the collection may keep an internal state to be aware of.

Getting ready

This section does not make use of any external libraries, so you can just start REPL and be ready.

How to do it...

To get a good grasp of how to use the different sorting methods, we will go through the most important functions first, and we will look at the under-the-hood functions in the next sub-section.

Using built-in sort

The built-in sort is easy to grasp and use. As with the usual Clojure functions, a new collection is created on applying sorting.

Let's see how to sort numbers, characters, and strings with simple code:

```
(sort [2 10 3 4 7])
; (2 3 4 7 10)

(sort ["a" "b" "e" "d" ])
; ("a" "b" "d" "e")
```

You may also think I have recorded the examples or typed things in, so let's also try it on a randomly generated collection. We start by generating a random ten-integer list:

```
(def to-sort
    (take 10
        (repeatedly
            #(rand-int 1000))))

(sort to-sort)
; (4 6 221 233 272 332 441 474 535 927)
```

Without any parameters, the `sort` function uses the default compare function. We can use a function of our choice:

```
(sort > [2 10 3 4 7])
; (10 7 4 3 2)

(sort < [2 10 3 4 7])
; (2 3 4 7 10)
```

As you would expect, `sort` also works on different collection types:

```
(sort < '(10 3 2 9))
; (2 3 9 10)
(sort < #{10 3 2 9})
; (2 3 9 10)
```

Let's add a bit of randomness so that we make sure we are not been cheated:

```
(sort
  <
        (repeatedly 5
            #(rand-int 1000)))
; (61 198 402 536 973)
```

Migrating to sort-by

The `sort-by` function is quite similar to `sort`, but the function that is used for comparison only takes one argument. If we want to sort strings by their length, we can use the `count` function directly:

```
(sort-by
 count
 ["this is the first string"
  "this is the second string"
  "another one"])
; ("another one" "this is the first string" "this is the second string")
```

This also works the same if we want to sort strings based on the first index of the character `"a"`:

```
(sort-by
 #(clojure.string/index-of % "a")
 ["ca" "bba" "al"])
; ("al" "ca" "bba")
```

Using sorted-set

`sorted-set` creates a slightly different internal data structure, of type `PersistentTreeSet`, that we will see in a bit more detail afterwards. For now, let's say we start with a structure that will be sorted, and keep on being sorted, even after adding new items to it:

```
; pass the values to sort directly to
; the sorted-set function
(sorted-set 2 1 3)
; #{1 2 3}

; call sorted-set on an existing set
; will return a new sorted set.
(apply sorted-set #{2 1 3})
; #{1 2 3}

; you can transform a sequence to a sorted set as well:
(apply sorted-set '(1 3 2 7 6 ))
; #{1 2 3 6 7}
```

We can, of course, also specify the function to do the sorting, just like with `sort`:

```
(apply
 sorted-set-by
 >
 #{2 1 3})
; #{3 2 1}
```

A very frequent usage of `sorted-set` is composing with `into`. `into` converts a data structure, taking all the elements of the input, to another one of a given type. You do remember basic usage of the `into` function, as follows:

```
(into [] (range 5))
; [0 1 2 3 4]
(into {} [[:a :b] [:c :d]])
; {:a :b, :c :d}
```

Creating a new tree with `sorted-set` and adding elements to it via `into` is therefore nicely suited and bird-friendly:

```
(into (sorted-set) [3 2 9])
; #{2 3 9}
```

Finally, as its name would tend to indicate, `sorted-set` returns a set. This means there will be no duplicate values in the resulting collection:

```
#{1 2 2 3}
; java.lang.IllegalArgumentException: Duplicate key: 2
```

Working with sorted collection subsets

Two functions from `clojure.core` are a great extension to `sorted-set`; they are `subseq` and `rsubseq` for, as you just found, creating sub-sequences or reverse sub-sequences from sorted sets. Both functions need a sorted set and will benefit from the internal data structure being extremely fast.

For example, let's say we want to find an element greater than 500 in a random list, and I am sure you do. We create the sorted set with a call to `sorted-set` then pass this as a parameter to `subseq` along with the test, `<`, and the key, `500`:

```
(subseq
 (apply sorted-set
        (take 10
              (repeatedly
                #(rand-int 1000)))))
```

```
    > 500)
;  (537 598 817 818 953 965)
```

`rsubseq` works in a similar way but returns a reverse version of the resulting sub-collection:

```
(rsubseq
    (apply sorted-set
          (take 10
                (repeatedly
                    #(rand-int 1000))))
    > 500)
;  (917 878 820 715 641 544)
```

Sorting Clojure maps

Sorting is not confined to one-dimensional collections; we can, and should, do some sorting on Clojure maps.

We will start by noticing that a call to the regular `sort` will sort on keys:

```
(sort {:c 2 :b 3})
;  ([:b 3] [:c 2])
```

`sort-by` will get us to the next level by being able to sort on desired keys. Since keywords are functions, we can use them to do the sorting (hint, we will go over this very soon):

```
(sort-by
 :price
 >
 [{:price  10 :product :apple}
  {:price 30 :product :tomato}
  {:price 5 :product :peanuts}])
```

Before you know it, we will recall the Clojure function `juxt`, which can create a combination of two functions. Calling `juxt` on a single entry map will return a vector containing the result of each call of `fn1`, `fn2` on the same structure, here, a map:

```
((juxt :price :quantity)
    {:price  10 :quantity 2})
;  [10 2]
```

The result may look surprising at first, but when you look at it in detail, we called `:price` on the map, got `10`, then called `:quantity` on the map, and got `2`.

This `juxt-ed` combination can be use to sort again through `sort-by`:

```
(sort-by
 (juxt :price :quantity)
 [{:price  10 :quantity 2}
  {:price 10 :quantity 1}
  {:price 5 :quantity 10}])

; ({:price 5, :quantity 10}
    {:price 10, :quantity 1}
    {:price 10, :quantity 2})
```

Since records also behave like maps, I am sure you will have some fun when applying the preceding `sort-by` to records:

```
(defrecord Person [first-name])
(sort-by
       :first-name
 [(->Person "nico")
  (->Person "Makoto")
  (->Person "Princess Peach")])

; (#chapter02.sorting.Person{:first-name "Makoto"}
    #chapter02.sorting.Person{:first-name "Princess Peach"}
    #chapter02.sorting.Person{:first-name "nico"})
```

Sorted map structure

`sorted-map` is the equivalent sorted data structure to `sorted-set`. We can use those two functions in very similar ways, and again, the preferred way here is to use them in conjunction with `into`, to convert from a regular map to a sorted map data structure.

The default `compare` behavior for `sorted-map` is to sort by keys:

```
(sorted-map :a 2 :b 3)
; {:a 2, :b 3}

(into (sorted-map) {:a 2 :b 3})
; {:a 2, :b 3}

(into (sorted-map) {2 :b 3 :a})
; {2 :b, 3 :a}
```

To define our own comparator, we will make use of `sorted-map-by`, which accepts a comparator as the first argument. Here, we see how to sort the entries based on their values:

```
(let [to-sort {:a 3 :b 5 :c 7 :d 2 :e 10 :f 1}]
  (into
    (sorted-map-by
      #(compare
             (get to-sort %1)
             (get to-sort %2)))
        to-sort))
; {:f 1, :d 2, :a 3, :b 5, :c 7, :e 10}
```

Are you sorted yet?

`sorted-map` and `sorted-set` are examples of sorted collections. Those are actually implemented as Java data structures, and implement the `Sorted` interface. To know if a collection is sorted or not, we refer to the `sorted?` method, which delegates its result to the simple fact of whether the data structure is implementing the `Sorted` interface or not. This is the Clojure snippet code for sorted:

```
(instance? clojure.lang.Sorted coll)
```

Thus, you can sort a map and check if it is indeed sorted:

```
(sorted?
  (sorted-map :a 2 :b 3))
; true
```

As we have seen, a sorted collection can be used as a parameter to `subseq` and `rsubseq`.

Be aware that just because a collection seems to be sorted, it does not mean `sorted?` will return `true`:

```
(sorted? [1 2 3])
; false
```

How it works...

We have been keeping this secret so far, but yes, functions in Clojure are all implementing an abstract class named `AFunction`. (At least on the JVM ....):

```
public abstract class AFunction extends AFn implements IObj, Comparator,
Fn, Serializable {
..
}
```

As we can see, `AFunction` implements the Java interface `java.util.Comparator`, and what that means in simple terms is that any Clojure function can be used directly as a comparator.

Let's see that again in action:

```
(sort
 #(< %1 %2)
 [1 2 3 0 -1])
(-1 0 1 2 3)
```

If we want to keep things as they are, or reverse them, we can always return `true` or `false`:

```
(sort
 (fn[_ _] true)
 [1 2 3 0 -1])
; (-1 0 3 2 1)

(sort
 (fn[_ _] false)
 [1 2 3 0 -1])
; (1 2 3 0 -1)
```

The `compare` function of any function, `AFunction`, simply checks the return value by invoking itself with two items:

```
public int compare(Object o1, Object o2){
    Object o = invoke(o1, o2);
    if(o instanceof Boolean)
    {
        if(RT.booleanCast(o))
                return -1;
        return RT.booleanCast(invoke(o2,o1))? 1 : 0;
    }
    Number n = (Number) o;
    return n.intValue();
}
```

So, if the function returns a Boolean and that Boolean is `true`, we suppose the first object is smaller. Then we compare the Boolean value of the reverse invoke call to find out if the values are equal or not.

Finally, if we're not in the Boolean domain, we use numeric values to compare:

```
(sort
 (fn [_ _] -1)
 [1 2 3 0 -1])
; (-1 0 3 2 1)
```

Clojure sort calls on the JVM eventually rely on the JVM's own sort implementation, which is a modified version of the merge sort algorithm.

There is more to explain about sorting on the JVM, but we'll leave it for now as it is out of the scope of this recipe.

In any case, sort in Clojure should be as fast as sort on Java collections.

There's more...

Sorting is a fun sport on its own and we could go through all sorts of algorithms. Here, we will focus on how to use sorting in day-to-day tasks.

Sorting lines of a file

In this small example, we will learn how to sort lines of text read from a file. The following example will load the whole file in memory, so it may not be appropriate for most big files, but we can see how to directly apply what we've learned about sorting to organize lines in a file:

```
; we will make use of the threading operator
(->>
    ; read the full file from memory
    (slurp "project.clj")
    ; split lines
    clojure.string/split-lines
    ; here we go. our custom sort, comparing line length with count
    (sort #(compare (count %1) (count %2)))
    ; join each element of the previous sequence with end of line
character
    (clojure.string/join "\n")
    ; put the result in a new file
    (spit "target/buffer.out"))
```

In this recipe, we have seen how to sort data structure with a call to `sort`, and `sort-by`, as well as other ways to compare items in a collection. We also saw how to create and keep a collection sorted. Finally, we saw how to apply sorting knowledge to real-world cases such as reading and parsing files.

Merging and splitting collections

Sometimes, you'd like to merge multiple collections into a single collection or split a single collection into multiple collections. Let's have a look these cases.

Getting ready

You only need REPL, described in the *Repl up!* recipe in `Chapter 1`, *Live Programming with Clojure*, and no additional libraries. Start REPL, and you can review the sample code in this recipe.

How to do it...

Let's see how to merge and split collections.

Using merge and merge-with for merging

The `merge` function merges multiple maps into a single map. If there are the same keys among maps in arguments, latter entries override former entries:

```
(merge {:a 1 :b 2 :c 3} {:c 4 :d 5 :e 6})
;;=> {:a 1, :b 2, :c 4, :d 5, :e 6}
(merge {:a 1 :b 2 :c 3} {:c 4 :d 5 :e 6} {:c 7 :f 4 :g 6})
;;=> {:a 1, :b 2, :c 7, :d 5, :e 6, :f 4, :g 6}
```

The `merge-with` function is more amazing:

```
(def nicos-fruits
  {:apple 10 :melon 15 :orange 2 :pear 12}
  )
;;=> #'collection.core/nicos-fruits

(def makotos-fruits
  {:apple 10 :orange 2 :lemon 8 :lime 9}
  )
```

```
#'collection.core/makotos-fruits
(merge-with + nicos-fruits makotos-fruits)
;;=> {:apple 20, :melon 15, :orange 4, :pear 12, :lemon 8, :lime 9}
```

Let's define a function that summarizes the fruits maps:

```
(defn summarize [& fruits]
  (apply merge-with +  fruits)
  )
;;=> #'collection.core/summarize
(summarize nicos-fruits makotos-fruits)
;;=> {:apple 20, :melon 15, :orange 4, :pear 12, :lemon 8, :lime 9}
```

The zipmap merges keys and values for maps

The zipmap function creates a map from a key list and a value list:

```
(zipmap [:a :b :c :d :e] [1 2 3 4 5])
;;=> {:a 1, :b 2, :c 3, :d 4, :e 5}
```

Using interleave

The interleave function interleaves its argument collections:

```
(apply assoc {} (interleave [:a :b :c :d :e] [1 2 3 4 5]))
;;=> {:a 1, :b 2, :c 3, :d 4, :e 5}
```

Using split-at and split-with to split collections

The split-at function splits collections by position. The split-with function splits collections with a conditional function:

```
(split-at 5 (range 10))
;;=> [(0 1 2 3 4) (5 6 7 8 9)]
(split-with (partial > 5) (range 10))
;;=> [(0 1 2 3 4) (5 6 7 8 9)]
```

How it works...

The `interleave` function returns a lazy sequence; we can define the following function:

```
(defn make-random-vars [n]
  (apply assoc {}
         (take (* n 2)
               (interleave (map #(keyword (str "x" (inc %))) (range))
                           (repeatedly #(float (rand 100)))
                           ))
         )
  )
(make-random-vars 5)
;;=> {:x1 72.97348, :x2 38.836014, :x3 96.239944, :x4 95.13157, :x5
81.230804}
(make-random-vars 10)
;;=> {:x9 85.312256, :x10 27.16199, :x4 10.890139, :x6 33.993263, :x7
61.26995, :x3 96.727, :x1 34.886852, :x8 60.126255, :x5 87.26598, :x2
30.690058}
```

There's more...

We will teach you more techniques here.

Using group-by to split collections

The `group-by` function groups by function argument. The following code groups people by company:

```
(group-by :company
'({:name "John" :company "facebook"}
  {:name "Tony" :company "twtter"}
  {:name "Andy" :company "google"}
  {:name "Sally" :company "twtter"}
  {:name "Peter" :company "google"}
  {:name "Sara" :company "facebook"}
    {:name "Linda" :company "twtter"}
  )
)
;;=> {"facebook"
 [{:name "John", :company "facebook"}
  {:name "Sara", :company "facebook"}],
 "twtter"
 [{:name "Tony", :company "twtter"}
  {:name "Sally", :company "twtter"}
```

```
   {:name "Linda", :company "twtter"}],
  "google"
  [{:name "Andy", :company "google"}
   {:name "Peter", :company "google"}]}
```

Using the filter function to split collections

The next sample demonstrates splitting collections using the `filter` function. The `split-into-two` function splits a collection into two collections according to whether its elements are odd or even. The `split-into-three` function splits a collection into three collections by taking out remainders of its elements:

```
(defn split-into-two [col]
  (list (filter odd? col)
        (filter even? col)
        )
  )
;;=> #'chapter03.core/split-into-two
(split-into-two (range 12))
;;=> ((1 3 5 7 9 11) (0 2 4 6 8 10))
(defn split-into-three [col]
  (list (filter #(= (rem % 3) 0) col)
        (filter #(= (rem % 3) 1) col)
        (filter #(= (rem % 3) 2) col)
        )
  )
;;=> #'chapter03.core/split-into-three
(split-into-three (range 12))
;;=> ((0 3 6 9) (1 4 7 10) (2 5 8 11))
```

How to become lazy

As you may know, laziness is a simple concept. It is the act of only doing the minimum required, or to postpone work until the very last moment. This is a conscious choice, and therefore must be applied with care.

One of the reasons Clojure is enjoyable as a programming language is because it makes it easy to be lazy; or, in simple computing terms, it only evaluates the minimum needed, when it is needed. Nothing extra.

So, why would you want to be lazy, or in other words, build lazy sequences? Obviously, to avoid unnecessary computations. An example of this is, say, if you have a mathematical formula or a repeating function defining a list of elements and you only want to use some of those elements. This is when you want to write a lazy sequence, and not evaluate all the elements of the list up front but only those that will be accessed and used at runtime.

In this recipe, we will see first how to use lazy sequences in Clojure, as well as create our own.

Getting ready

For this section, we do not need anything else but a running REPL. To prepare for laziness, though, we can have look at the source of the `lazy-seq` macro, which is the way we can create lazy collections:

```
(defmacro lazy-seq
 [& body]
  (list 'new 'clojure.lang.LazySeq (list* '^{:once true} fn* [] body)))
```

Without going into too much detail, we can see the Clojure code delegates calls to a Java object, LazySeq, https://github.com/clojure/clojure/blob/master/src/jvm/clojure/lang/LazySeq.java, defined from a single function.

The object itself holds a reference to the first object and to the next function call. The main implemented interface is ISeq. See https://github.com/clojure/clojure/blob/master/src/jvm/clojure/lang/ISeq.java for more details.

How to do it…

We will progressively see how laziness is put into action, then see how to create our own lazy sequences.

The iterate function

The `iterate` function is a simple way to get into lazy sequences. `iterate` builds a lazy sequence from a function and a starting value. For example, here we build an infinite sequence of integers, starting from zero, adding one at each iteration:

```
(iterate inc 0)
; (0 1 2 3 4 ....
; note the above will hang your REPL, if you don't use
```

```
;  (set! *print-length* 50)
;  to set the max number of items to print from collections.
```

This applies a function, inc, to the first element, 0, which gives 1. 1 is then the new seed of the sequence, and the realized sequence is made up of (0 1). At the next step, we apply inc to the new seed, 1, which gives 2, which is appended to the realized portion of the sequence to give (0 1 2) and the new seed is 2, and so on. The sequence produced will be as follows:

```
((inc 0) (inc (inc 0)) (inc (inc (inc 0)))  ...
;  (1 (inc 1) (inc (inc 1) ...)
;  (1 2 (inc 2)
;  and so on
```

We also compute (or we use the term realize), only when needed. Thus, from the full lazy-seq of iterate here, we only take the first five elements:

```
(take 5 (iterate inc 0))
(0 1 2 3 4)
```

Realized?

To partner with lazy sequences, we have the realized? function, which tells us whether a sequence or subsequence has been evaluated or not. Take the following example, which takes the first five elements of the previous lazy sequence:

```
(def a (take 5 (iterate inc 0)))
;  '#a
(realized? a)
;  false
(println a)
;  console shows: (0 1 2 3 4)
(realized? a)
;  true
```

We see that a has the possibility to be computed, but has not been evaluated until we actually refer to its value through the println function. realized? is very useful for checking whether a sequence has been fully computed or not.

Random sequences with repeatedly

Now, let's say we want to build a sequence of random integers. We similarly use another lazy sequence, producing a function named `repeatedly`. This function always calls to the same function, and does not depend on a current or previous seed:

```
(repeatedly #(rand-int 10))
; (5 7 2 10 9 2 10 9 8 10 5 0 7 7 10  ...)
```

Using the macro lazy-seq

To build a more generic lazy sequence, we can use the macro `lazy-seq`.

From the Clojure lazy page, `lazy-seq` takes a body of expressions that returns an `ISeq` or `nil`, and yields a seqable object that will invoke the body only the first time `seq` is called, and will cache the result and return it on all subsequent `seq` calls.

With this in mind, we can re-implement our random `int` to generate lazy sequences, as follows:

```
(defn rand-seq []
  (lazy-seq
    (cons
      (rand)
      (rand-seq))))
```

As we have seen before, we realize the first element using `(rand)` and then call upon ourselves again through the same method name `(rand-seq)`.

How it works...

In Clojure, the `lazy-seq` macro is implemented directly in Java. There are three key elements in this implementation:

- A head, or a seed, which is the top value of a sequence
- The sequence of realized or computed values
- The information necessary (a function, for example) to compute the other elements of the sequence

Let's see how `lazy-seq` can be represented with a small diagram:

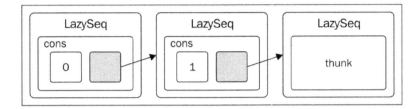

A `Thunk` is enough information for the other elements to be computed.

Note, lazy sequences are evaluated in chunks of around 30 elements, 32 to be precise, so some values are computed ahead of their actual need because this is usually more efficient that making function calls one by one.

Look at the following example:

```
(take 10 (cycle [1 2 3]))
```

Even though we are only accessing the first 10 values, the first 32 will be computed, to improve efficiency.

In `rand-seq`, we do not get stack overflows from `lazy-seq` calls because the realized part of the sequence is being cached, and only the next elements contain information on how to get computed.

There's more...

Lazy sequences is one of the core key concepts of this book. In this short section, we will see other ways to write lazy sequences, as well as forcing sequences to not be lazy and be realized as soon as possible.

Other lazy-seq-producing functions

We have seen two functions, `iterate` and `repeatedly`, and the more generic `lazy-seq` macro to generate lazy sequences in a generic way. As much as possible, Clojure sequences are lazy.

For example, the following table shows a list of lazy sequence-producing functions:

Name	Usage	Example
cycle	Cycles through a sequence or vector and generates an infinite sequence	(cycle [1 2 3])
repeat	Produces an infinite sequence of the same element	(repeat 1)
iterate	As we have seen, produces an infinite sequence of x, (f x) (f (f x))	(iterate inc 0)
range	Produces an infinite lazy sequence from a starting point	(range 10)
interleave	Produces a lazy-sequence made of one item of col1, then one item of col2, and so on	(interleave (cycle [:a :b]) (range))

Functions in `clojure.core` generate lazy sequences as well. See the following functions:

- map
- filter
- remove
- take, take-while
- drop, drop-last, drop-while

Force evaluation with doall

With all this laziness going around, you might wonder how to force evaluation of the lazy sequence ahead of it being accessed. We use a function named `doall`. `doall` forces the realization of all the elements in the lazy sequence. We can check this by calling `realized?` on the sequences, as shown here:

```
(def a
  (take 100 (map inc (cycle [1 2 3])))) 
(realized? a)
; false

(def  b
  (doall
    (take 100 (map inc (cycle [1 2 3]))))) 
(realized? b)
; true
```

Lazy evaluation with files

File reading is a good example of where you should be careful when using lazy sequences, and where it is actually important to pay attention to the order in which the Clojure code is executed. Take this example:

```
(def c  (with-open [rdr (clojure.java.io/reader "project.clj")]
            (interleave (line-seq rdr) (cycle "\n") )))
```

Nothing suspicious at first; you open a file and then use a function named `line-seq`, which you know produces a lazy sequence of each line of the opened file. `interleave` then appends an end-of-line character between lines.

So, with all confidence, you rush to the following:

```
(println c)
; and ...
; java.io.IOException: Stream closed
```

What has just happened? The `with-open` call actually also wraps a close stream call so that by the time the call returns `c`, the stream has already been closed. Eventually, `println` asks for the sequence to be realized, but with the stream being closed, things are going wonky.

A quick way to go around the problem is to simply force the execution:

```
(def e (with-open [rdr (clojure.java.io/reader "project.clj")]
            (apply str  (interleave (line-seq rdr) (cycle "\n") ))))

; (def e (with-open [rdr (clojure.java.io/reader "project.clj")]
;             (doall  (interleave (line-seq rdr) (cycle "\n") ))))
(println e)
```

This shows that functions that have side effects, such as requiring a state and access to data that is not shown in the code, need to be cautiously used with `lazy-seq`.

Apart from this particular example, `lazy-seq` is full steam ahead for efficiency.

The map function and calling rest

If you remember the `map` function, you would remember that `map`, in its simplest form, produces a lazy sequence of a function applied to every element of another sequence:

```
(map inc (range))
; (1 2 3 4 5 6 7 8 9 10 11 12 13 14 15 16 17 ...)
```

`map-s` gives a nice template to show how to build a lazy sequence using `lazy-seq`, `cons`, and `rest`:

```
(defn map-2
 ([f coll]
  (lazy-seq
   (when-let [s (seq coll)]
     (cons (f (first s)) (map-2 f (rest s)))))))

(map-2 inc (range 0 100))
```

We make use of the following:

- The `lazy-seq` macro, to evaluate the sequence in chunks.
- `cons` concatenates two elements.
- It realizes the first element of the sequence using `first`.
- It calls to itself to keep evaluating the rest of the sequence. `rest` here acts more or less as a pointer to what needs to remain evaluated.

Voila. We have seen how to get our laziness to a new level. No more excuses to not go out and have a great time.

3

Clojure Next

In this chapter, we will cover the following topics:

- Using destructuring techniques
- Using functional programming style
- Using threading macros
- Defining simple macros
- Defining more advanced macros
- Using protocols
- Defining multimethods
- Transducers for dummies
- Logic programming in Clojure

Introduction

This chapter is for Clojure programmers to jump to the next step and contains advanced concepts and techniques, including destructing, functional programming, and macros. Clojure's macros are very strongly inherited from Lisp. You will learn how to realize polymorphism in Clojure using protocol and multimethod. Finally, you will dive into the transducers and logic programming that take you to Clojure's fantastic world!

Using destructuring techniques

Destructuring can be used in `defn` and `let`. This technique provides flexible ways to extract values for bodies of functions or `let` expressions. Though destructuring looks a bit unusual for beginners of Clojure and programmers of other languages, it is effective for extracting desired values from the structural data of arguments and binding values.

Getting ready

This recipe uses the `math.numeric-tower` and `core.match` functions, so change the `:dependency` in the `project.clj` file as follows and restart the REPL, and be ready:

```
:dependencies
 [[org.clojure/clojure "1.8.0"]
  [org.clojure/math.numeric-tower "0.0.4"]
  [org.clojure/core.match "0.3.0-alpha4"]
  ]
```

How to do it...

Here, let's learn how to do sequential destructing and map destructing.

Sequential destructuring

Sequential destructuring is for extracting desired elements from sequence collections. In the following code, variables x, y, z bind to 1, 2, 3:

```
(let [[x y z] [1 2 3]]
 [x y z]
  )
;;=> [1 2 3]
```

Similarly, x, y, and z bind to 1, 2, and 3, and a, b, and c bind to "a", "b", and "c":

```
(let [[x y z] [1 2 3] [a b c] ["a" "b" "c"]]
     [x y z a b c]
      )
;;=> [1 2 3 "a" "b" "c"]
```

The variadic arguments feature accepts variable number of arguments we have already seen in Chapter 1, *Live Programming with Clojure*. In the following example, the z binds to (3 4):

```
(let [[x y & z] [1 2 3 4]]
 [x y z]
 )
:;=> [1 2 (3 4)]
```

Underscore (_) represents unused arguments explicitly:

```
(let [[x _ z] [1 2 3]]
 [x z]
 )
;;=> [1 3]
```

Using map destructuring

The map destructuring extracts desired values from maps. In the following example, the x, y, and z bind to 1, 2, and 3:

```
(let
    [{x :x y :y z :z} {:x 1 :y 2 :z 3}]
    [x y z])
;;=> [1 2 3]
```

The preceding expression looks a bit verbose. There is a simpler, shortcut expression of map destructuring, as follows:

```
(let
    [{:keys [x y z]} {:x 1 :y 2 :z 3}]
  [x y z])
;;=> [1 2 3]
```

If keys of maps are strings or symbols, use the :strs or :syms instead:

```
(let
   [{:strs [x y z]} {"x" 1 "y" 2 "z" 3}]
 [x y z])
 ;;=> [1 2 3]
(let
   [{:syms [x y z]} {'x 1 'y 2  'z  3}]
 [x y z])
;;=> [1 2 3]
```

If you would like to specify the default values, use the `:or` keyword and specify the default value. In the following example, the values of `:y` and `:z` are not specified in the map and as a result, the `y` and `z` bind to the default values:

```
(let
    [{:keys [x y z] :or {x 0 y 0 z 0}}
     {:x 1}
     ]
  [x y z])
  ;;=> [1 0 0]
```

Using the `:as` keyword, the followed variable binds to the map itself. In the following example, the `all` binds to `{:x 1 :a 2 :b 3}`:

```
(let
    [{:keys [x y z] :or {x 0 y 0 z 0} :as all} {:x 1 :a 2 :b 3}
     ]
  [x y z all])
  ;;=> [1 0 0 {:x 1, :a 2, :b 3}]
```

The following map-destructuring code extracts values from a nested map:

```
(let
    [{x :x y :y {a :a b :b} :z}
     {:x 1 :y 2 :z {:a 3 :b 4}}
     ]
  [x y a b])
  ;;=> [1 2 3 4]
```

The following code uses the shortcut style of nested-map destructuring:

```
(let
    [{:keys [x y] {:keys [a b]} :z}
     {:x 1 :y 2 :z {:a 3 :b 4}}
     ]
  [x y a b])
  :;=> [1 2 3 4]
```

How it works...

Using the destructuring technique properly makes function definitions simpler. Let's compare two versions of function definitions – one using sequence destructuring and one not using it:

```
(defn func1 [[x y z]]
  (+ x y z)
```

```
    )
;;=> #'chapter03.destucturing/func1
(func2 [1 2 3])
;;=> 6
(defn func2 [col]
    (+ (first col) (second col) (nth col 2))
    )
;;=> #'chapter03.destucturing/func2
(func2 [1 2 3])
;;=> 6
```

The comparison between using map destructuring and not using it is similar:

```
(defn func3 [{:keys [x y z]}]
    (+ x y z)
    )
;;=> #'chapter03.destucturing/func3
(func3 {:x 1 :y 2 :z 3})
;;=> 6
(defn func4 [col]
    (+ (:x col) (:y col) (:z col))
    )
;;=> #'chapter03.destucturing/func4
(func4 {:x 1 :y 2 :z 3})
;;=> 6
```

There's more...

Let's learn more advanced techniques for destructuring for string and using `core.match`.

Sequential destructuring for string

Sequential destructing can be used for string to pick up characters from strings. The following code gets the first, third, and fifth characters and returns a vector containing these characters:

```
(let [[a _ b _ c ] "Clojure"]
  [a b c])
;;=> [\C \o \u]
```

The following code eliminates the first three characters from a string:

```
(let [[_ _ _ & x] "Clojure"]
  (apply str x))
;;=> "jure"
```

Conditional destructing with core.match

The `core.match` is pattern matching library for Clojure. The `core.match` performs conditional destructing.

First, to make use of the `match` function in the `clojure.core.match`, do the following:

```
(require '[clojure.core.match :refer [match]])
;;=> nil
```

The `core.match` is a strong matching library for pattern matching. The following example shows a typical sequential pattern matching. In the following code, `[x y z]` matches _`[false true true]`_, and as a result, is evaluated to be 3:

```
(let [x false y true z true]
  (match [x y z]
         [false false false] 1
         [false false true]  2
         [false true true]   3
         :else 5))
;;=> 3
```

The following code is a map pattern-matching example. The given map matches the third pattern `{:a a :b b}` and b binds to 2:

```
(let [x {:a 3 :b 2 :c 1}]
  (match [x]
         [{:a 1 :b b}]   {:b1 b}
         [({:a 3 :b a} :only [:a :b])] {:a2 a}
         [{:a a :b b}]   {:a3 b}
         :else nil))
;;=> {:a3 2}
```

In the preceding example, we use the `:only` modifier. It matches keys of the given map that are `:a` and `:b`. The next code is a function that calculates the two- or three-dimensional distance between two points using `core.match`. The number of elements of function arguments should be exactly two or three, otherwise you'll get an error:

```
(require '[clojure.math.numeric-tower :as math])
(defn distance [x y]
    (match [x y]
           [[x1 y1][x2 y2]]
           (math/sqrt
            (+ (math/expt (- x2 x1) 2) (math/expt (- y2 y1) 2)))
           [[x1 y1 z1][x2 y2 z2]]
           (+ (math/expt (- x2 x1) 2) (math/expt (- y2 y1) 2) (math/expt (-
z2 z1) 2))
```

```
        :else :error
        )
  )
;;=> #'chapter03.destucturing/distance
(distance [0 0] [1 1])
;;=> 1.4142135623730951
(distance [0 0 0] [1 1 1])
;;=> 3
(distance [0 0 0] [1 1 1 1])
:error
```

Using functional programming style

In this recipe, we will show you how to define and use anonymous functions and have functions as arguments and return functions. Using the concepts and techniques described here correctly provides higher abstraction.

Getting ready

This section does not make use of any external library, so you can just start a REPL and be ready.

How to do it...

First, let's see some functions take functional arguments.

Functions taking functions as their arguments

Clojure functions such as map and reduce can take functions as arguments.

map

The map function has already been seen in the previous chapters. The map function takes a function as the first argument, applies it to all elements of collection arguments, and returns a lazy sequence.

In the following example, `map` applies `inc` to all elements of the collection:

```
(map inc [1 2 3 4 5])
;;=> (2 3 4 5 6)
```

The `map` function takes an arbitrary number of arguments and returns a lazy sequence. The following code applies + to five arguments:

```
(take 10 (map + (range) (range) (range) (range)(range)))
;;=> (0 5 10 15 20 25 30 35 40 45)
```

The number of iterations of `map` to collections is limited to the collection that has the smallest number of elements.

In the following code, the number of the arguments in the third collection is the smallest and returns a collection of 10 elements:

```
(map + (range) (range) (range 10) (range)(range))
;;=> (0 5 10 15 20 25 30 35 40 45)
```

reduce

The `reduce` function applies a binary operation to a collection. It applies a function to the first two elements, and then applies a function to the result and the next element until there is no element to reduce:

```
(reduce + [1 2 3 4 5])
;;=> 15
```

The preceding expression is calculated as follows:

```
(+ (+ (+ (+ 1 2) 3) 4) 5)
```

apply

The `apply` function accepts a variadic function as the first argument and applies it to collections. The following code applies the + to 1, 2, 3, 4, and 5:

```
(apply + [1 2 3 4 5])
;;=> 15
```

So, the preceding result is the same as (+ 1 2 3 4 5). The `apply` function can take any number of arguments before the final sequence collection:

```
(apply + 1 2 3 [4 5])
;;=> 15
```

The following code works with collections where the elements are a string:

```
(apply str ["Clojure" " " "programming" " " "cookbook"])
;;=> "Clojure programming cookbook"
```

The preceding is the same as (str "Clojure" " " "programming" " " "cookbook").

Using anonymous functions

Here, we will learn about anonymous functions in Clojure.

Anonymous functions using fn

Clojure can define anonymous functions used in arguments in functions or variable assignments using let or def. The fn function defines anonymous functions. The following code defines a simple anonymous function x + 2 for the map function:

```
(map (fn [x] (+ x 2)) [1 2 3 4 5])
;;=> (3 4 5 6 7)
```

The equivalent code using the defn is as follows:

```
(defn add2 [x]
  (+ x 2)
  )
;;=> #'chapter03.functional/add2
(map add2 [1 2 3 4 5])
;;=> (3 4 5 6 7)
```

The defn is a macro using the def and fn special forms. So, function defined by the defn is equivalent to function by the def and fn. The following code is using def and fn to define x + 2:

```
(def my-add2 (fn [x] (+ x 2)))
;;=> #'chapter03.functional/my-add2
(my-add2 3)
;;=> 5
```

The fn? function examines whether a symbol is defined by the fn:

```
(fn? add2)
;;=> true
(fn? my-add2)
;;=> true
```

The `fn` function can take variadic arguments as follows:

```
((fn [x y & rest] (apply * x y rest)) 1 2 3 4 5)
;;=> 120
```

Using function literals to define anonymous functions

Clojure has a syntax sugar to define anonymous functions more straightforward:

```
(map #(+ % 2) [1 2 3 4 5])
;;=> (3 4 5 6 7)
```

To define function literals, we have a preceding # and then the body of the function. The %
binds to a value. If there is more than one argument, %, %2, %3, and so on are used as
follows:

```
(#(+ % %2 %3) 1 2 3)
;;=> 6
```

Functions returning functions

Here, we will demonstrate functions returning functions as their returns.

constantly

The `constantly` function returns a function that returns a constant value. In the following
code, (`constantly` 0) returns the function that always returns zero:

```
(map (constantly 0) [1 2 3 4 5])
;;=> (0 0 0 0 0)
```

complement

The `complement` function takes a function as an argument and returns a function that
returns the complement of the given function. The following code returns `true` if an
argument is empty and returns `false` otherwise:

```
(def not-empty?
  (complement empty?))
;;=> #'chapter03.functional/not-empty?
(not-empty? [])
;;=> false
(not-empty? [1 2 3])
;;=> true
```

The following expression generates a set that contains random values smaller than 30:

```
(set (take 15 (repeatedly #(rand-int 30))))
;;=> #{7 20 4 21 29 28 25 3 2 14 18 8}
```

Therefore, the following code will be always true:

```
(defn larger-than-15? [n] (> n 15))
;;=> #'chapter03.functional/larger-than-15?
(let [x (set (take 15 (repeatedly #(rand-int 100))))]
  (= x
     (set (clojure.set/union
            (filter larger-than-15? x)
            (filter (complement larger-than-15?) x)
            )
          ))
  )
;;=> true
```

partial

Since some Clojure functions accept functions with a single argument, `partial` is useful to make a function that always returns a unary function.

The following example extracts elements larger than 10 from a vector using `partial`:

```
(filter (partial < 10) [1 21 34 12 2])
;;=> (21 34 12)
```

The following is the equivalent code using a function literal:

```
(filter #(< 10 %) [1 21 34 12 2])
;;=> (21 34 12)
```

comp

The `comp` composes a function from functions given as arguments.

The expression `(comp f2 f1)` applies `f1` to arguments and then applies `f2` to the results of `f1`. The `comp` applies functions from right to left. The following code increments the number and then negates it:

```
(map (comp - inc) [ 1 2 3 4 5])
;;=> (-2 -3 -4 -5 -6)
```

every-pred and some-fn

The `every-pred` function returns a function to test whether all predicates are true.

In the following code, `every-pred` returns a function that checks whether all tests for all arguments are passed or not:

```
2 < x < 12
x is odd number
```

There are two variations to be evaluated, `true` or `false`:

```
((every-pred odd? #(< % 12)  #(> % 2))  3  5 7)
;;=> true

((every-pred odd? #(< % 12)  #(> % 2)) 1 2 3)
;;=> false
```

Using `filter`, it tests each element of the sequence:

```
(filter (every-pred odd? #(< % 12)  #(> % 2)) [1 2 3 4 5])
;;=> (3 5)
```

In the following code, the `some-fn` function returns true if at least one of a given predicates returns true for any arguments.

In the following code, the first expression is evaluated to be true and the second expression to be false:

```
((some-fn even? #(= % 10) #(= % 1))  11 10 1)
;;=> true
((some-fn even? #(= % 10) #(= % 1))  3 5 7)
;;=> false
```

Using `filter` checks each element in a sequence:

```
(filter (some-fn even? #(= % 10) #(= % 1)) [11 10 1 2 3])
;;=> (10 1 2)
```

How it works...

We will explain how Clojure functions are first-class functions. We will also explain pure functions' characteristics.

Clojure functions are first-class functions

The first-class function can provide a high-level abstraction of code. High-level abstraction using first-class functions makes code compact and good perspective. It also increases productivity and extensibility compared to imperative languages such as Java.

Let's review how Clojure functions are first-class functions:

- Functions can be arguments of functions. Functions such as `map`, `reduce`, and `filter` take a function as the first argument.
- Functions can be returns of functions. The functions `comp` and `partial` return a function.
- Functions can be anonymous. Anonymous functions can be defined using `fn` or function literals.
- Functions can be assigned to variables or in data structures. `def` and `fn` can assign functions to variables.

Pure functions

The characteristics of pure functions are as follows:

- Referential transparency: The function always returns the same result with the same arguments.
- No side effects: The function doesn't cause any side effects.

Mathematical functions are pure functions. The + is a pure function, but the `rand` is not a pure function because it is not the same return value with the same argument:

```
(+ 1 2 3)
;;=> 6
(+ 1 2 3)
;;=> 6
(+ 1 2 3)
;;=> 6

(rand 10)
;;=> 1.4931178951826118
(rand 10)
;;=> 1.40702455780493
(rand 10)
;;=> 7.135082921360361
```

Pure functions provide us testability and avoid unintended behaviors causing problems. Clojure is not entirely a pure functional language, but it provides ways to minimize side effects, and functions have referential transparency.

There's more...

We will describe some related topics here.

reduce and apply

In some cases, both `reduce` and `apply` can be used. Let's measure their performance:

```
(time (reduce + (range 10000000)))
;;=> "Elapsed time: 386.814518 msecs"
;;=> 49999995000000
(time (apply + (range 10000000)))
;;=> "Elapsed time: 392.471789 msecs"
;=> 49999995000000
```

Performances are almost the same. The reason is that their implementations are similar.

loop and recur

Clojure runs on JVM and does not have the tail recursion optimization, which transforms a recursive call to a jump instruction. The following code fails with stack overflow when the argument is very large:

```
(defn factorial [n]
  (if (= n 1) 1 (* n (factorial (dec n))))
  )
;;=> #'chapter03.functional/factorial
(time (factorial 200000N))
;;=> StackOverflowError   clojure.lang.Numbers.toBigInt (Numbers.java:252)
```

Using `loop` and `recur` avoids the preceding problem and works fine:

```
(defn factorial-recur[n]
  (loop [c n ret 1]
    (if (< c 2)
      ret
      (recur  (dec c) (* ret c))
      )))
;;=>#'chapter03.functional/factorial-recur
```

```
(factorial-recur 20000N)
;;=> 181920632023034513482...
```

Using threading macros

Threading macros are the cherry on the pie of your Clojure code. We use them all the time, and for one very simple reason: they make your code more readable. We can think of threading macros as a way to directly see how the data flows through our well-crafted functions.

Threading macros, as the name suggests, are macros. The code you write is being rearranged before being compiled and evaluated.

In this short section, we will see how to use the two threading macros, -> and ->>, so that you can use and abuse them while having some Clojure fun.

This will also be used as a bridge to learn how to write our own macros in the following two recipes.

Finally, we will also see how this is used in context for a full-fledged Apache Spark integration.

Getting ready

For this recipe, nothing but a plain Clojure REPL is needed.

How to do it...

In this short section, we will review the main threading macros of the Clojure language.

Introducing the -> macro

In pseudo-code, we can use the -> macro as seen in the following, create something, and make it flow through a set of functions:

```
(-> something
    (function1)
    (function2)
    ...
    )
```

So, let's say we want to add 1 to a random integer. To do so, we would write the following:

```
(->   (rand-int 10)
      (+ 1))
; 5
```

The `rand-int` function gives us a new integer between 0 and 10 exclusive. In the preceding code, if that integer had been 4, then we call this 4 as the first parameter of the next function, which is `(+ 1)`.

So, `(+ 1)` actually turns into `(+ 4 1)`.

If we want to make a string of the final result, we would just add one more line using the most famous `str` function, as follows:

```
(-> 2
    (+ 1)
    (str))
; "3"
```

The brackets can be avoided when there is only one argument to the function:

```
(-> 2
    (+ 1)
    str)
; "3"
```

Introducing the ->> macro

The partner in crime of the `->` macro is the `->>` macro, which similarly threads function calls one after the other, but instead of applying the result of the previous function result as the first parameter, it is used as the last parameter.

In the following code, a value of 2 is passed as the second parameter of the minus function:

```
(->> 2
     (- 1))
; -1
```

You can see the difference right away by comparing it with the previous macro:

```
(-> 2
    (- 1))
; 1
```

A few common Clojure functions are particularly well adapted to this second macro, in particular, `map`:

```
(->> [1 2 3]
     (map inc))
;  (2 3 4)
```

The `into` function is another function that is very well suited and can be used to convert easily to a vector again at the end of the chain:

```
(->> [1 2 3]
     (map inc)
     (into []))
;  [2 3 4]
```

Introducing the cond-> and the cond->> macros

Now that we have seen the basics of two threading macros, we can build and expand on them with two other pretty useful ones, `cond->` and `cond->>`.

First let's quickly remind ourselves how to use `cond`, which takes a set of conditions and returns the value with the first matching test:

```
(let [speed 110]
     (cond
         (>= speed 130) "Too fast for love"
         (>= speed 100) "How many miles to babylon ..."
         (>= speed 80) "Your grand ma is calling"
         (>= speed 50) "City center"
         :else "Falling asleep"))
```

The `cond->` macro works in a similar way to matching clauses, but it does not stop after the first match and keeps on going until the end of the conditions:

```
(let [speed 110 count 0]
     (cond-> count
         (>= speed 130) inc
         (>= speed 100) inc
         (>= speed 80) inc
         (>= speed 50) inc
             ))
; number of matches
; 3
```

As you will have noticed in the preceding code, the `inc` function on each line is applied with the current value of `count` for each matching statement.

Similarly, `cond->>` does something similar, but the function for each matching statement behaves like `->>`:

```
(let [speed 110 count 0]
      (cond->> count
         (>= speed 130) inc
         (>= speed 100) inc
         (>= speed 80) inc
         (>= speed 50) inc
               ))
; 3
```

It returns the same result, but it becomes interesting when you want to apply a set of functions to a collection.

Let's say we want to compute the average speed of a set of speed records. We start by defining a simple `average` function:

```
(def average (fn [coll]
   (/ (reduce + coll) (count coll))))
```

Then our compute method will make use of `cond->>`, as follows:

```
(defn compute
  [speeds {:keys [apply-fn limit-to]}]
       (cond->> speeds
          limit-to (take limit-to)
          apply-fn average
               ))
```

Our `compute` function takes a collection of speed records and a map of parameters. Note that the second parameter is using a nice way of deconstructing the map and accessing the values of the map directly, through their key name.

Our first call will compute the average speed of the whole set:

```
(compute
  [110 90 150 10]
  {:apply-fn average})
;   90
```

Our second run will nicely compute the average of the first two:

```
(compute
  [110 90 150 10]
            {:apply-fn average :limit-to 2})
; 100
```

We could replace the `:apply-fn` with compute max or min, but since you still have a REPL opened, you can do this as an exercise.

Introducing some-> and some->>

The `some->` and `some->>` macros keep on building on our knowledge of those threading macros. They are mostly used to apply a series of steps to maps.

For example, let's say we want to check the size of the collection mapped to the `:speed` key:

```
(some-> {:speed [50 90]}
        :speed
        count
        )
; 2
```

`some->` applies the first function; here, this is a keyword (Remember? Yes, of course, keywords are functions). The keyword call does not return `nil`, so `some->` keeps on threading and moves on to the `count` function, which returns 2. Also note that `some->` helps guard against `nil` values, as the threading stops as soon as the function called returns `nil`.

Similarly, we can thread through `->>` with `some->>` and apply a `map` function:

```
(some->> {:speed [50 90]}
        :speed
        (map inc)
        average
        )
; 71
```

A longer `some->>` threading example could include `calls` to `take`, and `filter` as well:

```
(some->> {:speed [50 90 100]}
        :speed
        (take 2)
        (map inc)
        (filter (fn[x] (> x 60)))
        average
```

```
        )
; 91
```

Again, as said previously, this is really nice to present very readable code. You know what each steps is doing – it is passing the data from one step to the other.

Sweet, isn't it?

How it works...

So what happens under the hood of those macros? As surprising as it is, not much; the macros simply reorder each function call. See what happens when we use macroexpand-1 to show us the code generated by the -> macro:

```
(macroexpand-1
   ` (-> 2
        (+ 1)
        (+ 2)))
; (clojure.core/+ (clojure.core/+ 2 1) 2)
```

Similarly, with the ->> macros, the code generated would look like a simple code reorganization, where the first function call is the innermost call, and then we build more and more beautiful brackets around it:

```
(macroexpand-1
   ` (->> 5
        (- 1)
        (- 2)))
; (clojure.core/- 2 (clojure.core/- 1 5))
```

As we have seen when introducing some->, the nil guard shows clearly when expanding a sum macro:

```
(macroexpand-1 '  (some-> {:speed [50 90]}
         :speed
         ))
; (clojure.core/let [G__12916 {:speed [50 90]}] (if (clojure.core/nil?
G__12916) nil (clojure.core/-> G__12916 :speed)))
```

How it works is pretty easy to grasp, but I am pretty sure you'll be okay with skipping a few autogenerated function names at this stage, so let's see what's more!

There's more…

We actually left out one of those threading macros for the end because historically, it has been added slightly later and because it somehow combines both the -> and the ->> ways.

Introducing as->

The main difference with as-> is that it is the only one where you can position the parameter for threading at will. -> passes the value as the first parameter, ->>, as the last parameter, and as-> does both through a clever but very simple name binding.

Back to your speed collection example, we bind the input map to the variable name s and then thread that s through different functions:

```
(as-> {:speed [50 70 100]} s
      (get s :speed)
      (take 2 s)
      (average s)
      )
; 60
```

Note that this is the part that makes as-> stand out, and we can specify the position where s appears in each function call.

So, s is the first parameter of get, but the result of that get function is then passed as the last parameter of the next functions, take, and so on.

Another simple example, where we conj, map, and into like Clojure freaks:

```
(as-> [1 2 3] $
      (conj $ 5)
      (map inc $)
      (into [] $)
      )
; [2 3 4 6]
```

Break the limits and build the impossible.

Flambo preview

We will come back to it in a later recipe, but let's have a quick look at `flambo`, a Clojure-friendly way of writing Apache Spark jobs. Just like Hadoop in the early days, Spark aims to make large computation tasks a breeze, and this is made even simpler through Clojure. `flambo` uses threading pretty much all over the place.

Following is how to create a simple character count job in `flambo`:

```
(ns com.fire.kingdom.flambit
  (:require [flambo.api :as f]))
  (->
   (f/text-file sc "data.txt")
   ;sc here means spark context, basically the reference to spark
   (f/map (f/fn [s] (count s)))
   (f/reduce (f/fn [x y] (+ x y))))
```

You see how short and brief this is. We will not look into the Flambo API in detail, so let's translate the preceding superb code into standard Clojure. We want to do a word count, so we build two helper functions, one to split text into words and the other to calculate frequencies:

```
(defn split-words [text]
 "split text into a list of words"
 (re-seq #"\w+" text))

(defn calculate-frequencies [words]
 "convert list of words to a word-frequency hash"
 (reduce (fn [words word] (assoc words word (inc (get words word 0))))
 {}
 words))
```

The threading macro now comes into action and we can pipeline all this with what we have seen so far:

```
(->
   (slurp "LICENSE")
   (split-words)
   (count))
; 1711 ... as far as the current license file goes ;)
```

Already in plain simple Clojure code, we've seen how this is put in action. The `slurp` call reads the text into a string, which is then split into words, and finally, we count the number of words through a simple call to `count`.

Flambo uses the exact same kind of threading syntax that make distributed jobs so easy to write.

In this recipe, we have presented the different Clojure threading macros and have seen how they pass an initial and moving data structure through a set of functions, sometimes given test conditions.

In the end, we also had a quick example of how this is used in a real-world application, with spark computing.

Defining simple macros

Macros in Clojure allow you to redefine the processing flow and generate code through a simple but very Clojure-esque defmacro construct.

This section will guide us through writing some of those building blocks and reading some macro code from the original from Clojure.

Getting ready

Macro-biotics and a spoon are all you need for this recipe. No other agricultural produce required.

How to do it...

All you ever wanted to know about writing simple Clojure macros is in this section. Keep on writing those simple macros until it finally makes sense.

Your first macro

Well, here you go. Your first macro is here:

```
(defmacro my-very-first-macro []
  (list println "FIRST"))
```

Okay, that was kind of a fast introduction to something that deserves description; it's time to bring you upto speed.

First, the `defmacro` routine requires a name and some parameters. There you go, we give it the name `my-very-first-macro` and, being a bit on the greedy side, no parameter whatsoever.

Now to the body of the macro itself. A macro should return a list. Why a list? Remember that with Clojure, data is code. That returned list will be what the code will be expanded or pre-compiled to by the Clojure compiler.

Here we have:

```
(list println "FIRST")
```

When typed in an REPL, that list will expand to the following:

```
; (#object[clojure.core$println 0xe1e81f5 "clojure.core$println@e1e81f5"]
"FIRST")
```

So basically, you have a list made of two elements: a function and a string. This list is ready to be compiled and can then be evaluated like the usual Clojure code.

To evaluate the list, we can use the `eval` function that will evaluate the Clojure code:

```
(eval (list println "FIRST"))
; nil, but "FIRST" is printed in the console ..
```

Right, so we now understand that a macro is generating Clojure code, which is a list:

```
(my-very-first-macro)
; nil, but "FIRST" is printed in the console ..
```

We think we are writing `(my-very-first-macro)`, but the code generated is actually the following:

```
(println "FIRST")
; yes, this is a list!
```

Your second macro

The second macro will build on the first one by simply making use of parameters in the macro definition.

Our second macro will be a macro that multiplies its input by three. To do so, we want to write something with `defmacro`, which returns a list made of `*`, 3, and the input.

Try it:

```
(defmacro x3 [ arg ]
  (list * 3 arg ))
```

To use it, we use that as a regular code `eval` with the following:

```
(x3 2)
; 6
```

We do understand that the code generated is a list of three elements:

```
(* 3 arg)
```

The call to the macro will generate code and then evaluate it:

```
; 6
```

Macros allow you to evolve the language in some ways not previously thought of. You can recreate control flows and make things behave in completely new ways. Superb, but let's go back a few steps to see what's going on behind the scenes.

How it works...

We have already seen in the previous recipe on threading macros that we can use `macroexpand-1` to see what a macro actually expands to.

Here we apply `macroexpand` to the first macro we wrote, `my-very-first-macro`:

```
(macroexpand-1 '(my-very-first-macro))
```

We get the code that is generated by the macro:

```
(#object[clojure.core$println 0xe1e81f5 "clojure.core$println@e1e81f5"]
"FIRST")
```

Feels extremely familiar, right? And so it should be, this is the code we saw in detail when we wrote the following:

```
(list println "FIRST")
; ...
```

Now, our second macro should not feel so different, and seeing what code is actually being compiled does not bring a lot of surprises:

```
(macroexpand-1 '(x3 2))
; (clojure.core/* 3 2)
```

Just to make it clear, all of the following are equivalent:

```
; evaluate the macro directly
(x3 2)
; 6

; eval the non compiled version of the macro.
(eval (quote (x3 2)))
; 6

; same with the quote version
(eval '(x3 2))
; 6


; eval the code generated by the macro
(eval (macroexpand-1 '(x3 2)))
; 6
```

So, now this is all making sense! We understand the two phases between the generated and evaluated Clojure code. Remember that code is data, but code, through macros, can generate more data, well, code.

We call this homoiconicity of a language due to the fact that the internal representation of a program is a data structure understood by the language itself.

There's more...

> *"Be careful–with quotations, you can damn anything."*

> *– Andre Malraux*

Sometimes you want to manipulate or return forms using their current structure and not their valued content. This is where *quote* comes into play.

Using quotes

Quote, or `'`, is the friendly brother of `eval`. It is something that tells the compiler to not evaluate the code coming after it, but instead return data in its current form.

Let's see how that works with a short example:

```
(quote (* 3 3))
; (* 3 3)

(str '(* 3 3))
; "(clojure.core/* 3 3)"
```

The quote tells the compiler to return the data structure `(* 3 3)` as is and not evaluate it. So, we write `(* 3 3)` and we get `(* 3 3)`, not its evaluated form, which in this case would be `9*`.

This comes in handy in the case of macros because we do want to generate a form that is a list of nonevaluated code.

So, a tricky question would be: what is the difference between those two macro definitions? Take a look at the following:

```
(defmacro hello2a[]
  '(+ 1 1))

(defmacro hello2b[]
    (+ 1 1))
```

As we can see, one has a quote and the other does not, but if we call `eval` on each of them, we do get the same result, no? Let's see:

```
(hello2a)
; 2
(hello2b)
; 2
```

What's up with this? So, we do remember we can use `macroexpand-1` to see the code that is generated by each macro. Let's not wait for Christmas and let's try it:

```
(macroexpand-1 '(hello2a))
; (+ 1 1)

(macroexpand-1 '(hello2b))
; 2
```

That's right. The generated code is very different. The first macro call returns a list of three elements, +, 1, and 1, while the second macro simply returns an integer, 2. Calling `eval` on each of those two forms returns the same result indeed, but their original form is completely different.

We are almost there. One last thing! We saw previously that we could write macros with arguments, and we can quickly write this with a quote, like the following:

```
(defmacro hello2c [arg]
  '(+ 1 arg))
```

Easy! Now look at the following:

```
(hello2c 3)
; clojure.lang.Compiler$CompilerException: java.lang.RuntimeException:
Unable to resolve symbol: arg in this context,
```

What happened here? Umm. Let's expand on that a bit more again:

```
(macroexpand-1 '(hello2c 3))
; (+ 1 arg)
```

The generated form is (+ 1 arg). But wait. We have not defined arg anywhere, so that cannot work. We want to generate code that is the value of arg, not arg itself. arg made sense in the context of generating code, but once the code has been generated, arg does not point to anything relevant.

In this case, we use a different quote: the backquote. The backquote gives us access to a templated version of the given form, to which we can apply customization.

It makes more sense with an example, so let's do it:

```
(defmacro hello2d [arg]
  `(+ 1 ~arg))
```

We are now introducing two different characters: unquote, or ~, and unquote splicing, or ~@. Think of unquote and unquote splicing as copy and paste, where you can insert the form directly in the generated code. So in the preceding code, the generated code should expand to the actual value of the arg, and not simply the arg string:

```
(macroexpand-1 '(hello2d 3))
; (clojure.core/+ 1 3)
```

Wow! This feels way better, doesn't it. Let's just confirm if it can be evaluated properly:

```
(hello2d 3)
;  4
```

Finally, unquote splicing makes sense with list, maps, and so on, but the copy/paste idea stays the same. One copy and pastes the list as is, while the other copies the forms one by one into the template:

```
(defmacro hello2e [& body ]
  `(apply str  ~body))

(defmacro hello2f [& body ]
  `(apply str  ~@body))


(macroexpand-1 '(hello2e "1" "2" "3"))
; (clojure.core/apply clojure.core/str ("1" "2" "3"))

(macroexpand-1 '(hello2f  "1" "2" "3"))
; (clojure.core/apply clojure.core/str "1" "2" "3")
```

Macros everywhere

In this recipe, we have seen how to create our very first macro, and moved along to grasping what compiled code is and when it occurs in the code lifecycle. We saw that Clojure was a homogenic language, meaning its internal structure and its representation were the same, and we linked this homogenic feature and macro concept together.

Defining more advanced macros

When we started thinking about the structure of the book, it all kind of made sense to talk about simple macros and advanced macros. Now, arriving at the topic, the author has to admit it is not so clear anymore. So, what do we mean when we talk about advanced macros? We tried to ask Canon, but they would not give us a proper answer.

In this recipe, we will therefore state that an advance macro is a macro that generates a form that changes the flow of the evaluation of the resulting code. In the previous recipe on simple macros, the macros were, well, simple, because the form generated was always the same. This recipe will expose macros that always generate the same code or where the control flow gets slightly more complicated. The goal of course is to easily be able to write convenient macro in your code.

Getting ready

While there is no specific preparation for this recipe, let's have a look at the `clojure.core` when we have a macro to guide us:

```
(defmacro when
  "Evaluates test. If logical true, evaluates body in an implicit do."
  {:added "1.0"}
  [test & body]
  (list 'if test (cons 'do body)))
```

With what we learned, we can rewrite it in a slightly more concise form with the backquote character:

```
(defmacro my-when
  [test & body]
  `(if ~test (do ~@body)))
```

The code generated is according to the plan:

```
(macroexpand-1
 '(my-when (odd? (rand-int 2))
   (println "hello")))
; (if (odd? (rand-int 2)) (do (println "hello")))
```

Good. Now the thing we are interested in doing for advanced macros is to generate more advanced code. So, following through this example, we will write a macro that randomly generates code.

The macro in the following code does not take a test as an input parameter anymore, just a body. We mostly moved code around, but look! The unquote symbol is no longer at start of the body of the macro, it is now nested inside the `if` statement.

Remember the macro body needs to return a Clojure form. The macro in the following code will randomly return either the passed body list wrapped in a `do`, or an empty list:

```
(defmacro random-when
  [& body]
  (if (odd? (rand-int 2))
    `(do ~@body)
    (list)
    ))
```

Try the following a few times in your REPL and you will see that the code generated is not always the same:

```
(macroexpand-1
  '(random-when
      (println "Hello")))
; ()
; OR
; (do (println "Hello"))
```

A very silly example it is, but that should open your mind to new tracks and adventures for ever more advanced macros!

How to do it...

We will look at two small examples to see how some slightly advanced macros can facilitate your developer's life and make your evening glass of wine easier to grasp.

Tracking when code was started

The first sample will be a macro that generates things for us, the time `init` was called, and a function that tells us how long the system has been up.

The macro is making use of two calls to `def` - one for a simple value and the other for a function:

```
(defmacro track-init[]
  `(do
    (def init (System/currentTimeMillis))
    (def up (fn [] (- (System/currentTimeMillis) init)))))
  )
```

The call to the Java platform's `System` class is a bit overwhelming, but basically we just want to access the current time. Expand the generated code as follows:

```
(macroexpand-1
    '(track-init))
```

We see what looks like standard Clojure, defining one value and a function:

```
(do
  (def my-very-first-macro/init
      (java.lang.System/currentTimeMillis))
  (def my-very-first-macro/up
```

```
(clojure.core/fn []
 (clojure.core/-
 (java.lang.System/currentTimeMillis)
 my-very-first-macro/init)))) 
```

Except you did not write this code, the only thing you wrote in the first place was that call to track-init macro:

```
(track-init)
```

Now, in the namespace, the macro was called, therefore in the same namespace we have init and (up):

```
init
; 1449641148783

(up)
; 596928
```

This kind of macro, which generates code for you, can be very helpful during development, so be careful as this kind of macro can also leave some def-ed symbols about the place!

Logging a message with macro

In the second example, we will simply look at a dumb log macro that gives an output message when the log level is sufficient and doesn't if not. Umm. Yes. I miss the days of 20 logging frameworks to rule none of them. (But that is history.)

So, the following defines a top log level that could be automatically loaded from a file, but I leave that to the reader. We also define the log macro that gives output of the code only if the log level is set to DEBUG:

```
(def LOG_LEVEL "INFO")

(defmacro log [msg]
  (if (= LOG_LEVEL "DEBUG")
    `(println ~msg)))
```

In this case, when we call the macro using the following statement:

```
(log "hello3")
; ...
```

You got it right. Nothing is printed in the console. Now, let's say we `def` the log level again, (hmmm ... this is not the recommended way of doing things but bear with us here):

```
(def LOG_LEVEL "DEBUG")
```

When calling the `log` macro again, messages are shown in the console:

```
(log "hello3")
; .. hello3 in the console
```

We will let the reader check the code generated for each case with `macroexpand-1`, as usual:

```
(macroexpand-1
 '(log "hello3"))
; (println "hello3")
```

How it works...

I guess we have seen quite a bit on what the underlying process is when playing with macros. Let's have a look at one of the macros that is all over the Internet to create an iterative language looking for loop.

The code for the loop macro is only slightly more difficult than what you have seen so far. Notice how the return form of the macro is a list, through backquote, and how the body `steps` are wrapped in a `do`:

```
(defmacro my-for-loop [ [sym init check change] & steps]
     `(loop [~sym ~init value# nil]
        (if ~check
          (let [new-value# (do ~@steps)]
            (recur ~change new-value#))
          value#)))
```

The one new thing you may have noticed is the # sign here and there, for example, `new-value#`. The sharp sign is an indication that you would like to get a generated, qualified name for a variable or a function:

```
gensym is the longer version of this #.
(gensym "hello")
; hello6075
```

If we were not using `gensym` or `#`, we would try to get the value of, say, `new-value`, which is not defined when the macro code is generated and thus would throw an error.

To generate your own loop, you would then call the macro as defined, with four parameters and a body:

```
(my-for-loop
  [ i 0 (< i 10) (inc i)]
  (println
   (str "- " (rand-int i))))
; this is the part where you look at the console
```

After just a bit of clean up, the generated code looks like the following, which is mostly a simple loop, but we'll admit that the preceding was easier on the eyes:

```
(loop [i 0 value nil]
  (if (< i 10)
    (let [new-value
          (do (println (str "- " (rand-int i))))]
      (recur (inc i) new-value))
    value))
```

A nice way to write your own macro is actually to first write what you want the generated code from the macro to be like, then work your way backward to the `defmacro` exercise.

Voila!

There's more...

There's more, but not much as far as macros are concerned. Macros are fast, so be sure to use them when you can.

To finish on my favorite example, we will quickly have a look at the deftest macro from `clojure.test`.

deftest

Without all the boilerplate, this is how the `deftest` macro looks. You have to admit that you are not surprised by the macro-specific syntax anymore, are you?

```
(defmacro deftest
  [name & body]
  (when *load-tests*
    `(def ~(vary-meta name assoc :test `(fn [] ~@body))
          (fn [] (test-var (var ~name))))))
```

What is surprising here is that the only thing the `deftest` macro is actually doing is creating functions through `def`, with simply some metadata attached to it. The new function is simply defined in the current namespace.

To run tests then, the `run-tests` function will actually look for those macro-defined functions that have the proper metadata, and will then execute them.

As a quick reminder, to create and run tests from the REPL, we simply need to call `deftest`:

```
(require '[clojure.test :refer :all])

(deftest  my-test []
  (is (= 1 1)))

 (run-tests)

;macro.clj:
;Testing my-very-first-macro
;macro.clj:
;Ran 1 tests containing 1 assertions.
;macro.clj:
;0 failures, 0 errors.
```

Hopefully that gives you new ideas for creating macros and how to put them in context!

Using protocols

Protocols provide polymorphism between different data types. Defining protocols are defining Java's interfaces in fact. We can define protocols for Clojure's records and types. It is also possible to define protocols for Java classes.

Getting ready

This section does not make use of any external library, so you can just start a REPL and be ready.

How to do it...

Let's start with defining records and types, and then look at how to define and use protocols.

Defining a record

Here, we will define a record of the author. We have shown how to express the author Sir Conan Doyle using a map in Chapter 2, *Interacting with Collections*:

```
{:name "Arthur Ignatius Conan Doyle"
 :born "22-May-1859"
 :died "7-July-1930"
 :occupation ["novelist" "short story writer" "poet" "physician"]
 :nationality "scottish"
 :citizenship "United Kingdom"
 :genre ["Detective fiction", "fantasy", "science fiction", "historical
novels", "non-fiction"]
 :notable-works ["Stories of Sherlock Holmes" "The Lost World"]
 :spouse ["Louisa Hawkins" "Jean Leckie"]
 :no-of-children 5
 }
```

Now we will define the preceding map using a record. To define a record, use the defrecord and specify the record name and its attributes as fields. Here we defined the Author record, which has 10 fields:

```
(defrecord Author
    [name
     born
     died
     occupation
     nationality
     citizenship
     genre
     notable-works
     spouse
     no-of-children
     ])
;;=> chapter03.protocols.Author
```

Then, let's define Conan Doyle using the `Author` record. To define it, use the `->Author` and then enumerate values of fields:

```
(def doyle
  (->Author
    "Arthur Ignatius Conan Doyle"
    "22-May-1859"
    "7-July-1930"
    ["novelist" "short story writer" "poet" "physician"]
    "scottish"
        "United Kingdom"
    ["Detective fiction", "fantasy", "science fiction", "historical novels",
"non-fiction"]
    ["Stories of Sherlock Holmes" "The Lost World"]
    ["Louisa Hawkins" "Jean Leckie"]
    5
    ))
;;=> #'chapter03.protocols/doyle
```

Another way to create a record of the `Author` is to use the `map->Author`:

```
(def christie
    (map->Author {
                      :name
                      "Agatha Mary Clarissa Miller"
                      :born
                      "15-September-1890"
                      :died
                      "12-January-1976"
                      :occupation
                      ["novelist" "short story writer" "playwright"
"poetnovelist"]
                      :nationality
                      "england"
                      :citizenship
                    "United Kingdom"
                      :genre
                      ["murder mystery" "thriller" "crime fiction" "detective"
"romance"]
                      :notable-works
                      ["Murder on the Orient Express"
                    "The Murder of Roger Ackroyd"
                    "Death on the Nile"
                    "The Murder at the Vicarage"
                    "Partners In Crime"
                    "The ABC Murders"
                    "And Then There Were None"
                    "The Mousetrap"]
```

```
                            :spouse
                            ["Archibald Christie" "Sir Max Mallowan"]
                            :no-of-children
                            1
                          }
                        )
       )
;;=> #'chapter03.protocols/christie
```

To access fields, use keywords such as :name or :genre:

```
(:name doyle)
;;=> "Arthur Ignatius Conan Doyle"
(:name christie)
;;=> "Agatha Mary Clarissa Miller"
(:genre doyle)
;;=> ["Detective fiction" "fantasy" "science fiction" "historical novels"
"non-fiction"]
(:genre christie)
;;=>["murder mystery" "thriller" "crime fiction" "detective" "romance"]
```

Defining a type

Clojure's types are Java class but they have fewer features than records. To define type, use the deftype:

```
(deftype Point [x y])
;;=> chapter03.protocols.Point
```

To create an instance of the type, use the constructor of Java inter-op. To access the fields of a type instance, use Java inter-op:

```
(def pos1 (Point. 1 2))
;;=> #'chapter03.protocols/pos1
(.x pos1)
;;=> 1
(.y pos1)
;;=> 2
```

Defining a protocol

Now, let's define a protocol and use it. First, define the `Point` record:

```
(defrecord Point [x y])
;;=> chapter03.protocols.Point
```

The following code defines the `IPoint` protocol. It has `move` and `distance` functions.
Protocols are Java interfaces and their functions are Java methods:

```
(defprotocol IPoint
  "A simple protocol for flying"
  (move [self delta])
  (distance [self])
  )
;;=> IPoint
```

Then, using `_extend-protocol`, define an implementation:

```
(require '[clojure.math.numeric-tower :as math])
;;=> nil
(extend-protocol IPoint
  Point
  (move [self delta]
    (->Point
      (+ (.-x self) (delta 0))
      (+ (.-y self) (delta 1))))
    (distance [self]
      (math/sqrt
        (+
        (* (.-x self) (.-x self))
        (* (.-y self) (.-y self)))
        )))
;;=> nil

(def pos1 (Point. 1 2))
;;=> #'chapter03.protocols/pos1
[(.-x pos1)(.-y pos1)]
;;=> [1 2]
(distance pos1)
;;=> 2.23606797749979
(def pos2 (move pos1 [1 2]))
;;=> #'chapter03.protocols/pos2
[(.-x pos2)(.-y pos2)]
;;=> [2 4]
(distance pos2)
;;=> 4.47213595499958
```

Now we will define the three-dimensional point, `Point3D`, using type. The difference with `Point` is that `Point3D` is not a record:

```
(deftype Point3D [x y z]
  IPoint
    (move [self delta]
    (Point3D.
     (+ (.-x self) (delta 0)) (+ (.-y self) (delta 1)) (+ (.-z self) (delta
2)))))
    (distance [self]
      (math/sqrt
       (+
        (* (.-x self) (.-x self))
        (* (.-y self) (.-y self))
        (* (.-z self) (.-z self))))))))
;;=> chapter03.protocols.Point3D
(def pos3 (Point3D. 1 2 3))
;;=> #'chapter03.protocols/pos3
[(.-x pos3) (.-y pos3) (.-z pos3)]
;;=> [1 2 3]
(def pos4 (move pos3 [1 1 1]))
;;=> #'chapter03.protocols/pos4
[(.-x pos4) (.-y pos4) (.-z pos4)]
;;=> [2 3 4]
(distance pos4)
;;=> 5.385164807134504
```

How it works...

Here, we will learn how records and types are implemented and how they differ.

Records and types are Java classes

Clojure's records are Java classes. In the example of the `Author`, the `Author` defined is a Java class. The `->Author` and `map->Author` are factory classes, and `doyle` and `christie` are instances of the class:

```
(class Author)
;;=> java.lang.Class
(class Point)
;;=> java.lang.Class
```

We can use field accessors of java-inter-op, which we will describe in depth in a later chapter:

```
(.-occupation christie)
;;=> ["novelist" "short story writer" "playwright" "poetnovelist"]
(.-x (Point. 10 2))
;;=> 10
```

The `defrecord` and `deftype` generate accessors for their elements. So, we can also use them for records and types:

```
(.y (Point. 10 2))
;;=> 2
(.nationality doyle)
;;=> "scottish"
```

Access to fields of records or types is faster than access to values by hash search, and it's better to use records or types for performance-sensitive cases.

Differentiating between records and types

There are some differences between records and types. Records provide more features than types do. Type provides no functionality other than a constructor with fields.

`defrecord` provides a complete implementation of a persistent map, including value-based equality and hashCode.

Record implements a lot of Clojure interfaces, whereas type implements only the `clojure.lang.IType`:

```
(supers Author)
;;=> #{clojure.lang.IKeywordLookup clojure.lang.ILookup
clojure.lang.Seqable java.lang.Object java.lang.Iterable clojure.lang.IMeta
clojure.lang.IHashEq clojure.lang.IPersistentMap clojure.lang.Counted
java.io.Serializable java.util.Map clojure.lang.IPersistentCollection
clojure.lang.IObj clojure.lang.Associative clojure.lang.IRecord}
(supers Point3D)
;;=> #{java.lang.Object clojure.lang.IType}
(def x (Point. 1 1))
;;=> #'chapter03.protocols/x
(def y (Point. 1 1))
;;=> #'chapter03.protocols/y
(= x y)
;;=> true
```

Record supports a value-based equality and hashCode. See the following code:

```
(defrecord PointRecord [x y])
;;=> chapter03.protocols.PointRecord
(= (PointRecord. 10 5)
   (PointRecord. 10 5)
   )
;;=> true
(deftype PointType [x y])
;;=> chapter03.protocols.PointType
(= (PointType. 10 5)
   (PointType. 10 5)
   )
;;=> false
```

Records are immutable and persistent. Clojure's record implements the
`clojure.lang.IPersistentMap`, we can access records using functions for `map`. Fields of
types can be mutable. We will show a technique for this later in this recipe.

There's more...

Here, we will show you a mutable protocol and type to update these field mutably.

Defining a mutable protocol and type

Here, we will show a mutable type to update a field mutably. We use the `IEditPoint`
protocol and define four methods. The `setX` and `setY` do destructive updates:

```
(defprotocol IEditPoint
  (getX [this])
  (setX! [this val])
  (getY [this])
  (setY! [this val])
  )
;;=> IEditPoint
```

Then we will define the `MutablePoint` type and implement four methods. The keyword
`^:volatile-mutable` defines mutable variables. The `set!` performs a destructive update:

```
(deftype MutablePoint [^:volatile-mutable x ^:volatile-mutable y]
  IEditPoint
  (getX [this] (. this x))
  (setX! [this val] (set! x val))
  (getY [this] (. this y))
```

```
    (setY! [this val] (set! y val))
    )
;;=> chapter03.protocols.MutablePoint
```

Now we will test how mutable updates work. The initial value of the `mutable-point` is (5, 3). We will change it to (10, 1):

```
(def mutable-point (MutablePoint. 5 3))
;;=> #'chapter03.protocols/mutable-point
(.getX mutable-point)
;;=> 5
(.getY mutable-point)
;;=> 3
(.setX! mutable-point 10)
;;=> 10
(.setY! mutable-point 1)
;;=> 1
(.getX mutable-point)
;;=> 10
(.getY mutable-point)
;;=> 1
```

Defining multimethods

Defining multimethods is another way to realize polymorphism. The multimethod has a strong dispatch mechanism for polymorphism. Let's see how it works.

Getting ready

You need to add the `math.numeric-tower` to your `project.clj` file to run samples (or any other dependency management you are using):

```
:dependencies
  [[org.clojure/clojure "1.8.0"]
   [org.clojure/math.numeric-tower "0.0.4"]
                 ]
```

How to do it...

Let's see how to define and use multimethods.

Defining a multimethod

The `defmulti` creates new multimethods, and the `defmethod` creates and implements a new method of multimethod associated with a dispatch value.

The following code shows an example of the `defmulti` of the calculation of the volume of shapes. The first argument is the name of the multimethod and the second argument is the dispatch function:

```
(defmulti volume :shape)
;;=> nil
```

Now we will define a method for the calculation of cube:

```
(defmethod volume :cube [shape]
  (* (:length shape)(:length shape)(:length shape))
  )
;;=> #multifn[volume 0x4f6134c8]
(volume {:shape :cube :length 10})
;;=> 1000
```

Then we will define a method for the rectangular parallelepiped. It calculates a cubic capacity:

```
(defmethod volume :rectangular-parallelepiped [shape]
  (* (:length shape)(:width shape)(:height shape))
  )
;;=> #multifn[volume 0x3695e4a4]
(volume {:shape :rectangular-parallelepiped :length 2 :width 3 :height 4})
;;=> 24
```

We will define another shape ball. The calculation is 4 / 3 (Pi radius **3):

```
(defmethod volume :ball [shape]
  (/ (* (. Math PI) (:radius shape) (:radius shape)(:radius shape) 4.C)
3.0)
  )
;;=> #multifn[volume 0x3695e4a4]
(volume {:shape :ball :radius 2})
;;=> 33.510321638291124
```

How it works...

Multimethods dispatch by function specified as the first argument. In the preceding example, the :shape is a function to dispatch.

When the expression (volume {:shape :cube :length 10}) is called, the function :shape is applied as follows:

```
(:shape {:shape :cube :length 10})
;;=> :cube

Then the following method is called.
(defmethod volume :cube [shape]
  (* (:length shape)(:length shape)(:length shape))
  )
;;=> #multifn[volume 0x4f6134c8]
```

There's more...

If there are no expected arguments specified for multimethods, it causes an error, as follows:

```
(volume {:shape :cone :length 10 :height 20})
IllegalArgumentException No method in multimethod 'volume' for dispatch
value: :cone   clojure.lang.MultiFn.getFn (MultiFn.java:156)
```

If you don't want to see such a message, use defmethod with :default as follows:

```
(defmethod volume :default [shape] nil)
;;=> #multifn[volume 0x4f6134c8]
(volume {:shape :cone :length 10 :height 20})
;;=> nil
```

Transducers for dummies

To be very honest, the first time transducers were presented, like a few other things by Rich Hickey, creator of Clojure, it felt like it was ahead of its time. Just even understanding the concepts was quite a task, never mind using them.

In this recipe, we will slowly look at how to use a transduce call, from the very first baby steps to some more pragmatic examples.

We will also go through the different terms used when dealing with transducers. Finally, we will also see how to apply parallelism to transducers using `core.async`.

So relax, grab a bit of coffee, and let's get ready.

Getting ready

If you remember the `into` function, you will remember that it takes all the elements from one collection and puts them in a different collection. You will mostly want to do so because the collection types are different or you want to get a sorted collection.

So, to turn a range-generated sequence into a vector, you would use `into`:

```
(into []
    (range 10))
; [0 1 2 3 4 5 6 7 8 9]
```

Nothing is complicated so far; the first parameter of `into` is the target collection, while the second one is the input.

Now, `into` has a second version with three parameters, where now the second parameter is a transducer. Let's add some elements from a source collection, but select odd elements only to insert on the target vector.

This is how we would write it:

```
(into []
      (filter odd?)
      (range 10))
; [1 3 5 7 9]
```

`(filter odd?)` here is a transducer function.

Remember that `filter` usually takes two parameters, a condition and a collection:

```
(filter odd? [1 2 3])
; (1 3)
```

In `(filter odd?)`, we call `filter` without the collection parameter, which has the effect of returning not a result, but a function, which is also a reducer.

An immediate way of using a transducer and validating its output is through the `sequence` function, which lazily creates another sequence going through a transformation slash a transducer:

```
(sequence (filter odd?) [1 2 3])
; (1 3)
```

This is very similar to the preceding `into` example, except `into` is not lazy, but reduces or computes its result directly:

```
(class
    (sequence (filter odd?) [1 2 3]))
; clojure.lang.LazySeq

(class
    (into []
       (filter odd?)
       (range 10)))
; clojure.lang.PersistentVector
```

Alright, now we get what a transducer is more or less, let's see how to perform a transducing operation without stress.

How to do it...

`transduce` is similar to `reduce`, but we will make use of additional transducers. `transduce` turns a collection into another collection through a transducer, then reduces the result to the reducing function.

Following are the two functions, `reduce` and `transduce`, one after the other to compare their usage with + as the reducing function and `(range 5)` as the input collection:

```
(reduce +
    (range 5))
; 10

(transduce
 (filter odd?)
 +
 (range 5))
; 4
```

The result of the transduce call is indeed very similar to a call for reduce after applying a filter to the original collection:

```
(reduce
 +
 (filter odd? (range 5)))
; 4
```

Except…yes, now is the time to see a bit more how that works under the hood.

How it works…

Transducers are not so easy to grasp at first, so we will take a bit of time to see what they are made of and then start writing our own, step by step.

Composable functions

Transducers are first of all composable functions. So, composing a transducer with another transducer will return a new transducer. One of the most useless transducers you could have will be to inc elements first then apply dec. Composition of transducers can be done with comp:

```
(sequence
 (comp
  (map inc)
  (map dec))
    [1 2 3 4])
; (1 2 3 4)
```

Wow! Great! In this fantastic recipe, the reader can also get to learn how to write code that does literally nothing.

We can see that the resulting transducer used here applies two transformations, one after the other, and just by random luck, it just so happens that they are cancelling each other out.

Inserting elements

Transducers can also create new elements along the processing. The `interpose` function has a transducer version that can be used to insert generated elements in the resulting sequence:

```
(sequence
 (comp
  (map inc)
  (interpose 1)
  )
 [1 2 3 4])
; (2 1 3 1 4 1 5)
```

So, we also see that the resulting collection can have a very different number of elements from the original collection and that elements can be added or removed along the transducer pipeline.

Let's see how we can write a transducer from scratch that removes elements through processing.

Writing your own transducers

So, what is the signature of a transducer? Or, more precisely, how do we write one in Clojure code?

A `transduce` operation can be seen as a pipeline of element-per-element processing. So, to define a transducer, we need the following:

- An `init` step before any new values have been added to the pipeline
- A `step` step to process one element of the pipeline
- A `last` step to complete the processing

Equally, a transducer is a function being understood in the context of a reduction, therefore the `reducing` function will be a parameter in the creation of that function.

Now, taking all this into account and extracting the important part of the original Clojure filter function, we come up with the following function:

```
(defn my-transfilter [rf]
      (fn
        ; init step
        ([] (rf))
```

```
; step
([result input]
    (if (odd? input)
      (rf result input)
      result))

; last  step
([result] (rf result))

))
```

There is quite a bit involved in the preceding code sample, but nothing surprising as such, with the presentation work we have done up to now.

Our transducer is a simple odd-filtering pipeline. The first and last steps of the pipeline are delegating calls directly to the reducing function, and the main step of processing does the extra bit of either filtering and applying the resulting function to the newly coming element, or simply not doing any processing and returning the existing result of the transducing pipeline.

If we try to illustrate this, we could come up with the following:

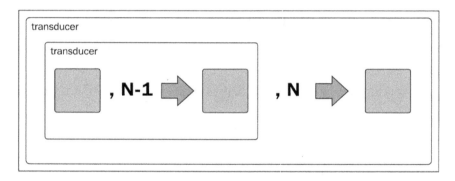

In the preceding diagram, the red arrow is the result of applying the reducing function on the result, in blue, and a new coming value from the pipeline, **N-1** and **N**.

Is there a way to stop the pipeline and ask for the end of the pipeline processing you may ask? Yes indeed…

Short circuit

If you remember, `reduce` can be short-circuited with `reduced`. That tells the processing to stop right there and avoid unnecessary computation. The following example stops the processing and ends once a value greater than 5 has been added to the reducing pipeline:

```
(reduce

 (fn [result new-value]
   (if (< 5 new-value)
     (reduced result)
     (+ result new-value)))

 (range 10))
; 15
```

This, by the way, is equivalent to the following:

```
(+ 5 (+ 4 (+ 3 (+ 2 (+ 1 (+))))))
```

We can reuse the same kind of idea when writing our transducer, so a slightly modified and agreed kind of silly version could be as follows:

```
(defn my-transfilter [rf]
      (fn
        ; init
        ([] (rf))
        ; step
        ([result input]
          (reduced 1))
        ; last
        ([result] (rf result))

        ))

(transduce
  my-transfilter
  +
  [ 1 3 8 7])
; 1
```

The processing stops at the first real pipeline processing, and short-circuits all processing to simply return 1. This makes it easy for you to define a way to end the processing of the pipeline on a certain condition straight from the definition of the transducer.

Neat, huh?

There's more...

Phew. It has been quite a transducing ride so far, no? But one more pattern is coming along. With transducers being completely context-unaware, we can easily parallelize their use with `core.async`. Let's quickly see how!

Transducers with core.async

To play with `core.async`, we will, just like before, add the dependencies to the `project.clj` file:

```
:dependencies [
        ...
        [org.clojure/core.async "0.2.385"]
        ]
```

Then, restart the REPL and start by calling `require` to add the functions needed to the current namespace:

```
(require '[clojure.core.async :refer (chan buffer pipeline put! take!)])
```

Next comes the meat of the French course with the `apply-transducer` function, which will create the glue between the in channel and the out channel using the pipeline function from `core.async`. Pipeline needs a thread-count parameter as well as the transducer function. The rest is now pretty intuitive:

```
(defn apply-transducer
  [in xf]
  (let [
        out (chan 8)
        thread-count 2
        ]
    (pipeline thread-count out xf in)
    out))
```

With this in our suitcase, we can define `core.async` in and out channels as follows:

```
(def in (chan))
(def out (apply-transducer in (filter odd?)))
```

Now, put some values in the preceding defined channel:

```
(put! in 3)
(take! out (fn [x] (println x)))
; 3 in the console

(put! in 4)
(take! out (fn [x] (println x)))
;  nothing printed ... the element has been filtered.
```

This technique can be very useful for handling real-time stream processing, for example, doing encryption or decryption on the fly from Internet of Things devices like Raspberry PI! When doing monitoring, this could also be used to remove irrelevant values or too-noisy values and avoid too much output.

Summing things up

It has been a long ride, but now we have it. We came all the way from knowing very little about transducers to seeing how they can be created and combined and how they process data through something similar to a pipeline, and, finally, we saw a specifically defined `pipeline` function in `core.async` that can help us apply transducing techniques to real-time stream processing.

Define a transducer that now replays this recipe one more time and reduce itself into a nice cup of coffee.

Logic programming in Clojure

> *"Logic will get you from A to B. Imagination will take you everywhere."*
>
> *– Albert Einstein*

This recipe is going to be a *hell of a ride* recipe. Strap yourself in. Get a shot of tequila. This is hardcore. So many fun things to learn! But first, what is logic programming? In one sentence, I would say:

Logic programming is a technique that enables you to find goals, given a set of statements or facts.

Again, this is the author's way of presenting logic programming. There is much more academic language being used on the Internet if you are interested. Anyway. What does that mean in easy-to-read terms? Let's see an example.

Say you want to find all the solutions where *x* is not equal to 2, and *x* is in the list (1 2 3). Or say, you want to find all the friends of your friends, not your direct friends, that live in Japan, but not in Tokyo.

This is the type of problem logic programming usually helps you solve.

While there is good amount of tutorials available on the subject, in this recipe, we will take a slightly different angle and actually look at how logic programming and `core.logic` can help generate data given a set of constraints.

Getting ready

Getting ready for logic is simple Clojure-wise, less so logic-wise. Let's review how to import the proper libraries and how to run the first set of logic examples.

Baby logic steps

The only dependency you need in your Clojure project to get started is on `core.logic` itself:

```
[org.clojure/core.logic "0.8.10"]
```

To check if everything is set up properly, we can already copy and paste our first logic program as follows:

```
(ns chapter03.logic
(:use [clojure.core.logic])
(:require [clojure.core.logic.fd :as fd]))

(run* [q]
    (== q 1))
; (1)
```

Two Clojure imports, and our first goal!!! Find all the values of q that equal 1. No need for a computer or a book to find the answer. Let's look at the wording used here instead:

- run* tells the logic engine to find all the values.
- q is the goal. There may be intermediate goals in the logic program, but we are only interested in q, which is called a logic var here, or lvar.
- (== q 1) is the constraint. This says to find all the values that are equal to 1.

Our first baby steps; many more coming.

Getting to know the "o" vocabulary

For some reason, out of scope here, core.logic uses function naming. Apart from the naming, their usage is actually pretty straightforward, so let's review the main ones. We will go quickly through them, so make sure you type them in the REPL and experiment a bit to get accustomed to the language.

conso: check for vector association

Here we look for a list of items q, such that q results from 1 concatenated to a list of items (2 3):

```
(run* [q]
  (conso 1 [2 3] q))
; ((1 2 3))
```

Note that this is one result, and that result is (1 2 3).

resto: check for the rest of a vector

Here we look for a var, such that this var equals the rest of vector [1 2 3 4]:

```
(run* [q]
  (resto [1 2 3 4] q))
; ((2 3 4))
```

Note that this is one result, and that result is (2 3 4).

membero

Keep going on. We want to find a value q, such that 7 is a member of [1 3 8 q]:

```
(run* [q]
    (membero 7 [1 3 8 q]))
; (7)
```

Of course, we can have multiple statements while looking for a result. Let's say we want to find q such that q is a member of [1 2 3] and a member of [2 3 4]. This is pretty much a vector intersection:

```
(run* [q]
   (membero q [1 2 3])
   (membero q [2 3 4]))
; (2 3)
```

That gives us two solutions: q can either be 2 or 3.

Statements can be mixed, of course. Say we want to find members of [1 2 3] that are not 2:

```
(run* [q]
      (!= q 2)
      (membero q [1 2 3]))
; (1 3)
```

As seen here, both 1 and 3 are valid solutions.

appendo: appending list

See how we look for q such that the concatenation of two known lists results in q, or the concatenation of a known list and q returns a known list:

```
(run* [q] (appendo [1 2] [3 4] q))
; ((1 2 3 4))
(run* [q] (appendo [1 2] q [1 2 3 4]))
; ((3 4))
```

Note, there is only one solution each time, and each time it is a list.

conde

The logic function `conde` does not end in o, but it is quite useful. It works like OR. See how we check that q is either 1 or 2:

```
(run* [q]
      (conde
        [(== q 1)]
        [(== q 2)]))
; (1 2)
```

Matche

Matche does all your pattern matching magic. In this example, we want to do pattern matching against an array of five elements [1 2 3 4 5]. We want to find q such that it is similar to [1 q], where a is any value, and q denotes a subarray, and [1 * q] is equal to [1 2 3 4 5]. The underscore sign is a wildcard, and the dot sign denotes that what is coming after is, or should, be a subarray:

```
(run* [q]
  (fresh [a]
    (== a [1 2 3 4 5])
    (matche [a]
            ([ [1 _ . q ]]))))
; ((3 4 5))
```

Item 2 of the array is being ellipsed by the wildcard; the only possible value of q is a list of elements (3 4 5).

Going through just a bit more, `matche` understands multiple conditions for each pattern. If q is "first" in the following code, we have a solution through the first pattern. For the second one, whatever q is, no match is possible, since a does not match [1 1 . _]:

```
(run* [q]
  (fresh [a]
    (== a [1 2 3 4 5])
    (matche [a]
            ([ [1 2 . [3 4 5] ]]
             (== q "first"))
            ([ [1 1 . _] ]
             (== q "second")))))
; ("first")
```

Beginner logic

We have seen some basic logic functions, so now, going further, let's go through a few proper `core.logic` techniques.

Keeping fresh

Sometimes, you want to put a condition on things that are not directly related to the goal we are looking for. In this case, we declare a new logic variable through `fresh`. What this means is that the logic computing goes into finding an answer for the new variable, but the result only contains our usual `q`, which is what we are interested in.

Say we want `q` such that `q` is equal to `[a b]`, where a is 4 and b is 5:

```
(run* [q]
  (fresh [a b]
    (== 4 a)
    (== b 5)
    (== [a b] q)))
; ([4 5])
```

We can, of course, apply the same functions we have already seen to a and b or any new logic var introduced by `fresh`.

Finding only one result

Back to the preceding example, instead of finding all the possible answers, we may just be looking for one. In this case, we use a slightly different version of `run`, not `run**`, but `run 1*`:

```
(run 1 [q]
    (conde
        [(== q 2)]
        [(== q 3)]))
; (2)
```

The 1 is indeed the number of answers we are looking for.

Mature logic

Logic power increases with age and usage of the `fd` namespace.

Range of values

We can define a range of constraints for our answer through `fd/in`, `fd/domain`, and `fd/interval`.

The following searches for `q` such that `q` is one of 1, 2, 3, 4 ,5 and `q*q = r`, with `r` being in between `1` and `10`. This is shown in the following example:

```
(run* [q]
   (fresh [r]
     (fd/in q (fd/domain 1 2 3 4 5))
     (fd/in r (fd/interval 1 10))
     (fd/* q q r)))
; (1 2 3)
```

`domain` is a list of values, `interval` is a Clojure range, and `in` defines *appartenance*. `fd/` then does a logic __ operation.

In the following, we use `fd/eq` to define equality, but the applied concepts are the same:

```
(run 1 [q]
   (fresh [a b]
     (fd/in a (fd/interval 0 10000))
     (fd/eq (= 4 (* a a)))
     (== q a)))
; (2)
```

Note that `membero` can also be used in a similar way, so to mark a range constraint with `membero`, you would use regular Clojure code, as seen in the following:

```
(run* [q]
   (fresh [r]
     (fd/in q (fd/domain 1 2 3 4 5))
     (membero r (range 1 10))
     (fd/* q q r)))
```

Alright, we have seen an impressive amount already! One more shot of tequila and let's move on to generating some fun data!

How to do it...

Now that we have had enough tequila and we have seen a lot of the building blocks of `core.logic`, we are ready to put some code together and be able to generate data. We will start with some simple examples and build up along the way, so be sure to try everything at the REPL yourself.

Generating data

So, we want to generate a set of data of vectors [a b], such that a and b are in between 0 and 10, and a − b = 2. With what we have seen previously, this becomes:

```
(run* [q]
          (fresh [a b]
            (fd/in a b (fd/interval 0 10))
            (fd/eq (= 2 (- a b)))
            (== q [a b])))
; ([2 0] [3 1] [4 2] [5 3] [6 4] [7 5] [8 6] [9 7] [10 8])
```

Note that we have generated all the possible permutations, which is quite cool!

Another version combining earlier techniques; we want to find all possible permutations such that a is in between 0 and 5 and q such that q is a concatenation of a and [2 3]. This is done easily using what we know already:

```
(run* [q]
    (fresh [a]
      (fd/in a (fd/interval 0 5))
      (conso a [2 3] q)))
; ((0 2 3) (1 2 3) (2 2 3) (3 2 3) (4 2 3) (5 2 3))
```

Generating more data with more logic variables

Finding multiple values in `core.logic` simply requires looking for more than one q. Let's call them c1 c2 c3 and put a few constraints on them. All of c1, c2, and c3 are in the interval 1 to 20 and are such that c3 is 5 and c2 − c1 = c3. There are quite a few solutions, so we will limit ourselves to five possible solutions:

```
(run 5 [c1 c2 c3]
      (fd/in c1 c2 c3 (fd/interval 1 20))
      (fd/eq
        (= (- c2 c1) c3)
        (= c3 5)))
; ([1 6 5] [2 7 5] [3 8 5] [4 9 5] [5 10 5])
```

We now understand that more and more logic can be used to generate data. With just a bit more logic, we can take it where we are sure we only generate distinct tuples:

```
(run 5 [c1 c2 c3]
      (fd/in c1 c2 c3 (fd/interval 1 20))
      (fd/distinct [c1 c2 c3])
      (fd/eq
        (= (- c2 c1) c3)
        (= c3 5)))
; ([1 6 5] [2 7 5] [3 8 5] [4 9 5] [6 11 5])
```

Using a project

Stepping back a bit, and since you have tried a few things on your own at the REPL, you may have noticed that this does not work:

```
(run* [c1 c2 c3]
      (fd/in c1 c2 c3 (fd/interval 1 20))
      (== (+ c1 c3) 5))
; clojure.core.logic.LVar cannot be cast to java.lang.Number
```

This is because c_1 and c_3 are logic variables and we ask them to compare to an integer. When called from within the `fd/eq` directive, as was done previously, this does not show up. If you want to do it outside `fd/eq`, you can use project to enforce a logic var to be turned into its value:

```
(run* [a b c]
  (fd/in a b c (fd/interval 0 3))
  (fd/distinct [a b c])
  (project [a]
    (== 2 a)))
; ([2 0 1] [2 1 0] [2 0 3] [2 3 0] [2 1 3] [2 3 1])
```

How it works...

David Nolen, author of `core.logic`, has gone into superb detailed programming to make sure this implementation of logic programming was showing superb performance.

In the test cases, we actually found a reference to *Finite Domain Constraint Programming in Oz. A Tutorial* (`http://zeus.inf.ucv.cl/~jrubio/docs/2010-2/ICI%20662/Material/FiniteDomainProgramming.pdf`), and the relevant code is as follows:

```
(run* [c1 c2 c3 c4 c5 c6 c7 c8 c9 :as vs]
```

```
(everyg #(fd/in % (fd/interval 1 9)) vs)

(fd/distinct vs)

(fd/eq

  (= (- c4 c6) c7)
  (= (* c1 c2 c3) (+ c8 c9))
  (< (+ c2 c3 c6) c8)
  (< c9 c8))

  (project [vs]
   (everyg
    (fn [[v n]] (fd/!= v n) )
     (map
      vector
      vs
      (range 1 10)))))
```

This is actually the piece of code that inspired me. I hope it has the same impact on the reader! We have seen almost every keyword needed to ready this, but let's go through it step by step.

We are looking at vectors of logic variables, marked as c1...c9, and we will further reference this vector as `vs`:

```
(run* [c1 c2 c3 c4 c5 c6 c7 c8 c9 :as vs]
```

The first constraint is that each logic variable of the set will be in the interval 1 to 9. Here, `everyg` applies the same constraint to all the `lvars` of vector `vs`:

```
(everyg
   #(fd/in % (fd/interval 1 9))
   vs)
```

We want to make sure all `lvars` are distinct; we have seen this `fd/distinct` previously:

```
(fd/distinct vs)
```

Now that we have a set of relational constraints to apply, we use `fd/eq` to achieve this:

```
(fd/eq
    (= (- c4 c6) c7)
    (= (* c1 c2 c3) (+ c8 c9))
    (< (+ c2 c3 c6) c8)
    (< c9 c8))
```

Before the last part, a quick reminder on a forgotten usage of Clojure map: map can work with more than two parameters. Yes, indeed. In that case, the first parameter function of map receives multiple inputs. map will then be called step by step until one of the 2...*n* parameters runs out of elements:

```
(map #(hash-map %1 %2)
     (take 5 (range 0 10))
     (range 1 10))

; ({0 1} {1 2} {2 3} {3 4} {4 5})
```

OK!

The last part is quite overwhelming but very interesting. We want to impose a constraint on the value of each lvar. This is done through project, to work on the value, and everyg, to apply a constraint on a vector of variables:

```
(project [vs]

  (everyg

  (fn [[v n]] (fd/!= v n) )

   (map
    vector
    vs
    (range 1 10)))))
```

With all the elements in mind, we realize this means that we want to make sure that each logic variable does not have a value equal to its position. So c1 cannot take value 1, c2 cannot take value 2, and so on.

Running the preceding code is somewhat easy to generate, but complicated to replicate with other techniques. Let's enjoy:

```
;    ([4 3 1 8 9 2 6 7 5])
```

Phew!! What a ride again! But at last, that hardcore piece of code now finally looks readable to us.

There's more...

Two final usages of `core.logic` that we would like to present are the validation of results of a function over which we have no control, and also how to work with external data.

Validating the results of a function

So we have this function where we know the output, but we want to figure out what the input could have been, knowing the range of possible inputs.

This is the function we want to test in regular Clojure code:

```
(defn test-me [ x ]
  (* x x))
```

The interval of values is as follows:

```
(def interval (range 10))
```

Now we are looking for possible values, where the function to test returns either 9 or 16 and some made-on-the-spot constraints on the input.

Here, we use `membero` to limit possible solutions to a finite domain and `project` to work on values:

```
(run* [c1 c2 c3]

  (membero c1 interval)
  (membero c2 interval)
  (membero c3 interval)

  (fd/eq
    (= (- c2 c1) c3))

  (project [c3]
    (conde
      [(== (test-me c3) 16)]
      [(== (test-me c3) 9)])))
```

```
; ([0 3 3] [0 4 4] [1 4 3] [1 5 4] [2 5 3] [2 6 4] [3 6 3] [3 7 4] [4 7 3]
  [4 8 4] [5 8 3] [5 9 4] [6 9 3])
```

Note that this is also a nice way to generate data.

Working with external data

Here we will load data from a CSV file, but it could very well be from a database or an external API. The file contains the following three rows:

```
1,2,3
2,3,5
6,2,2
```

We can skip the boring part of parsing the CSV file to Clojure code:

```
(use '[clojure.string :only (split)])
(defn parse-rows
  [file]
    (let [rows (split (slurp file) #"\n" )]
      (map (fn[x]
         (map #(Integer/parseInt %)
           (split x #","))) rows)))
```

Now, our function to convert from data to something core.logic can understand will be unify:

```
(defn query [q file]
  (fn [b]
    (to-stream
      (map (fn [result] (unify b q result))
           (parse-rows file)))))
```

Note that unify does the same as ==, yes, the same == we have seen up to now.

Before moving on, make sure the resources/logic-rows.csv file contains data, as seen previously:

```
1,2,3
2,3,5
6,2,2
```

Having our custom data structure ready, we can run some constraints on the input CSV file and find some instances of q:

```
(run* [q]
      (fresh [a]
      (query a "resources/logic-rows.csv")
      (conso 1 q a)))
; ((2 3))
```

Anyone still here? Fantastic!

So, we went through a crash course on logic programming and core.logic, and then moved on to generating data and reading some difficult logic code. We also saw how to validate functions, or how to find the input from their output, and finally, how to make use of external data and integrate them in our core logic set of constraints.

4
File Access and the Network

In this chapter, we will cover the following topics:

- Manipulating files and directories
- Manipulating various formats of files – XML, JSON, YAML, and EDN
- Making use of Clojure HTTP client
- Using queues and topics in the RabbitMQ
- Using Kafka
- Using MQTT
- Streaming access to provide high performance
- Using Apache Camel to connect everything

Introduction

In this chapter, we will learn about file access and network. First, we will have a look at how to manipulate files and directories. Then, we will learn how to read and write various file formats. Later, we will learn to access messaging middleware and protocols such as HTTP, AMQP, MQTT, RabbitMQ, and Kafka. Finally, we will learn Apache Camel, which is a mediation framework.

Manipulating files and directories

In this recipe, we will show you how to read from files and write to files. Then we will learn how to create, delete, and list files and directories.

Getting ready

This recipe does not make use of any external library, so you can just start a REPL and be ready. As we manipulate files and directories, be careful to not delete files or directories and not overwriting the contents of your important files through inattention. We will make use of the source code of Clojure on the GitHub, so you need to install the `git` client to obtain the source.

How to do it...

Let's learn how to read and write files. We will also learn how to create and delete files and directories. Then we will see how to list files and directories.

spit and slurp

The `spit` writes a string to a file and the `slurp` reads the contents of a file as string:

```
(spit "/tmp/hello.txt" "Hello World Nico!" )
;;=> nil
```

The `spit` with the `:append true` option appends a string to an existing file:

```
(spit "/tmp/hello.txt" "\nHello World Makoto!" :append true)
;;=> nil
```

The following code reads a file content into a string:

```
(slurp "/tmp/hello.txt")
;;=> "Hello World Nico!\nHello World Makoto!"
```

The next code creates a vector whose elements are string lines of the file:

```
(-> (slurp "/tmp/hello.txt")
    (clojure.string/split #"\n")
    )
;;=> ["Hello World Nico!" "Hello World Makoto!"]
```

Reader and writer with with-open

The example code counts the number of lines of the /etc/passwd. The clojure.java.io/reader opens /etc/passwd and returns java.io.BufferedReader. The line-seq returns the lines of text from the reader as a lazy sequence of strings. The with-open automatically closes the reader after execution of the body of the expression:

```
(with-open [rdr (clojure.java.io/reader "/etc/passwd")]
  (count (line-seq rdr))
  )
```

The next code is an example for writing a file using the with-open, which closes the writer after the execution of the doseq:

```
(with-open [w (clojure.java.io/writer "/tmp/test.txt")]
  (doseq [x (range 1 11)]
    (.write w (str "Hello no" x " !\n"))))
(print (slurp "/tmp/test.txt"))
;;=> Hello no1 !
;;=> Hello no2 !
;;=> Hello no3 !
;;=> Hello no4 !
;;=> Hello no5 !
;;=> Hello no6 !
;;=> Hello no7 !
;;=> Hello no8 !
;;=> Hello no9 !
;;=> Hello no10 !
;;=> nil
```

Creating a file and directory

In the following code, the clojure.java.io/make-parents creates the parent directory of /tmp/foo/test.txt (/tmp/foo). Then, the spit creates a file under the directory and writes text to the file:

```
(let [f "/tmp/foo/test.txt"]
  (clojure.java.io/make-parents f)
  (spit f "Hello!")
  )
;;=> nil
(slurp "/tmp/foo/test.txt")
;;=> "Hello!"
```

Copying a file

The example copies /tmp/foo/test.txt to /tmp/test.txt:

```
(clojure.java.io/copy
 (clojure.java.io/file "/tmp/foo/test.txt")
  (clojure.java.io/file "/tmp/test.txt")
  )
;;=> nil
```

Deleting a file and a directory

Deleting a directory containing files causes an IOException as follows:

```
(clojure.java.io/delete-file "/tmp/foo")
;;=> IOException Couldn't delete /tmp/foo
;;=> clojure.java.io/delete-file (io.clj:426)
```

So, delete all files under the directory first and then delete the empty directory:

```
(clojure.java.io/delete-file "/tmp/foo/test.txt")
;;=> true
(clojure.java.io/delete-file "/tmp/foo")
;;=> true
```

If you try to delete a file or directory that does not exist, it causes an exception. If you don't want to see such an exception, use the true flag:

```
(clojure.java.io/delete-file "/tmp/foo")
;;=> IOException Couldn't delete /tmp/foo  clojure.java.io/delete-file
(io.clj:426)
(clojure.java.io/delete-file "/tmp/foo" true)
;;=> true
```

Listing files and directories in a directory

Java's method listFile in the java.io.File class lists files and directories directly under the specified directory:

```
(doseq [x (.listFiles (clojure.java.io/file "."))]
  (if (.isDirectory x) (print "[D] ")(print "[F] "))
    (println (.getPath x))
    )
[F] ./CHANGELOG.md
[D] ./images
```

```
[F]  ./.nrepl-port
[F]  ./README.md
[D]  ./test
[F]  ./project.clj
[F]  ./chapter04.md
[D]  ./src
[D]  ./doc
[D]  ./dev-resources
[F]  ./.gitignore
[D]  ./target
[F]  ./.hgignore
[D]  ./resources
[F]  ./LICENSE
nil
```

Clojure's function `file-seq` lists files recursively:

```
(doseq [x (file-seq (clojure.java.io/file "."))]
  (if (.isDirectory x) (print "[D] ")(print "[F] "))
    (println (.getPath x))
    )
[D]  .
[F]  ./CHANGELOG.md
[D]  ./images
[F]  ./images/rabbitmq.png
[F]  ./images/kafka-topic.png
[F]  ./images/kafka.png
[F]  ./images/zookeeper.png
[F]  ./.nrepl-port
[F]  ./README.md
[D]  ./test
[D]  ./test/chapter04
[F]  ./test/chapter04/core_test.clj
[F]  ./project.clj
[F]  ./chapter04.md
[D]  ./src
[D]  ./src/chapter04
[F]  ./src/chapter04/kafka.clj
[F]  ./src/chapter04/core.clj
[F]  ./src/chapter04/files.clj
[F]  ./src/chapter04/rabbitmq.clj
```

How it works...

Let's look at how `slurp` and `spit` work and then see how `with-open` works.

slurp and spit

As the `slurp` reads the whole file content into a string, it consumes a lot of memory if the file is very large. Similarly, as the `spit` writes a file from a string one at a time, it consumes a large amount of memory if the target file is very large. In such cases, use reader or writer with sequence read/sequence write instead.

with-open macro

The `with-open` macro uses `try` and `finally`. Reader or writer is closed by the `close` method in the `finally` clause. The object used in the `with-open` must have `open` and `close` methods. We can understand how the `with-open` works using the `macroexpand-1` as follows:

```
(macroexpand-1
  '(with-open [rdr (clojure.java.io/reader "/etc/passwd")]
     (count (line-seq rdr))
     ))
;;=> (clojure.core/let
;;=>    [rdr (clojure.java.io/reader "/etc/passwd")]
;;=>    (try
;;=>      (clojure.core/with-open [] (count (line-seq rdr)))
;;=>      (finally (. rdr clojure.core/close))))
```

There's more...

Let's learn how to read web contents via HTTP. Then, we will have a look at a small application to examine Clojure source files.

Reading HTTP resource

The `slurp`, `spit`, `clojure.java.io/reader`, and `clojure.java.io/writer` can make use not only for files but also of HTTP and network sockets.

The following code reads from a Clojure document site:

```
(slurp "http://clojuredocs.org")
;;=> <!DOCTYPE html>
;;=> <html><head><meta content="width=device-width, maximum-scale=1.0"
name="viewport">
;;=> <meta content="yes" name="apple-mobile-web-app-capable">
;;=> ......
```

```
;;=> </script></body></html>
```

The next code counts the number of bytes of the website. Since the `line-seq` eliminates newline, we add 1 to the byte size:

```
(with-open [rdr (clojure.java.io/reader "http://clojuredocs.org")]
  (->> (line-seq rdr)
       (map (fn [s] (inc (count (.getBytes s "UTF-8"))))) )
       (reduce +)))
;;=> 40261
```

Examining the source code

Now we will show you a little complex example. In this example, we will list the names of source files of Clojure and count the numbers of lines of these files.

The `get-source-files` returns the sequence of file objects (`java.io.File`) whose file name has the specific extension. The `re-matches` tests whether a file name matches a regular expression pattern. Such a regular expression is generated by the `re-pattern` as follows:

```
(re-pattern (str ".*\\." "clj"))
;;=> #".*\.clj"
(re-matches #".*\.clj" "foo.clj")
;;=> "foo.clj"
(re-matches #".*\.clj" "foo.java")
;;=> nil
```

The `get-source-files` filters files with the specific file extension (default is `.clj`.):

```
(defn get-source-files [path & {:keys [ext] :or {ext "clj"}}]
  (let [f (file-seq (clojure.java.io/file path))
        regex (re-pattern (str ".*\\." ext))]
    (->> f
         (filter #(comp not (.isHidden %)))
         (filter #(.isFile %))
         (filter #(re-matches regex (.getPath %) ))
         )
    )
  )
;;=> #'chapter04.files/get-source-files
```

Let's test the `get-source-files`:

```
(get-source-files ".")
;;=> (#object[java.io.File 0x5696f6cb "./project.clj"]
;;=>  ...
;;=>  #object[java.io.File "0x4f085b88" "./src/chapter04/rabbitmq.clj"])
```

Then we will show you how the `count-lines` counts the number of lines of the given file:

```
(defn count-lines [fname]
  (with-open [rdr (clojure.java.io/reader fname)]
    (count (line-seq rdr)))
  )
;;=> #'chapter04.files/count-lines
```

We use `count-lines` as follows:

```
(count-lines "./src/chapter04/rabbitmq.clj")
;;=> 32
```

Let's look at the `get-source-lines`, which returns a vector of a pair of file paths and the number of lines in it:

```
(defn get-source-lines [p & {:keys [ext] :or {ext "clj"}}]
  (map
   (fn [x]
     (let [p (.getPath x)]
       [p (count-lines p)]
       )) (get-source-files p :ext ext))
  )
;;=> #'chapter04.files/get-source-lines
```

Let's test the `get-source-lines`:

```
(get-source-lines ".")
;;=> (["./project.clj" 18] ["./src/chapter04/kafka.clj" 235]
;;=>  ...
;;=>  ["./src/chapter04/camel.clj" 103]
   ;;=> ["./src/chapter04/rabbitmq.clj" 296])
```

Let's apply the preceding code for the Clojure source code. So, we will get the Clojure source code on GitHub using `git clone` first:

```
$ git clone https://github.com/clojure/clojure.git
```

Then, we will pick up the file names of Clojure source files and count the number of lines of these files:

```
(get-source-lines "./clojure")
;;=> (["./clojure/test/clojure/test_clojure/pprint.clj" 20]
;;=>  ["./clojure/test/clojure/test_clojure/multimethods.clj" 234]
;;=>  ["./clojure/test/clojure/test_clojure/macros.clj" 113]
;;=>  ["./clojure/test/clojure/test_clojure/data_structures.clj" 1303]
;;=>  .....
;;=>  ["./clojure/test/clojure/test_clojure/protocols.clj" 676]
;;=>  ["./clojure/test/clojure/test_clojure/fn.clj" 55]
;;=>  ["./clojure/test/clojure/test_clojure/other_functions.clj" 355]
;;=>  .....
```

The following code counts the total number of lines of Clojure source code:

```
(reduce + (map second (get-source-lines "./clojure")))
;;=> 36584
```

We can also examine source files of Java:

```
(get-source-lines "./clojure" :ext "java")
;;=> (["./clojure/test/java/reflector/IBar.java" 20]
;;=>  ["./clojure/test/java/clojure/test/ReflectorTryCatchFixture.java" 22]
;;=>  ["./clojure/test/java/compilation/TestDispatch.java" 15]
;;=>  ["./clojure/src/jvm/clojure/main.java" 39]
;;=>  ;=>  .....
;;=>  ["./clojure/src/jvm/clojure/java/api/Clojure.java" 100]
;;=>  ["./clojure/src/jvm/clojure/asm/Opcodes.java" 358]
(reduce + (map second (get-source-lines "./clojure" :ext "java")))
;;=> 58676
```

We can also examine Clojure source and Java source at a time!

```
(reduce + (map second (get-source-lines "./clojure" :ext "(java|clj)")))
;;=> 95260
```

It would be nice!

Manipulating various formats of files – XML, JSON, YAML, and EDN

There are many formats available to exchange data between different systems these days, but the most important ones seems to be quite stable for some time with a list of XML, JSON, YAML, and, more recently, MessagePack and EDN, a subset of the Clojure notation.

Each of these formats has some strong points, so this recipe will show us how to read and parse data through those different formats, and also when you might want to use each of them.

Getting ready

This recipe will make use of the standard libraries in the Clojure world to parse the different data formats. These are the full set of dependencies that we will need in our `projects.clj` file:

```
[clj-yaml "0.4.0"] ; parse yaml
[cheshire "5.5.0"] ; parse json
[org.clojure/data.xml "0.1.0-beta1"] ; parse xml
[com.cognitect/transit-clj "0.8.285"] ; library for both json and msgpack
[org.clojure/tools.reader "1.0.0-alpha2"] ; EDN ! Clojure
[clojure-msgpack "1.1.2"] ; Message pack
[clojurewerkz/balagan "1.0.5"] ; manipulating clojure data structure
[org.clojure/core.async "0.2.374"] ; async ...
```

This actually turned into a dependency galore, so make sure you only write the ones you will actually use for your own project.

How to do it...

In sequence, we will go through the different formats and see some round-tripping encoding/decoding functions. As we will see, all the libraries eventually convert the input format to Clojure, and so we can work directly on the Clojure structures to retrieve the information we need.

XML

This may be the most famous or infamous data format. XML is the most verbose of all the presented formats, but it has the advantage of being present in most environments.

Parsing is done through the `data.xml` library:

```
(use 'clojure.data.xml)
```

Here, we will access the remote `weather.gov` service to send us the latest weather updates from the US. KSFO stands for San Francisco because it is always so sunny in the bay:

```
(def input-xml
  (slurp "http://w1.weather.gov/xml/current_obs/KSFO.rss"))

(def xml
  (parse (java.io.StringReader. input-xml)))
```

The XML `var` contains a lazy sequence on the elements of the parsed XML input. Every parsed element will look like the following structure:

```
#clojure.data.xml.node.Element{:tag :channel, :attrs {}, :content ...}
```

An XML element is a set of a tag, attributes, and content.

The returned Clojure data structure corresponds directly to the parsed XML, without the extra verboseness, so now we can use our beloved threading macros to navigate the parsed document:

```
(->> xml
 (:content)
 first
 (:content)
 (map #(:content %))
 first)
; ("Weather at San Francisco, San Francisco International Airport...")
```

Generating XML works the other way around, where we use the `element` function to create elements in the same data structure as previously:

```
(element :friend {"age" 23} "Chris")
; #clojure.data.xml.node.Element{:tag :friend, :attrs {"age" 23}, :content
("Chris")}
```

We can, of course, construct more complex data structures, with the body of each element being simply the last parameter of the `element` function:

```
(let [tags
      (element :friends {}
        (element :friend {"age" 23} "Chris")
        (element :friend {"age" 32} "Nick")
        (element :friend {"age"  45} "Ray"))]
  (println (indent-str tags)))
```

We will properly emit XML as shown in the following structure:

```
<?xml version="1.0" encoding="UTF-8"?>
<friends>
  <friend age="23">Chris</friend>
  <friend age="32">Nick</friend>
  <friend age="45">Ray</friend>
</friends>
```

JSON

In JSON, you will use the Cheshire library, which claims to be the fastest JSON parsing library. We want to retrieve some weather data, and as the programmable web wants, a lot of data is encoded with JSON because of its simplicity.

We start by call `require` on the `cheshire.core` namespace:

```
(require '[cheshire.core :refer :all])
```

Then `slurp` some web data from the `api.openweathermap.org` endpoint:

```
(def url
  "http://api.openweathermap.org/data/2.5/box/city?bbox=12,32,15,37,10&cluster=yes&appid=9220dd1ac43dcaf7091d8c07a8a46efb")
(def slurped
  (slurp url))
```

Finally, we use the threading macro again to access the data we want. `parse-string` is the `cheshire` function that turns the JSON data to a Clojure data structure:

```
(-> slurped
  parse-string
  (get "list"))
; [{"id" 2208791, "name" "Yafran", "coord" {"lon" 12 ...
```

Looks like it will be sunny tomorrow!

Now turning a Clojure data structure to a JSON data structure makes use of the `generate-string` function from Cheshire:

```
(generate-string {:friends {:friend "nico" :age 15}})
; "{"friends":{"friend":"nico","age":15}}"
```

The cool thing with the Cheshire library is its direct support for the `SMILE` data format, which is a binary version of the JSON format:

```
(generate-smile {:friends {:friend "nico" :age 15}})
; #object["[B" 0x41708227 "[B@41708227"]
```

Not very human readable, but rather compact. Round-tripping on the `smile` generated byte data; we can get our as follows:

```
(parse-smile
 (generate-smile {:friends {:friend "nico" :age 15}}))
 ; {"friends" {"friend" "nico", "age" 15}}
```

Some nice options to remember, pretty printing is available to generate human readable JSON:

```
(println
 (generate-string {:friends {:friend "nico" :age 15}} {:pretty true}))
```

Calling `generate-string` with the `{:pretty true}` parameter will return a nicely indented and readable JSON document:

```
{
  "friends" : {
    "friend" : "nico",
    "age" : 15
  }
}
```

Also, when you generate a JSON document, a function parameter is available to modify keys as needed, most of the time to convert between Clojure keywords and regular strings. Here we simply convert all the keys to uppercase:

```
(parse-string
    "{"friends":{"friend":"nico","age":15}}"
    (fn [k] (keyword (.toUpperCase k))))
; {:FRIENDS {:FRIEND "nico", :AGE 15}}
```

JSON is quite ubiquitous in the API world, and being able to parse data from remote services using it, it is always quite useful. JSON also fits well when you need it to be human readable so as to make your API very explicit and easy to understand. To connect to other systems out there, JSON seems like a welcome de facto choice.

YAML isn't a markup language

At this point, you might start to notice that most data formats work in a similar fashion in Clojure. Basically, you give a generic Clojure data structure to a generator or a parser, and convert back and forth to the required format.

Let's have a quick look at how YAML, which is not a markup language, can be generated from Clojure using the wrapper `clj-yaml`.

First, let's require the namespace:

```
(require '[clj-yaml.core :as yaml])
```

Then pass a generic Clojure data structure to the `generate-string` function:

```
(yaml/generate-string
  [{:name "John", :age 33}
   {:name "Nick", :age 27}])
```

Quite straightforwardly, the function returns the following:

```
- {name: John, age: 33}
- {name: Nick, age: 27}
```

The `parse-string` function allows us to get some YAML text turned into Clojure data structure:

```
(yaml/parse-string "
- {name: John, age: 33}
- name: Nick
  age: 27
")
```

This will give you a familiar sequence of elements:

```
({:name "John", :age 33} {:name "Nick", :age 27})
```

YAML is quite useful in the DevOps configuration world, and is able to parse those files and do some preliminary checks from Clojure.

MessagePack, Clojure library

MessagePack is described as being like JSON, but light and small. It is actually in a binary serialization format and is impressively fast and small. The Clojure library itself has no third-party dependency.

We start by requiring the `msgpack.core` namespace:

```
(ns chapter04.somemsgpack
  (:require [msgpack.core :as msg])
  (:require msgpack.clojure-extensions))
```

We can now use the `pack` and `unpack` methods to turn Clojure data structure to and from bytes. Let's turn our friend Nick to bytes first:

```
(msg/pack
    {:friends {:friend "Nick" :age 15}})
; #<byte[] [B@60280b2e>
```

Now let's free our friend from its byte form through a simple round-tripping example using pack/unpack:

```
(msg/unpack
    (msg/pack
        {:friends {:friend "Nick" :age 15}}))
; {:friends {:friend "Nick" :age 15}}
```

This MessagePack library also works smoothly with streams to read through very large binary files. We will make use of Java classes `DataInputStream` and `DataOutputStream` to handle the large streaming, and see that we can use those stream with the `pack-stream` and `unpack-stream` functions.

We start by importing the necessary Java classes and the `io` namespace:

```
(use 'clojure.java.io)
(import
    '(java.io.DataOutputStream)
    '(java.io.DataInputStream))
```

Now we can write the content of our list of friends to a file named `pack.dat`:

```
(with-open [o (output-stream "pack.dat")]
  (let [data-output (java.io.DataOutputStream. o)]
    (msg/pack-stream
        {:friends {:friend "Nick" :age 15}} data-output)))
```

As a quick reminder, by using `with-open`, we make sure the stream is properly closed when we are finished processing.

Now reviving our list of friends to Clojure, we can use the `unpack-stream` function:

```
(with-open [i (input-stream "pack.dat")]
  (let [data-input (java.io.DataInputStream. i)]
    (msg/unpack-stream data-input)))
; {:friends {:friend "Nick" :age 15}}
```

This actually means that very big Clojure data structures can be saved this way, without using as much memory. Another feature is to allow you to use your own custom encoders, for example, to encode Clojure records you may have defined. Custom encoders are available in the `macros` namespace:

```
(require '[msgpack.macros :refer [extend-msgpack]])
```

Now let's define a record, `Friend` that has one attribute, `name`:

```
(defrecord Friend [name])
```

We will tell `msgpack` that this special `Friend` structure will be encoded using the byte equivalent of the name attribute. Similarly, to retrieve a `Friend` record from bytes, we will pass the byte value to the `->Friend` function:

```
(extend-msgpack
  Friend
  100
  [p] (.getBytes (:name p))
  [bytes] (->Friend (String. bytes)))
```

We can now round-trip through our friend Nick:

```
(msg/unpack
    (msg/pack
        [(->Friend "Nick") 5 "test"]))
; (#chapter04.somemsgpack.Friend{:name "Nick"} 5 "test")
```

MessagePack is one of the new kids on the block for data serialization, but it sure is getting more and more attention. Redis has native support for MessagePack, making the format really attractive to be used from Clojure to dispatch job to other systems.

Now we have learnt quite extensively how to convert back and forth to different serialization formats, so let's have a look at how we can actually transform Clojure data structure through a query.

How it works...

So, now that we can turn all sorts of data in the Clojure landscape, we will make use of another trick to modify those structures.

Usually Clojure favors zippers to navigate up and down data structures. Now `balagan` is a library that helps you navigate and modify structures through a path-like query system:

Promptly, let's require it into our running namespace:

```
(require '[clojurewerkz.balagan.core :as b])
```

Now supposing our friend Nick still wants to play around with us, we are going to bring him back in and add some bits of information. This is going to look like a simple, but not too simple, Clojure map:

```
(def friend
  {:name "Nick"
   :birth {:year 1985 :place "Japan"}
   :nickname "nickthegreat"})
```

Now, let's say we would like to retrieve the year our friend Nick was born. We will construct a vector that will describe a path to go and fetch it. We are going to make use of the `select` function here:

```
(b/select friend
          [:birth :year])
; (1985)
```

That is pretty straightforward. Now, for some more fun, we can actually use wildcards throughout the `:*` path directive. So, replacing `:birth` with the wildcard gives the following:

```
(b/select friend
          [:* :year])
; (1985)
```

This is sweet as well.

As a side feature, if you use those data structures to do some configuration, `balagan` can actually trigger functions based on selectors by using the `with-paths` function:

```
(b/with-paths
  friend
  [:birth]  (fn [value path]
              (println "I am born in " (value :place))))
```

The preceding function will print the following in the console:

```
I am born in Japan
```

`with-paths` also supports multiple paths:

```
(b/with-paths
  friend
  [:name]
     (fn [value _]
         (println "My name is " value))))
  [:birth]
     (fn [value path]
             (println "I am born in " (value :place))))
```

While dispatching calls is also nice, our main goal is actually to update those data structures. This is done in the exact same way by calling the `balagan` function `update`. The function gets a data structure, a series of vectorized paths, and a value or a function for each path.

In its simplest form, we may just want to add a new field to confirm that our friend is a cool dude:

```
(b/update friend
    [] (b/add-field :nice-friend true) )
; {:name "Nick", :birth {:year 1985, :place "Japan"}, :nickname
"nickthegreat", :nice-friend true}
```

Note that in pure Clojure tradition, a new data structure is returned and the original is not touched.

If you've just realized you got the birth date wrong, you may want to update it. This is done by setting directly a value instead of using the `add-field` function:

```
(b/update friend
    [:birth :year] 1986)
; {:name "Nick", :birth {:year 1986, :place "Japan"}, :nickname
"nickthegreat"}
```

Each path directive, if it defines a function, gets passed the data structure as input, so you can make data-dependent computations. For example, to add an age field, we will make use of the `mk-path` function and an anonymous function that does some simple arithmetic:

```
(b/update friend
    (b/mk-path [:age]) #(- 2016 (-> % :birth :year)))
; {:name "Nick", :birth {:year 1985, :place "Japan"}, :nickname
"nickthegreat", :age 31}
```

Removing a field is also quite easy, again using path and an associated function:

```
(b/update friend
    [] (b/remove-field :nickname))
; {:name "Nick", :birth {:year 1985, :place "Japan"}}
```

And, as you notice, this works with a slightly more complicated path as well:

```
(b/update friend
    [:birth] (b/remove-field :place))
; {:name "Nick", :birth {:year 1985}, :nickname "nickthegreat"}
```

That's it! The cycle is closed. We can parse data in a format, update it, and convert it to another format at will.

There's more...

One more thing…what we have not done yet in this recipe is convert from Clojure to Clojure.

Extensible Data Notation

Extensible Data Notation, EDN in short, is a subset of the Clojure language that helps transporting Clojure data structure as standard text. Datomic, the Cognitect functional database, is making use of EDN to transfer data from its storage to the client. You can also use EDN to send data between a ClojureScript client and a Clojure server, making every part of your infrastructure be in Clojure.

The standard read-string function from clojure.core works fine:

```
(read-string
    "{:friends [{:friend {:name "Nick" :age 23}}]}")
; {:friends [{:friend {:name "Nick" :age 23}}]}
```

But there is also a tools.reader available for both Clojure and ClojureScript that can read text to Clojure data structure:

```
(require '[clojure.tools.reader.edn :as edn])

(edn/read-string
"{:friends [{:friend {:name "Nick" :age 33}}]}")

; {:friends [{:friend {:name "Nick", :age 23}}]}
```

Round-tripping is easy as well:

```
(edn/read-string
 (str
  {:friends [{:friend {:name "Nick" :age 23}}]}))

; {:friends [{:friend {:name "Nick", :age 23}}]}
```

Note that this also works with Clojure records. If we define a list of friends through record:

```
(defrecord Friend [name])
(def friends
     [(Friend. "Nico")
       (Friend. "Makoto")
       (Friend. "Nick")])
```

We can confirm that the type is maintained even after round-tripping:

```
(pr-str friends)
(read-string (pr-str friends))
(def read-friends (read-string (pr-str friends)))
(type (first read-friends))
(first read-friends)
```

Similarly, the record types are maintained even after round-tripping through files:

```
(spit "target/text.txt" (pr-str friends))
(read-string (slurp "target/text.txt"))
```

Voila! No more secrets on Clojure data structures and file formats for you now.

Making use of Clojure HTTP client

For retrieving simple HTTP requests, `http-kit` is a library of choice when the simple `slurp` function from `clojure.core` does not provide enough flexibility. While `http-kit` is both a server and a client, this recipe will only look at the client side of things.

Getting ready

Including the `http-kit` library into our project is now relatively straightforward. Let's add the following line to the `project.clj` file:

```
[http-kit "2.1.18"]
```

How to do it...

A simple request to retrieve the weather data, as we have seen before in the parsing JSON section, is quite simply done by calling the `get` function of `http-kit`. The function returns a promise by default, meaning the call will run in the background and block when trying to get the result by calling `deref` or `@`.

Let's get set quickly with the namespace and the target URL to retrieve weather data from the `openweathermap` API endpoint:

```
(ns chapter04.somehttp1
  (:require [org.httpkit.client :as http]))

(def url
  (str
  "http://api.openweathermap.org/data/2.5/box/city?"
  "bbox=12,32,15,37,10"
  "&"
  "cluster=yes"
  "&"
  "appid=2de143494c0b295cca9337e1e96b00e0"))
```

A `get` request with `http-kit` is straightforwardly done through the `get` function:

```
(http/get url)
```

Now, the returned `var` from `get` is not a result, but a promise on the result. This means that to synchronously get the result from `http get`, we actually need to call the preceding request prefixed with `@`:

```
@(http/get url)
```

This request will actually be made and the main thread will block until you get either an answer or a timeout.

The request returns a different map depending on success or error:

```
{:opts ... : status ... :headers.... :body ...}
{:opts ... :error ...}
```

`:opts`	**These are the details of the sent HTTP request**
`:status`	This is the HTTP status
`:headers`	These are the HTTP headers
`:body`	This is the content of the response

:error	This is the error message and is only present if the request failed

Usually, you would want to destructure on the keys to make it easy to process the different parts of the response:

```
(let [{:keys [status headers body error] :as resp} @(http/get url)]
  (println status))
; 200
```

Retrieving the content of body works about the same, so go ahead and have a few tries on your favorite website. http-kit supports the whole set of HTTP request types and a full set of options for sending those requests.

How it works...

On top of default parameters when sending a request, one of the hidden treasures is to be able to reuse the underlying TCP connection through the settings of the keepalive parameter:

```
(time
  (let [resp @(http/get url {:keepalive 60000})]
    (println (:opts resp))))
```

Calling the same code twice in a row will produce significant speed increase due to the fact that we do not need to open another TCP connection the second time. See for yourself!

```
; first time
; "Elapsed time: 514.686061 msecs"
; second time
; "Elapsed time: 77.74604 msecs"
```

The get function, and its more generic request implementation, supports a wide range of options; the main ones are shown in the following snippet:

```
(http/request
{:url ... ; the url to send the request to
:method :get              ; :post :put :head or other
:user-agent "User-Agent string"
:oauth-token "your-token"
:headers {"X-header" "value" "ApiToken" "123"}
:query-params {"param1" "foo, bar"} ; those are added to the URL
:form-params {"param2" "foo, bar"} ; those parameters are send in the body
of the request
:body (json/encode {"key" "value"}) ; you can set your serialization
strategy, here json
```

```
:basic-auth ["user" "pass"] ; add your basic credentials here
:keepalive 3000          ; As we have seen, allow to reuse the TCP
connection
:timeout 1000      ; set the reading timeout
:insecure? true ; Need to contact a server with an untrusted SSL cert?
:multipart [] ; files to upload, see below
:max-redirects 10 ; Max number of redirects to follow
:follow-redirects false ; do we allow being redirected ? no !
})
```

Through the `request` function, you, of course, have access to all the different HTTP request types:

```
get,delete,head,
post,put,options,patch,propfind,proppatch,lock,unlock,report,acl,copy,move
```

To easily see the content of your HTTP request, you can use a service-like `requestb.in` that shows the content of your last 20 requests to a given endpoint.

Register an endpoint in the service and replace the ID in the following examples.

Trying what we have seen so far, a simple request would look like the following:

```
(let [{:keys [status headers body error] :as resp}
      @(http/get "http://requestb.in/tp6d3jtp"
       {:keepalive 120000 :query-params {:a 1}})]
  (println body))
```

Nice! Let's reuse the same service to upload our file content. In this case, we use the `:multipart` element in the map request to specify the filename, the content of the file, and the name of the HTTP parameter in the body of the request:

```
(let [{:keys [status headers body error] :as resp}
  @(http/get "http://requestb.in/tp6d3jtp"
          {:multipart [
                  {:name "file"
                   :content (clojure.java.io/file "resources/test1.json")
                   :filename "test1.json"}]
           :keepalive 120000})]
  (println body))
```

`test1.json` would be as follows:

```
[
{ "name":"Amy" , "grade1": 35 , "grade2": 41 , "grade3": 53},
{ "name":"Bob" , "grade1": 44 , "grade2": 37 , "grade3": 28},
{ "name":"Charles" , "grade1": 68, "grade2": 65 , "grade3": 61},
{ "name":"David" , "grade1": 72 , "grade2": 78 , "grade3": 81}
```

```
]
```

There's more...

To conclude this recipe, there is one more thing we will look at: asynchronous requests. And yes, let's plug this with `core.async` to show where Clojure really shines.

async HTTP and core async

`http-kit` supports one more mode of sending requests, and this is through the use of a call back instead of blocking while waiting for the result call. For example, taking the previous example to the `requestb.in` call, we had the following:

```
(let [{:keys [status headers body error] :as resp}
      @(http/get "http://requestb.in/tp6d3jtp"
        {:keepalive 120000 :query-params {:a 1}})]
   (println body))
```

The `request` function has a support for a different arity and a different number of parameters, and the last one is providing a callback for the call:

```
(http/get
; endpoint
"http://requestb.in/tp6d3jtp"
; options
{:keepalive 120000 :query-params {:a 1}}
; callback
(fn [{:keys [status headers body error opts]}]
  (println body)))
```

The callback will be called whenever the request has returned.

We can plug this to a `core.async` channel so that the response will be pushed to a channel whenever the response is retrieved:

```
(ns chapter04.async
  (:require [org.httpkit.client :as http])
  (:require [clojure.core.async :as async]))

(defn async-get [url result]
  (http/get url {:keepalive 60000}
  #(async/go (async/>! result %))))
```

We can then go through the finish line, send `async` HTTP request, pipe the result to a channel, and then, finally, do some simple reading from the same channel:

```
(time
    (let [c (async/chan) res (atom [])]

    ;; send requests
    (doseq [i (range 1 3)]
      (async-get
        (format
        "http://requestb.in/tp6d3jtp?requestnumber=%d" i) c))
    ;; gather results
    (doseq [_ (range 1 3)]
      (swap! res conj (async/<!! c)))
    @res
    ))
```

Of course, we could do some more processing and encoding, but we will leave it as an exercise for you.

Using queues and topics in the RabbitMQ

RabbitMQ is a multiprotocol message broker and one of the most popular brokers. RabbitMQ is written in Erlang; however, it provides client libraries for some major language such as Java, .NET, Ruby, and Erlang. In this recipe, we will show you producers and consumers using Langohr, which supports AMQP 0-9.1.

Getting ready

Here we will look at how to set up RabbitMQ server and Langohr in the project.

Installing RabbitMQ

You need to install RabbitMQ, a multiprotocol messaging broker first. We will use a Docker image for RabbitMQ:

```
$ docker run -d --hostname my-rabbit --name some-rabbit rabbitmq:3
```

The following image shows the output of the preceding command:

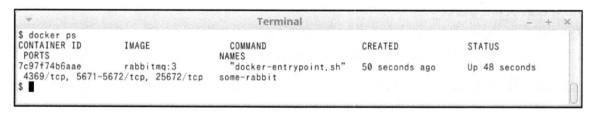

Then, we will check to see the container for RabbitMQ is running as follows:

```
$ docker ps
```

We can see the output in the following image, if the container launches successfully:

```
$ docker ps
CONTAINER ID          IMAGE          COMMAND                CREATED          STATUS
PORTS                                NAMES
7c97f74b6aae          rabbitmq:3     "docker-entrypoint.sh"  50 seconds ago   Up 48 seconds
4369/tcp, 5671-5672/tcp, 25672/tcp   some-rabbit
$ █
```

After launching the RabbitMQ container, we need to know the `ip` address of the container used by the client. To obtain it, we will issue the following Docker command:

```
$ docker inspect --format '{{ .NetworkSettings.IPAddress }}' some-rabbit
172.17.0.2
```

The output of the command is as follows:

```
                                   Terminal                          _  +  ×
$ docker inspect --format '{{ .NetworkSettings.IPAddress }}' some-rabbit
172.17.0.2
$ █
```

We will use Langohr, which is a Clojure library to access RabbitMQ. To make use of it, we need to add the `com.novemberain/langohr` to your `project.clj`:

```
:dependencies [
              [org.clojure/clojure "1.8.0"]
              [com.novemberain/langohr "3.3.0"]]
```

How to do it...

There are variations in exchange patterns for AMQP, but we will start with the most basic (default) exchange pattern.

Producing hello world messages and consuming them

We will demonstrate to you how to produce messages. Then we will learn how to receive them.

Declaring the namespace and loading Langohr libraries and IP address of the Docker container

Here we will declare the namespace and load some libraries for `langohr`:

```
(ns chapter04.rabbitmq
  (:require [langohr.core      :as core]
            [langohr.channel   :as channel]
            [langohr.queue     :as queue]
            [langohr.consumers :as consumers]
            [langohr.basic     :as basic]
            [langohr.exchange  :as exchange]
  ))
```

We also need to define *host* var, which is the IP address RabbitMQ is serving in the Docker container which we have examined:

```
(def *host* "172.17.0.2")
```

Defining a producer function

The following is the code of the function to produce a message:

```
(defn simple-producer [qname payload]
  (with-open
    [conn (core/connect {:host *host*})*})
     ch (channel/open conn)]
    (println "producing message to exchange " qname " payload = " payload)
    (queue/declare ch qname {:exclusive false :auto-delete false})
    (basic/publish
      ch "" qname payload {:content-type "text/plain" :type "message"})))
;;=> #'chapter04.rabbitmq/simple-producer
```

First, the producer connects to the RabbitMQ server using `langohr.core/connect`. Then it opens a channel of the connection using `langohr.channel/open`.

After that, the producer declares a queue by `langohr.queue/declare` and publishes a message by `langohr.basic/publish`.

Defining a message handler and consumer

We will define a message handler used by consumer:

```
(defn message-handler
  [ch {:keys [content-type delivery-tag type] :as meta} ^bytes payload]
  (println
    (str "Received a message payload : " (String. payload "UTF-8")  " , tag :
" delivery-tag)))
;;=> #'chapter04.rabbitmq/message-handler
```

The message handler has three parameters: channel, metadata, and payload. The example message handler simply prints metadata and payload.

Then, we will define a consumer. The consumer gets a connection, opens a channel, and then consumes messages published by the producer. The `langohr.consumers/subscribe` is used to obtain messages:

```
(defn simple-consumer [qname]
  (with-open
    [conn (core/connect {:host *host*})*})
```

```
    ch (channel/open conn)]
    (println (str "simple-consumer is connected with id:
"(.getChannelNumber ch)))
    (consumers/subscribe ch qname message-handler {:auto-ack true})))
;;=> #'chapter04.rabbitmq/simple-consumer
```

Testing producer and consumer

Let's test how the `producer` and `consumer` functions work.

Running the `producer` puts a message `"Hello !"` into the `"queue1.cookbook"` queue:

```
(simple-producer "queue1.cookbook" "Hello !")
;;=> producing message to exchange  queue1.cookbook  payload =  Hello !
;;=> nil
```

Then, let's run the consumer to obtain messages from the queue. The message handler in the consumer prints the channel properties and the message payload:

```
(simple-consumer "queue1.cookbook")
;;=> simple-consumer is connected with id: 1
;;=> Received a message payload : Hello ! , tag : 1
;;=> amq.ctag-8hfyoaVHtPAt_qKs1S7Hxg
```

It's very nice to receive a message!

Using blocking consumer

In the previous example, the `simple-consumer` exits after consuming all messages in the specified queue using the `langohr.consumers/subscribe`. This is a nonblocking consumer. We will now define a blocking consumer, which consumes messages in a queue forever until it will be terminated by others. Let's see the blocking consumer as follows:

```
(defn blocking-consumer [qname]
  (with-open
    [conn (core/connect {:host *host*})*})
    ch (channel/open conn)]
    (println (str "simple-consumer is connected with id:
"(.getChannelNumber ch)))
    (consumers/blocking-subscribe ch qname message-handler {:auto-ack
true})))
;;=> #'chapter04.rabbitmq/blocking-consumer
```

The preceding blocking consumer code is similar to the nonblocking consumer code defined in the previous section. We will use the `langohr.consumers/blocking-subscribe` instead. When we run the `blocking-consumer`, we use `future` to run it on a background thread:

```
(def f (future (blocking-consumer "queue1.cookbook")))
;;=> Consumer is connected with id: 1
;;=> #'chapter04.rabbitmq/f
```

Let's run the producer. We will run the `producer` function three times, and these invocations generate three messages. So, the `blocking-consumer` receives three messages in the background:

```
(simple-producer "queue1.cookbook" "Hello !")
;;=> produced a message =>  Hello !
;;=> nil
;;=> Received a message payload : Hello ! , tag : 1
(simple-producer "queue1.cookbook" "Hello !")
;;=> produced a message =>  Hello !
;;=> nil
;;=> Received a message payload : Hello ! , tag : 2
(simple-producer "queue1.cookbook" "Hello !")
;;=> produced a message =>  Hello !
;;=> nil
;;=> Received a message payload : Hello ! , tag : 3
```

To cancel the background thread, use the `future-cancel`.

```
(future-cancel f)
;;=> true
```

How it works...

AMQP stands for Advanced Message Queuing Protocol. It is an open standard for business messages between application and organization. RabbitMQ is the multiprotocol message broker and supports AMQP 0-9-1.

Connect to broker and open channel

In the preceding example, the `simple-producer` and `simple-consumer` connect to the broker and open a channel:

```
(with-open
  [conn (core/connect {:host *host*})*})
```

```
        ch (channel/open conn)]
....
    )
```

The `langohr.core/connect` connects to the broker, and the `langohr.channel/open` opens a channel for publishing and subscribing.

The `langohr.core/connect` can specify additional parameters using a map structure:

```
(core/connect {:host *host* :port 5672 :username "guest" :password "guest"
:vhost "/"})`
```

The `langohr.channel/open` takes the optional parameter of channel number to identify channels by numbers:

```
(channel/open conn 1)
```

How producer works

Let's walk through code to learn how producer works.

Declaring queue

After connecting to a broker and opening a channel, producer declares an exchange to publish.

The `langohr.queue/declare` declares a queue to use and associates with a channel:

```
(queue/declare ch qname {:durable false :exclusive false :auto-delete
false})
```

Mandatory parameters are a channel and a queue name. Additional parameters are the following queue properties:

- `:durable true`: This creates a durable queue, which enables the queue and messages in the queue survive after the event of broker reboot
- `:exclusive true`: This creates an exclusive queue, which can only be accessed by the current connection, and is deleted when the connection closes
- `:auto-delete true`: This deletes the queue after the application ends

Producing messages

Producer produces messages to the exchange. The `langohr.basic/publish` publishes messages to exchange. Parameters are a channel, exchange type, routing-key, payload, and optional properties. In the preceding example, the default exchange type(="") is used:

```
(basic/publish
  ch "" key payload {:content-type "text/plain" :type "message"}))
```

How consumer works

The following diagram depicts an exchange and queue as examples:

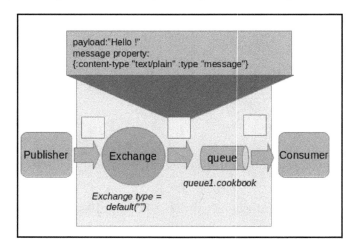

Consumer messages

After connecting to a broker and opening a channel, consumer subscribes messages from queue:

```
(consumers/subscribe ch qname message-handler {:auto-ack true})
```

Message handler is a function that is called when a message arrives. If `:auto-ack` is `true`, the broker remains messages until consumer confirms the message. If `:auto-ack` is `false`, the broker removes a message, when the broker sends to consumers.

Defining message handler

Message handler is a function when consumer receives messages. There are two parameters for message handler. The first parameter is a metadata of the message. The second one is a payload of the message. Since payload is a byte array, we convert it to a string:

```
(defn message-handler
  [ch {:keys [content-type delivery-tag type] :as meta} ^bytes payload]
  (println
    (str "Received a message payload : " (String. payload "UTF-8")  " , tag
: "  delivery-tag)))
```

There's more...

Now, we will explain more exchange types such as fanout exchange and topic exchange.

Using fanout exchange

The fanout exchange distributes messages to multiple queues at a time. We will define `fanout-producer` and `fanout-consumer`. The `langohr.exchange/fanout` specifies the fanout exchange type for both the producer and consumer:

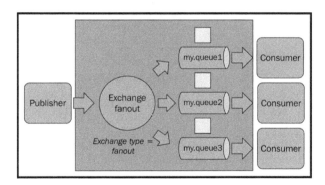

fanout-producer

Here we will define the `fanout-producer`. The `langohr.exchange/declare` declared the exchange to be the fanout exchange type:

```
(defn fanout-producer [ex  payload]
  (with-open
    [conn (core/connect {:host *host*})*})
```

```
      ch (channel/open conn)]
    (println "producing message to exchange " ex  " payload = " payload)
    (exchange/declare ch ex "fanout" {:durable false :auto-delete false})
    (basic/publish ch ex "" payload)))
;;=> #'chapter04.rabbitmq/fanout-publisher
```

fanout-consumer

The following code is the `fanout-consumer`. The `langohr.exchange/declare` declares the exchange to be the fanout exchange type. Then, the `langohr.queue/declare` declares a consumer queue, and the `_langohr.queue/bind` binds the exchange and queue:

```
(defn fanout-consumer [ex qname & {:keys [num] :or {num 1}}]
  (let [handler
        (fn [ch {:keys [delivery-tag]} payload]
          (println (format " [%d-%d] %s" (.getChannelNumber ch) delivery-
tag (String. payload "UTF-8"))))]
    (with-open [conn (core/connect)
                ch (channel/open conn num)]
      (println "starting consumer ...")
      (exchange/declare ch ex "fanout" {:durable false :auto-delete false})
      (queue/declare ch qname {:durable false :auto-delete false})
      (queue/bind ch qname ex)
      (consumers/blocking-subscribe ch qname handler
                                    {:auto-ack true}))))
;;=> #'chapter04.rabbitmq/fanout-consumer
```

Running the fanout consumers

We will run three fanout consumers on background threads:

```
(def f1 (future (fanout-consumer "fanout.exchange" "my.queue1" :num 1)))
;;=> starting consumer ...
;;=> #'chapter04.rabbitmq/f1
(def f2 (future (fanout-consumer "fanout.exchange" "my.queue2" :num 2)))
;;=> starting consumer ...
;;=> #'chapter04.rabbitmq/f2
(def f3 (future (fanout-consumer "fanout.exchange" "my.queue3" :num 3)))
;;=> starting consumer ...
;;=> #'chapter04.rabbitmq/f3
```

Testing fanout consumers

Then, the `fanout-publisher` publishes a message; three consumers receive the message published by the producer:

```
(fanout-producer "fanout.exchange" "hello world !")
;;=> producing message to exchange  my.exchange  payload =  hello world !
;=>  [1-1] hello world !
;=>  [2-1] hello world !
;=>  [3-1] hello world !
;;=> nil
```

Lastly, we will clean up the background threads:

```
(for [x [f1 f2 f3]]
  (future-cancel x))
;;=> [true true true]
```

Using topic exchange

The fanout exchange distributes messages to multiple queues at a time. We will define `topic-publisher` and `topic-consumer`. Topic exchange routes messages by routing key patterns:

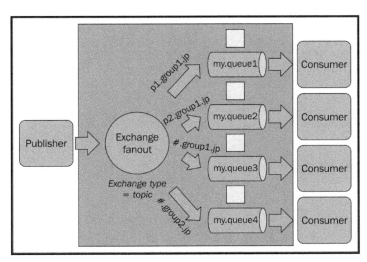

Topic-publisher

We will show you the `topic-producer` as follows:

```
(defn topic-producer [ex key payload]
  (with-open
    [conn (core/connect {:host *host*})*})
     ch (channel/open conn)]
    (println "producing message to exchange " ex "/"  key " payload = "
payload)
    (exchange/declare ch ex "topic" {:durable false :auto-delete false})
    (basic/publish ch ex key payload)
      )
  )
;;=> #'chapter04.rabbitmq/topic-publisher
```

The `langohr.exchange/declare` declares the exchange to be the topic exchange type.
Then, the `langohr.basic/publish` publishes messages to the exchange with a routing
key.

Topic-consumer

The `topic-consumer` is as follows:

```
(defn topic-consumer [ex topic qname & {:keys [num] :or {num 1}}]
  (let [handler
        (fn [ch {:keys [delivery-tag]} payload]
          (println (format " [%d-%d] %s" (.getChannelNumber ch) delivery-
tag (String. payload "UTF-8"))))]
    (with-open [conn (core/connect)
                ch (channel/open conn num)]
      (println "starting consumer ...")
      (queue/declare ch qname {:durable false :auto-delete false})
      (exchange/declare ch ex "topic" {:durable false :auto-delete false})
      (queue/bind ch qname ex {:routing-key topic})
      (consumers/blocking-subscribe ch qname handler
                              {:auto-ack true})))))
;;=> #'chapter04.rabbitmq/topic-consumer
```

The preceding code is the `topic-consumer`. The `langohr.exchange/declare` declares
the exchange to be the topic exchange type. Then, the `langohr.queue/declare` declares a
consumer queue, and the _langohr.queue/bind` binds the exchange and queue.

Running the topic consumers

We will run four topic consumers, and each consumer accepts different routing key patterns as follows:

Thread no.	Routing key pattern	Queue name
1	p1.group1.jp	my.queue1
2	p2.group1.jp	my.queue2
3	#.group1.jp	my.queue3
4	#.group2.jp	my.queue4

Each routing key pattern of topic consumer matches with a routing key in a message that is distributed to a queue of the consumer. The character # matches any number of characters.

We are using the `future` to run four consumers concurrently:

```
(def f1 (future (topic-consumer "topic.exchange1" "p1.group1.jp"
"my.queue1" :num 1)))
;;=> starting consumer ...
;;=> #'chapter04.rabbitmq/f1
(def f2 (future (topic-consumer "topic.exchange1" "p2.group1.jp"
"my.queue2" :num 2)))
;;=> starting consumer ...
;;=> #'chapter04.rabbitmq/f2
(def f3 (future (topic-consumer "topic.exchange1" "#.group1.jp" "my.queue3"
:num 3)))
;;=> starting consumer ...
;;=> #'chapter04.rabbitmq/f3
(def f4 (future (topic-consumer "topic.exchange1" "#.group2.jp" "my.queue4"
:num 4)))
;;=> starting consumer ...
;;=> #'chapter04.rabbitmq/f4
```

Testing the topic consumers

We will test topic consumers by publishing messages. In the following case, the message of the routing key is p1.group1.jp. So, it matches p1.group1.jp and #.group1.jp:

```
(topic-producer "topic.exchange1" "p1.group1.jp" "hello p1.group1.jp")
;;=> producing message to exchange  topic.exchange1 / p1.group1.jp  payload
=  hello p1.group1.jp
;;=>  [3-1] hello p1.group1.jp
;;=>  [1-1] hello p1.group1.jp
```

Similarly, the routing key p2.group1.jp matches p2.group1.jp and #.group1.jp since # is a wildcard:

```
(topic-producer "topic.exchange1" "p2.group1.jp" "hello p2.group1.jp 1")
;;=> producing message to exchange  topic.exchange1 / p2.group1.jp  payload
= hello p2.group1.jp 1
;;=>  [3-2] hello p2.group1.jp 1
;;=>  [2-2] hello p2.group1.jp 1
```

The routing key p3.group1.jp only matches #.group1.jp:

```
(topic-producer "topic.exchange1" "p3.group1.jp" "hello p3.group1.jp 1")
;;=> producing message to exchange topic.exchange1 / p3.group1.jp  payload
= hello p1.group2.jp 1
;;=>  [3-3] hello p3.group1.jp 1
```

The routing key p4.group2.jp only matches #.group2.jp:

```
(topic-producer "topic.exchange1" "p4.group2.jp" "hello p1.group2.jp 1")
;;=> producing message to exchange  topic.exchange1 / p4.group2.jp  payload
= hello p1.group2.jp 1
;;=>  [4-2] hello p1.group2.jp 1
```

Finally, we will stop the threads:

```
(for [x [f1 f2 f3 f4]]
  (future-cancel x))
;;=> [true true true true]
```

See also

For an understanding of the AMQP concepts, refer to https://www.rabbitmq.com/tutorials/amqp-concepts.html.

The AMQP 0.9.1 reference guide can be found at https://www.rabbitmq.com/amqp-0-9-1-reference.html.

For the AMQP home page, refer to http://www.amqp.org/.

Using Kafka

Apache Kafka is a fast, scalable, durable, and distributed messaging system developed by LinkedIn. We will use Kafka using `clj-kafka`. It's a Clojure wrapper.

Getting ready

We need to install Kafka for this recipe. The installation steps of Kafka are as follows.

Downloading Kafka 0.8.2.2

First, download Kafka 0.8.2.2 using the `wget` command:

```
$ wget
http://ftp.kddilabs.jp/infosystems/apache/kafka/0.8.2.2/kafka_2.11-0.8.2.2.
tgz
```

Then, extract Kafka files from the downloaded TAR file:

```
$ tar xzvf kafka_2.11-0.8.2.2.tgz
```

Start ZooKeeper and Kafka server

Go to the Kafka directory and run ZooKeeper and Kafka server:

```
$ cd kafka_2.11-0.8.2.2
$ bin/zookeeper-server-start.sh config/zookeeper.properties
```

The preceding ZooKeeper startup command will show you the following output:

```
Terminal
$ bin/zookeeper-server-start.sh config/zookeeper.properties
[2016-09-13 06:57:23,269] INFO Reading configuration from: config/zookeeper.properties (org.apache.zookeeper.server.quorum.QuorumPeerConfig)
[2016-09-13 06:57:23,271] INFO autopurge.snapRetainCount set to 3 (org.apache.zookeeper.server.DatadirCleanupManager)
[2016-09-13 06:57:23,271] INFO autopurge.purgeInterval set to 0 (org.apache.zookeeper.server.DatadirCleanupManager)
[2016-09-13 06:57:23,271] INFO Purge task is not scheduled. (org.apache.zookeeper.server.DatadirCleanupManager)
[2016-09-13 06:57:23,271] WARN Either no config or no quorum defined in config, running  in standalone mode (org.apache.zookeeper.server.quorum.QuorumPeerMain)
[2016-09-13 06:57:23,286] INFO Reading configuration from: config/zookeeper.properties (org.apache.zookeeper.server.quorum.QuorumPeerConfig)
[2016-09-13 06:57:23,286] INFO Starting server (org.apache.zookeeper.server.ZooKeeperServerMain)
[2016-09-13 06:57:23,294] INFO Server environment:zookeeper.version=3.4.6-1569965, built on 02/20/2014 09:09 GMT (org.apache.zookeeper.server.ZooKeeperServer)
[2016-09-13 06:57:23,294] INFO Server environment:host.name=phenix (org.apache.zookeeper.server.ZooKeeperServer)
[2016-09-13 06:57:23,294] INFO Server environment:java.version=1.8.0_92 (org.apache.zookeeper.server.ZooKeeperServer)
[2016-09-13 06:57:23,294] INFO Server environment:java.vendor=Oracle Corporation (org.apache.zookeeper.server.ZooKeeperServer)
[2016-09-13 06:57:23,294] INFO Server environment:java.home=/usr/local/oss/jdk1.8.0_92/jre (org.apache.zookeeper.server.ZooKeeperServer)
[2016-09-13 06:57:23,294] INFO Server environment:java.class.path=/usr/local/oss/kafka_2.11-0.8.2.2/bin/../core/build/dependant-libs-2.10.4*/*.jar:/usr/local/o
ss/kafka_2.11-0.8.2.2/bin/../examples/build/libs/kafka-examples*.jar:/usr/local/oss/kafka_2.11-0.8.2.2/bin/../contrib/hadoop-consumer/build/libs/kafka-hadoop-
consumer*.jar:/usr/local/oss/kafka_2.11-0.8.2.2/bin/../contrib/hadoop-producer/build/libs/kafka-hadoop-producer*.jar:/usr/local/oss/kafka_2.11-0.8.2.2/bin/../c
lients/build/libs/kafka-clients*.jar:/usr/local/oss/kafka_2.11-0.8.2.2/bin/../libs/jopt-simple-3.2.jar:/usr/local/oss/kafka_2.11-0.8.2.2/bin/../libs/kafka-clien
ts-0.8.2.2.jar:/usr/local/oss/kafka_2.11-0.8.2.2/bin/../libs/kafka_2.11-0.8.2.2-javadoc.jar:/usr/local/oss/kafka_2.11-0.8.2.2/bin/../libs/kafka_2.11-0.8.2.2-sca
ladoc.jar:/usr/local/oss/kafka_2.11-0.8.2.2/bin/../libs/kafka_2.11-0.8.2.2-sources.jar:/usr/local/oss/kafka_2.11-0.8.2.2/bin/../libs/kafka_2.11-0.8.2.2-test.jar
:/usr/local/oss/kafka_2.11-0.8.2.2/bin/../libs/kafka_2.11-0.8.2.2.jar:/usr/local/oss/kafka_2.11-0.8.2.2/bin/../libs/log4j-1.2.16.jar:/usr/local/oss/kafka_2.11-0
.8.2.2/bin/../libs/lz4-1.2.0.jar:/usr/local/oss/kafka_2.11-0.8.2.2/bin/../libs/metrics-core-2.2.0.jar:/usr/local/oss/kafka_2.11-0.8.2.2/bin/../libs/scala-librar
y-2.11.5.jar:/usr/local/oss/kafka_2.11-0.8.2.2/bin/../libs/scala-parser-combinators_2.11-1.0.2.jar:/usr/local/oss/kafka_2.11-0.8.2.2/bin/../libs/scala-xml_2.11-
1.0.2.jar:/usr/local/oss/kafka_2.11-0.8.2.2/bin/../libs/slf4j-api-1.7.6.jar:/usr/local/oss/kafka_2.11-0.8.2.2/bin/../libs/slf4j-log4j12-1.6.1.jar:/usr/local/oss
/kafka_2.11-0.8.2.2/bin/../libs/snappy-java-1.1.1.7.jar:/usr/local/oss/kafka_2.11-0.8.2.2/bin/../libs/zkclient-0.3.jar:/usr/local/oss/kafka_2.11-0.8.2.2/bin/../
libs/zookeeper-3.4.6.jar:/usr/local/oss/kafka_2.11-0.8.2.2/bin/../core/build/libs/kafka_2.10*.jar (org.apache.zookeeper.server.ZooKeeperServer)
[2016-09-13 06:57:23,294] INFO Server environment:java.library.path=/usr/java/packages/lib/amd64:/usr/lib64:/lib64:/lib:/usr/lib (org.apache.zookeeper.server.Zo
oKeeperServer)
[2016-09-13 06:57:23,294] INFO Server environment:java.io.tmpdir=/tmp (org.apache.zookeeper.server.ZooKeeperServer)
[2016-09-13 06:57:23,294] INFO Server environment:java.compiler=<NA> (org.apache.zookeeper.server.ZooKeeperServer)
[2016-09-13 06:57:23,295] INFO Server environment:os.name=Linux (org.apache.zookeeper.server.ZooKeeperServer)
[2016-09-13 06:57:23,295] INFO Server environment:os.arch=amd64 (org.apache.zookeeper.server.ZooKeeperServer)
[2016-09-13 06:57:23,295] INFO Server environment:os.version=3.19.0-37-generic (org.apache.zookeeper.server.ZooKeeperServer)
[2016-09-13 06:57:23,295] INFO Server environment:user.name=makoto (org.apache.zookeeper.server.ZooKeeperServer)
[2016-09-13 06:57:23,295] INFO Server environment:user.home=/home/makoto (org.apache.zookeeper.server.ZooKeeperServer)
[2016-09-13 06:57:23,295] INFO Server environment:user.dir=/usr/local/oss/kafka_2.11-0.8.2.2 (org.apache.zookeeper.server.ZooKeeperServer)
[2016-09-13 06:57:23,303] INFO tickTime set to 3000 (org.apache.zookeeper.server.ZooKeeperServer)
[2016-09-13 06:57:23,303] INFO minSessionTimeout set to -1 (org.apache.zookeeper.server.ZooKeeperServer)
[2016-09-13 06:57:23,303] INFO maxSessionTimeout set to -1 (org.apache.zookeeper.server.ZooKeeperServer)
[2016-09-13 06:57:23,311] INFO binding to port 0.0.0.0/0.0.0.0:2181 (org.apache.zookeeper.server.NIOServerCnxnFactory)
```

Then, we will start `kafka-server`:

$ bin/kafka-server-start.sh config/server.properties

The preceding command will show you the following output:

```
Terminal
$ bin/kafka-server-start.sh config/server.properties
[2016-09-13 06:57:40,250] INFO Verifying properties (kafka.utils.VerifiableProperties)
[2016-09-13 06:57:40,270] INFO Property broker.id is overridden to 0 (kafka.utils.VerifiableProperties)
[2016-09-13 06:57:40,270] INFO Property log.cleaner.enable is overridden to false (kafka.utils.VerifiableProperties)
[2016-09-13 06:57:40,270] INFO Property log.dirs is overridden to /tmp/kafka-logs (kafka.utils.VerifiableProperties)
[2016-09-13 06:57:40,270] INFO Property log.retention.check.interval.ms is overridden to 300000 (kafka.utils.VerifiableProperties)
[2016-09-13 06:57:40,271] INFO Property log.retention.hours is overridden to 168 (kafka.utils.VerifiableProperties)
[2016-09-13 06:57:40,271] INFO Property log.segment.bytes is overridden to 1073741824 (kafka.utils.VerifiableProperties)
[2016-09-13 06:57:40,271] INFO Property num.io.threads is overridden to 8 (kafka.utils.VerifiableProperties)
[2016-09-13 06:57:40,271] INFO Property num.network.threads is overridden to 3 (kafka.utils.VerifiableProperties)
[2016-09-13 06:57:40,271] INFO Property num.partitions is overridden to 1 (kafka.utils.VerifiableProperties)
[2016-09-13 06:57:40,271] INFO Property num.recovery.threads.per.data.dir is overridden to 1 (kafka.utils.VerifiableProperties)
[2016-09-13 06:57:40,271] INFO Property port is overridden to 9092 (kafka.utils.VerifiableProperties)
[2016-09-13 06:57:40,272] INFO Property socket.receive.buffer.bytes is overridden to 102400 (kafka.utils.VerifiableProperties)
[2016-09-13 06:57:40,272] INFO Property socket.request.max.bytes is overridden to 104857600 (kafka.utils.VerifiableProperties)
[2016-09-13 06:57:40,272] INFO Property socket.send.buffer.bytes is overridden to 102400 (kafka.utils.VerifiableProperties)
[2016-09-13 06:57:40,272] INFO Property zookeeper.connect is overridden to localhost:2181 (kafka.utils.VerifiableProperties)
[2016-09-13 06:57:40,272] INFO Property zookeeper.connection.timeout.ms is overridden to 6000 (kafka.utils.VerifiableProperties)
[2016-09-13 06:57:40,298] INFO [Kafka Server 0], starting (kafka.server.KafkaServer)
[2016-09-13 06:57:40,299] INFO [Kafka Server 0], Connecting to zookeeper on localhost:2181 (kafka.server.KafkaServer)
[2016-09-13 06:57:40,305] INFO Starting ZkClient event thread. (org.I0Itec.zkclient.ZkEventThread)
[2016-09-13 06:57:40,310] INFO Client environment:zookeeper.version=3.4.6-1569965, built on 02/20/2014 09:09 GMT (org.apache.zookeeper.ZooKeeper)
[2016-09-13 06:57:40,310] INFO Client environment:host.name=phenix (org.apache.zookeeper.ZooKeeper)
```

Create topic

Create topic names `test`:

```
$ bin/kafka-topics.sh --create --zookeeper localhost:2181 --replication-
factor 1 --partitions 1 --topic test
```

```
Terminal                                                          - + x
$ bin/kafka-topics.sh --create --zookeeper localhost:2181 --replication-factor 1 --partitions 1 --topic test
Created topic "test".
$ █
```

Check whether it exists:

```
$ bin/kafka-topics.sh --zookeeper localhost:2181 --list
```

```
Terminal                                                          - + x
$ bin/kafka-topics.sh --zookeeper localhost:2181 --list
test
$ █
```

Run a console consumer

Run a console consumer in order to check whether Clojure producer works:

```
$ bin/kafka-console-consumer.sh --zookeeper localhost:2181 --topic test
```

Using clj-kafka

In this recipe, we will use `clj-kafka`, which is a Clojure library for Kafka:

```
(defproject chapter04 "0.1.0"
:dependencies [[org.clojure/clojure "1.8.0"]
                          [clj-kafka "0.3.4"]])
```

How to do it...

Let's learn how to publish messages into Kafka topics and how to consume messages from topics.

Declaring the namespace and load Clojure library

At first, we will declare a namespace and libraries used by this recipe:

```
(ns chapter04.kafka
  (:require
  [clj-kafka.producer :as p]
  [clj-kafka.core :as core]
  [clj-kafka.consumer.zk :as zk]
  [clj-kafka.new.producer :as new]
  [clj-kafka.consumer.simple :as simple]
  [clj-kafka.admin :as admin]
  ))
;;=> nil
```

Producing messages

Define parameters for the producer configuration as a map as follows:

```
(def producer-config
  {"metadata.broker.list" "localhost:9092"
   "serializer.class" "kafka.serializer.DefaultEncoder"
   "partitioner.class" "kafka.producer.DefaultPartitioner"}
  )
;;=> #'chapter04.kafka/producer-config
```

We will produce four messages using the `clj-kafka.producer/send-message`. The following code sends a string to the `test` topic:

```
(p/send-message (p/producer producer-config)
    (p/message "test" (.getBytes "Hi hello !")))
;;=> nil
(p/send-message (p/producer producer-config)
    (p/message "test" (.getBytes "Hi hello !")))
;;=> nil
(p/send-message (p/producer producer-config)
    (p/message "test" (.getBytes "Hi hello !")))
;;=> nil
(p/send-message (p/producer producer-config)
    (p/message "test" (.getBytes "Hi hello !")))
;;=> nil
```

Consuming a messages

Now, let's look at how to consume messages from the topic. The following code defines the configuration for the consumer:

```
(def consumer-config {
                        "zookeeper.connect" "localhost:2181"
                        "group.id" "test-consumer-group1"
                        "auto.offset.reset" "smallest"
                        "zookeeper.connection.timeout.ms" "5000"
                        "consumer.timeout.ms" "5000"
                        "auto.commit.enable" "true"
             })
;;=> #'chapter04.kafka/consumer-config
```

Then, the consumer reads two messages from the `test` topic:

```
(def x (core/with-resource [c (zk/consumer consumer-config)]
        zk/shutdown
        (doall (take 1 (zk/messages c "test")))
        ))
;=> #'chapter04.kafka/x
```

The preceding code returns a lazy sequence of the `clj_kafka.core.KafkaMessage` and its payload can access by value as follows:

```
(-> (first x)
    :value
    (String. "UTF-8")
    )
;;=> "Hi hello !"
```

How it works…

Now, we will have a look at how the Kafka producer and consumer work.

Producing messages

Producer produces messages using the `clj-kafka.producer/send-message` with a producer object and a message.

The first parameter of the `send-message` is producer object. To create that object, use the `clj-kafka.producer/producer` with configuration properties as follows:

Property	Default value	Description
`metadata.broker.list`	`""`	List of addresses (`"host:port"`) to access Kafka broker.
`serializer.class`	`kafka.serializer.DefaultEncoder`	The serializer class for messages. The default encoder takes a byte[] and returns the same byte[].
`partitioner.class`	`kafka.producer.DefaultPartitioner`	The partitioner class for partitioning messages among subtopics. The default partitioner is based on the hash of the key.
`request.required.acks`	`0`	`0` means that the producer never waits for an acknowledgement from the broker. `1` means that the producer gets an acknowledgment after the leader replica has received the data. `-1` means that the producer gets an acknowledgment after all in-sync replicas have received the data.

producer.type	sync		Sync/async producer.

Consuming messages

The `clj-kafka.consumer.zk/messages` consumes a lazy sequence of `KafkaMessage` messages from the topic. The first parameter of the `messages` is a consumer connection and the second one is a topic name.

To create consumer, use the `clj-kafka.consumer.zk/consumer` with the consumer properties as follows:

Property	Default	Description
zookeeper.connect	" "	ZooKeeper connection string in the form `hostname:port`.
group.id	" "	A string that uniquely identifies the group of consumer processes to which this consumer belongs.
auto.offset.reset	largest	What to do when there is no initial offset in ZooKeeper or if an offset is out of range: `smallest` – automatically resets the offset to the smallest offset `largest` – automatically resets the offset to the largest offset anything else – throws an exception to the consumer
zookeeper.connection.timeout.ms	6000	The max time that the client waits while establishing a connection to ZooKeeper.
consumer.timeout.ms	-1	Throws a timeout exception to the consumer if no message is available for consumption after the specified interval.
auto.commit.enable	true	If `true`, periodically commits to ZooKeeper the offset of messages already fetched by the consumer. This committed offset will be used when the process fails as the position from which the new consumer will begin.

The `clj-kafka.consumer.zk/messages` returns a lazy sequence of the `clj_kafka.core.KafkaMessage`. The `KafkaMessage` is defined as follows:

```
(defrecord KafkaMessage [topic offset partition key value])
```

The `clj-kafka.core/with-resource` is a macro and takes the following three parameters:

- `binding`: This is a binding of the consumer connection
- `close` function: This is called when function exits
- `body`: This is the function body

As ZooKeeper remembers offsets where each consumer has the same group ID, consuming a topic with the same group ID increments its offset as follows:

```
(core/with-resource [c (zk/consumer consumer-config)]
  zk/shutdown
  (doall (take 1 (zk/messages c "test"))))
;;=> (#clj_kafka.core.KafkaMessage{:topic "test", :offset 1, :partition 0,
:key nil, :value #object["[B" 0x2076f724 "[B@2076f724"]})
(core/with-resource [c (zk/consumer consumer-config)]
  zk/shutdown
  (doall (take 1 (zk/messages c "test"))))
;;=> (#clj_kafka.core.KafkaMessage{:topic "test", :offset 2, :partition 0,
:key nil, :value #object["[B" 0x4d0d3a0b "[B@4d0d3a0b"]})
(core/with-resource [c (zk/consumer consumer-config)]
  zk/shutdown
  (doall (take 1 (zk/messages c "test"))))
;;=> (#clj_kafka.core.KafkaMessage{:topic "test", :offset 3, :partition 0,
:key nil, :value #object["[B" 0x125f8cd0 "[B@125f8cd0"]})
```

There's more...

Here, we will learn how to create a new topic.

Creating a new topic

The following code creates a new topic named `"test-topic"`:

```
(with-open [zk (admin/zk-client "127.0.0.1:2181")]
  (let [topic "test-topic"]
  (if-not (admin/topic-exists? zk topic)
    (admin/create-topic zk topic
```

```
                        {:partitions 1
                         :replication-factor 1
                         :config {"cleanup.policy" "compact"}}}))
      )
  )
;;=> nil
```

See also

For the Apache Kafka home page, refer to `http://kafka.apache.org/`.

For the Kafka quick start guide, refer to `http://kafka.apache.org/documentation.html#quickstart`.

Using MQTT

As they say these days, the **Internet of things** (**IoT**) is bringing up a third industrial revolution. Devices will be talking to each other more and more to share information, real time, and the need for a low power, secure protocol to connect those devices together is greater than ever.

What is MQTT? It is an OASIS-approved standard, machine-to-machine super lightweight transport protocol for publishing and subscribing activities.

MQTT client are always connected to what is called an MQTT broker, never to each other.

The MQTT protocol itself is based on top of TCP/IP, and both the MQTT client and the MQTT broker require a TCP/IP stack.

MQTT has been designed specifically for IoT and is well suited for a wide range of scenarios such as:

- Ad hoc social networking
- Hospitals in need of immediate analysis on real-time data collected from patients going through
- Environmental monitoring through the use of sensors in remote and rural areas such as seaside or mountains
- Internal monitoring of cars to collect and send information on the different parts of the car in real time
- Gambling machines distributed around a casino but that must regularly communicate with a central server

- Cashier that sends transaction information and receives price updates over slow networks

As you can see, the MQTT protocol has been designed with low memory and low processing power devices, and a restricted networking environment.

Getting ready

We need a few things to get ready for this recipe, so we will install the broker, install a UI for our machine to check visually messages, and, lastly, configure our Clojure environment to be ready to talk to all those components.

Installing the MQTT broker

To be ready to try and get a sense of the protocol, we need a small broker, meaning a component that will receive and broadcast messages according to their topics.

While a few brokers are available, we recommend you use Mosquitto. It has an easy installer, or you can also compile it easily from the source code. On Macintosh, the following should do it for you:

```
brew install mosquitto
```

Of course, there are Linux packages and Windows installers also available. Once installed, start the broker simply from the command line with the following:

```
mosquitto
```

And observe something along those lines:

```
1452329996: Using default config.
1452329996: Opening ipv4 listen socket on port 1883.
1452329996: Opening ipv6 listen socket on port 1883.
```

While we are at it and before we start to send any message, let's also install a helper graphical client.

MQTT graphical client

Again there are quite a few available clients, so make sure you get something that works for you. But here we will recommend the one named MQTT-spy, which a Java-based client, doesn't get in the way, and lets us see the different messages going through the broker.

The download is a JAR file, and to start the file is either a simple double click or again from the command line:

```
java -jar mqtt-client/mqtt-spy-0.4.0-beta-b4-jar-with-dependencies.jar
```

This will bring the following welcome screen:

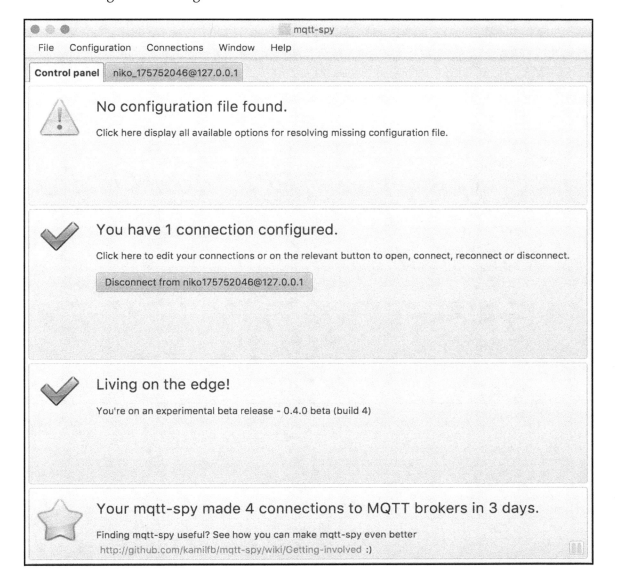

Clicking on the first or the second box will either create a set of default connections for you or directly connect you to the local broker we started previously:

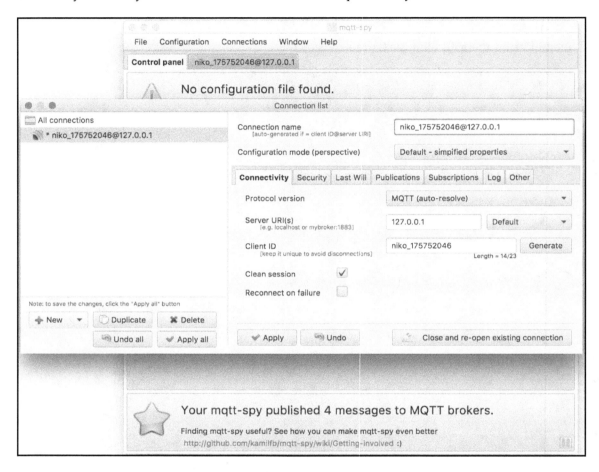

Once done, the connection screen should be something similar to the following, and this is where we will see the messages flowing through:

Send our first MQTT message

To make it slightly interesting, we are going to send a message from the command line and see it showing on the MQTT spy interface.

In the preceding UI, let's subscribe to a topic, which we will name `topic/hello`. This is done by entering the topic as shown in the following screenshot:

We can now press the **Subscribe** button and be ready:

Now let's send our message from the command line. On the command line, there are actually two useful scripts:

- `mosquitto_pub`
- `mosquitto_sub`

They both use a similar set of parameters, so it is also easy to just try sending messages over different connection settings.

To publish a message, we will use the `mosquitto_pub` script and tell it to connect to localhost, and then indicate the topic and, finally, the message:

```
mosquitto_pub -h localhost -t topic/hello -m "one more cup of coffee?"
```

On *Enter*, our MQTT spy screen should have gotten the message, as shown in the following screenshot:

Nice. It is not only easy to send messages with MQTT, but it is also easy to subscribe to different topics and debug the messages.

But while running a graphical client might be easy on a laptop or a home computer, embedded devices with low resources and a low-memory footprint most of the time do not have this chance, so we will use the other MQTT command we presented previously to subscribe to messages, `mosquitto_sub`.

The command works the same as the pub version, except we do not set the message parameter:

```
mosquitto_sub -h localhost -t topic/hello
```

The script starts and outputs nothing yet, but let's resend the same message for more coffee because the waiter did not get it the first time:

```
Nicolass-MacBook:chapter04 niko$ mosquitto_sub -h localhost -t topic/hello
one more cup of coffee?
```

Now you can see that our running subcommand has retrieved the message properly. And you can also see that the MQTT spy window is displaying a second message.

Getting some Clojure

Finally, we just add a small MQTT library to our `project.clj` to get all set from the Clojure side:

```
[clojurewerkz/machine_head "1.0.0-beta9"]
```

Et voila! Now let's have some fun.

How to do it...

In this receipe, we will see how to publish and subscribe to messages from Clojure. The `machine_head` library is a classic, and the following code will look very sensible to most of us:

```
(ns chapter04.mqtt-pub
  (:require [clojurewerkz.machine-head.client :as mh]))

(let [id (mh/generate-id)
      c  (mh/connect "tcp://127.0.0.1:1883" id)]
    (mh/publish c "topic/hello" "hello from Clojure!")
    (mh/disconnect c))
```

We start by requiring the library with the mh prefix, preparing an ID for the connection, and connecting through a regular socket on `tcp` protocol.

We then send a message pretty much in the same way we did on the command line, on top of the connection parameter, a topic and a message.

As seen in the MQTT spy UI, the message on the `topic/hello` is shown as follows:

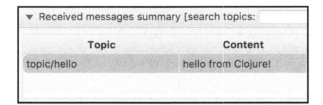

The subscribe side of things will not look too scary either, and the following small snippet shows us how to subscribe to a topic and act on the messages coming through the `topic/hello` again.

We are also showing here how to keep:

```
; start with regular Clojure import and require directive
(ns chapter04.mqtt
  (:require [clojurewerkz.machine-head.client :as mh]))

; set up the connection
(def id (mh/generate-id))
(def c  (mh/connect "tcp://127.0.0.1:1883" id))

; set up a ref to keep track of the number of messages
(def i  (ref 0))

; define a callback on the topic/hello topic
(def s  (mh/subscribe c {"topic/hello" 0}
       (fn [^String topic meta ^bytes payload]
         (println "-> " (String. payload))
         (dosync (alter i inc)))))
```

At this point, you can use either the `mosquitto_pub` command line or the MQTT spy UI to send a few messages to the MQTT topic. The Clojure code will pick up your messages and display them in the console as per the handler we have defined:

```
chapter04 0.1.0-SNAPSHOT[stdout]:   ->  one more cup of coffee?
chapter04 0.1.0-SNAPSHOT[stdout]:   ->  one more cup of coffee?
```

And we can also confirm the number of messages received:

```
(println "messages count " @i)
; mqtt.clj:   messages count  2
```

Finally, to close the MQTT connection, you call disconnect on the `mqtt` connection variable:

```
(mh/disconnect c)
```

How it works...

How it works in real life would require you to walk to your IoT room, grab your Arduino board, and do some Arduino coding.

This section supposes you have done some Arduino coding earlier, which means some simple C programming.

The MQTT library for Arduino has some nice and simple examples to get you running, so we will go through the simplest example quickly.

The following code snippet takes you to the same level we had with command line, UI, and the Clojure code:

```c
// Arduino imports for serial communication, ethernet and MQTT.
#include <SPI.h>
#include <Ethernet.h>
#include <PubSubClient.h>

// network settings
byte mac[]    = {  0xDE, 0xED, 0xBA, 0xFE, 0xFE, 0xED };
IPAddress ip(172, 16, 0, 100);
IPAddress server(172, 16, 0, 2);

// callback that will receive the MQTT messages
void callback(char* topic, byte* payload, unsigned int length) {
  // handle message code
}

// ethernet et mqtt clients
EthernetClient ethClient;
PubSubClient client(server, 1883, callback, ethClient);

// standard arduino setup function
void setup()
{
  Ethernet.begin(mac, ip);
  if (client.connect("arduinoClient")) {
    client.publish("arduino/out","hello world");
    client.subscribe("arduino/in");
  }
}
// standard arduino loop function.
void loop()
{
  client.loop();
}
```

You can picture pretty well now how the Arduino board can send measure results to the broker, for example, temperature or wind, and the Clojure code can react directly to messages coming from the board itself.

You can also see how the Clojure code could subscribe to measures coming from different devices and then send commands to a different set of boards.

A really simple but nice example would be to take sound measures from the Arduino board and then change the intensity of lighting of the room straight from the intensity of the conversation.

Reverbly, we could monitor online earthquake measures coming from the Internet and dispatch alarms or preventive measures to a set of Arduino devices through MQTT when the earthquake occurs.

There's more...

While Arduino may be the most famous platform for IoT, the Raspberry Pi surely has an impressive hardware that makes it attractive to be a broker itself.

Here, we will not go through an example of setting the Raspberry Pi board itself, but we will quickly look at how we can emulate things in VirtualBox to get a feeling of how the board could be programmed and deployed.

We have included a torrent file to retrieve a full image of a Raspberry Pi operating system. Note that, while running in a virtual box, and the connected sensors are not physically there, the OS itself behaves exactly same as to when running on a real board.

First, let's grasp the ova file, which is an image for VirtualBox through the given torrent file. aria2c is a favorite command line torrent client, but you are, of course, free to use your favorite one:

```
aria2c RaspberryPi.VirtualBox/RaspberryPi.ova.torrent
```

The `RaspberryPi.ova` is now in your local machine. Double-clicking on it will import it in `VirtualBox`. For our testing purpose, we will change the network settings so that it uses the host settings to connect to the Internet, as shown in the following screenshot:

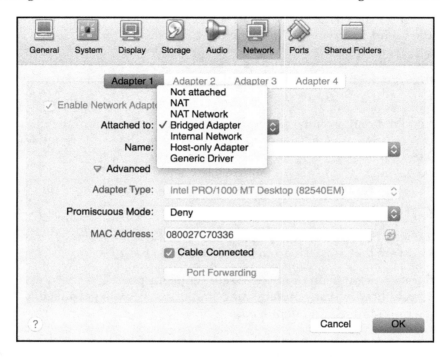

We need to simply make sure to use the **Bridged Adapter**.

The Raspberry image is now ready to be booted, so let's click on **Start** and after a few seconds, the Raspberry is running!

Using the login `rpi/password` we can enter the Raspberry emulated system.

First let's fix the network settings by editing the `/etc/network/interfaces` file, which tells the Raspberry how to connect to the Internet:

```
# The primary network interface
auto correct
iface eth1 inet dhcp
```

Like a regular Debian/Ubuntu-based system, we will add a package repository:

```
apt-get install  python-software-properties
apt-add-repository ppa:mosquitto-dev/mosquitto-ppa
apt-get update
```

And then we can retrieve the `mosquitto` software easily using the standard `apt-get` command install:

```
apt-get install mosquitto mosquitto-clients
```

So, we are back to the getting ready of this recipe where we would get the command line running. We will start the `mosquitto` broker on the Raspberry Pi first:

mosquitto

And then supposing your emulated Raspberry Pi IP address is `192.168.100.103`, the Clojure code becomes only slightly changed with a new IP:

```
(ns chapter04.mqtt-pub
  (:require [clojurewerkz.machine-head.client :as mh]))

(let [id (mh/generate-id)
      c  (mh/connect "tcp://192.168.100.103:1883" id)]
  (mh/publish c "topic/hello" "hello from Clojure!")
  (mh/disconnect c))
```

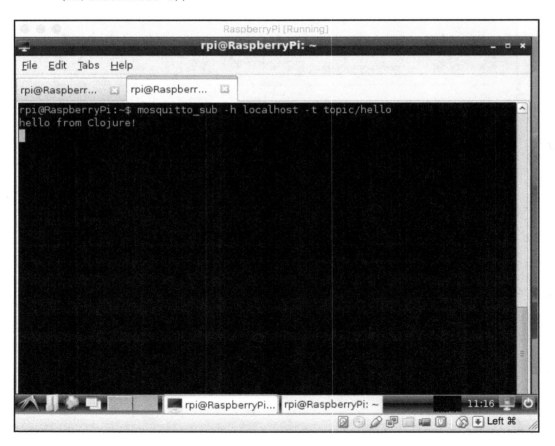

In real life, the nonemulated Raspberry Pi board does have enough power to do standard processing to relay messages from lower energy devices, or to make some decision on whether to send a message or now.

Note that Clojure also runs on the Raspberry Pi, so you can run the Clojure code we have seen in this recipe.

So much in one recipe, that is probably time to get dinner.

Streaming access to provide high performance

This recipe will take a look at how to parse and write large amount of data. Since XML is probably the most verbose of data formats, we will look briefly at how to generate large amount of junk data and then how to process those in a memory efficient way.

Getting ready

The `data.xml` library is our library of choice here, so let's add it to the `project.clj` if it is not already:

```
[org.clojure/data.xml "0.1.0-beta1"]
```

We will also make use of the core Java streaming and zipping functions that are available in the JVM. We know we can access host functions just by importing them in the current namespace, so nothing more to prepare here.

How to do it...

So that's it. Let's go for a large dump of data onto our file system. We will create an XML element.

Streaming out

We get ready by pulling the proper namespaces for XML and for writing to streams:

```
(use 'clojure.data.xml)
(use '[clojure.java.io :only [writer output-stream]])
```

Now, we can generate XML elements and emit them directly into a text file. This is done by opening a `write` on the file and then emitting the XML:

```
(with-open [o (writer "data-set-1.xml")]
  (doseq [i (range 1 10)]
             (.write o (str (element :friend {"age" "23"} (str "Friend"
i))))
             (.write o "\n")))
```

Note that this can also be done in parallel with a basic `pmap` call. While the data order is lost in a way, the data is generated way more rapidly:

```
(with-open [o (writer "test_1.xml")]
  (doall
   (pmap
   #(.write o
       (str
           (element :friend
               {"age" "23"}
               (str "Friend" %)) "\n"))
   (range 1 10)))))
```

Note that in this case, we need to use `doall` to force the execution before getting out of the scope of `with-open`, otherwise we will get a stream closed exception.

While this is generating a large file with one XML per line, a proper XML file would look like the following:

```
(with-open [o (writer "test_2.xml")]
(.write o "<friends>\n")
(doseq [i (range 1 10)]
  (.write o
      (str
       (element :friend
           {"age" "23"}
           (str "Friend" i))
          "\n")))")))
(.write o "</friends>\n"))
```

Now increase the range value to about 10,000,000 to get a nice 500 MB file of data. You can also note that the memory usage did not increase so much and stayed relatively stable.

Let's now analyze the data back in!

Streaming in

```
(use '[clojure.java.io :only [reader input-stream]])

(with-open [in (reader (input-stream "test_2.xml"))]
   (doall
    (filter
     #(= "Friend3" (first (:content %)))
     (:content (clojure.data.xml/parse in)))))

; (#clojure.data.xml.node.Element{:tag :friend, :attrs {:age "23"},
:content ("Friend3")})
```

Again, we need to call `doall` again to make sure we do the processing while the file is still opened. How big the file is does not seem to much affect memory consumption, and we are streaming the file properly directly through the `data.xml` parse method, which returns a lazy sequence of XML elements.

Streaming with line-seq

In the case where line-by-line processing is possible, we can make use of the `line-seq` function, which will build a lazy sequence of items.

When we generated sample data files, we had a file that had a not-so-XML version; it was one XML element per line:

```
(with-open [in (reader (input-stream "test_1.xml"))]
 (doall

 (filter
  #(= "Friend1"
     (first (:content (parse
     (java.io.StringReader. %)))))

 (line-seq in))))
```

In this case, we `line-seq` reads one line at a time from the buffered reader, and the processing is then lazily one, meaning one element at a time.

How it works...

Now streaming can easily be made even better through the usual usage of `core.async`. At this stage, you should be getting used to deal with the channels, so let's go quickly through the setup of the namespace and the two core async channels we will use:

```
(use 'clojure.data.xml)
(use '[clojure.java.io :only [writer reader input-stream output-stream]])
(require '[clojure.core.async :as async])

(def in-chan (async/chan))
(def out-chan (async/chan))
```

Now the resulting thread, the one that will show the data, will simply be printing data coming from the out channel. This translates to a `core.async` thread as follows:

```
(async/thread
  (while true
    (let [data (async/<!! out-chan)]
      (println data))))
```

We will use a second thread that will parse and filter data coming from the input channel. The parsing we have seen in the previous section, and the code stays the same. We just wrap all this in a similar fashion into a `core.async` thread:

```
(async/thread
  (while true
    (let [data (async/<!! in-chan)]
      (if  (= "Friend1"(first (:content (parse (java.io.StringReader.
data)))))
      (async/>!! out-chan data)))))
```

After reading from the input channel, if the data is matching, we will put it onto the out channel, the one that the previous thread should read from.

Lastly, we reuse `pmap` and `line-seq` to do the simple reading from the

```
(with-open [in (reader (input-stream "test_1.xml"))]
(doall
 (pmap
 #(async/>!! in-chan %)
  (line-seq in))))
```

Suppose the `test_0.xml` file content is as follows:

```
<friend age="23">Friend1</friend>
<friend age="23">Friend4</friend>
...
```

Then the output of the reading with `core-async` simply goes through a one-by-one flow, as seen in the following diagram:

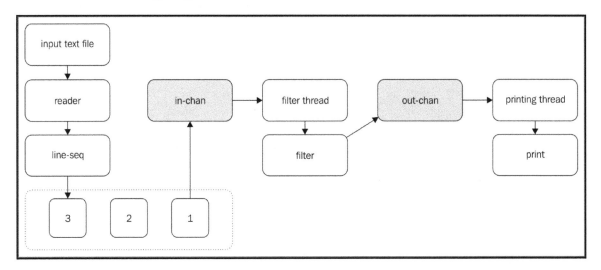

There's more...

The same parsing and handling techniques of data could be also applied to reducers:

```
(require '[clojure.core.reducers :as r])
(use 'clojure.data.xml)
(use '[clojure.java.io :only [writer reader input-stream output-stream]])

(with-open [in (reader (input-stream "test_1.xml"))]
  (into []
    (r/filter
    (fn[x]
      (= "Friend1"
      (first (:content (parse
      (java.io.StringReader. x)))))))
    (line-seq in))))
```

This has the drawback of loading more data in memory than needed, but processing is easier to read and concise.

If multiple actions are to be taken while handling the data, transducers could also be added to the mix. We leave that to the curiosity of the reader!

Using Apache Camel to connect everything

Apache Camel is a rule-based routing and mediation engine that provides the Enterprise Integration Patterns using an API or declarative Java domain-specific language to configure routing and mediation rules.

Getting ready

In this recipe, we will use the Java Camel library. So, you need to add the `org.apache.camel/camel-core` to your `project.clj`:

```
(defproject chapter04 "0.1.0"
:dependencies [[org.clojure/clojure "1.8.0"]
               [org.apache.camel/camel-core "2.16.1"]
```

How to do it...

Here, we will learn basic uses of Camel from Clojure.

Importing Camel classes

The following code imports the Camel classes that we will use:

```
(ns chapter04.camel
  (:import [org.apache.camel.impl DefaultCamelContext]
           [org.apache.camel.builder RouteBuilder]
           [org.apache.camel.main Main]
           [org.apache.camel Exchange]
           [org.apache.camel Processor]
           ))
```

Your first ride on Camel with Clojure

Let's write a simple Camel code that moves files from one directory to the other. The following code is to move a file from /tmp/in to /tmp/out:

```
(def ctx
  (let [context (DefaultCamelContext.)]
    (.addRoutes context (proxy [RouteBuilder] []
                          (configure [] (.. this
                                            (from
"file:/tmp/in?noop=false")
                                            (to "file:/tmp/out")))))
    context
    ))
#'chapter04.camel/ctx
```

Start the context:

```
(.start ctx)
;;=> nil
```

Then create a file under the /tmp/in:

$ echo hello Makoto ! > /tmp/in/makoto.txt

The Camel code checks under the /tmp/in and moves to /tmp/out:

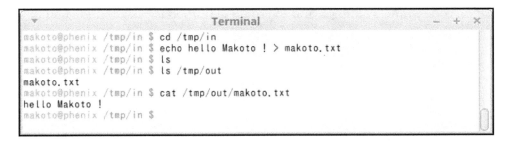

Let's stop Camel as follows:

```
(.stop ctx)
;;=> nil
```

Writing more Clojure idiomatic code with Camel

The preceding code is simpler compare to the following Java code:

```java
public class FileToFile {
    public static void main(String args[]) throws Exception {
        CamelContext context = new DefaultCamelContext();
        context.addRoutes(new RouteBuilder() {
            public void configure() {
                from("file:/tmp/in?noop=false")
                .to("file:/tmp/out");
            }
        });
        context.start();
    }
}
```

Using macro makes application code simpler. We will define a helper function that implements `org.apache.camel.builderRouteBuilder` and a macro:

```clojure
(defn create-builder [builder]
  (proxy [RouteBuilder] [] (configure [] (builder this))))
;;=> #'chapter04.camel/create-builder
(defmacro add-routes [ctx & body]
  `(.addRoutes ~ctx (create-builder (fn [~'this] (.. ~'this ~@body)))))
;;=>#'chapter04.camel/add-routes
```

Using macro, code is much simpler, and the route definition is easy to understand:

```clojure
(defn file-to-file []
  (let [context (DefaultCamelContext.)]
    (add-routes context
            (from "file:/tmp/in?noop=false")
            (to "file:/tmp/out")
            )
    context
    ))
;;=> #'chapter04.camel/file-to-file
```

We can start and stop the router using `.start` and `.stop`, respectively:

```clojure
(def ctx (file-to-file))
;;=> #'chapter04.camel/ctx
(.start ctx)
;;=> nil
(.stop ctx)
;;=> nil
```

How it works...

The preceding code uses file endpoints. We will show you major parameters for the endpoint as follows:

Name	Default value	Description
noop	false	If `true`, the file is not moved or deleted in any way. This option is good for read only data or for ETL type requirements.
append	true	When writing, do we append to the end of the file or replace it?
consumer.delay	500	Milliseconds before the next poll of the file/directory.

There's more...

Let's define a very simple processor that transforms messages between the file endpoints. To write a processor, we have to implement a `process` method in the `org.apache.camelProcessor` class. We will use the Clojure `proxy` function to implement this method. Our simple processor echoes an inbound string and adds a string `"Hello "` on it and sends it to the outbound:

```
(defn get-payload-as-string[ex]
  (-> ex .getIn (.getBody (class ""))))
;;=> #'chapter04.camel/get-payload-as-string
(def simple-processor
  (proxy [Processor][]
    (process [exchange]
      (let [payload
            (get-payload-as-string exchange)])]
        (println payload)
        (-> exchange .getOut (.setBody (str "Hello " payload)))))))
#'chapter04.camel/processor
```

So, let's define a new context using the processor:

```
(defn file-to-file-with-processor []
  (let [context (DefaultCamelContext.)]
    (add-routes context
            (from "file:/tmp/in?noop=false")
            (process simple-processor)
            (to "file:/tmp/out"))
    context))
;;=> #'chapter04.camel/processor
```

The following code runs Camel:

```
(def ctx (file-to-file-with-processor))
;;=> #'chapter04.camel/ctx
(.start ctx)
;;=> nil
```

Let's run the following commands:

```
$ echo Makoto  > /tmp/in/makoto.txt
$ echo Nico  > /tmp/in/nico.txt
```

Echo strings are displayed on your console, and file contents are converted, as shown in the following screenshot:

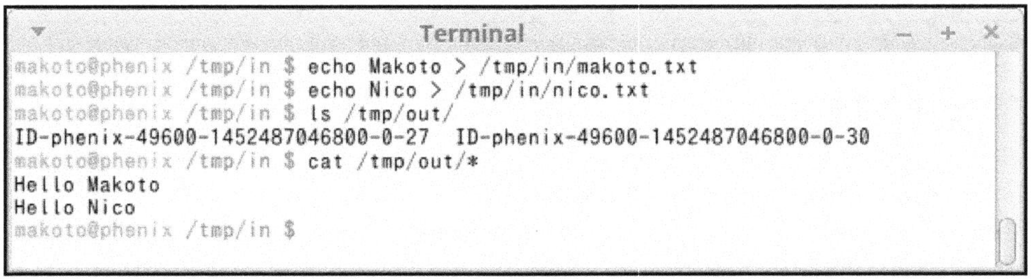

```
▼                          Terminal                      —  +  ✕
makoto@phenix /tmp/in $ echo Makoto > /tmp/in/makoto.txt
makoto@phenix /tmp/in $ echo Nico > /tmp/in/nico.txt
makoto@phenix /tmp/in $ ls /tmp/out/
ID-phenix-49600-1452487046800-0-27   ID-phenix-49600-1452487046800-0-30
makoto@phenix /tmp/in $ cat /tmp/out/*
Hello Makoto
Hello Nico
makoto@phenix /tmp/in $
```

See also

You can have a look at the Apache Camel home page at http://camel.apache.org/.

5

Working with Other Languages

In this chapter, we will cover the following topics:

- Calling Java methods and accessing Java objects from Clojure
- Extending Java superclasses and implementing Java interfaces
- Calling Clojure from Java
- Calling Scala from Clojure
- ClojureCLR
- ClojureScript

Introduction

Clojure runs on the **Java Virtual Machine** (**JVM**), and the Clojure language provides full access to Java. Java has huge assets and we can use all of them from Clojure. This is one of the great advantages of Clojure, which is also callable from Java.

In this chapter, you will see how to instantiate objects from classes and how to access Java objects, including methods and fields, and also learn ways to inherit superclasses and ways to implement interfaces.

You will also learn how to use Clojure on Microsoft's .Net and JavaScript, using ClojureCLR and ClojureScript. This chapter will introduce to you how to set up ClojureCLR and ClojureScript environments and how to smoothly write code on them.

Calling Java methods and accessing Java objects from Clojure

Though the Clojure language looks quite different from Java, Clojure provides full access to Java. This enables Clojure to make use of huge Java assets very efficiently. In general, calling Java assets from Clojure is much simpler and results in less code than calling them from Java. Another big advantage is REPL, which makes programming fun and faster.

Getting ready

In this recipe, we don't use an external library, so the only necessary thing is to start REPL to run code.

How to do it...

We will learn how to instantiate objects, call instance and class methods, access fields and inner classes, and reference classes. Then, we will learn how to manipulate Java arrays.

Instantiating objects

To instantiate an object from a class, use the following syntax:

```
(ClassName. arg1 arg2 ...)
```

For instance, to instantiate a new `String` object the syntax is as follows:

```
(String. "abc")
;;=> "abc"
(Integer. 1)
;;=> 1
```

Calling instance methods

To call Java methods, the syntax is as follows:

```
(.method-name object arg1 arg2  ...)
```

The following code calls the Java `concat` method:

```
(.concat "Hello " "Makoto")
;;=> "Hello Makoto"
```

Calling class methods

The syntax for calling static methods (that is, class methods) is as follows:

```
(class-name/method-name arg1 arg2  ...)
```

Or:

```
(. class-name method-name arg1 arg2 ...)
```

The following code is to get a float value from a string:

```
(Float/valueOf "1000.0")
;;=> 1000.0
(. Float valueOf "1000.0")
;;=> 1000.0
```

Another example is to get the Japanese timezone using the static method:

```
(import 'java.util.TimeZone)
(def time-zone (TimeZone/getTimeZone "Asia/Tokyo" ))
;;=> #'chapter05.calling-java/time-zone
(.getDisplayName time-zone (java.util.Locale. "en_US"))
;;=> "Japan Standard Time"
```

Accessing instance fields

Direct access to instance fields is not recommended in Java, so it's not often we access instance fields. However, there is a way to access these fields. The syntax is as follows:

```
(. field-name object)
```

We will access instance fields of `java.awt.Point` as follows:

```
(import java.awt.Point)
;;=> java.awt.Point
(def p (Point. 100 200))
;;=> #'chapter05.calling-java/p
(. p x)
;;=> 100
(. p y)
```

```
;;=> 200
```

The syntax for setting instance values is as follows:

```
(set! (.field-name object) value)
```

The following code is to update the instance field of `java.awt.Point`:

```
(set! (.x p) 300)
;;=> 300
(. p x)
;;=> 300
```

Accessing class fields

The syntax for accessing static fields is as follows:

```
class-name/field-name
```

The following code gets the value of the natural logarithm:

```
Math/E
;;=> 2.718281828459045
```

Accessing inner classes

The following syntax is to access static inner classes:

```
class-name$inner-class-name/static-field-name
```

Or:

```
(class-name$inner-class-name/static-method-name arg1 arg2 ..)
```

The following example accesses the static values NEW and TERMINATED in an inner class of the `Thread` class:

```
(def t (Thread.))
;;=> #'chapter05.calling-java/t
(.getState t)
;;=> #object[java.lang.Thread$State 0xc736e3e "NEW"]
(= (.getState t) Thread$State/NEW)
;;=> true
(.start t)
;;=> nil
(= (.getState t) Thread$State/TERMINATED)
```

The next example shows how to access methods in an inner class. At the time of creating a thread, its state is NEW. After the thread is started, it terminates immediately and the state becomes TERMINATED:

```
(Thread$State/values)
;;=> #object["[Ljava.lang.Thread$State;" 0x3efd737c
"[Ljava.lang.Thread$State;@3efd737c"]
(Thread$State/valueOf "NEW")
;=> #object[java.lang.Thread$State 0xc736e3e "NEW"]
```

Referencing classes

To refer to classes, use their class name as follows:

```
String
;;=> java.lang.String
(= String (Class/forName "java.lang.String"))
;;=> true
(= java.lang.String (Class/forName "java.lang.String"))
;;=> true
```

Using arrays

To create arrays in Java, use into-array:

```
(def str-array (into-array '("a" "b" "c" "d" "e")))
;;=> #'chapter05.calling-java/str-array
```

To access arrays, use aget:

```
(aget str-array 0)
;;=> "a"
```

Arrays in Java are not immutable, so we can change the value of the element using aset:

```
(aset str-array 0 "x")
;;=> "x"
(aget str-array 0)
;;=> "x"
```

`long-array` creates arrays whose elements are the `long` type of Java primitives. We will compare the performance with an array whose elements are Java's long objects:

```
(time
 (let [n 10000000
       a (long-array (range n))]
   (reduce + a)))
;;=> "Elapsed time: 1339.504072 msecs"
;;=> 49999995000000
(time
 (let [n 10000000
       a (into-array (range n))]
   (reduce + a)))
;;=> "Elapsed time: 6101.370939 msecs"
;;=> 49999995000000
```

The following code creates Java's `byte-array`:

```
(byte-array (map int [\C \l \o \j \o \u \r \e]))
;;=> #object["[B" 0x590f9b92 "[B@590f9b92"]
(String. (byte-array (map int [\C \l \o \j \o \u \r \e])))
;;=> "Clojoure"
```

The following code is to create a two-dimensional array:

```
(def mat1 (make-array Double/TYPE  10 10))
;;=> #'chapter05.calling-java/mat1
(aget mat1 9 9)
;;=> 0.0
```

To specify, `Double/TYPE` generates an array whose elements are double primitive types.

How it works...

We will summarize ways to interoperate Java and compare its syntax with Java calls. Then we will explain how Clojure does not inherit Java's checked exceptions.

Summary of how Clojure accesses Java methods and objects

In the following table, we summarize how Clojure can invoke Java methods and access Java objects:

Action	Syntax	Clojure code	Java code
Creating instances	`(ClassName. arg1 arg2 ...)`	`(String. "abc")`	`new String("abc");`
Calling instance methods	`(.method-name object arg1 arg2 ...)`	`(.concat "Hello " "Makoto")`	`String s = "Hello "; s.concat("Makoto");`
Calling class methods	`(class-name/method-name arg1 arg2 ...)`	`(Float/valueOf "1000.0")`	`Float.valueOf("1000.0");`
Accessing instance fields	`(. field-name object)`	`(. (java.awt.Point. 100 200) x)`	`Point new java.awt.Point(100 200); p.x;`
Accessing class fields	`class-name/field-name`	`Math/E`	`Math.E;`
Accessing fields of inner classes	`class-name$inner-class-name/static-field-name`	`Thread$State/NEW`	`Thread.State.NEW;`
Calling methods of inner classes	`(class-name$inner-class-name/static-field-name arg1 arg2 ..)`	`(Thread$State/values)`	`Thread.State.values() ;`
Referencing classes	`class-name`	`java.lang.String`	`Class.forName("java.lang.String");`

Clojure does not inherit Java's checked exception

In Java, checked exceptions are checked at compile time. Using Java, checked exceptions should be handled by a try-catch block or methods should declare the exception using the `throws` keyword. Otherwise the program will give an error at compile time.

The following Java code causes an error at compile time:

```
class CheckedException
{
    public static void main(String args[])
    {
    Thread.sleep(1000);
    }
}

$ javac CheckedException.java
CheckedException.java:3: error: unreported exception InterruptedException;
```

```
must be caught or declared to be thrown
        Thread.sleep(10000);
                    ^
1 error
```

To avoid the preceding error, we need to modify the code as follows:

```
public class CheckedException {
    public static void main(String args[])  {
    try {
        Thread.sleep(10000);
    } catch (InterruptedException e) {
        System.out.println("Interrupt occured");
    }
    }
}
```

Generally, checked exceptions tend to not be liked. Scala also does not inherit checked exceptions. Clojure is the same, and the following code works fine:

```
(Thread/sleep 1000)
```

Summary of array accesses

In the following table, we summarize Java's array accesses from Clojure and equivalent code using Java:

Action	Clojure	Java
Creating a one-dimensional array	(long-array 10)	new long[10];
Creating a two-dimensional array	(make-array Double/TYPE 10 10))	new Double[10][10];
Getting an element of an array	(aget str_array 0)	str_array[0];
Setting a value to an element of an array	(aset str_array 0 "x")	str_array[4] = "x";

Print strings of Java's primitives

We often see unusual expressions such as the following when we generate an array whose element type is primitive:

```
(int-array [1 2])
;;=> #object["[I" 0x4d307a58 "[I@4d307a58"]
```

In the preceding example, "`[I`" stands for an array of int. Similarly, the next example generates the two-dimensional array with `Double/TYPE`:

```
(make-array Double/TYPE  10 10)
;;=> #object["[[D" 0x77570b3c "[[D@77570b3c"]
```

In the preceding example, "`[[D`" stands for two-dimensional array of type double. The following table shows how Java primitives are printed:

Type	String
Short	"S"
Integer	"I"
Long	"J"
Float	"F"
Double	"D"
Byte	"B"
Char	"C"
Boolean	"Z"

There's more...

We will learn how to use more advanced topics in this section.

Chained calls with the double-dot macro

The `..` macro expands into a member access (`.`) of the first member on the first argument, followed by the next member on the result. Using (`..`) chains calls from Java methods. The code to get `JAVA_HOME` from REPL is as follows:

```
(.. System getenv (get "JAVA_HOME"))
```

```
;;=> "/usr/local/oss/jdk1.8.0_65"
```

The preceding is equivalent to:

```
(. (. System getenv) (get "JAVA_HOME")).
(macroexpand-1 '(.. System getenv (get "JAVA_HOME")))
;;=> (..(.. (. System getenv) (get "JAVA_HOME"))
```

Using the doto macro

The code to apply multiple methods on the same object using Java's interop is as follows:

```
(doto (java.util.HashMap.)
  (.put "key1" "value1")
  (.put "key2" "value2")
  (.put "key3" "value3")
  )
;;=> {"key1" "value1", "key2" "value2", "key3" "value3"}
```

Using the doto macro makes the code simpler:

```
(let [hash (java.util.HashMap.)]
    (.put hash "key1" "value1")
    (.put hash "key2" "value2")
    (.put hash "key3" "value3")
    hash
    )
;;=> {"key1" "value1", "key2" "value2", "key3" "value3"}
```

Using reflections

clojure.reflect reflects Java's classes. The following code gets the signature of methods that start with "get" using reflection:

```
(use 'clojure.reflect)
;;=>nil
(use 'clojure.pprint)
;;=>nil
(->> (clojure.reflect/reflect java.lang.String)
    :members
    (filter #(.startsWith (str (:name %)) "get"))
    (clojure.pprint/pprint))
;;=>({:name getChars,
;;=>   :return-type void,
;;=>   :declaring-class java.lang.String,
;;=>   :parameter-types [int int char<> int],
```

```
;;=>   :exception-types [],
;;=>   :flags #{:public}}
;;=> {:name getBytes,
;;=>   :return-type byte<>,
;;=>   :declaring-class java.lang.String,
;;=>   :parameter-types [],
;;=>   :exception-types [],
;;=>   :flags #{:public}}
;;=> ....
```

Extending Java superclasses and implementing Java interfaces

Java provides a superclass and interface mechanism to provide encapsulation and extendibility. Let's have a look at how to extend existing Java superclasses and implement Java interfaces in Clojure.

Getting ready

In this chapter, we will learn how to define subclasses and how to implement superinterfaces. We will use Jackson and other libraries. So, the :dependencies section in your project.clj as follows:

```
:dependencies [[org.clojure/clojure "1.8.0"]
               [org.clojure/math.numeric-tower "0.0.4"]
               [com.fasterxml.jackson.core/jackson-core "2.7.0"]
               [com.fasterxml.jackson.core/jackson-databind "2.7.0"]
               [com.fasterxml.jackson.core/jackson-annotations "2.7.0"]
               ]
```

How to do it...

Let's learn how to use proxy to implement Java interfaces.

Using proxy

`proxy` generates an anonymous class for superclasses and interfaces. In the previous recipe, we used the `java.lang.Thread` class. We will implement `java.lang.Runnable` when we instantiate:

```
(def t
  (Thread.
       (proxy [java.lang.Runnable] []
         (run [] (println "Thread is called ..."))
         )))
;;=> #'chapter05.proxy/t
(.start t)
;;=> Thread is called ...
;;=> nil
```

`proxy` can extend superclasses. The following code overrides the default method of the `java.util.HashMap`:

```
(def m
  (proxy [java.util.HashMap][0.75 10]
    (put [k v] (println "key=" k "value=" v " is goint to be inserted")
    (proxy-super put k v))))
;;=> #'chapter05.proxy/m
(.put m 1 1)
    (doto (java.util.HashMap.)
      (.put 1 1)
      )
;;=> key= 1 value= 1  is goint to be inserted
;;=> {{1 1}}
```

The second `proxy` parameter is the constructor parameter of the `HashMap`. The `proxy-super` calls supermethods.

Using reify for implementing interfaces

We can also implement interfaces using `reify`. The following code is the `reify` version of implementing `java.lang.Runnable`:

```
(def t
  (Thread.
  (reify
    java.lang.Runnable
    (run [this]
      (println "Thread is called ...")
      ))))
```

```
;;=> #'chapter05.proxy/t
(.start t)
;;=> Thread is called ...
;;=> nil
```

How it works...

`proxy` and `reify` are similar, but the following differences apply:

- `reify` does not support extending superclasses, but `proxy` does
- `reify` requires object references for the parameter list, but `proxy` doesn't
- The performance of `reify` is better than that of `proxy`

There's more...

When we are writing Java code, we sometimes define anonymous classes to define methods for specific purposes but not used by others. We can do the same thing in Clojure.

Defining anonymous classes in Clojure

Inline definition of anonymous classes is a common technique in Java:

```java
import java.util.List;
import java.util.Arrays;
import java.util.Collections;
import java.util.Comparator;

public class ComparatorTest {
    public static void main(String [] args) {
      List<Integer> list = Arrays.asList(1, 3, 2, 5, 8);
      Collections.sort(list, new Comparator<Integer>() {
            @Override
                public int compare(Integer o1, Integer o2) {
                return Integer.compare(o1, o2);
            }
        });
      System.out.println(list);
```

We will try to write the equivalent code in Clojure as follows:

```clojure
(defn list-sort [li]
  (java.util.Collections/sort li
```

```
    (reify java.util.Comparator
      (compare [this x y]
        (Integer/compare x y)))))
;;=> #'chapter05.proxy/list-sort
(def l1 (java.util.ArrayList. [3 1 5 2 4]))
;;=> #'chapter05.proxy/l1
(clojure.pprint/pprint l1)
;;=> [3 1 5 2 4]
;;=> nil
(list-sort l1)
;;=> nil
(clojure.pprint/pprint l1)
;;=> [1 2 3 4 5]
;;=> nil
```

Using annotations

We can make use of Java annotations in Clojure. Example code using Jackson to handle JSON and use Java annotations is as follows:

```
(import [com.fasterxml.jackson.databind ObjectMapper)]
;;=> com.fasterxml.jackson.databind.ObjectMapper
(import [com.fasterxml.jackson.annotation JsonCreator JsonProperty])
;;=> com.fasterxml.jackson.annotation.JsonProperty
(deftype ^{JsonProperty {}}
    Employee
    [^{:tag String JsonProperty "name"} name
     ^{:tag String JsonProperty "dept"} dept
     ^{:tag long JsonProperty "salary"} salary
     ]
  )
;;=> chapter05.proxy.Employee
```

The preceding code defines the Employee class with name, dept, and salary fields. The next code instantiates an Employee object:

```
(def makoto (->Employee "Makoto" "Development" 10000))
;;=> #'chapter05.proxy/makoto
```

We can get a JSON string using writeValueAsString of the ObjectMapper class as follows:

```
(.writeValueAsString (ObjectMapper.) makoto)
;;=> {"name":"Makoto","dept":"Development","salary":10000}
```

Calling Clojure from Java

In this recipe, we will learn how to define Java classes in Clojure and call them from Java.

Getting ready

To include Java sources in a Leiningen project, we create the `project.clj` as follows and restart the REPL:

```
(defproject chapter05 "0.1.0-SNAPSHOT"
  :description "FIXME: write description"
  :url "http://example.com/FIXME"
  :license {:name "Eclipse Public License"
            :url "http://www.eclipse.org/legal/epl-v10.html"}
  :java-source-paths ["src/java"]
  :aot [chapter05.calling-from-java]
  :prep-tasks [
               ["compile" "chapter05.calling-from-java"]
               "javac" "compile" ]
  :main chapter05.TestHello
  :dependencies [[org.clojure/clojure "1.8.0"]
                 ])
```

How to do it...

We will take a look at how we define Java classes that can be called from Java.

Defining a simple named class using gen-class

The following code is a very simple code to print string using `proxy`:

```
(ns chapter05.calling-from-java)
(gen-class
 :name cljbook.chapter05.Hello
 :methods [^:static [hello [String] void]])
;;=> nil
(defn- -hello
  [s]
  (println (str "Hello " s)))
;;=> nil
```

We write the following code to call the `hello` method in the `Hello` class written in Clojure:

```
package chapter05;
import cljbook.chapter05.Hello;
public class TestHello {
    public static void main(String[] args) {
    Hello.hello("makoto");
    }
}
```

`TestHello.java` is located under `src/java/chapter05`. We will invoke the Clojure code in `src/chapter05/calling_from_java.clj`.

So, let's go to your terminal and issue a command as follows:

```
$ lein run -m chapter05.TestHello
Compiling 1 source files to /home/makoto/clojure/clojure-packt-
book/chapter05/target/classes
Hello makoto
```

Defining a class with instance methods and constructors in Clojure

Here, we will learn how to define instance methods and constructors using `gen-class`. Our code defines the `Person` class in the `cljbook.chapter05` package, which has three constructors and two pairs of getters/setters for 22 fields:

```
(gen-class
 :name cljbook.chapter05.Person
 :state state
 :init init
 :prefix "-"
 :main false
 :constructors {
              [] []
              [String] []
              [String String] []}
 :methods [
          [setCountry [String] void]
          [getCountry [] String]
          [setName [String] void]
          [getName [] String]])
;;=> nil
```

`-init` defines three constructors:

```
(defn -init
  ([]  [[]  (atom {:name nil :country nil})])
  ([name]  [[]  (atom {:name name :country nil})])
  ([name country]  [[]  (atom {:name name :country country})])))
;;=> #'chapter05.calling-from-java/-init
```

`set-value` and `get-value` are utility functions to update and refer a map in the `Person`
object:

```
(defn set-value
  [this key value]
      (swap! (.state this) into {key value}))
;;=> #'chapter05.calling-from-java/set-value
(defn get-value
  [this key]
  (@(.state this) key))
;;=> #'chapter05.calling-from-java/get-value
(defn -setName [this name]
  (set-value this :name name))
;;=> #'chapter05.calling-from-java/-setName
```

The following are getters and setters for the `name` and `country` fields:

```
(defn  -getName
  [this]
  (get-value this :name))
;;=> #'chapter05.calling-from-java/-getName
(defn -setCountry [this country]
  (set-value this :country country))
;;=> #'chapter05.calling-from-java/-setCountry
(defn  -getCountry
  [this]
  (get-value this :country))
  ;;=> #'chapter05.calling-from-java/-getCountry
```

Now, we will test this in the REPL as follows:

```
(compile 'chapter05.calling-from-java)
;;=> chapter05.calling-from-java

(def p1 (cljbook.chapter05.Person.))
;;=> #'chapter05.calling-from-java/p1
(.setName p1 "Makoto")
;;=> nil
(.setCountry p1 "Japan")
;;=> nil
```

```
(.getName p1)
;;=> makoto
(.getCountry p1)
;;=> Japan
(def p2 (cljbook.chapter05.Person. "Nico" "France"))
;;=> #'chapter05.calling-from-java/p2
(.getName p2)
;;=> Nico
(.getCountry p2)
;;=> France
```

So, we will write a Java class to call the `Person` object as follows:

```
package chapter05;
import cljbook.chapter05.Person;
public class TestPerson {
    public static void main(String[] args) {
    Person p1 = new Person();
    p1.setName("Makoto");
    p1.setCountry("Japan");
    System.out.println(p1.getName() + " from " + p1.getCountry());

    Person p2 = new Person("Nico","France");
    System.out.println(p2.getName() + " from " + p2.getCountry());
    }
}
```

Let's run the Java code as follows:

```
$ lein run -m chapter05.TestPerson
Compiling 1 source files to /home/makoto/clojure/clojure-packt-
book/chapter05/target/classes
Makoto from Japan
Nico from France
```

Creating a JAR file callable from Java

Here we will create single JAR file callable from Java. The command `lein uberjar` that creates a standalone JAR file includes the application code and all dependent libraries:

```
                                   Terminal                          — + x
$ lein uberjar
Warning: specified :main without including it in :aot.
Implicit AOT of :main will be removed in Leiningen 3.0.0.
If you only need AOT for your uberjar, consider adding :aot :all into your
:uberjar profile instead.
Compiling chapter05.calling-from-java
Compiling 8 source files to /home/makoto/clojure/clojure-packt-book/chapter05/target/classes
Warning: skipped duplicate file: chapter05/TestInterface.class
Created /home/makoto/clojure/clojure-packt-book/chapter05/target/chapter05-0.1.0-SNAPSHOT.jar
Created /home/makoto/clojure/clojure-packt-book/chapter05/target/chapter05-0.1.0-SNAPSHOT-standalone.jar
$
```

The JAR file is located in the `target` directory under the top directory of the project:

```
                                   Terminal                          — + x
$ ls -l target/
合計 6044
-rw-r--r-- 1 makoto makoto 5957261  2月  1 05:02 chapter05-0.1.0-SNAPSHOT-standalone.jar
-rw-r--r-- 1 makoto makoto  221051  2月  1 05:02 chapter05-0.1.0-SNAPSHOT.jar
drwxr-xr-x 6 makoto makoto    4096  2月  1 05:02 classes
drwxr-xr-x 2 makoto makoto    4096  2月  1 05:02 stale
$
```

The name of the JAR file is `chapter05-0.1.0-SNAPSHOT-standalone.jar`. Now, let's create the following Java source file, located in the project and named `TestPerson.java`:

```java
import cljbook.chapter05.Person;
public class TestPerson {
    public static void main(String[] args) {
        Person p1 = new Person();
        p1.setName("Makoto");
        p1.setCountry("Japan");
        System.out.println(p1.getName() + " from " + p1.getCountry());

        Person p2 = new Person("Nico","France");
        System.out.println(p2.getName() + " from " + p2.getCountry());
    }
}
```

Let's compile and run the preceding Java code:

```
$ javac TestPerson.java -cp target/chapter05-0.1.0-SNAPSHOT-standalone.jar
$ java -classpath .:target/chapter05-0.1.0-SNAPSHOT-standalone.jar
TestPerson
Makoto from Japan
Nico from France
```

```
                        Terminal                    —  +  ✕
$ javac TestPerson.java -cp target/chapter05-0.1.0-SNAPSHOT-standalone.jar
$ java -classpath target/chapter05-0.1.0-SNAPSHOT-standalone.jar:. TestPerson
Makoto from Japan
Nico from France
$
```

How it works...

We will explain how to code `project.clj` so it is callable from Java. We also show what **ahead-of-time (AOT)** compilation is.

The project.clj for generating Java classes

The following is the `project.clj` for this recipe:

```
(defproject chapter05 "0.1.0-SNAPSHOT"
  :description "FIXME: write description"
  :url "http://example.com/FIXME"
  :license {:name "Eclipse Public License"
            :url "http://www.eclipse.org/legal/epl-v10.html"}
  :java-source-paths ["src/java"]
  :aot [chapter05.calling-from-java]
  :prep-tasks [
               ["compile" "chapter05.calling-from-java"]
               "javac" "compile" ]
  :main chapter05.TestHello
  :dependencies [[org.clojure/clojure "1.8.0"]
                 ])
```

The `:java-source-paths` keyword declares Java source code paths, and the Java source files are located under the `src/java` directory in our case. The `:aot` keyword declares Clojure source files to apply the AOT compilation. We declare the file `chapter05/calling-from-java.clj` should be compiled and generates a class file for callers. This is necessary for the callers to invoke classes written in Clojure.

The `:prep-tasks` keyword controls the order of compilation. Our definition is as follows:

```
:prep-tasks [
            ["compile" "chapter05.calling-from-java"]
            "javac" "compile" ]
```

In the preceding example, tasks will be executed in the following order:

1. The compilation of `chapter05.calling-from-java` first compiled by `javac` second.
2. Then, all Java source files are compiled by `javac`.

The rest of the Clojure files are then compiled.

AOT compilation

By default, Clojure compiles all source code when it loads into JVM bytecode on-the-fly. But AOT compilation is used in the following situations:

- To generate named class files for use by Java
- When we don't want to deliver source code
- To reduce application startup times

We use the AOT option for generating a named class to be called by Java code in this recipe.

There's more...

We will learn how to define interfaces and implementations in Clojure that can be called from Java.

Defining an interface and implementing a class callable from Java

`definterface` defines Java interfaces in Clojure and implements these interfaces in `deftype`. The following `definterface` declares a Java interface of the `Calculation`, which has the `getX`, `setX`, `add_`, and `_sub` methods. Then the `_deftype` of `MyInt` implements these methods:

```
(definterface Calculation
  (^long getX [])
```

```
  (^void setX [^long value])
  (^long add [^long x])
  (^long sub [^long x]))
;;=> chapter05.calling_from_java.Calculation
(deftype MyInt [^long x]
  Calculation
  (getX [this] (.x this))
  (setX [this val] (set!  (.x this) val))
  (add [this x] (+ (.x this) x))
  (sub [this x] (- (.x this) x)))
  ;;=> chapter05.calling_from_java.MyInt
```

Then, let's test the code as follows:

```
(def myInt (MyInt. 15))
(.add myInt 30)
;;=> 45
(.sub myInt 11)
;;=> 4
(.getX myInt)
;;=> 15
(.setX myInt 10)
;;=> nil
(.getX myInt)
;;=> 10
```

We will write Java code to call the implementation of the interface written in Clojure as follows:

```java
package chapter05;
import chapter05.calling_from_java.MyInt;
public class TestInterface {
    public static void main(String[] args) {
    MyInt myInt = new MyInt(15);
    System.out.println("add result = " + myInt.add(30));
    System.out.println("sub result = " + myInt.sub(11));
    System.out.println("x = " + myInt.getX());
    myInt.setX(10);
    System.out.println("x = " + myInt.getX());
    }
}
```

We will check to see the Java code call the interface written in Clojure:

```
$ lein run -m chapter05.TestInterface
Compiling 2 source files to /home/makoto/clojure/clojure-packt-
book/chapter05/target/classes
add result = 45
```

```
sub result = 4
x = 15
x = 10
```

Using Maven for Clojure and Java projects

We will demonstrate how to convert an existing Leiningen project into a Maven project to create a mixed project using Clojure and Java. Now let's start!

```
$ lein pom
```

Let's look at the generated pom.xml. Dependent JARs (such as Clojure JAR and Jackson-related JARs) used in Clojure are declared in the dependencies section in the pom.xml:

```
<dependencies>
    <dependency>
      <groupId>org.clojure</groupId>
      <artifactId>clojure</artifactId>
      <version>1.8.0</version>
    </dependency>
    <dependency>
      <groupId>org.clojure</groupId>
      <artifactId>math.numeric-tower</artifactId>
      <version>0.0.4</version>
    </dependency>
    <dependency>
      <groupId>com.fasterxml.jackson.core</groupId>
      <artifactId>jackson-core</artifactId>
      <version>2.7.0</version>
    </dependency>
    <dependency>
      <groupId>com.fasterxml.jackson.core</groupId>
      <artifactId>jackson-databind</artifactId>
      <version>2.7.0</version>
    </dependency>
    <dependency>
      <groupId>com.fasterxml.jackson.core</groupId>
      <artifactId>jackson-annotations</artifactId>
      <version>2.7.0</version>
    </dependency>
  </dependencies>
</project>
```

The following command runs the Java class of the TestPerson and prints the results:

```
$ mvn exec:java -Dexec.mainClass=chapter05.TestPerson
```

```
Terminal                                                    –  +  x
$ mvn exec:java -Dexec.mainClass=chapter05.TestPerson
[WARNING]
[WARNING] Some problems were encountered while building the effective settings
[WARNING] Expected root element 'settings' but found 'pluginGroups' (position: START_TAG seen <p
luginGroups>... @1:14)  @ /home/makoto/.m2/settings.xml, line 1, column 14
[WARNING]
[INFO] Scanning for projects...
[INFO]
[INFO] ------------------------------------------------------------------------
[INFO] Building chapter05 0.1.0-SNAPSHOT
[INFO] ------------------------------------------------------------------------
[INFO]
[INFO] --- exec-maven-plugin:1.4.0:java (default-cli) @ chapter05 ---
Makoto from Japan
Nico from France
[INFO] ------------------------------------------------------------------------
[INFO] BUILD SUCCESS
[INFO] ------------------------------------------------------------------------
[INFO] Total time: 1.855 s
[INFO] Finished at: 2016-02-02T01:47:07+09:00
[INFO] Final Memory: 12M/208M
[INFO] ------------------------------------------------------------------------
$
```

Now, let's add the clojure-maven-plugin to run the Clojure REPL using a maven command:

```xml
<plugin>
    <groupId>com.theoryinpractise</groupId>
    <artifactId>clojure-maven-plugin</artifactId>
    <version>1.3.10</version>
    <executions>
      <execution>
        <id>compile</id>
        <phase>compile</phase>
        <goals>
            <goal>compile</goal>
        </goals>
      </execution>
      <execution>
        <id>test</id>
        <phase>test</phase>
        <goals>
            <goal>test</goal>
        </goals>
```

```
        </execution>
      </executions>
   </plugin>
```

```
▼                              Terminal                         — + ×
$ mvn clojure:repl
[WARNING]
[WARNING] Some problems were encountered while building the effective settings
[WARNING] Expected root element 'settings' but found 'pluginGroups' (position: START_TAG seen <pluginGroups>... @1:14
) @ /home/makoto/.m2/settings.xml, line 1, column 14
[WARNING]
[INFO] Scanning for projects...
[INFO]
[INFO] ------------------------------------------------------------------------
[INFO] Building chapter05 0.1.0-SNAPSHOT
[INFO] ------------------------------------------------------------------------
[INFO]
[INFO] >>> clojure-maven-plugin:1.3.10:repl (default-cli) > test-compile @ chapter05 >>>
[INFO]
[INFO] --- build-helper-maven-plugin:1.7:add-source (add-source) @ chapter05 ---
[INFO] Source directory: /home/makoto/clojure/clojure-packt-book/chapter05/src/java added.
[INFO]
[INFO] --- maven-resources-plugin:2.6:resources (default-resources) @ chapter05 ---
[WARNING] Using platform encoding (UTF-8 actually) to copy filtered resources, i.e. build is platform dependent!
[INFO] Copying 0 resource
[INFO]
[INFO] --- maven-compiler-plugin:3.1:compile (default-compile) @ chapter05 ---
[INFO] Changes detected - recompiling the module!
[WARNING] File encoding has not been set, using platform encoding UTF-8, i.e. build is platform dependent!
[INFO] Compiling 8 source files to /home/makoto/clojure/clojure-packt-book/chapter05/target/classes
[INFO]
[INFO] --- clojure-maven-plugin:1.3.10:compile (compile) @ chapter05 ---
[INFO]
[INFO] --- maven-resources-plugin:2.6:testResources (default-testResources) @ chapter05 ---
[WARNING] Using platform encoding (UTF-8 actually) to copy filtered resources, i.e. build is platform dependent!
[INFO] Copying 0 resource
[INFO]
[INFO] --- maven-compiler-plugin:3.1:testCompile (default-testCompile) @ chapter05 ---
[INFO] Nothing to compile - all classes are up to date
[INFO]
[INFO] <<< clojure-maven-plugin:1.3.10:repl (default-cli) < test-compile @ chapter05 <<<
[INFO]
[INFO] --- clojure-maven-plugin:1.3.10:repl (default-cli) @ chapter05 ---
Clojure 1.8.0
user=>
```

Calling Scala from Clojure

In this recipe, we will integrate Clojure and Scala. We will configure a mixing project using Leiningen.

Getting ready

We create a project by `lein new clojure-scala` and `project.clj` as follows:

```
(defproject clojure-scala "0.1.0-SNAPSHOT"
  :description "FIXME: write description"
  :url "http://example.com/FIXME"
  :license {:name "Eclipse Public License"
            :url "http://www.eclipse.org/legal/epl-v10.html"}
  :dependencies [[org.clojure/clojure "1.8.0"]
                 [org.scala-lang/scala-library "2.11.7"]]
  :plugins [[io.tomw/lein-scalac "0.1.2"]]
  :scala-source-path "src/scala"
  :scala-version "2.11.7"
  :prep-tasks ["scalac"]
  :main clojure-scala.core
  )
```

After modifying the `project.clj`, start the REPL.

How to do it...

We will explain how Clojure code calls Scala methods and how to access fields defined in Scala. We will use Leiningen and the plugin for Scala. This assumes that Clojure projects using Leiningen make use of existing Scala libraries such as Kafka and Spark.

Using Leiningen to develop Scala and Clojure

Create `Main.scala` under the `src/scala` directory:

```
package chapter05
object Main {
  def hello(txt: String) = {
    "hello from Scala: " + txt + " !"
  }
}
class Calculation {
  def factorial(n: BigInt): BigInt = {
    if (n <= 1) 1  else  n * factorial(n - 1)
  }
  def add(a:Int, b:Int):Int = a + b
}

class MyTuple {
  def tuple(x:Int, y:Int) = (x,y)
}
```

To compile Scala source code, do the following:

```
$ lein scalac
```

```
Terminal                                                    — + x
$ lein scalac
Compiling 1 source file to /home/makoto/clojure/clojure-packt-book/chapter05/clojure-scala/target/classes
$
```

We need to restart the REPL after modifying and compiling Scala source code to test from Clojure.

Importing Scala classes

Then we will test Scala code from Clojure's REPL. The following code imports Scala classes:

```
(ns clojure-scala.core)
;;=> nil
```

Calling instance methods

Let's start with calling instance methods from Scala. It is the same as calling Java's instance methods:

```
(import 'chapter05.Calculation)
;;=> chapter05.Calculation
(.add calc 10 2)
;;=> 12
(import 'scala.math.BigInt)
;;=> scala.math.BigInt
(import 'java.math.BigInteger)
;;=> java.math.BigInteger
(.factorial calc (BigInt. (BigInteger. "25")))
;;=> 15511210043330985984000000
```

Calling `factorial` is a bit complicated. The code converts to Scala's `scala.math.BigInt`.

Calling singleton methods

Calling Scala's singleton methods is the same as calling Java's static methods:

```
(import 'chapter05.Main)
;;=> chapter05.Main
(Main/hello "Makoto")
;;=> "hello from Scala: Makoto !"
```

```
(import 'chapter05.MyTuple)
;;=> chapter05.MyTuple
(def tuple1 (MyTuple/tuple 1 5))
;;=> #'clojure-scala.core/tupl1e
```

Accessing tuples

To access tuples, use _1, _2, and so on:

```
(._1 tuple1)
;;=> 1
(._2 tuple1)
;;=> 5
```

Accessing Scala fields

Let's access Scala fields from Clojure. In Scala, declaring a field generates accessor methods automatically, but method names are different from Java:

```
package chapter05
import scala.beans.BeanProperty

class Student {
  var name   = new String("")
  var address = new String("")
  }

class Person {
  @BeanProperty var name : String = _
  @BeanProperty var address  : String = _
}
```

To generate getter/setter methods for Java, use the BeanProperty annotations in the preceding code. The following code shows how to access Scala fields from Clojure. To access the default fields of a Scala class, use .field_name and .filedname\$eq for the getter and setter, respectively:

```
(import 'chapter05.Person)
;;=> chapter05.Person
(import 'chapter05.Student)
;;=> chapter05.Student
(def s (Student.))
;;=> #'clojure-scala.core/s
(.name_$eq s "Nico")
;;=> nil
(.name s)
```

```
;;=> "Nico"
(def p (Person.))
;;=> #'clojure-scala.core/person
(.setName p "Makoto")
;;=> nil
(.getName p)
;;=> "Makoto"
(.address_$eq p "Japan")
;;=> nil
(.address p)
;;=> "Japan"
```

How it works...

In `project.clj`, we added the Scala library as follows:

```
:dependencies [[org.clojure/clojure "1.8.0"]
               [org.scala-lang/scala-library "2.11.7"]]
```

The following plugin enables the compilation of Scala source code by `lein-scalac`:

```
:plugins [[io.tomw/lein-scalac "0.1.2"]]
```

We have specified the Scala source path and the version of Scala by `:scala-source-path` and `:scala-version`, respectively:

```
:scala-source-path "src/scala"
 :scala-version "2.11.7"
```

We use `:prep-tasks` to compile the Scala source code ahead of the compilation of the Clojure code:

```
:prep-tasks ["scalac"]
```

There's more...

SBT is the de facto standard build tool for Scala, and a lot of Scala projects use SBT. We use Scala DSL to describe project configuration for SBT. Here we will learn how Scala calls Clojure in an SBT project. We will use the Clojure plugin for SBT. In this example, we will learn how to use SBT for a mixing project using the Scala and Clojure languages.

Using SBT

We will demonstrate how to create an SBT-based project. In the example, Scala code calls methods defined by Clojure. So, let's go !

Creating an SBT-based project

Let's create an SBT project first:

```
$ mkdir sbt-scala-clojure
$ cd sbt-scala-clojure
$ mkdir project
```

Create `build.sbt` as follows:

```
seq(clojure.settings :_*)
libraryDependencies += "org.clojure" % "clojure" % "1.8.0"
```

`project/plugins.sbt_` specifies the `sbt-clojure` plugin:

```
// Comment to get more information during initialization
//logLevel := Level.Debug
logLevel := Level.Info
//lazy val root = project.in(file(".")).dependsOn(clojurePlugin)

//lazy val clojurePlugin = file("../../sbt-clojure")
addSbtPlugin("com.unhandledexpression" % "sbt-clojure" % "0.1")
```

Writing source code

We will create the Clojure source code under `src/main/clojure`:

```
(ns helloworld)
(gen-class
 :name cljbook.chapter05.HelloWorld
 :methods [#^{:static true} [sayHello [] void]])
(defn -sayHello []
  (println "Hello world from Clojure!"))
(gen-class
   :name cljbook.chapter05.Calculator
   :methods
   [#^{:static false} [add [long long] long]
    #^{:static false} [sub [long long] long]])
(defn -add [this a b]
  (+ a b))
(defn -sub [this a b]
  (- a b))
```

The preceding Clojure code has two classes: `cljbook.chapter05.HelloWorld` and `cljbook.chapter05.Calculator`. Then, we will look at Scala code. The following is the Scala code for calling classes defined in Clojure:

```scala
import cljbook.chapter05.HelloWorld
import cljbook.chapter05.Calculator
object Main {
  def main(args: Array[String]) = {
    println("I'm calling methods defined by Clojure from Scala.")
    HelloWorld.sayHello();
    val calc = new Calculator
    println("add: "+calc.add(1,2))
    println("sub: "+calc.sub(10,5))
  }
}
```

The following screenshot is the directory for this project:

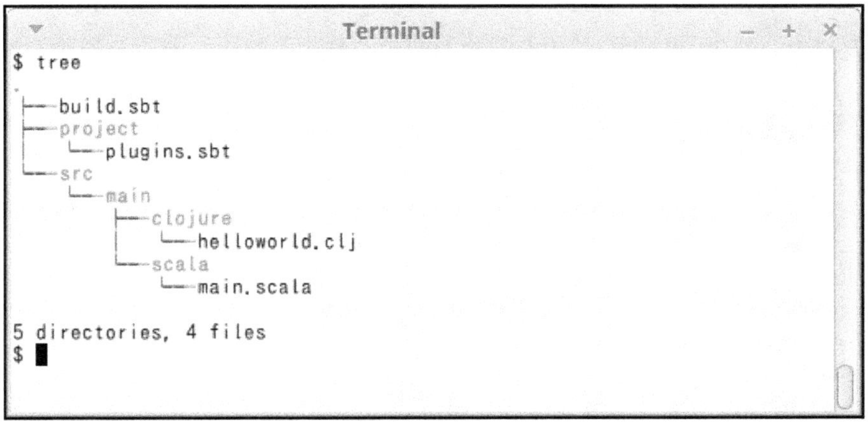

```
Terminal                              _  +  ✕
$ tree
.
├──build.sbt
├──project
│   └──plugins.sbt
└──src
    └──main
        ├──clojure
        │   └──helloworld.clj
        └──scala
            └──main.scala

5 directories, 4 files
$ ▮
```

Then run the following:

```
$ sbt run
```

```
                                        Terminal                                    - + x
$ sbt run
[info] Loading global plugins from /home/makoto/.sbt/0.13/plugins
[info] Loading project definition from /home/makoto/clojure/clojure-packt-book/chapter05/sbt-scala-clojure/project
[info] Set current project to sbt-scala-clojure (in build file:/home/makoto/clojure/clojure-packt-book/chapter05/sbt-scala-clojure/)
[info] Updating {file:/home/makoto/clojure/clojure-packt-book/chapter05/sbt-scala-clojure/}sbt-scala-clojure...
[warn] Multiple dependencies with the same organization/name but different versions. To avoid conflict, pick one version:
[warn]   * org.clojure:clojure:(1.5.1, 1.8.0)
[info] Resolving org.fusesource.jansi#jansi;1.4 ...
[info] Done updating.
[info] Start Compiling Clojure sources
No need to call RT.init() anymore
[info] Compiling 1 Scala source to /home/makoto/clojure/clojure-packt-book/chapter05/sbt-scala-clojure/target/scala-2.10/classes...
[info] Running Main
I'm calling methods defined by Clojure from Scala.
Hello world from Clojure!
add: 3
sub: 5
[success] Total time: 4 s, completed 2016/02/04 10:03:54
$
```

ClojureCLR

ClojureCLR is a way to use and port your Clojure code to a .NET runtime. There are different levels in achieving this integration; why you want to run your Clojure code on the CLR is going to be at the root of your usage and of its different patterns. You may simply have stumbled upon some fantastic looking Clojure code, but with all those brackets you are not sure if you can debug it or not yet, so you just want to embed the `clj` algorithm and be able to run this on the command line or through a Windows native interface. You may be tempted to create Windows User Interfaces from the usual Clojure REPL, which is also possible using ClojureCLR. You may also want to distribute you Clojure code into a Windows **Dynamic-link Library** (**DLL**) and give it to a customer so he can call it natively.

In this recipe, we will look at all those different options and will also learn how to be productive on the CLR.

While working through this recipe, you will also realize, again, how the memory footprint of .NET programs is often lower than their Java VM counterparts, which makes a nice argument for Clojure when running on memory-limited environments.

Writing this recipe made the author wanting to write more C# and other related .NET code and even to write some mobile apps. Now it's your turn to get excited.

Getting ready

There is actually quite a lot we need to do to get ready for this recipe. Also, make sure to not go around the web and try to combine indications from other web sources with this one. Things have gotten a lot better over time with regard to installation and integration, so there is no need to revert to outdated instructions.

First, on Windows, it is recommended you install Visual Studio.

 All examples in this recipe have been written using the Community Edition. Quite a few of the screenshots will be taken from there.

There is no particular plugin needed, but the examples in this chapter will make use of a few C# examples.

Along the way, we will also look at how to integrate the mono IDE from Xamarin Studio. Mono allows you to run .NET code on non-Windows machines; thus, you do not need to run the Windows-only Visual Studio and instead you can run your nicely integrated .NET and Clojure code everywhere.

Installing Visual Code Studio and creating a project

This should be a no-brainer, apart from the required disk space, which takes up almost 10GB of your precious SSD drive:

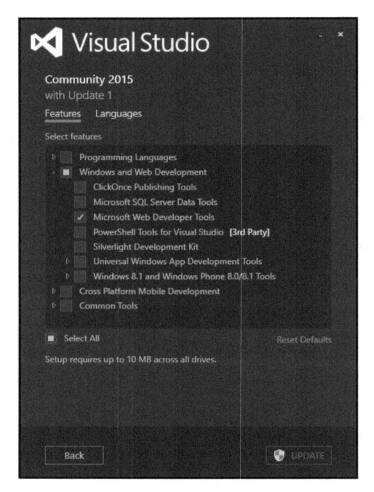

Once the install is finished, you will create a new command line-based C# project, as shown in the following screenshot:

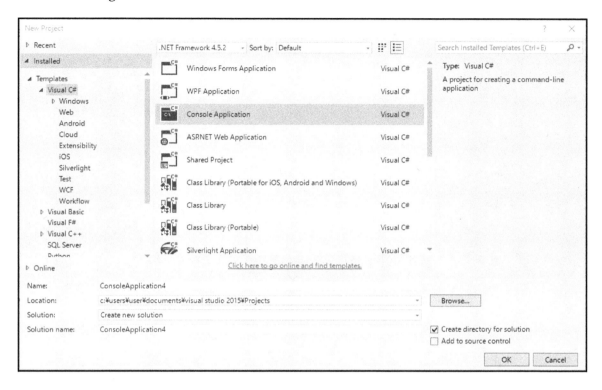

Creating a new project will take you to a very familiar setup. To get ready to use our project with Clojure, we will use the NuGet package manager, which is the de facto standard in .NET for installing the Clojure libraries:

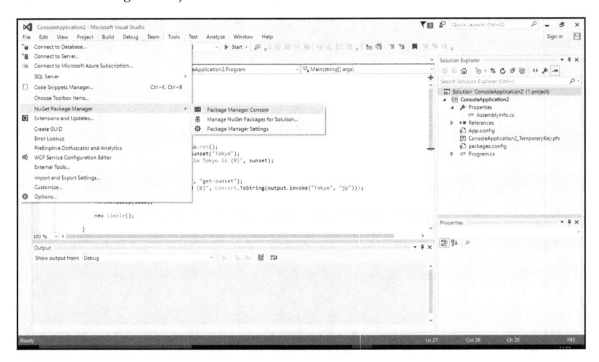

Now we will install the Clojure libraries into the current project. In the NuGet console, type the following:

```
Install-Package Clojure -Version 1.7.0
```

Now NuGet will grab the basic stuff for you:

```
Package Manager Console
Package source: nuget.org            ⚙   Default project: ConsoleApplication4                 ⎚
PM> Install-Package Clojure
Package 'Clojure.1.7.0' already exists in project 'ConsoleApplication2'
PM> Install-Package Clojure
Attempting to gather dependencies information for package 'Clojure.1.7.0' with respect to project 'ConsoleApplication4', targeting
'.NETFramework,Version=v4.5.2'
Attempting to resolve dependencies for package 'Clojure.1.7.0' with DependencyBehavior 'Lowest'
Resolving actions to install package 'Clojure.1.7.0'
Resolved actions to install package 'Clojure.1.7.0'
Adding package 'Clojure.1.7.0' to folder 'c:¥users¥user¥documents¥visual studio 2015¥Projects¥ConsoleApplication4¥packages'
Added package 'Clojure.1.7.0' to folder 'c:¥users¥user¥documents¥visual studio 2015¥Projects¥ConsoleApplication4¥packages'
Added package 'Clojure.1.7.0' to 'packages.config'
Successfully installed 'Clojure 1.7.0' to ConsoleApplication4
PM>
```

A note here: ClojureCLR version 1.8.0 could not be successfully tested before this book came out so that is why we stick to a slightly older version. For our purposes here, that will not be a problem.

You are now ready to execute your first bits of Clojure code from your C# project.

Let's stick in some usual interop code in the core of the main application:

```csharp
using System;
using clojure.lang;
using System.Threading;
using clojure.clr.api;

namespace firstclojure
{
class Program
    {
      {
        static void Main(string[] args)
        {
          IFn load = clojure.clr.api.Clojure.var("clojure.core", "load-
string");
          Console.WriteLine(Convert.ToString(load.invoke("(+ 1 1)")));
          Thread.Sleep(1000);
        }
      }
    }
}
```

Executing the preceding, and assuming the installation went fine, the following will show up:

```
2
```

This means that the Clojure code has effectively been compiled using the `load-string` method, and has been `eval-ed`. We're sleeping a bit more in the end, so we have time to see the message. It is worth noting that the Objects explorer window shows a reference to the core Clojure libraries:

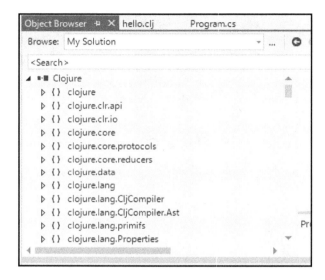

Looking through the hierarchy, we can see the different methods that are available, and actually Visual Studio does a good job of showing you options while you type code.

This is very basic, and we will see how to do more interaction with Clojure later on.

For now, since the workflow is very similar, let's have a look at how to get ready on a platform-independent environment when using Mono Studio.

Installing Mono Studio IDE

For those of us who do not have the chance to work on Windows, we can revert to installing Xamarin Studio. There will be some more gymnastic around, so if you are on Windows, probably sticking with the comfort of Visual Studio is a better option:

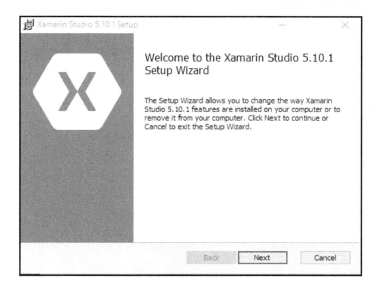

Once the setup is done, the new project flow should feel similar; you can create a new command line-based project:

We will need to install Clojure through NuGet as well:

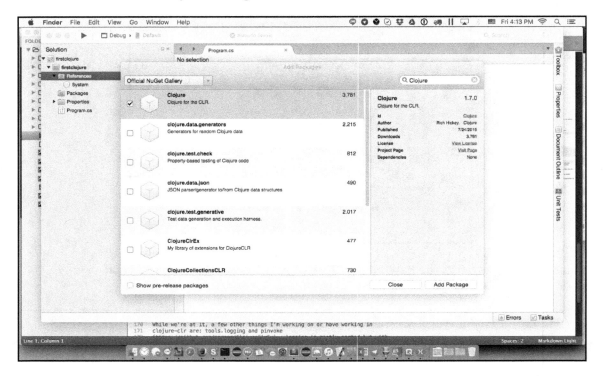

Although it seems that we still need to insert the libraries one by one, at this stage make sure you are grabbing the CLR binaries from the Clojure website at `https://github.com/clojure/clojure-clr/wiki/Getting-binaries`.

Once you have extracted the content of the ZIP file, do add all the DLLs to the current project. Refer to all of the Dynamic Libraries in the unzipped folder:

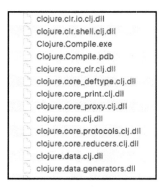

Add them to the references of the project, as shown in the following screenshot:

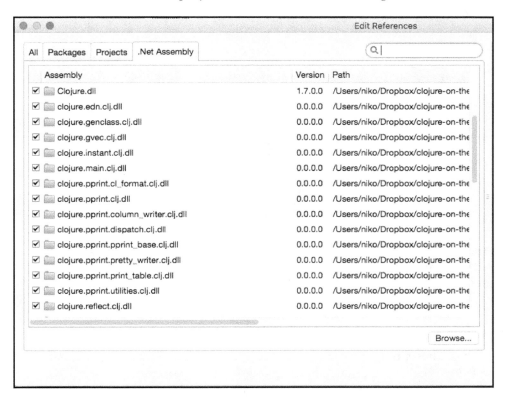

This is thought to be a temporary work around for CLJCLR-48, which is being investigated. Apart from that, you are good! So, let's reuse almost the same code. Here we are making explicit that the function should be loaded from the clojure.core namespace. Then we can make reference to that function in standard .NET code:

```
using System;
using clojure.lang;
using System.Threading;
using clojure.clr.api;

namespace firstclojure
{
    class MainClass
    {
        public static void Main (string[] args)
        {
            IFn load = Clojure.var("clojure.core", "load-string");
```

```
            Console.WriteLine(Convert.ToString(load.invoke("(reduce *
    (range 2 10))")));
            Console.WriteLine ("Hello World!");
            Thread.Sleep (1000);
        }
    }
}
```

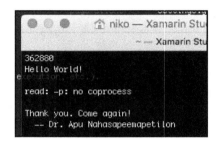

Now we suppose that at this stage we are able to add both libraries in Visual Studio and Xamarin Studio, the second one being based on the mono runtime, a different .NET runtime implementation..

Lein CLR

Leiningen has a basic plugin that supports developing Clojure code that can be compiled and used from .NET, or vice versa, helping us use .NET code from Clojure. To create a new CLR-based project, the Leiningen CLR plugin can be used transparently using the `lein clr` template. So, to create a new project, supposing you have Leiningen installed at this stage, you can simply type the command:

```
lein new lein-clr bonjour-clr
```

A new Clojure project will be created, but before you can run any of the CLR-based commands, you need to define a system variable CLRCLR14_40, which should point to the downloaded Clojure .NET binaries, as seen earlier in the Xamarin section:

There are other ways to do this, but you will probably agree with me that this was the fastest one. At this point, if you are not on Windows, you will need to point some PATH variables to the Mono Framework, which should be downloaded with the Xamarin Studio install; if not, now is a good time to do it. On MacOS, something like the following, should get you sorted:

```
export PATH=$PATH:/Library/Frameworks/Mono.framework/Home/bin
```

That's it. Now that you are all set, let's just quickly run the code loaded by default using the following command prompt:

```
lein clr run -m bonjour-clr.core "this is a test"
; Received args: this is a test
```

Wow. Sweet. You'll also be surprised to see that the Clojure code knows nothing about its host, as you can confirm from the main file:

```
(ns bonjour-clr.core)

(defn foo
  "I don't do a whole lot."
  [x]
  (println x "Hello, World!"))

(defn -main
  [& args]
  (apply println "Received args:" args))
```

How to do it...

Now that we are all ready, we will go through a few things with the CLR, such as calling .NET code straight from Clojure and going through the different ways of running Clojure code from .NET. So get ready.

Calling .NET code from Clojure

Even though you are now in the land of .NET, you really do not want to throw away the REPL advantages of Clojure. Let's see how to set it up and use it.

Starting an REPL

This is going to be an easy one, but most of the code we write in Clojure for the .NET platform can be run directly using the Leiningen CLR plugin. So, for example, to start a .NET REPL, simply type the following:

```
lein clr repl
```

You can check this is no cheat, by typing the following two lines:

```
(System.Reflection.Assembly/LoadWithPartialName "System.Windows.Forms")
(System.Windows.Forms.MessageBox/Show "Hello world")
```

This will show a familiar-looking Windows Alert Box:

You have to like the conciseness of the code. If we go through it quickly, the first line loads the required library or DLL using a system call. Here we want to load the `SystemSystem.Windows.Forms` library:

```
(System.Reflection.Assembly/LoadWithPartialName "System.Windows.Forms")
```

The second line is a regular Clojure interop, using the static method `Show` from the class `System.Windows.Forms.MessageBox`. Note that the class is only available because we loaded the DLL/Library beforehand.

```
(System.Windows.Forms.MessageBox/Show "Hello world")
```

Working with IO

The next sample will show you how to call a few more .NET methods. First, we can recall how to use the `WriteLine` method from C#:

```
(System.Console/WriteLine "Now we use Console Writeline")
```

This is functionally equivalent to the Clojure function `println`, but here we are explicitly calling on the C# method.

Next, we want to output something to a file; this will be done through the `StreamWriter` class and the `WriteLine` method. Note that we create .NET objects in Clojure the same way we do for Java, with a dot. The successive calls to `WriteLine` and `Close` are done on an instance of the .NET object, using again the dot notation:

```
(let [filename "test.txt" file  (System.IO.StreamWriter. filename)]
  (.WriteLine file "===Hello Clojure ===")
  (.Close file))
```

Avoiding all explicit call to .NET, you could also retrieve the content of the newly created files using the `slurp` function:

```
user=> (println (slurp "test.txt"))
; ===Hello Clojure ===
```

Parsing some XML using C# code

We will quickly look at an example on how to parse XML from Clojure on .NET because this will be the base of our integration example in the next section. For this example, we will load the `System.Xml` library, as we have seen before, using the following:

```
(System.Reflection.Assembly/LoadWithPartialName "System.Xml")
; #object[RuntimeAssembly 0xf097c6 "System.Xml, Version=4.0.0.0,
Culture=neutral, PublicKeyToken=b77a5c561934e089"]
```

A note for later would be to confirm that the DLL is loaded properly, as seen in the echo message when typed on the console. `LoadWithPartialName` outputs some information showing that, from that newly loaded library, we will import a few classes, the same ones we used with Java interop. The `ns` declaration makes it easy to hold all of those together so:

```
(ns hello.parsing
  (:import [System.Xml XmlReader])
  (:import [System.IO StringReader])
  (:import [System.Text]))
```

Here, you can note how the XML definition is completely defined through the usual Clojure code:

```
(def xml "<bookstore>
      <book genre='autobiography' publicationdate='1981-03-22'
ISBN='1-861003-11-0'>
          <title>The Autobiography of Benjamin Franklin</title>
          <author>
              <first-name>Benjamin</first-name>
              <last-name>Franklin</last-name>
          </author>
          <price>8.99</price>
      </book>
    </bookstore>")
```

Finally, we will load the `XmlReader` from a C# `StringReader`, and then using some obscure C# Sax parsing methods we can access the name of the book:

```
(let [reader (XmlReader/Create (StringReader. xml))]
  (.ReadToFollowing reader "title")
```

```
(println
  (.ReadElementContentAsString reader)))
; The Autobiography of Benjamin Franklin
```

That was rather concise! In the next example, we will take it a step further by calling a remote web service.

Calling a REST API using Clojure/C#

In this example, we will take it from the XML parsing from the previous example to parse a response from a remote web service. The remote web service will be Yahoo Weather, and we will make it so that we can find the sunset time for a specific location.

If you are starting from a fresh REPL, or at the top of your file, start by importing the XML Library as done previously:

```
(System.Reflection.Assembly/LoadWithPartialName "System.Xml")
; #object[RuntimeAssembly 0xf097c6 "System.Xml, Version=4.0.0.0,
Culture=neutral, PublicKeyToken=b77a5c561934e089"]
```

On top of the XML parsing-related classes, we will import the C# `WebClient`, which will send the HTTP request for us:

```
(ns hello.net
  (:import [System.Net WebClient])
  (:import [System.Xml XmlReader])
  (:import [System.IO StringReader])
  (:import [System.Text])
  (:import [System.Text Encoding]))
```

In pure Clojure, we will create a function that will create the API endpoint from a string concatenation. This is mostly documented in the Yahoo API usage, and only the city and country have been extracted to bring a bit of fun:

```
(defn api-uri [city country]
  (str
"https://query.yahooapis.com/v1/public/yql?q=select%20astronomy.sunset%20fr
om%20weather.forecast%20where%20woeid%20in%20(select%20woeid%20from%20geo.p
laces(1)%20where%20text%3D%22"
    city
    "%2C%20"
    country
"%22)&format=xml&env=store%3A%2F%2Fdatatables.org%2Falltableswithkeys"))
```

The preceding function can then be called as follows:

```
(api-uri "Tokyo" "Japan")
; ... a long string ...
```

Let's define a `uri` ref as the return of the last function call; remember the * notation to refer to previous results at the REPL:

```
(def uri *1)
```

And let's use that URI endpoint to query the sunset using the `WebClient`:

```
(.GetString Encoding/UTF8 (.DownloadData (WebClient.) uri))
; "<?xml version="1.0" encoding="UTF-8"?>\n<query
xmlns:yahoo="http://www.yahooapis.com/v1/base.rng" yahoo:count="1"
yahoo:created="2016-02-09T02:04:09Z" yahoo:lang="en-
US"><results><channel><yweather:astronomy
xmlns:yweather="http://xml.weather.yahoo.com/ns/rss/1.0" sunset="5:15
pm"/></channel></results></query><!-- total: 9 -->\n<!-- main-37493228-
cac5-11e5-b8c6-9cb6548278d0 -->\n"
;
```

Provided you are not behind a proxy and you are connected to the Internet, the preceding call will return the XML response from the Yahoo Web Service. Linked with parsing calls from the previous example, we can now create a function that will query the web service and return only the value we want from the attribute sunset of the tag:

```
(defn get-sunset [city country]
  (let [
    uri (api-uri city country)
    res (.GetString Encoding/UTF8 (.DownloadData (WebClient.) uri))
    reader (XmlReader/Create (StringReader. res))
  ]
  (doto reader
    (.ReadToFollowing "astronomy"
"http://xml.weather.yahoo.com/ns/rss/1.0")
    (.MoveToAttribute "sunset"))
  (str (.Value reader))))
```

This comes up nicely, and we now have a method to query sunset time from everywhere. So let's travel to Paris in a bit!

```
(get-sunset "Paris" "France")
; 6:00pm, at the time of the book writing ;)
```

UI Prototyping

Now to wrap this all up, we will go the extra step of setting up a basic **user interface** (**UI**) to our wonderful function that calls the Yahoo API. First, we will build a very simple UI and then we will enhance our example to call the API based on a ComboBox! Excited? Sure you are!

We start by loading and referring to the usual set of classes:

```
(System.Reflection.Assembly/LoadWithPartialName "System.Windows.Forms")

(ns hello.simpleui
  (:import [System.Windows.Forms Button Form Label])
  (:import [System.Drawing Size Point]))
```

Then, we define a new component for the overall UI using a `let` block:

```
(let [
  form (Form.)
  load-btn (Button.)
  title-label (Label.)
  title-string "A very simple UI! "]
```

We then create a standard label; note the interop and calls to setters are done using `.set_` calls to the different fields:

```
(doto title-label
  (.set_Text title-string)
  (.set_Location (Point. 12 12))
  (.set_Size (Size. 360 22)))
```

To build an interactive button, we use `gen-delegate`, which allows us to plugin to the native Event Handling system. The block of `gen-delegate` is the body of the callback that will be called when the event is triggered. Here we change the text of the preceding label and print a string on the console:

```
(doto load-btn
  (.set_Name "loadButton")
  (.set_Location (Point. 12 78))
  (.set_Text "Button 1")
  (.set_Size (Size. 360 22))
  (.add_Click
   (gen-delegate EventHandler [sender args]
      (.set_Text title-label "clicked button1 !")
      (System.Console/WriteLine "Now we use Console Writeline"))))
```

We do all this by adding the preceding two UI controls to the form and then showing the form itself:

```
(doto (.Controls form)
  (.Add title-label)
  (.Add load-btn))

(doto form
  (.set_Text title-string)
  (.set_Size (Size. 400 200))
  .ShowDialog))
```

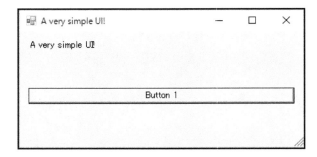

Putting it all together

By changing the top namespace to include the code you wrote for the Yahoo API, you will now add a ComboBox object to be able to select a city and send the request when the ComboBox selection has been updated:

```
(ns hello.simpleui2
  (:use [hello.net])
  (:import [System.Windows.Forms ComboBox MessageBox Button Form Label])
  (:import [System.Drawing Size Point]))
```

Now on to the ComboBox core code; the import part is on the add_SelectedIndexChanged call. The event itself is SelectedIndexChanged, and the CLR interop with Clojure allows you to register the handler through the prefixed function with add_, as shown in the following:

```
(.AddRange
  (.get_Items combo)
  (into-array ["osaka" "Tokyo" "Sapporo"]))

(doto combo
  (.set_Location (Point. 12 78))
  (.set_Size (Size. 360 22))
```

```
(.add_SelectedIndexChanged
  (gen-delegate EventHandler [sender args]
    (let [city  (str (.Text combo)) ]
    (MessageBox/Show (str "sunset time in " city  " : " (hello.net/get-
sunset city "jp") ))))))
```

The rest of the code is rather easy to go along, and you will notice, of course, the call to the `get-sunset` function that you wrote earlier on. On running all this through the REPL or through the command `lein clr run -m hello.simpleui2`, you will now be able to get the sunset times for all those beautiful Japanese cities:

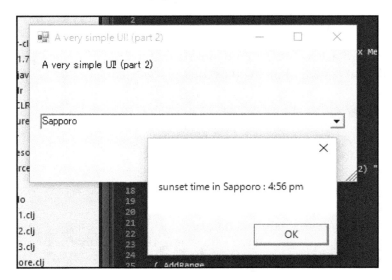

How it works...

Now that you have seen through an extensive list of CLR interops, it is time to see how all this works when calling Clojure code from .NET. Things get a little bit more complicated, so you will have to stay focused. First of all, you want to be able to generate executables and Dynamic Libraries from the Clojure code you are writing. Once this is all going smoothly, we will switch to importing those generated objects into a Visual Studio project, and for the sake of completeness, a Xamarin Mono-based project as well.

Compiling Clojure code for .NET

Back to the `hello.net` namespace that you have created earlier on, by adding the usual interop glue; we can add a main method that will be the main entry point when calling the executable:

```
(defn -main[& args]
  (println (get-sunset (first args) "jp")))
```

We also make sure that the `:gen-class` directive is present in the namespace definition:

```
(ns hello.net
  (:gen-class))
```

From the command line, the expected outcome is that, taking a city as a parameter, the runtime will call the Yahoo API. Let's check that with the run command of the Leiningen CLR plugin:

```
lein clr run -m hello.net "Osaka"
; 5:34 pm
```

You are good. (You are right?) Now to make this reusable, we will make use of the compile command of the Leiningen CLR plugin to compile one namespace:

```
lein clr compile hello.net
```

Note that this will compile the required namespaces as well. If all goes well, in the `target\clr\bin` folder, you now have a few more files, notably the two newly generated ones – the DLL and the EXE files:

```
-a----        2016/02/09    17:21        10240 hello.net.clj.dll
-a----        2016/02/09    17:21         4608 hello.net.exe
```

Those files are executables, provided you added the required Clojure and Microsoft DLLs as explained previously. On the command line, this time, no plugin required! This is pure .NET code:

```
.\hello.net.exe Osaka
; 5:34 pm
```

Sweet!

To be even more ready for the next step, we will add a specific method to be generated and exposed through the DLL. This is done at the `:gen-class` directive level:

```
(:gen-class
    :methods [[#^{:static true} getsunset [String] String]])
```

This tells the compiler to expose a function named `getsunset`, which takes a string as input parameter, in the brackets, and returns a string, the right-most string definition. For this to work, we actually do need to add a new method to the Clojure code of the `hello.net` namespace since exposed method definitions need to be using the – prefix by default:

```
(defn -getsunset [this city]
    (get-sunset city "jp"))
```

Let's rerun the Leiningen CLR plugin, to make sure you have the latest code with:

```
lein clr compile hello.net
```

Still here? Great! Let's go for some more C# adventures!

Adding Clojure code to a Visual Studio project

So, we are back to Visual Studio now, and let's create a brand new C#-based command line application. On the newly created project, make sure you have added the Clojure library through NuGet first as you saw previously and then add the references to our newly compiled binaries:

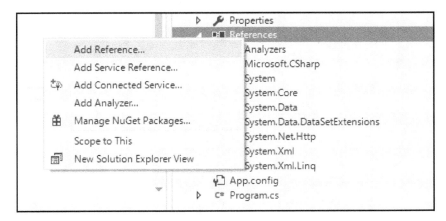

You need to browse to the `target\clr\bin` folder and then select both the `.dll` and `.exe` files, as shown in the following screenshot:

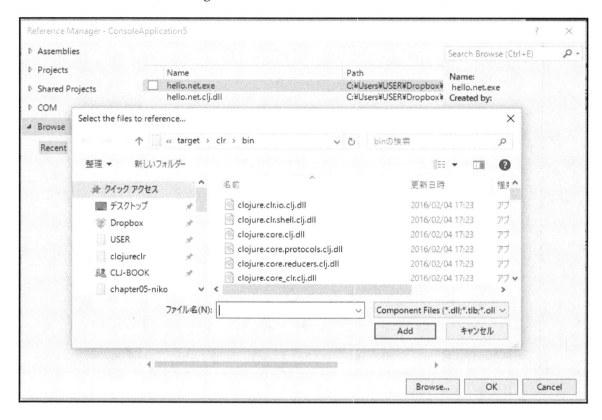

The dependencies are now shown in your project:

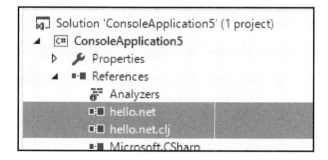

You are now ready to add C# code to call the newly added library:

```
hello.net fromclojure = new hello.net();
string sunset = fromclojure.getsunset("Tokyo");
Console.WriteLine("Sunset today in Tokyo is {0}", sunset);
Thread.Sleep(5000);
```

Note a few things. We need to create a new object instance to call the generated code. But then the Clojure-compiled code really looks like any other C# library around.

Make sure you fix the imports as proposed by Visual Studio. Let's click on the Windows-like **Start** button!

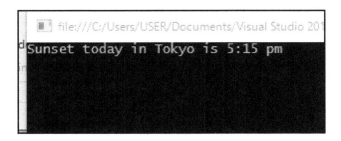

Running Clojure code using Clojure.RT

There is actually another slightly different method to call the Clojure code using the `clojure.lang.RT` class. This call has a `load` method that works as a `require` directive. This works very much in the same way as the regular Java interop if you remember:

```
RT.load("hello.net");
IFn output =  RT.var("hello.net", "get-sunset");
Console.WriteLine("Second method {0}", output.invoke("Tokyo", "jp"));
```

So, we create an IFn object, which works or maps to a Clojure function through the `RT.var` call. Then, you can `invoke` this resulting IFn object, with the desired parameter, here `Tokyo`.

Using Xamarin Mono Studio

If you have been following all this properly, and even if you are not on a Windows machine, the last part of this recipe will actually be a breeze. On the Xamarin C# project we created previously, we will also add references to the DLL and EXE files that were generated. This is done in two steps. First, open the `References` dialog, as shown in the following screenshot:

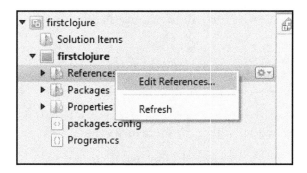

Then, browse and select the .NET assembly, as shown in the next screenshot:

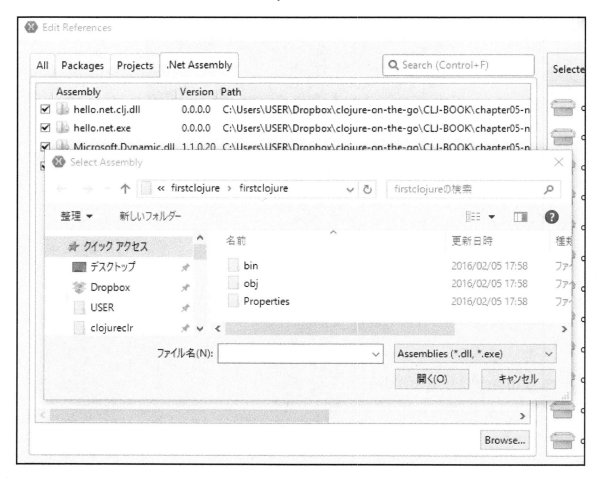

The code for the Xamarin IDE is the exact same as the code written for Visual Studio, so the same C# code comes along:

```
...
namespace firstclojure
{
    class MainClass
    {
        public static void Main (string[] args)
        {
            hello.net fromclojure = new hello.net();
            string sunset = fromclojure.getsunset("Tokyo");
            Console.WriteLine("Sunset today in Tokyo is {0}", sunset);
            Thread.Sleep (2000);
        }
    }
}
```

Running this will bring you the usual sunset times!

Time to get this recipe to its natural sunset conclusion, don't you think?

There's more...

To make things complete, we need to explore calling a library coded in C# from Clojure. This is very similar to calling a regular .NET namespace, but it is nice to be in charge of both sides of the code. So, let's say you have coded a fantastic library in Visual Studio after creating a new Library project:

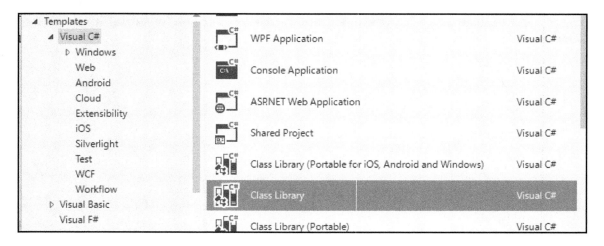

The code may look a bit…hmm…insipid, at this stage, but it will be your task to spice it up later. Here we go with a simple `compute` function that returns the value of an input plus 1:

```
namespace ClassLibrary1
{
    public class Class1
    {
        public int compute(int a)
        {
            return a + 1;
        }
    }
}
```

When you build the library from Visual Studio, or Xamarin for that matter, you will get a DLL file, which we can load with either `LoadWithPartialName`, if the path can be guessed by the runtime, or `LoadFrom`, to specify the full path to the DLL:

```
; (System.Reflection.Assembly/LoadWithPartialName "ClassLibrary1")
(System.Reflection.Assembly/LoadFrom "ClassLibrary1.dll")
```

In Clojure code, we can reference the code through an `import` call, specifying both the namespace and the Class we want to load:

```
(ns hello-clr2.core
    (:import [ClassLibrary1 Class1])
    (:gen-class)
    )
```

Finally, we can make use of the C# `compute` function you wrote previously:

```
(defn -main
  [& args]
  (println  (.compute (Class1.) (first args))))
```

A regular call to the main function either through `lein` or directly through a compiled EXE file will do it!

```
lein clr run -m hello-clr2.core 10
; 11
```

The next step for .NET integration is to fly the skies and be able to script the Unity engine with Clojure and...guess what! The `arcadia` project has this in store for you! Go and have some fun.

ClojureScript

ClojureScript is Clojure targeted at running on the JVM. While it might sound like yet another platform to run Clojure on, this one actually exposes your code to a quite tremendously larger audience and proposes to clean up some parts of the spaghetti code. Since this is not a book on ClojureScript, the goal of this recipe is to get you into your ClojureScript adventure so that you can feel at ease and start producing clean Clojure for the JVM.

Getting ready

While there are a few Leiningen templates out there to get you ready in no time, we will actually look at how to get ready from scratch. So, nothing is required up front apart from your usual command line `lein` client.

In an empty folder of your choice, start by creating a new `project.clj` file with the following content:

```
(defproject cljs-one "0.1.0-SNAPSHOT"
  :dependencies [[org.clojure/clojure "1.8.0"]
                 [org.clojure/clojurescript "1.7.228"]]
  :plugins [[lein-cljsbuild "1.1.2"]]
  :cljsbuild {
    :builds [{:source-paths ["src"]
              :compiler {
                :output-to "out/one.js"
```

```
                :output-dir "out"}}]})
```

You will notice that we have added a dependency on ClojureScript itself and one other oddity, the `cljsbuild` plugin for Leiningen. The plugin will help you compile Clojure code to JavaScript. For this to work, the ClojureScript compiler needs a few details contained in the `:cljsbuild:builds` section of the `project.clj` file:

```
{:source-paths ["src"]
 :compiler {
   :output-to "out/one.js"
   :output-dir "out"}}
```

What we are telling the compiler here is that the ClojureScript files are located in the `src` folder, that the compiled file should be `out/one.js`, and that, finally, other compiled files should be going to the `out` folder.

This is pretty much it, so let's create a `src/core.cljs` file and add some familiar-looking Clojure code in it:

```
(ns core)
(enable-console-print!)
(println "I'm home!")
```

The `enable-console-print` function allows to bind the printing function to the JavaScript console object. So, you can expect the preceding code to print a nice welcoming message on the developer console of your favorite browser. Project and source code are now ready, so on the command line you will now tell the ClojureScript plugin to compile the code, according to the rules we have set in `project.clj`, and the once parameter tells the compiler to compile only once, and then exit:

```
lein cljsbuild once

; Compiling ClojureScript...
; Compiling "out/one.js" from ["src"]...
; WARNING: core is a single segment namespace at line 1 src/core.cljs
; Successfully compiled "out/one.js" in 1.682 seconds.
```

Now that was great, but we would love to actually see the results of this. Usually, to run JavaScript, you have probably used something called HTML, which would load your JavaScript code as needed. ClojureScript relies on Google's **Closure** (yes that is a *s*), to load code according, among other things, to their namespace definition. So in an `index.html` at the root of your project folder, write the following code:

```
<html>
    <body>
        <script src="out/goog/base.js" type="text/javascript"></script>
```

```
        <script src="out/one.js" type="text/javascript"></script>
        <script type="text/javascript">goog.require("core");</script>
    </body>
</html>
```

The first HTML import script directive tells the page to load the Closure library. The second script import directive tells the page to load our compiled code. And, finally, the third script directive requires the code, meaning to load it, and since we did not create a function but just pure code, this will effectively, and finally, run the code you wrote previously.

That's it, you can now go and open the index.html page in anything but **Internet Explorer (IE)**. Just teasing, even IE will do.

How to do it...

Now that you have the basics on your local machine, from here this is going to be a road to JavaScript freedom.

Autocompiling your code

Instead of have to run the `cljsbuild once` command each time, there is actually a second mode for the `cljsbuild` plugin. And, yes, you have guessed it, it is called `auto`:

```
lein cljsbuild auto
```

With the preceding command, any change to the `core.cljs` file will trigger a new compilation of your code. In the ClojureScript file, let's update the Clojure code with the following code:

```
(ns core)
(enable-console-print!)

(time
  (sort
    (reverse
      (range 10 100))))
```

The first two lines are identical, but now we use the `time` macro to evaluate a function and print the time it took to perform the evaluation. On saving the file, the `auto` mode of the plugin will detect the changes, and the console where Leiningen is running will show a nice message:

```
Compiling "out/one.js" from ["src"]...
```

You can then reload the HTML page and see that the console has a new message printed from the Clojure code you wrote previously:

```
"Elapsed time: 1.305000 msecs"
```

Fibonacci'ed

It would not be fun if we did not try to run standard Clojure code here, would it? In the same `core.cljs`, let's add an untouched Clojure-based version of Fibonacci:

```
(def fib-seq
  ((fn rfib [a b]
     (lazy-seq (cons a (rfib b (+ a b)))))
   0 1))
(prn (take 20 fib-seq))
; in the console ..
; (0 1 1 2 3 5 8 13 21 34 55 89 144 233 377 610 987 1597 2584 4181)
```

How it works...

That was a pretty smooth ride up to now, but we have not tried to interact with standard JavaScript code ourselves yet, so let's do it now!

Interacting with JavaScript

To interact with JavaScript, ClojureScript exposes the window object as the reference `js`. Let's try it with the ever-fashionable `alert` dialog box:

```
(js/alert "I'm home!")
```

Provided that the Leiningen `cljsbuild` command is still running, reloading the HTML page will bring you the familiar:

Using jQuery from ClojureScript

So let's say you want to convert some jQuery code to ClojureScript. Since we have the `js` element available to us, we should be able to do that more or less smoothly. A standard jQuery `div` toggling example could look the following:

```
$(document.body).click(function () {
  if ($("div:first").is(":hidden")) {
    $("div").slideDown("slow");
  } else {
    $("div").hide();
  }
});
```

In the preceding code, we show and hide `div` elements based on clicks on the HTML body element. First, of all, let's add the script `import` directive in the HTML file as usual:

```
<script src="http://ajax.aspnetcdn.com/ajax/jQuery/jquery-2.2.0.min.js"
type="text/javascript"></script>
```

Actually, before converting the whole piece of code together, let's simply try to grab mouse clicks and print some messages. So, this would be the following jQuery part:

```
$(document.body).click(function () {
  ..
}
```

The print click function we define as follows, in standard Clojure code:

```
(defn click-fn[]
    (println "Clicked!"))
```

Now that you have the handler, let's react on mouse clicks. The DOM element we are targeting is body. We access the JavaScript exposed jQuery object from ClojureScript via js/jQuery and we call it with the parameter "body":

```
(js/jQuery "body")
```

We have the body element as a jQuery object, so let's use the click function. In usual Clojure interop, the .click dispatching can be used:

```
(.click
    (js/jQuery "body")
    click-fn)
```

Suppose you have some text in the index.html page, say:

```
<body>
Click me!
...
</body>
```

That's right, now is the time to show some mouse-clicking power !! And yes, the message shows up, as shown in the following screenshot:

Now the full ClojureScript version of the preceding jQuery code becomes easy to write. Let's create a new callback function click-slide-fn:

```
(defn click-slide-fn[]
    (if (.is (js/jQuery "div:first") ":hidden")
        (.slideDown (js/jQuery "div") "slow")
        (.hide (js/jQuery "div"))))
```

And let's replace the code handling the click with the new callback:

```
(.click
    (js/jQuery "body")
    click-slide-fn)
```

To check the `div` are playing with us nicely, let's add some colors and some `div` elements, the whole HTML page looks like this:

```
<html>
<head>
  <style>
    div {
        background:#ccff55; margin:3px; width:80px;
        height:40px; display:none; float:left;
    }
  </style>
</head>
<body>
  Click me!
  <div></div>
  <div></div>
  <div></div>
  <script src="http://ajax.aspnetcdn.com/ajax/jQuery/jquery-2.2.0.min.js"
type="text/javascript"></script>
  <script src="out/goog/base.js" type="text/javascript"></script>
  <script src="out/one.js" type="text/javascript"></script>
  <script type="text/javascript">goog.require("core");</script>
</body>
```

Note that if we want to make it look like a bit more jQuery-like, we can bind the js/jQuery object to the dollar sign again:

```
(def $ js/jQuery)

(defn click-slide-fn[]
    (if (.is ($ "div:first") ":hidden")
        (. ($ "div") slideDown "slow")
        (. ($ "div") hide)))
(.click
    ($ "body")
    click-slide-fn)
```

Wow. That was fun.

Creating a ClojureScript library

ClojureScript libraries can also be packaged as JAR files. This is actually entirely similar to standard Clojure, so a regular Leiningen `jar` command would do it. Let's try it in our current JavaScript project:

```
lein jar
```

And we can simply check the content:

```
~/D/c/C/c/s/cljs-three >>> jar tvf target/cljs-two-0.1.0-SNAPSHOT.jar
   117 Wed Feb 10 13:50:28 JST 2016 META-INF/MANIFEST.MF
  1895 Wed Feb 10 13:50:28 JST 2016 META-INF/maven/cljs-two/cljs-
two/pom.xml
   401 Wed Feb 10 13:50:28 JST 2016 META-INF/leiningen/cljs-two/cljs-
two/project.clj
   401 Wed Feb 10 13:50:28 JST 2016 project.clj
   ...
   428 Wed Feb 10 13:42:24 JST 2016 core.cljs
```

Locally, we will actually use the `install` command to make the library available to other projects:

```
lein install
; Installed jar and pom into local repo.
```

In `project.clj`, you can now add a dependency on the newly created library, the usual Clojure way:

```
[cljs-two "0.1.0-SNAPSHOT"]
```

And, in a new ClojureScript file, you can reference the previous library ClojureScript code, just as if it was here:

```
(ns core2
    (:require [core]))


(def $ js/jQuery)

(.click
    ($ "body")
    core/click-slide-fn)
```

And it still clicks!

Using a third-party library

This small section will be a simple follow-up to using third-party ClojureScript libraries. Here we want to try the ClojureScript money library, a library that helps you play with Canvas. Your `project.clj` will contain an added reference to a release number:

```
[rm-hull/monet "0.2.2"]
```

Now you can make use of the money namespaces, just as we have seen previously:

```
(ns core
  (:require [monet.canvas :as canvas]))
(def canvas-dom
    (.getElementById js/document "canvas"))
(def monet-canvas
    (canvas/init canvas-dom "2d"))
(canvas/add-entity monet-canvas :background
 (canvas/entity {:x 0 :y 0 :w 600 :h 600}
  nil
  (fn [ctx val]
    (-> ctx
        (canvas/fill-style "#ccff55")
        (canvas/fill-rect val)))))
```

There's more...

Wouldn't it be nice if you could connect to the ClojureScript REPL and play with it in real time? This is where we can use the ClojureScript REPL available with the `cljsbuild` plugin!

Running in the REPL

To achieve a connection, we will ask the ClojureScript code to explicitly open a socket connection to our soon to come REPL. The browser REPL is part of ClojureScript and can be called as shown in the following:

```
(ns core
    (:require
        [clojure.browser.repl :as repl]))

(repl/connect "http://localhost:9000/repl")
```

To be able to open connections from the browser to the outside world, or here, the REPL, you need to be actually in hosted mode. In the `project.clj` file, we will add a plugin to host the local directory, especially the `index.html` page. The plugins section should now look like the following:

```
:plugins [
        [lein-cljsbuild "1.1.2"]
      [lein-simpleton "1.3.0"]
      ]
```

Simply start hosting files on port `8000`, with the following command:

lein simpleton 8000

Last step now, the command to start the ClojureScript REPL is as follows:

lein trampoline cljsbuild repl-listen

Connecting to the REPL socket is done by opening the `index.html` page at `http://localhost:8000/index.html`. You will have a nice familiar prompt available for you:

```
cljs.user=> (js/alert "Connected to the REPL!")
```

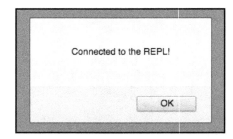

And yes! This is live and connected to the browser. You can send code and it will compile code on-the-fly from ClojureScript to JavaScript and will be executed on the browser VM.

What a journey!

Compiling code for both Clojure and ClojureScript

To finish this recipe properly, we will show how to simply call Clojure code from ClojureScript, and the very good news today is, close to nothing. See for yourself! We will write the Fibonacci code we had earlier in a regular Clojure file:

```
(ns example.shared)
(def fib-seq
  ((fn rfib [a b]
     (lazy-seq (cons a (rfib b (+ a b)))))
   0 1))
```

The ClojureScript file will reference this later on, so your new code can simply reference the Clojure code:

```
(ns example.hello
  (:require
    [example.shared :as shared]))
(js/alert (take 5 shared/fib-seq))
```

To compile all this, just make sure you have separate folders for ClojureScript files and regular Clojure files. This is done in `project.clj` by adding where the Clojure files are located:

```
:source-paths ["src-clj"]
```

And telling the ClojureScript compiler where the `cljs` file are:

```
:builds {
    :dev
    {:source-paths ["src-cljs"]
     :compiler {:output-to "out/seven.js"
                :output-dir "out"
                :optimizations :none}}}
```

Et voila. All your Clojure-based algorithms can be reused for the web! Now it's your turn to go and explore.

6
Concurrency and Parallelism

In this chapter, we will cover the following topics:

- Solving concurrent problems using Clojure
- Distributed actor-based dev with Akka
- Using Spyglass and Couchbase to share state between JVMs
- Reactive programming with meltdown
- Bridging core.async
- On Quasar/Pulsar

Introduction

In this chapter, we will learn about the concurrency and parallelism that Clojure provides. First, we will take a look at concurrency and parallelism features. Next, we will try to use Scala's Akka library and Spyglass. Then we will learn Quasar/Pulsar, which are fibers, channels, and actors for Clojure and Java used in Netflix. Finally, we will have a look at meltdown, a nice Clojure wrapper for Reactor, which is a toolkit for asynchronous programming, event passing, and stream processing.

Solving concurrent problems using Clojure

In this recipe, we will learn Clojure's atoms, refs, and agents. Then we will have a look at Clojure's parallel features.

Getting ready

In this recipe, we will not use an external library. So, the only necessary thing is to start REPL to run code.

How to do it...

Clojure provides solutions for the concurrency problem. Clojure's vars defined in `def` are ensured only in single thread and are not safe in concurrent environments. Clojure provides three types of resources for concurrent problem. Here, we will introduce you atoms, refs, and agents that work in concurrent environments.

Using atoms

Atoms provide a way to manage shared, synchronous, and independent states.

Creating and referring atom

The `atom` function sets the initial value to atom. The following code initializes the atom to `1` and sets the atom to the var `x`:

```
(def x (atom 1))
;;=? #'chapter06.concurrency/x
```

So, the value of `x` binds to `Atom` instance:

```
x
;;=> #<Atom@541e8f8d: 1>
```

To see the values of the atoms, use the `deref` macro or the reader macro @:

```
(deref x)
;;=> 1
@x
;;=> 1
```

Updating atom

There are a couple of ways to update atoms. The `swap` atomically applies a function to the original value and sets the atom to it:

```
(swap! x inc)
;;=> 2
@x
;;=> 2
(swap! x (partial + 1))
;;=> 3
```

The following image shows how the atom value changes by `swap`:

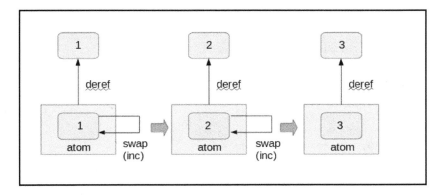

The `reset!` function sets the value of atom regardless of the current value of atom:

```
(reset! x 1)
;;=> 1
x
;;=> #<Atom@541e8f8d: 1>
```

Using validator

There is a validation mechanism for atom. Atom's validators check values of atoms. The following code checks the atom value should be less than 5:

```
(def y (atom 1 :validator (partial > 5)))
;;=> #'chapter06.concurrency/y
(swap! y (partial + 2))
;;=> 3
(swap! y (partial + 2))
;;=> IllegalStateException Invalid reference state
clojure.lang.ARef.validate (ARef.java:33)
```

Using CAS operation

Compare-and-swap (**CAS**) is an atomic instruction used in concurrent environments and achieves synchronization between race conditions. In Clojure, the `compare-and-set!` function updates the value of the `new-value` atom if the current value of the atom equals the `old-value`. The syntax is as follows:

```
(compare-and-set! atom old-value new-value)
```

The next function we define gets the current value of the atom, sleeps for the interval, and updates the value of atom using the `compare-and-set!`:

```
(defn cas-test! [my-atom interval]
  (let [v @my-atom u (inc @my-atom)]
    (println "current value = " v ", updated value = " u)
    (Thread/sleep interval)
    (println "updated " (compare-and-set! my-atom v u))))
;;=> #'chapter06.concurrency/cas-test!
```

Let's define an atom and see how `compare-and-set!` works:

```
(def x (atom 1))
;;=> #'chapter06.concurrency/x
```

The following test code updates twice by CAS operations, but both updates are successful since two updates occur sequentially and no race condition occurs:

```
(do
  (cas-test! x 20)
  (cas-test! x 30))
;;=> current value =  1 , updated value =  2
;;=> updated  true
;;=> current value =  2 , updated value =  3
;;=> updated  true
```

The following diagram depicts how two updates change the value of x:

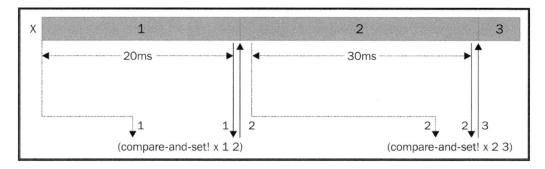

In the following code, concurrent updates cause a race condition, and the later update fails since the original value has been updated by the other:

```
(do
  (def x (atom 1))
  (future (cas-test! x 20))
  (future (cas-test! x 30)))
;;=> current value =  1 , updated value =  2
;;=> current value =  1 , updated value =  2
;;=> updated   true
;;=> updated   false
```

In the following diagram, two updates make a race condition, and the later update fails because the earlier update changes the value of the x:

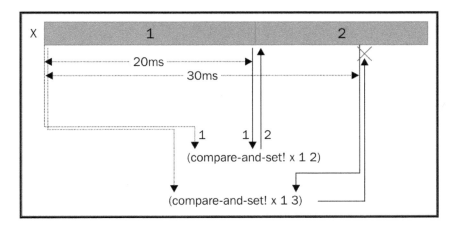

Software Transactional Memory using ref and dosync

Software Transactional Memory (STM) provides transactional accesses to multiple resources on memory. STM coordinates multiple resources in a transaction and provides consistency, atomicity, and isolation. Inside dosync, resources defined by ref are coordinated.

Let's look at how STM works in Clojure. In the following example code, we use the ref, dosync, and alter functions for STM transactions.

Creating ref

The ref function creates a ref with an initial value. makoto-account and nico-account exist. They are credit balances for two customers. The ref function creates a ref, whose value is a map:

```
(def makoto-account (ref {:name "Makoto Hashimoto" :amount 1000}))
;;=> #'chapter06.concurrency/makoto-account
(def nico-account (ref {:name "Nicolas Modrzyk" :amount 2000}))
;;=> #'chapter06.concurrency/nico-account
```

Updating refs using alter

Then, the following transfer! function executes a transaction moving the amount of money between the from account and the to account:

```
(defn transfer! [from to amount]
  (dosync
    (println "transfer money from " (:name @from) " to " (:name @to) "
amount = " amount " begins")
    (alter from assoc :amount (- (:amount @from) amount))
    (Thread/sleep 500)
    (alter to assoc :amount (+ (:amount @to) amount))
    (println "Now, " (:name @from) " amount is  " (:amount @from) " and "
(:name @to) " amount is " (:amount @to))
    ))
;;=> #'chapter06.concurrency/transfer!
```

There are a couple of alter calls inside the dosync in the transfer! function that form a transaction. Let's test to transfer 10 dollars from Makoto to Nicolas:

```
(transfer! makoto-account  nico-account 10)
;;=> transfer money from  Makoto  to  Nicolas  amount =  10  begins
::=> Now,  Makoto  amount is  990  and  Nicolas  amount is  2010
;;=> nil
```

```
@nico-account
;;=> {:name "Nicolas Modrzyk", :amount 2010}
(deref makoto-account)
;;=> {:name "Makoto Hashimoto", :amount 990}
```

Great! It works correctly.

Then, let's run two transactions concurrently and see how they work. The first transaction transfers 200 dollars from Makoto to Nico and the second transaction transfers 300 dollars in the same direction:

```
(do
    (future
        (transfer! makoto-account nico-account 200))
    (future
        (transfer!  makoto-account nico-account 300)))
;;=> transfer money from  Makoto Hashimoto  to  Nicolas Modrzyk  amount =
200  begins
;;=> #<Future@473dad05: :pending>
;;=> transfer money from  Makoto Hashimoto  to  Nicolas Modrzyk  amount =
300  begins
;;=> transfer money from  Makoto Hashimoto  to  Nicolas Modrzyk  amount =
300  begins
;;=> transfer money from  Makoto Hashimoto  to  Nicolas Modrzyk  amount =
300  begins
;;=> transfer money from  Makoto Hashimoto  to  Nicolas Modrzyk  amount =
300  begins
;;=> transfer money from  Makoto Hashimoto  to  Nicolas Modrzyk  amount =
300  begins
;;=> Now,  Makoto Hashimoto  amount is  790  and  Nicolas Modrzyk  amount
is  2210
;;=> transfer money from  Makoto Hashimoto  to  Nicolas Modrzyk  amount =
300  begins
;;=> Now,  Makoto Hashimoto  amount is  490  and  Nicolas Modrzyk  amount
is  2510
```

The second transaction waits for the completion of the first one. The second transaction tries to update the same `ref` but fails five times because the update of the same `ref` is blocked by the first `transfer!` After the completion of the first transaction, the second transaction performs updates successfully.

Using ensure

The `ensure` function protects refs from trying to update while a preceding update is in progress. In the following code, the `ensure-transfer!` function adds `ensure` to `transfer`:

```
(defn ensure-transfer! [from to amount]
  (dosync
    (ensure from)
    (println "transfer money from " (:name @from)
             " to " (:name @to) " amount = " amount " begins")
    (alter from assoc :amount (- (:amount @from) amount))
    (Thread/sleep 500)
    (alter to assoc :amount (+ (:amount @to) amount))
    (println "Now, " (:name @from) " amount is  " (:amount @from)
             " and " (:name @to) " amount is " (:amount @to))))
;;=> #'chapter06.concurrency/ensure-transfer!
```

Let's test the preceding code:

```
(do
    (future
      (ensure-transfer! nico-account makoto-account 100))
    (future
      (ensure-transfer! nico-account makoto-account 200)))
;;=> transfer money from  Nicolas Modrzyk  to  Makoto Hashimoto  amount =
100  begins
;;=> Now,  Nicolas Modrzyk  amount is  2410  and  Makoto Hashimoto  amount
is  590
;;=> transfer money from Nicolas Modrzyk  to  Makoto Hashimoto  amount =
200  begins
;;=> Now,  Nicolas Modrzyk  amount is  2210  and  Makoto Hashimoto  amount
is  790
```

The subsequent transaction does not try to update until the proceeding transaction has completed.

Using watcher and a refined transaction code

Using watcher traces modifications of refs. We will look at how it works. The following `add-watcher` function adds a watcher for a `ref`:

```
(defn add-watcher [ref]
  (add-watch ref :watcher
             (fn [_ _ old-state new-state]
               (prn "---- ref changed --- " old-state " => " new-state)
               )))
```

```
;;=> #'chapter06.concurrency/add-watcher
(add-watcher makoto-account)
;;=> #ref[{:status :ready, :val {:name "Makoto Hashimoto", :amount 1000}}
0x52f5973a]
(add-watcher nico-account)
;;=> #ref[{:status :ready, :val {:name "Nicolas Modrzyk", :amount 2000}}
0x7ecca962]
```

Then, we will refine the former `ensure-transfer!` function and change the name to `refined-transfer!`:

```
(defn refined-transfer! [from to amount]
  (dosync
   (ensure from)
   (if (<=  (- (:amount @from) amount) 0)
     (throw (Exception. "insufficient amount")))
   (alter from assoc :amount (- (:amount @from) amount))
   (Thread/sleep 500)
   (alter to assoc :amount (+ (:amount @to) amount))))
;;=> #'chapter06.concurrency/refined-transfer!
```

Let's set values of refs using `ref-set`:

```
(do
   (ref-set makoto-account {:name "Makoto Hashimoto" :amount 1000})
   (ref-set nico-account {:name "Nicolas Modrzyk" :amount 2000}))
;;=> IllegalStateException No transaction running
clojure.lang.LockingTransaction.getEx (LockingTransaction.java:208)
```

Oops! `ref_set` should be called inside `dosync`. Let's try again:

```
(dosync
   (ref-set makoto-account {:name "Makoto Hashimoto" :amount 1000})
   (ref-set nico-account {:name "Nicolas Modrzyk" :amount 2000})
   )
;;=> "---- ref changed --- " {:name "Nicolas Modrzyk", :amount 2000} " => "
{:name "Nicolas Modrzyk", :amount 2000}
;;=> "---- ref changed --- " {:name "Makoto Hashimoto", :amount 1000} " =>
" {:name "Makoto Hashimoto", :amount 1000}
;;=> {:name "Nicolas Modrzyk", :amount 2000}
```

The updates are successful and the watcher detects the modifications and prints messages. Now, let's test the `refined-transfer!` function concurrently:

```
(do
    (future
       (refined-transfer! makoto-account nico-account 100))
    (future
```

```
        (refined-transfer! nico-account makoto-account 300))
    )
;;=> #<Future@4c041c9: :pending>
;;=> "---- ref changed --- " {:name "Nicolas Modrzyk", :amount 2000} " => "
{:name "Nicolas Modrzyk", :amount 2100}
;;=> "---- ref changed --- " {:name "Makoto Hashimoto", :amount 1000} " =>
" {:name "Makoto Hashimoto", :amount 900}
;;=> "---- ref changed --- " {:name "Nicolas Modrzyk", :amount 2100} " => "
{:name "Nicolas Modrzyk", :amount 1800}
;;=> "---- ref changed --- " {:name "Makoto Hashimoto", :amount 900} " => "
{:name "Makoto Hashimoto", :amount 1200}
```

It works fine!

Let's check in the `refined-transfer!` whether the control that the balance must not be negative works correctly. The following expression moves 1,500 dollars from Makoto to Nico but Makoto's balance is 1,200 dollars:

```
(refined-transfer! makoto-account nico-account 1500)
;;=> Exception insufficient bound   chapter06.concurrency/transfer!/fn-
-20708 (form-init8938610057865502322.clj:87)
```

Using commute

Let's look at another example using STM. The following function starts a transaction, sleeps 500 ms, and adds value to the `ref` variable:

```
(defn alter-add! [var val]
  (dosync
   (Thread/sleep 500)
   (alter var  (partial + val))))
;;=> #'chapter06.concurrency/alter-add!
```

Let's run five threads concurrently and measure how long it takes to finish all updates using the `future` calls:

```
(do
  (def v1 (ref 10))
  (time
   (doseq
     [x [
         (future (alter-add! v1 10))
         (future (alter-add! v1 10))
         (future (alter-add! v1 10))
         (future (alter-add! v1 10))
         (future (alter-add! v1 10))
         ]]
```

```
     (@x))
  (println @v1)
  )
;;=> "Elapsed time: 2504.52562 msecs"
;;=> 60
;;=> nil
```

In the preceding code, using the `alter` in the `dosync` blocks other access to the same ref. So, it takes 500 ms * 5 = 2.5 sec to finish. Let's look at the same update using the `commute`. The `commute-add!` uses `commute` instead of `alter`.

The `commute` is a function that updates refs inside `dosync` similar to `alter`. The difference is that commit using `alter` is in order, whereas commit using `commute` is out of order. `alter` checks the current (updated) value and committing value. If they are the same, the commit takes place. Otherwise there is no committing action and retries. `commute` does not check the difference when commit takes place. So, let's try the `commute` version as follows:

```
(defn commute-add! [var val]
  (dosync
    (Thread/sleep 500)
    (commute var  (partial + val))))
;;=> #'chapter06.concurrency/commute-add!
```

We will measure the performance of updates using `commute`:

```
(do
  (def v1 (ref 10))
  (time
    (doseq
        [x [(future (commute-add! v1 10))
            (future (commute-add! v1 10))
            (future (commute-add! v1 10))
            (future (commute-add! v1 10))
            (future (commute-add! v1 10))]]
      (@x))
  (println @v1)
  )
;;=> "Elapsed time: 503.967362 msecs"
;;=> 60
```

The `commute` version is faster than `alter` and runs on a highly concurrent environment, but the update operation should be commutative.

Using agents

Agents mutate states asynchronously. Here, we will learn how to create agents and update their values.

Creating agents

To create an agent, we will use `agent` with an initial value. We will define `simple-agent`, whose state is zero and is going to be updated asynchronously:

```
(def simple-agent (agent 0))
;;=> #'chapter06.concurrency/simple-agent
simple-agent
;;=> #agent[{:status :ready, :val 0} 0x3aa1d3cc]
```

Updating agents

To update the existing agents, use `send` with an update function. The following example shows updating `simple-agent` with `inc` and the result of the agent value will be 1:

```
(send simple-agent inc)
;;=> #agent[{:status :ready, :val 0} 0x3aa1d3cc]
@simple-agent
;;=> 1
```

Let's see the next example where the agent expresses the name and location:

```
(def makoto-agent (agent {:name "Makoto" :location [100 200]}))
;;=> #'chapter06.concurrency/makoto-agent
```

The `move` function moves `dx` and `dy` and takes `t` ms:

```
(defn move [a dx dy t]
  (println "moving takes " t "msecs")
  (Thread/sleep t)
  (assoc a :location
         [(+ ((:location a) 0) dx)
          (+ ((:location a) 1) dy)]))
;;=> #'chapter06.concurrency/move

(do
  (send makoto-agent move 10 20 1000)
  (println makoto-agent)
  (await makoto-agent)
  (println makoto-agent))
;;=> moving takes  1000 msecs
```

```
;;=> #agent[{:status :ready, :val {:name Makoto, :location [100 200]}}
0x34a8e8f]
;;=> #agent[{:status :ready, :val {:name Makoto, :location [110 220]}}
0x34a8e8f]
```

How it works...

Here, we will summarize three reference types, STM and `alter/commute`.

Summary of three reference types in Clojure

Concurrent operations can be classified as coordinated/uncoordinated and synchronous/asynchronous.

Coordinated/uncoordinated

A coordinated operation keeps consistency between multiple resources. We previously saw an example of transferring money between accounts. That requires a coordinated operation. On the other hand, an uncoordinated operation only keeps the consistency for a single resource.

Synchronous/asynchronous

A synchronous operation waits for its execution. An asynchronous operation only fires execution and does not wait.

We summarize these three reference types in the following table:

Left align	Coordinated	Uncoordinated
Synchronous	Refs	Atoms
Asynchronous	—	Agents

How STM works in Clojure

STM supports concurrent access to shared resources. STM does not use a lock-based synchronization. Instead, it uses **Multiversion of Concurrency Control** (**MVCC**) for solving concurrent updates to shared resources.

Using MVCC, each transaction has a private copy of the state and checks whether the state is not updated by another transaction. If there is no update by another transaction, the transaction commits, otherwise that transaction rolls back and retries.

Traditional transactions of a database mechanism have the property of **ACID** (**Atomicity, Consistency, Isolation, and Durability**). However, since STM does not persist states, it does not have the Durability characteristic.

Alter and commute

The `commute` is faster than the `alter` when the order of updates does not matter. It makes no difference to when concurrent processes update a counter, the result is the same. You can use `commute` in such cases.

There's more...

We will show functions related to parallelism here. Let's start with `promise` and `deliver`.

promise and deliver

`promise` delays it's execution until `deliver` sets it value. Let see a simple example. There are x, y, and z defined by `promise`:

```
(def x (promise))
;;=> #'chapter06.concurrency/x
(def y (promise))
;;=> #'chapter06.concurrency/y
(def z (promise))
;;=> #'chapter06.concurrency/z
```

In the following code, the thread is waiting for realizations of x and y by `deliver`:

```
(future
  (do (deliver z (+ @x @y))
      (println "z value : " @z)))
```

The var z is not still realized:

```
(realized? z)
;;=> false
```

Then we will realize x and y by `deliver`:

```
(deliver x 1)
;;=> #promise[{:status :ready, :val 1} 0x2f5df579]
```

```
(deliver y 1)
;;=> #promise[{:status :ready, :val 1} 0x1614985]
;;=> z value :   2
```

When both values of x and y are set, z is calculated, and thread created by `future` exits:

```
@z
;;=> 2
```

We will show you another example. We are assuming that multiple products are ready and a shipment instruction has occurred.

In the following code, the `Order` record has the `name`, `price`, and `qty` properties:

```
(defrecord Order [name price qty])
;; => chapter06.concurrency.Order
```

The `merge-products` function calculates a total price and merges product info as a vector:

```
(defn merge-products [m1 m2]
  {:total-price
   (+ (* (.price x) (.qty x)) (* (.price y) (.qty y)))}
  [m1 m2])
;; => #'chapter06.concurrency/merge-products
```

The `ship-products_ issues` function orders when two products are ready to ship:

```
(defn ship-products [x y z]
  (deliver z (merge-products @x @y))
  (println "We can ship products  " @z))
;; => #'chapter06.concurrency/ship-products
```

The `deliver-product` function notifies that the product is ready to ship with its price:

```
(defn deliver-product [p name price]
  (deliver p [name price]))
;; => #'chapter06.concurrency/deliver-product
```

Then we will define the `product-a`, `product-b`, and `shipping-ab` functions accordingly:

```
(def product-a (promise))
;; => #'chapter06.concurrency/product-a
(def product-b (promise))
;; => #'chapter06.concurrency/product-b
(def shipping-ab (promise))
;; => #'chapter06.concurrency/shipping-ab
```

Let's run the `ship-products` function, which waits for `product-a` and `product-b` to be ready:

```
(future (ship-products product-a product-b shipping-ab))
;; => #future[{:status :pending, :val nil} 0x347af059]
```

The `product-a` and `product-b` is ready to ship, the _ship-products calculates a total price and orders a shipment:

```
(deliver product-a (->Order "book" 10.1 5))
;; => #promise[{:status :ready, :val #chapter06.concurrency.Order{:name
"book", :price 10.1, :qty 5}} 0x1a198bfe]
(deliver product-b (->Order "pencil" 2.1 10))
;; => #promise[{:status :ready, :val #chapter06.concurrency.Order{:name
"pencil", :price 2.1, :qty 10}} 0x458b44f6]
;;=> We can ship products  [#chapter06.concurrency.Order{:name book, :price
10.1, :qty 5} #chapter06.concurrency.Order{:name pencil, :price 2.1, :qty
10}]
```

pmap, pcalls, and pvalues

Let's learn about `pmap`, `pcalls`, and `pvalues` here. All three functions are related to parallelism and use multicores. The `pmap` function is the multithreaded version of `map`. The `pcalls` and `pvalues` functions create, execute, and join multithreads easily.

The `pmap` function makes use of multicores effectively. It assigns threads per processing of an element. However, to assign too small a task to a thread causes overhead and is slower than the original `map`:

Let's study the performance aspect of `pmap`. In the following code, it calculates the volume of the cube from the length of the side:

```
(time (doall (map #(* % % %) (repeatedly 100 rand))))
;;=> "Elapsed time: 78.548941 msecs"
(time (doall (pmap #(* % % %) (repeatedly 100 rand))))
;;=> "Elapsed time: 184.195486 msecs"
```

For the preceding example, the original `map` is faster. Assuming that the calculation takes more time, `pmap` is faster:

```
(time (doall (map #(do (Thread/sleep 10) (* % % %)) (repeatedly 100
rand))))
;;=> "Elapsed time: 1012.360687 msecs"
(time (doall (pmap #(do (Thread/sleep 10) (* % % %)) (repeatedly 100
rand))))
```

```
;;=> "Elapsed time: 156.927029 msecs"
```

pcalls

pcalls executes functions in parallel and returns a lazy sequence of their values:

```
(pcalls fn-1 fn-2 fn-3 ...)
```

The following code calls a sum of 0 – 9999999 and 10000000 – 19999999 concurrently and waits for the results as a sequence:

```
(time
 (println
     (apply pcalls
            [(fn [] (reduce + (range 10000000)))
             (fn [] (reduce + (range 10000000 20000000)))
            ])))
;;=> (49999995000000 149999995000000)
;;=> "Elapsed time: 454.398538 msecs"
;;=> nil
```

pvalues

pvalues is a macro and returns a lazy sequence of the values of the expressions, which are evaluated in parallel:

```
(pvalues expr-1 expr-2 expr-3 ...)
```

The following code is an example usage of pvalues. It's similar to pcalls, but its arguments are expressions:

```
(time
 (println
  (let [fn1 (fn [num-list] (reduce + num-list))]
    (pvalues (fn1 (range 0 10000000)) (fn1 (range 10000000 20000000))))))
;;=> (49999995000000 149999995000000)
;;=> "Elapsed time: 578.047634 msecs"
;;=> nil
```

See also

Haskell also supports STM; for more information, refer to http://book.realworldhaskell.org/read/software-transactional-memory.html.

Distributed actor-based dev with Akka

Akka is a concurrent, distributed, and fault-tolerant framework and runtime environment developed by Lightbend (formerly Typesafe). It supports the actor model initially developed in Erlang. So, Akka is greatly inspired by Erlang's actor.

The following image shows collaborating tasks by sending messages among actors. Actors send messages via mail boxes. Receiving actors check their mail boxes and process them. Actors can organize hierarchies. Parent actors can request their subtasks to child actors:

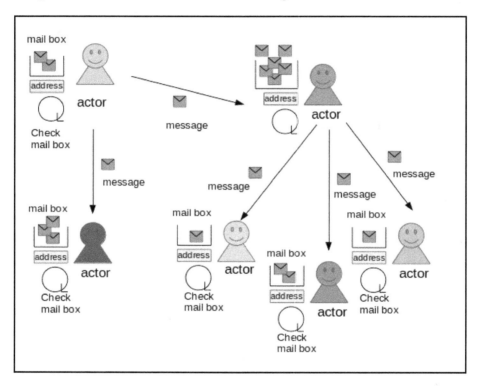

Akka itself is developed in Scala but it supports Java. We will use Okku, a Clojure wrapper for Akka.

Getting ready

The `okku` is a small wrapper for Akka. We need to add the `okku` to your `project.clj` file to run samples (or any other dependency management you are using):

```
:dependencies
  [[org.clojure/clojure "1.8.0"]
   [org.clojure.gaverhae/okku "0.1.5"]
```

How to do it...

Let's learn how to use Akka via `okku`!

Your first okku

Let's declare `okku.core` and some `akka` libraries to use:

```
(ns chapter06.akka
  (:require  [okku.core :as okku])
  (:import [akka.actor Actor Props]
           [akka.event.Logging]))
;;=> nil
```

`okku/actor-system` creates a new actor system with its name:

```
(def actor-system (okku/actor-system "actor-system-1"))
;;=> #'chapter06.akka/actor-system
```

Shutdown actor system as follows:

```
(.shutdown actor-system)
;;=> nil
```

Create an actor system with name, hostname, and port as follows:

```
(def actor-system (okku/actor-system "actor-system-1" :hostname "localhost"
:port 9999))
;;=> #'chapter06.akka/actor-system
```

Now, we will define `actor-1`, which receives a message and prints it, as follows:

```
(def actor-1
  (okku/spawn
   (okku/actor
    (okku/onReceive [m]
```

```
                            (println m)))
     :in actor-system :name "print-m"))
;;=> #'chapter06.akka/actor-1
```

The `tell` function sends a message to an actor:

```
(defn tell [actor message]
  (.tell actor message nil))
;;=> #'chapter06.akka/tell
```

Now, let's send a string message and make sure the actor receives a message:

```
(tell actor-1 "Hello Akka Actor !")
;;=> Hello Akka Actor !
;;=> nil
```

Then, we will send a map message:

```
(tell actor-1 {:name "Makoto" :country "Japan" :message "Hello !"})
;;=> {:name Makoto, :country Japan, :message Hello !}
;;=> nil
```

Creating actors

`okku/actor` creates `akka.actor.props`, and `okku/spawn` creates `Actor` objects using props. The following code generates the `props` object:

```
(def print-props
    (okku/actor
        (okku/onReceive [m]
                        (println m))))
;;=> #'chapter06.akka/print-props
```

`okku/spawn` creates actors using `props` as follows:

```
(def print-actor
  (okku/spawn
   print-props
   :in actor-system :name "print-actor3"))
;;=> #'chapter06.akka/print-actor
```

Then, send a message to `print-actor`:

```
(tell print-actor "hello !")
;;=> hello !
;;=> nil
```

Dispatching messages

okku has the `dispatch-on` function to dispatch messages with message types. The following `print-actor-by-key-props`:

```
(def print-actor-by-key-props
    (okku/actor
     (okku/onReceive [{type :type message :message}]
                     (okku/dispatch-on type
                                        :normal (println "message: "
message)
                                        :emergency (println "emagency !!!!
: " message)
                                        :else (println "unhandled
type")))))
;;=> #'chapter06.akka/print-actor-by-key-props
(def print-actor-by-key
  (okku/spawn print-actor-by-key-props
              :in actor-system
              :name "print-actor-by-key")
  )
;;=> #'chapter06.akka/print-actor-by-key
```

Let's send two types of messages!

```
(tell print-actor-by-key {:type :normal :message "I'm very happy !"})
;;=> message: I'm very happy !
;;=> nil
(tell print-actor-by-key {:type :emergency :message "I don't have money.
Please give me some !"})
;;=> emergency !!!! :  I don't have money. Please give me some !
;;=> nil
```

The following is another example of dispatch on classes:

```
(def print-actor-by-type-props
    (okku/actor
     (okku/onReceive [message]
                     (okku/dispatch-on (class message)
                                        clojure.lang.PersistentVector
(println "vector => "message)
                                        clojure.lang.PersistentArrayMap
(println "array-map => "message)
clojure.lang.PersistentHashMap (println "hash-map => "message)
                                        :else (println "unhandled type")
                                        ))))
;;=> #'chapter06.akka/print-actor-by-type-props
(def print-actor-by-type
```

```
    (okku/spawn print-actor-by-type-props
                :in actor-system
                :name "print-actor-by-type")
    )
;;=> #'chapter06.akka/print-actor-by-type
```

Let's test the preceding code:

```
(tell print-actor-by-type [1 2 3])
;;=> vector =>  [1 2 3]
;;=> nil
(tell print-actor-by-type {:a 1 :b 2})
;;=> array-map =>  {:a 1, :b 2}
;;=> nil
(tell print-actor-by-type {:v1 1 :v2 2 :v3 3 :v4 4 :v5 5 :v6 6 :v7 7 :v8 8
:v9 9})
;;=> hash-map =>  {:v1 1, :v2 2, :v3 3, :v4 4, :v5 5, :v6 6, :v7 7, :v8 8,
:v9 9}
;;=> nil
```

How it works...

We will explain actor systems and actors in okku.

Actor system

Actor systems are entry points for actors and manage actors. We can create actors from actor systems. We defined actor-system in the preceding section. Let's see the definition as follows:

```
actor-system
;;=> #object[akka.actor.ActorSystemImpl 0x59236b90 "akka://actor-system-1"]
(class actor-system)
;;=> akka.actor.ActorSystemImpl
```

Okku's actor system is akka.actor.ActorSystemImpl, which is a subclass of akka.actor.ActorSystem, as shown in the following image:

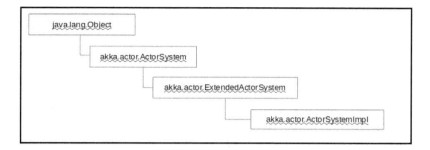

Actor systems have their addresses. The address of our actor system is `akka://actor-system-1`.

Understanding actors

Actors have internal states similar to objects in object-oriented systems. However, actors don't have public methods. Instead, actors communicate via mail boxes. Actors usually process messages asynchronously. By default, they process messages in the order of their arrival but it can process different orders using priorities.

Actors sometimes delegate their tasks to child actors. Parent actors generate children and they request subtasks to their child actors. This workflow is explained in the following illustration:

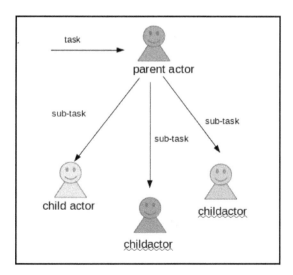

Okku's actor `akka.actor.RepointableActorRef` is created by `okku/spawn__`:

```
print-actor
;;=> #object[akka.actor.RepointableActorRef 0x186dd109 "Actor[akka://actor-
system-1/user/print-actor#-652953659]"]
(class print-actor)
;;=> akka.actor.RepointableActorRef
```

Actors are created under an actor system. In the preceding example, `print_actor` is created as follows:

```
akka://actor-system-1/user/print-actor.
```

There's more…

We will learn an advanced usage for Okku in this recipe.

Calling remote actors

Here, we will show you how to communicate with remote actors. We will create a new `akka` project named `akka-service` and will define `hello-actor` under `actor-system-1`:

$ lein new akka-service

Go to the `akka-service_` directory and modify `_project.clj` as follows:

```
:dependencies [
               [org.clojure/clojure "1.8.0"]
               [org.clojure.gaverhae/okku "0.1.5"]
               ]
```

We have to add the `main:` section as follows:

```
:main akka-service.core
```

Modify `src/akka-service/core.clj` as follows and save it:

```
(ns akka-service.core
  (:require [okku.core :as okku]))
(def actor-system (okku/actor-system "actor-system-1"
                                     :hostname "localhost" :port 2552))
(defn -main [& args]
  (println "launching akka service ...")
  (okku/spawn
```

```
(okku/actor
  (okku/onReceive [m]
                  (println m)))
  :in actor-system :name "hello-actor")
)
```

The following command runs actor system and actor on localhost, and the port number is 2552:

$ lein run

The following image shows the output of the preceding command:

```
                                     Terminal                                  - + x
$ lein run
Reflection warning, /tmp/form-init5972461126656481952.clj:1:902 - call to static method invokeStaticMethod on clojure.lang.Reflector can't
be resolved (argument types: unknown, java.lang.String, unknown).
Reflection warning, okku/core.clj:18:7 - call to akka.routing.RoundRobinRouter ctor can't be resolved.
Reflection warning, okku/core.clj:35:5 - call to method getConfig can't be resolved (target class is unknown).
Reflection warning, okku/core.clj:42:5 - call to method withFallback can't be resolved (target class is unknown).
Reflection warning, okku/core.clj:62:5 - call to static method load on com.typesafe.config.ConfigFactory can't be resolved (argument types:
 unknown).
Reflection warning, okku/core.clj:79:12 - call to static method ask on akka.pattern.Patterns can't be resolved (argument types: akka.actor.
ActorRef, unknown, unknown).
Reflection warning, okku/core.clj:79:6 - reference to field map can't be resolved.
Reflection warning, okku/core.clj:89:27 - call to static method create on scala.concurrent.duration.Duration can't be resolved (argument ty
pes: unknown, unknown).
Reflection warning, okku/core.clj:104:3 - call to method withRouter can't be resolved (target class is unknown).
Reflection warning, okku/core.clj:114:30 - call to akka.actor.Address ctor can't be resolved.
Reflection warning, okku/core.clj:115:30 - call to akka.actor.Address ctor can't be resolved.
Reflection warning, okku/core.clj:122:3 - call to method withDeploy can't be resolved (target class is unknown).
Reflection warning, okku/core.clj:159:47 - reference to field unwrapped on java.lang.Object can't be resolved.
Reflection warning, okku/core.clj:180:45 - reference to field settings on java.lang.Object can't be resolved.
Reflection warning, okku/core.clj:180:45 - reference to field config can't be resolved.
Reflection warning, okku/core.clj:180:45 - reference to field root can't be resolved.
Reflection warning, okku/core.clj:183:5 - call to method actorFor on java.lang.Object can't be resolved (no such method).
[INFO] [09/18/2016 20:39:09.899] [main] [Remoting] Starting remoting
[INFO] [09/18/2016 20:39:10.086] [main] [Remoting] Remoting started; listening on addresses :[akka.tcp://actor-system-1@localhost:2552]
[INFO] [09/18/2016 20:39:10.087] [main] [Remoting] Remoting now listens on addresses: [akka.tcp://actor-system-1@localhost:2552]
Reflection warning, akka service/core.clj:9:3 - call to method actorOf can't be resolved (target class is unknown).
launching akka service ...
```

Now, we will access the preceding actor system and actor from the different REPL. So, let's start another REPL as follows:

$ lein repl

Then, define namespace and load `okku` library. After that, create an actor system named `actor-system-2` and get the reference of the remote actor:

```
(ns okku-client.core
  (:require [okku.core :as okku]))
;;=> nil
(defn tell [actor message]
  (.tell actor message nil))
;;=> #'okku-client.core/tell
(def actor-system
  (okku/actor-system "actor-system-2" :hostname "localhost" :port 2553))
```

```
;;=> #'okku-client.core/actor-system
(def actor-ref (okku/look-up
        "akka.tcp://actor-system-1@localhost:2552/user/hello-actor"
          :in actor-system))
;;=> #'okku-client.core/actor-ref
```

The name of the remote actor system is `actor-system-1` and its port is `2552`. The path to the target actor is `/user/hello-actor/`.

Let's invoke the remote actor via the reference:

```
(tell actor-ref  "hello remote akka !")
;;=> nil
```

We can see the message in another REPL:

Request and reply

We will implement request/reply messages between actors. Since communications between actors are asynchronous, receivers should reply to messages explicitly using `okku.core/!`

Let's restart the actor system:

```
(.shutdown actor-system)
;;=> nil
(def actor-system (okku/actor-system "actor-system-1" :hostname
"localhost"))
;;=> #'chapter06.akka/actor-system
```

We will define `stock-service-requester` and `stock-service-requester-actor` to request the current stock price of the company. `declare` for `stock-service-actor` is necessary because it will be defined after the definition of `stock-service-requester`:

```
(declare stock-service-actor)
;;=> #'chapter06.akka/stock-service-actor
(def stock-service-requester
  (okku/actor
    (okku/onReceive [{t :type m :message}]
                    (okku/dispatch-on t
                                      :request
                                      (tell stock-service-actor m)
                                      :reply
                                      (do
                                        (println (str "price of "  (:company
m) " is " (:price m)))))))))
;;=> #'chapter06.akka/stock-service-requester
(def stock-service-requester-actor
  (okku/spawn
    stock-service-requester
    :in actor-system))
;;=> #'chapter06.akka/stock-service-requester-actor
```

Then, we will define `stock-service` and `stock-service-actor`:

```
(def stock-service
  (let [stocks {"google" 10.0 "amazon" 200.0 "facebook" 10.0 "twitter" 20.0
"inkedin"  5.0}]
    (okku/actor
      (okku/onReceive [{company :company}]
                      (okku/! stock-service-requester-actor
                              {:type :reply :message {:company company
:price (stocks company)}})))))
;;=> #'chapter06.akka/stock-service
(def stock-service-actor
  (okku/spawn
    stock-service
    :in actor-system))
;;=> #'chapter06.akka/stock-service-actor
```

The `stock-service` receives a company name and returns the corresponding price. Let's get stock prices for Google and Amazon as follows:

```
(tell stock-service-requester-actor {:type :request :message {:company
"google"}})
;;=> price of google is 10.0
;;=> nil
(tell stock-service-requester-actor {:type :request :message {:company
```

```
    "amazon"}})
;;=> price of amazon is 200.0
;;=> nil
```

The following image depicts the relationships between actors and how the messages are:

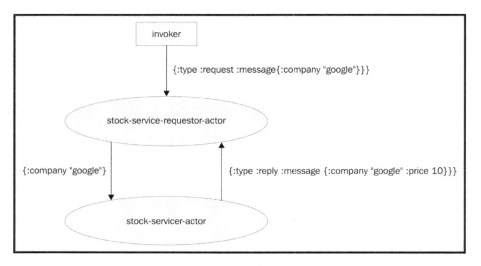

See also

Visit Akka home page at `http://akka.io/`.

Using Spyglass and Couchbase to share state between JVMs

Spyglass is a very fast Memcached client to share states between JVMs.

Spyglass is a future complete client to support almost all of the Memcached protocol operations, as well as binary and text protocols. Spyglass supports not only synchronous accesses to Memcached but also asynchronous accesses to it.

We will use a Couchbase Server as a Memcached server and access it using Spyglass.

Getting ready

Installing Couchbase and setting up Memcached takes several steps. We will instruct you how to do them.

Setting up dependencies in project.clj

You need to add the `spyglass` to your `project.clj` file to run samples (or any other dependency management you are using):

```
:dependencies
  [[org.clojure/clojure "1.8.0"]
   [clojurewerkz/spyglass "1.0.0"]]
```

Setting up Couchbase Server as a Memcached server

Couchbase Server is an awesome ultrascale document-oriented NoSQL Server. Couchbase Server can be set up as a Memcached server. We will set up Couchbase Server using `docker-compose`.

Using docker-compose to start Couchbase Server

We assume that Docker is already installed on your PC. Follow these simple steps to start Couchbase Server.

Creating a directory and a file for docker-compose

Let's create a `docker-compose` directory and `docker-compose.yaml` under it:

```
$ cd (your-directory)
$ mkdir docker-couchbase-41
$ cd docker-couchbase-41
```

Create and edit `docker-compose.yaml`:

```
couchbase1:
  image: arungupta/couchbase
  volumes:
    - /export/var/couchbase/node41-1:/opt/couchbase/var
couchbase2:
  image: arungupta/couchbase
  volumes:
```

```
      - /export/var/couchbase/node41-2:/opt/couchbase/var
couchbase3:
  image: arungupta/couchbase
  volumes:
      - /export/var/couchbase/node41-3:/opt/couchbase/var
  ports:
      - 8091:8091
      - 8092:8092
      - 8093:8093
      - 11210:11210
```

Start Couchbase cluster

The following command starts a three node Couchbase cluster using `docker-compose`:

```
$ docker-compose up -d
```

```
$ docker-compose up -d
Unable to find image 'docker/compose:1.5.0' locally
1.5.0: Pulling from docker/compose

f5f17db9ef7c: Pull complete
1a5d7604b84c: Pull complete
edb9562a1a85: Pull complete
83f27339e1ae: Pull complete
fe338db44539: Pull complete
fd10e3d2c1a4: Pull complete
a3ed95caeb02: Pull complete
Digest: sha256:146e95775e3e1a79e0e31632d3b1842f84debed41a222188eb73d6c95163175b
Status: Downloaded newer image for docker/compose:1.5.0
dockercouchbase41_couchbase1_1 is up-to-date
Starting fa82e35b4f dockercouchbase41_couchbase3_1
Starting dockercouchbase41_couchbase2_1
```

Check if Docker processes are running

We will then check if Docker processes are running. `docker ps` shows the status of Docker processes, and `docker-compose ps` shows the status of `docker-compose` processes:

```
$ docker ps
$ docker-compose ps
```

```
$ docker ps
CONTAINER ID     IMAGE               COMMAND              CREATED        STATUS        PORTS
                                             NAMES
96e137dfc3cc     arungupta/couchbase "/entrypoint.sh /opt/" 3 minutes ago  Up 3 minutes  8091-8093/tcp, 11207/tcp, 11210-11211/tcp, 18091-18
092/tcp                                     dockercouchbase41_couchbase2_1
ca9790431358     arungupta/couchbase "/entrypoint.sh /opt/" 3 minutes ago  Up 3 minutes  0.0.0.0:8091-8093->8091-8093/tcp, 11207/tcp, 11211/
tcp, 0.0.0.0:11210->11210/tcp, 18091-18092/tcp  dockercouchbase41_couchbase3_1
6bb9483dff68     arungupta/couchbase "/entrypoint.sh /opt/" 3 minutes ago  Up 3 minutes  8091-8093/tcp, 11207/tcp, 11210-11211/tcp, 18091-18
092/tcp                                     dockercouchbase41_couchbase1_1
$ docker-compose ps
          Name                        Command              State                    Ports
-----------------------------------------------------------------------------------------------------
dockercouchbase41_couchbase1_1  /entrypoint.sh /opt/couchb ...   Up            11207/tcp, 11210/tcp, 11211/tcp,
                                                                                18091/tcp, 18092/tcp, 8091/tcp,
                                                                                8092/tcp, 8093/tcp
dockercouchbase41_couchbase2_1  /entrypoint.sh /opt/couchb ...   Up            11207/tcp, 11210/tcp, 11211/tcp,
                                                                                18091/tcp, 18092/tcp, 8091/tcp,
                                                                                8092/tcp, 8093/tcp
dockercouchbase41_couchbase3_1  /entrypoint.sh /opt/couchb ...   Up            11207/tcp, 0.0.0.0:11210->11210/tcp,
                                                                                11211/tcp, 18091/tcp, 18092/tcp,
                                                                                0.0.0.0:8091->8091/tcp,
                                                                                0.0.0.0:8092->8092/tcp,
                                                                                0.0.0.0:8093->8093/tcp
$
```

```
$ docker inspect --format '{{ .NetworkSettings.IPAddress }}'
dockercouchbase41_couchbase1_1
    172.17.0.3
$ docker inspect --format '{{ .NetworkSettings.IPAddress }}'
dockercouchbase41_couchbase2_1
    172.17.0.5
$ docker inspect --format '{{ .NetworkSettings.IPAddress }}'
dockercouchbase41_couchbase3_1
    172.17.0.4
```

```
$ docker inspect --format '{{ .NetworkSettings.IPAddress }}' dockercouchbase41_couchbase1_1
172.17.0.3
$ docker inspect --format '{{ .NetworkSettings.IPAddress }}' dockercouchbase41_couchbase2_1
172.17.0.5
$ docker inspect --format '{{ .NetworkSettings.IPAddress }}' dockercouchbase41_couchbase3_1
172.17.0.4
$
```

Summary of Couchbase cluster

We summarize Couchbase cluster's node names and Docker process names IP addresses and Couchbase installation directories in the following table:

Node	Docker process name	IP address	Couchbase installation directory
couchbase1	dockercouchbase41_couchbase1_1	172.17.0.3	/export/var/couchbase/node41-1
couchbase2	dockercouchbase41_couchbase1_2	172.17.0.5	/export/var/couchbase/node41-2
couchbase3	dockercouchbase41_couchbase1_3	172.17.0.4	/export/var/couchbase/node41-3

Using Couchbase web administrator console

Let's set up a cluster consists of three nodes.

Logging into the web console

If you start Couchbase successfully, you can access the web administrator console by opening the following URL: `http://localhost:8091`

You are asked a username and its password, so enter `Administrator` and `password`, respectively, as shown in the following screenshot:

If you can log in into the console, the following page appears. If you fail to log in, please check the username and password are correct:

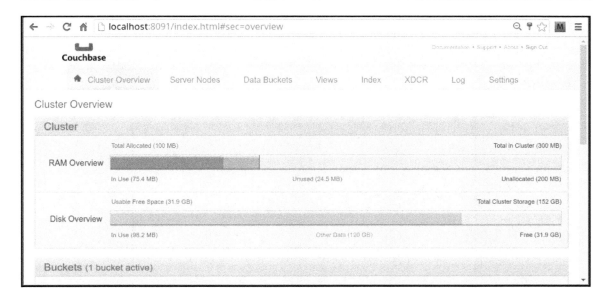

Adding nodes to the cluster

We will add two nodes into the cluster. Go to the server nodes tab by clicking on **Server Nodes** in the browser, as shown in the following screenshot:

On the preceding page, only the node whose IP is 172.17.0.4 joins the cluster.

Adding Cluster

Let's add the nodes172.17.0.3 and 172.17.0.5. Click on **Add Server** and enter 172.17. 0.3 as the **Server IP Address** and password as **Password**, as shown in the following screenshot:

Click on **Add Server** and enter 172.17. 0.5 as the **Server IP Address** and password as **Password**, as shown in the next screenshot:

After adding the two servers, we will see the following page, which shows that a rebalance is necessary. Rebalance distributes the same amount of data among cluster nodes.

Click on the **Rebalance** option and wait for the rebalance to finish:

The following screenshot shows that the rebalance is in progress:

Defining Memcached bucket

Go to the **Data Bucket** tab and click on the **Create New Data Bucket** option:

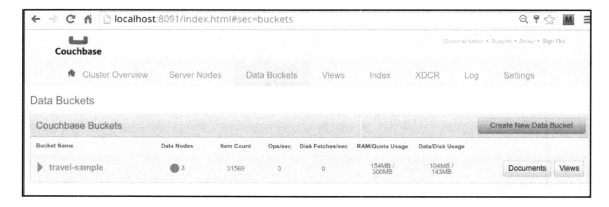

Let's specify the parameters for the new Memcached bucket:

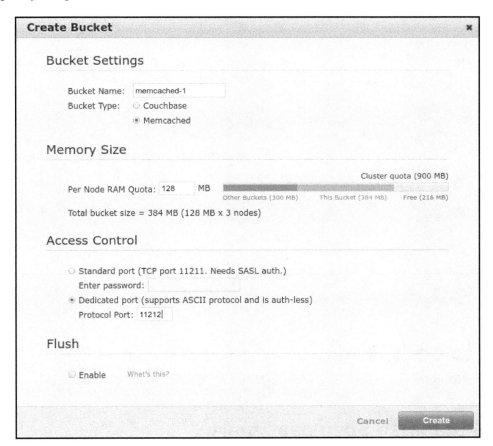

We review the parameters in the following table:

Parameter	Value
Bucket Name	memcached-1
Bucket Type	Memcached
Per Node Ram Quota	128 or higher
Access Control	Dedicated port
Protocol Port	11212

In the following screenshot, we can see that the `memcached-1` bucket has been created:

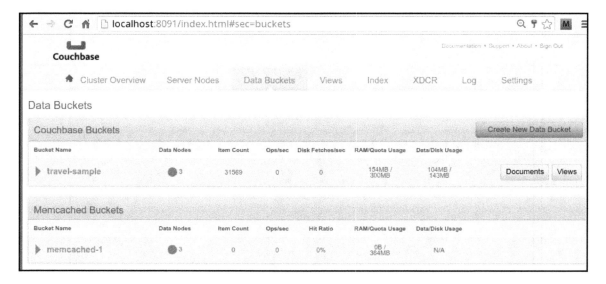

Now, we can use Couchbase Server as a Memcached server!

How to do it...

So, let's try Spyglass to manipulate Memcached on Couchbase we defined previously.

Defining to use Spyglass library

Let's define `clojurewerkz.spyglass.client` first:

```
(ns spyglass-example.core
  (:require [clojurewerkz.spyglass.client :as c]))
```

Connecting server

To connect a Memcached server, use `clojurewerkz.spyglass.client/text-connection`:

```
(def tc (c/text-connection
        "172.17.0.3:11212 172.17.0.4:11212 172.17.0.5:11212"))
;;=> #'spyglass-example.core/tc
```

The `text-connection` parameter is a string that may have multiple addresses separated by space, as shown previously.

Set values

The syntax to set a value is as follows:

```
(clojurewerkz.spyglass.client/text-connection connection key time-to-live-in-second value)
```

Let's set keys to different data types:

```
(c/set tc "key-1" 0 "Hello !")
;;=> #clojurewerkz.spyglass.OperationFuture[{:status :ready, :val true}
0x50b6f787]
(c/set tc "key-1" 0 "Hello !")
;;=> #clojurewerkz.spyglass.OperationFuture[{:status :ready, :val true}
0x50b6f787]
(c/set tc "key-2" 0 1)
;;=> #clojurewerkz.spyglass.OperationFuture[{:status :ready, :val true}
0x81bbd8a]
(c/set tc "key-3" 0  [1 2 3])
;;=> #clojurewerkz.spyglass.OperationFuture[{:status :ready, :val true}
0x2e6b1c50]
```

Get values from another REPL

Let's start another REPL so that we can share data on memory between JVMs:

```
$ lein repl
```

After the REPL is ready, let's get values:

```
(ns spyglass-example.core
  (:require [clojurewerkz.spyglass.client :as c]))
;;=> nil
(def tc (c/text-connection
         "172.17.0.3:11212 172.17.0.4:11212 172.17.0.5:11212"))
;;=> #'spyglass-example.core/tc
(c/get tc "key-1")
;;=> "Hello !"
(c/get tc "key-2")
;;=> 1
(c/get tc "key-3")
;;=> [1 2 3]
```

Testing time to live

The following code shows the time to live parameter works correctly. We set that parameter to 3 seconds and check if the value expires after 3 seconds:

```
(let [tc (c/text-connection
          "172.17.0.3:11212 172.17.0.4:11212 172.17.0.5:11212")]
  (c/set tc "key-1" 3  "Hello !")
  (println (c/get tc "key-1"))
  (println "sleeping ....")
  (Thread/sleep 3100)
  (println (c/get tc "key-1"))
  (c/shutdown tc))
;;=> Hello !
;;=> sleeping ....
;;=> nil
```

Disconnecting

To disconnect, use `clojurewerkz.spyglass.client/shutdown`:

```
(c/shutdown tc)
;;=> nil
```

How it works...

We will briefly describe Memcached and Couchbase.

What is Memcached?

Memcached is a commonly used distributed key value system. It is very often used to get high performance to speed up websites by caching data and objects in memory to reduce access to a database.

Memcached was originally developed by Danga Interactive for LiveJournal, but is now used by many other systems, including Google, Facebook, Twitter, and other famous companies.

Memcached's APIs provide a very large hash table distributed across multiple machines. When the table is full, subsequent inserts cause older data to be purged in least recently used order.

Access Memcached from Telnet

Memcached supports Telnet access to manipulate cached data. Let's try it. Start the connection again in your REPL if you have shut it down:

```
(def tc (c/text-connection
         "172.17.0.3:11212 172.17.0.4:11212 172.17.0.5:11212"))
;;=> #'spyglass-example.core/tc
```

Let's go to your terminal and issue the Telnet to connect to the Memcached server:

```
$ telnet 172.17.0.3 11212
set key-1 0 60 5
test!
STORED
get key-1
VALUE key-1 0 5
test!
END
```

The preceding commands access Memcached using Telnet, go to your REPL and set a key-1 to a value and get it. So far, let's go to REPL get a value of the key-1:

```
(c/get tc "key-1")
;;=> "test!"
(c/set tc "key-2" 100 "Hello !")
;;=> #clojurewerkz.spyglass.OperationFuture[{:status :ready, :val true}
0x171ca0f1]
;;=> 1
```

Switch to your terminal again and issue the following:

```
get key-2
VALUE key-2 0 7
Hello !
END

quit
Connection closed by foreign host.
```

```
$ telnet 172.17.0.5 11212
Trying 172.17.0.5...
Connected to 172.17.0.5.
Escape character is '^]'.
set key-1 0 60 5
test!
STORED
get key-1
VALUE key-1 0 5
test!
END
get key-2
VALUE key-2 0 7
Hello !
END
quit
Connection closed by foreign host.
$ ■
```

Couchbase Server

Couchbase Server is a distributed NoSQL document database server with high performance, high scalability, and high availability. Couchbase cluster can consist up to hundreds of nodes to provide ultrahigh performance. A bucket in Couchbase is a set of documents similar to the DBMS database or schema.

There are two types of buckets:

- One is a Couchbase bucket type, which provides a JSON-based document database
- The other is a Memcached bucket type

We use the latter type. The following diagram is our Couchbase cluster running on Docker containers:

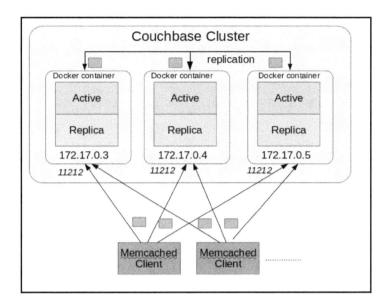

There's more...

There are three advanced topics for spyglass. Let's try them!

Using get-multi

get-multi gets values at a time. Let's test the following code:

```
(doseq [x (range 1 11)]
    (c/set tc (str "key-" x) 300 (str "Hello " x " !")))
;;=> nil
```

We will test the following code in the different REPL (JVM) to get the result:

```
(def x
  (c/get-multi tc (mapv #(str "key-" %) (range 1 11))))
  ;;=> #'spyglasbvs-example.core/x
(println x)
;;=> {key-2 Hello 2 !, key-9 Hello 9 !, key-8 Hello 8 !, key-3 Hello 3 !,
key-4 Hello 4 !, key-5 Hello 5 !, key-1 Hello 1 !, key-7 Hello 7 !, key-6
```

```
Hello 6 !}
;;=> nil
```

Using async-get

`async-get` gets the results asynchronously into `future`. To get the results, use `deref` or `@`:

```
(c/set tc "key-1" 300 "Hello !")
;;=> #clojurewerkz.spyglass.OperationFuture[{:status :ready, :val true}
0x3a7b844e]
(def x (c/async-get tc "key-1"))
;;=> #'spyglasbvs-example.core/x
(c/replace  tc "key-1" 300 "Good bye !")
;;=> #clojurewerkz.spyglass.OperationFuture[{:status :ready, :val true}
0xf0bd936]
(def x (c/async-get tc "key-1"))
;;=> #'spyglasbvs-example.core/x
@x
;;=> Good bye!
```

In the preceding code, `replace` is to replace the value of the existing key with a new value.

Using CAS operations

Memcached supports**CAS** operations to solve concurrency problems in multithreaded or multiprocess environment. Spyglass also supports it.

The next statement defines and sets `"key-1"` to 0:

```
(c/set tc "key-1" 0 0)
;;=> #clojurewerkz.spyglass.OperationFuture[{:status :ready, :val true}
0x4dc54398]
```

We need to start two REPLs using the following commands:

```
REPL-1
$ lein repl
REPL-2
$ lein repl
```

We will test concurrent updates for single value "key-1". So we run the following code from two REPLs.

In REPL-1:

```
(require '(clojurewerkz.spyglass [client :as c]))
;;=> nil
(defn apply-fn [tc k fn]
  (let [ret (c/get tc k)
        v (fn ret)]
    (c/replace tc k 0 v) ))
;;=> #'spyglasbvs-example.core/apply-fn
(def tc (c/text-connection
        "172.17.0.3:11212 172.17.0.4:11212 172.17.0.5:11212"))
;;=> #'spyglass-example.core/tc
```

In REPL-2:

```
(require '(clojurewerkz.spyglass [client :as c]))
;;=> nil
(defn apply-fn [tc k fn]
  (let [ret (c/get tc k)
        v (fn ret)]
    (c/replace tc k 0 v) ))
;;=> #'spyglasbvs-example.core/apply-fn
(def tc (c/text-connection
        "172.17.0.3:11212 172.17.0.4:11212 172.17.0.5:11212"))
;;=> #'spyglass-example.core/tc
```

And let's increment the "key-1" 10,000 times from two REPLs at the same time.

In REPL-1:

```
(time
 (dotimes [_ 10000]
   (apply-fn tc "key-1"  inc)
   ))
;;=> "Elapsed time: 2472.73951 msecs"
;;=> nil
```

In REPL-2:

```
(time
 (dotimes [_ 10000]
   (apply-fn tc "key-1"  inc)))
;;=> "Elapsed time: 2467.011652 msecs"
;;=> nil
```

Let's check `"key-1"` either in REPL-1 or REPL-2. It should be 20,000:

```
(c/get tc "key-1")
;;=> 17258
```

Wrong! There is a concurrency problem.

So let's do the same test using the CAS function. We will learn how CAS works. We will run the following code either in REPL-1 or REPL-2.

First of all, let's see how CAS works using a simple code.

`clojurewerkz.spyglass.client/gets` gets a current value and `clojurewerkz.spyglass.client/cas` updates the value using CAS. If the CAS update is successful, `cas` returns `:ok`. If it fails, it returns `:exists`.

Let's set `"key-1"` to 0 and get the CAS value for it:

```
(c/set tc "key-1" 0 0)
;;=> #clojurewerkz.spyglass.OperationFuture[{:status :ready, :val true}
0x7e0e69e5]
    (def cas-value (:cas (c/gets tc "key-1")))
    ;;=> 80010
    #'user/cas-value
```

The CAS value is `80010` in the preceding case. Then we will update `"key-1"` using the `cas` function:

```
(c/cas tc "key-1" cas-value 1)
;;=> ok
(c/get tc "key-1")
;;=> 1
```

The preceding CAS operation updates the CAS value and it fails to update using the previous CAS value:

```
(:cas (c/gets tc "key-1"))
;;=> 80011
(c/cas tc "key-1" cas-value 1)
;;=> :exists
```

So, let's define the modified version of function named `apply-fn-with-cas`, which updates a Memcached value using CAS. We will define `apply-fn-with-cas` in two REPLs.

In REPL-1:

```
(defn apply-fn-with-cas [tc k fn]
  (loop []
    (let [ret (c/gets tc k)
          v (fn (:value ret))]
      (when
          (= (c/cas tc k (:cas ret) v)  :exists)
        (recur)))))
;;=> #'spyglasbvs-example.core/apply-fn-with-cas
```

In REPL-2:

```
(defn apply-fn-with-cas [tc k fn]
  (loop []
    (let [ret (c/gets tc k)
          v (fn (:value ret))]
      (when
          (= (c/cas tc k (:cas ret) v)  :exists)
        (recur)))))
;;=> #'spyglasbvs-example.core/apply-fn-with-cas
```

In the latter case, `apply-fn-with-cas` retries an update.

Let's increment the `"key-1"` 10,000 times from two REPLs at the same time again.

In REPL-1:

```
(time
 (dotimes [_ 10000]
   (apply-fn-with-cas tc "key-1"  inc)))
;;=> "Elapsed time: 4287.262212 msecs"
;;=> nil
```

In REPL-2:

```
(time
 (dotimes [_ 10000]
   (apply-fn-with-cas tc "key-1"  inc)))
;;=> "Elapsed time: 4559.814013 msecs"
;;=> nil
```

There seem to be many collisions by concurrent updates and retries and it took time to complete. But the result is correct:

```
(c/get tc "key-1")
;;=> 20000
```

Finally, let's stop the containers of the Couchbase cluster.

```
$ docker-compose stop
```

See also

For further reading, please refer to the following links to Couchbase and Memcached protocol:

- Couchbase official site at `http://www.couchbase.com/`
- Memcached protocol at `https://github.com/memcached/memcached/blob/master/doc/protocol.txt`

Reactive programming with meltdown

Meltdown brings to Clojure the ease of reactive programming. Your code is now turned into a set of event definitions and listeners to those events. Your running code is now bound to a state (or a set of multiple states) and each part of the code, can now react from values of the state. The event stream becomes abstracted from the code.

Say you are implementing a brand new mail software; messages showing on your screen would be bound to a state or a part of the state. The visual representation of the e-mails is a direct translation of the state itself. If you need to replace or pull in new e-mails, you would add some messages to that state list.

Meltdown can also be used as a stream processing toolkit, meaning you can somehow pipe the processing of messages, and we will look at it in the last part of this recipe.

Getting ready

Here again, there is not much to do to get ready for this recipe, we will just add the meltdown coordinates to the list of dependencies of the project. We will also make use of MQTT connections later on to show the interaction between reactive programming and remote services, so let's add it together now:

```
:dependencies [
  [org.clojure/clojure "1.8.0"]
 [clojurewerkz/meltdown "1.1.0"]
  [clojurewerkz/machine_head "1.0.0-beta8"]
  [org.slf4j/slf4j-simple "1.6.1"]
]
```

We revert to `slf4j-simple` to avoid some annoying warning messages about loggers.

How to do it...

Reactive programming is based around a single point of event receiving and event dispatching, which, in meltdown terms, is named a reactor. First, we will see the basic interactions with a reactor.

Defining a reactor

Defining a reactor is done through a simple binding using a call to `def` to the proper `create` function of meltdown namespace, as shown in the following:

```
(require '[clojurewerkz.meltdown.reactor :as mr])
(def reactor (mr/create))
```

This reactive point can be seen as a common point of communication to a conversation with multiple participants. It could also be seen as a topic.

Now let's say you want to react to a message being sent to that point of communication or more precisely you want to have a function that will react to a message or a group of messages sent to the reactor.

The function will be executed when a message is sent to the reactor and a message key can be selected by our selector.

This is done as follows, where we start by requiring the proper namespace for selectors from meltdown and then define a selector and a function that will be called if needed:

```
(require '[clojurewerkz.meltdown.selectors :refer [$]])

; create a reactive function on a reactive point
(mr/on reactor
    ; selector
    ($ "key")
    ; function that will be executed when the selector has matched
(fn [event]
    (println event)))
```

Sending a message to a reactor

Now to the part where you send a message to the reactor, hope it will execute the function with the `println` block. To send a message, you will use the `notify` function of the main meltdown namespace followed by the reactor, the key, and the message itself, which can be of any type, but here we will use a simple map:

```
; send a message
(mr/notify reactor "key" {:my "payload"})
```

And so, if you had been typing all the preceding at the REPL and were checking at the console, you would see the `println` function being called and the event being printed:

```
{:data {:my payload}, :reply-to nil, :headers {}, :key key, :id #uuid
"42d33831-110b-11e6-f3e1-5dbaf4ef3e34"}
```

We can see that a message is made of a payload, contained in the `:data` key, which is the data associated with the message that we send. The message obviously has a unique ID and comes with a set of headers.

Going the sync way

Now this second way of sending message means that we want the message to do a kind of ping-pong with the sent message. A `receive-event` call is also using a selector and a reactor, but will also do some processing on the data:

```
(mr/receive-event
    ; we bind to a reactor
reactor
; define a selector
($ "hello-key")
```

```
; do some processing. And send some data back, here "response"
(fn [_] (Thread/sleep 2000)  "response"))
```

The second part involves sending the message itself using the `send-event` function. The first three arguments are the same as when using the `notify` function. The last parameter is a callback function that is called at the very end of the message transaction:

```
(mr/send-event
reactor
"hello-key"
"data"
(fn [event]
; print the data that was send by the receive-event
; definition above, so most likely "response"
 (println (:data event))
  (println "done")))
```

Since we have added a callback, you will notice a slight delay before the `"done"` message is being printed on the console. Note also that the `(:data event)` part in the callback properly receives data from the earlier definition.

How it works...

You saw the basic usage of reactors and how to send messages. In this section, we will quickly review how to work with selectors and follow up with a part showing how to build streams of processing by assembling or piping callback functions together.

Selectors

Till now you have seen how to select a given key using the dollar $ selector:

```
(require '[clojurewerkz.meltdown.selectors :refer [$]])
```

Selector can make use of a wild card to achieve something similar to a selection based on regular expressions.

Say you want to send and receive messages based on food and options, so you can define selectors using R as follows:

```
(require '[clojurewerkz.meltdown.selectors :as s :refer [R]])

(mr/on reactor
 (R "Burger.*")
 (fn [event] (println "Delicious Burger:" event)))
```

Now you can have wild pattern matching on notify calls to the reactor:

```
(mr/notify reactor "Burger.withbacon"  {:teh :payload})
(mr/notify reactor "Burger.withcheese" {:das :payload})
```

Note that the following message will obviously not call for anything on the reactor and no callback will be called:

```
(mr/notify reactor "Sushi.salmon" {:das :payload})
```

Keep playing around and see if you can get some nice sushi to your plate.

Streams

Streams are an abstraction, building on the concept of reactive programming that allows you to apply real-time transformations to messages or values coming to the streams.

Streams in meltdown can be seen as a root channel and functions applied to the channel.

There are four main functions for streams:

- `create`: This is where it all starts and you can define a new channel with it.
- `map*`: This is a helper function that acts just like the Clojure core map function but acts on values coming from the channel.
- `consume`: This is the last function of the composed function that acts on values. It will make use of the piping of functions using `map*` or something similar.
- `accept`: This sends values to the channel.

The following simple example shows you how to simply add `1` to integer values coming through the channel:

```
(require '[clojurewerkz.meltdown.streams :as ms :refer [create consume
accept map*]])

(def channel (ms/create))
(def incremented-values (map* inc channel))

(consume incremented-values (fn [i] (println "Incremented: " i)))
(accept channel 1)
; 2
(accept channel 2)
; 3

(ms/flush channel)
```

The interesting part with streams is that you can combine functions that are applied to the values in the channel. Here we reuse the almost same preceding example, but you can already see how functions are combined with each other by using a function based on map* as the input of another function based on map*:

```
(def channel (ms/create))
(def incremented-values (map* inc channel))
(def incremented-twice  (map* inc incremented-values))

(consume incremented-twice
 (fn [i] (println "Incremented twice: " i)))

(accept channel 1)
; 3
(accept channel 2)
; 4

(ms/flush channel)
```

Streams and reduce

It is also very easy to apply some reducing function to the stream using the reduce* function in the same ms meltdown namespace:

```
(require '[clojurewerkz.meltdown.streams :as ms :refer [create consume
accept reduce*]])

(def channel2 (ms/create))
(def res (atom nil))
(def sum (reduce* #(+ %1 %2) 0 channel2))
(ms/consume sum #(reset! res %))

(ms/accept channel2 1)
(ms/accept channel2 2)
(ms/accept channel2 3)
(ms/flush channel2)

@res
; 6
```

The preceding example also highlights the usage of flush, which has not really been required up to now. As with most Clojure code, evaluation is mostly lazy. So, flush forces all the values in the channel to be used and to go through all the functions applied on the streams.

Combining functions with a graph

Meltdown also has a namespace that offers what is called `stream-graph`. Think of it as easy-to-use syntactic sugar when you need to combine functions applied to your channels:

```
(require '[clojurewerkz.meltdown.stream-graph :refer :all])

(def res (atom 0))
(def channel (graph  (create)
                     (map* inc
                     (reduce* #(+ %1 %2) 0
            (consume #(reset! res %))))))
   (accept channel 1)
   (accept channel 2)
   (accept channel 3)

   (ms/flush channel)
@res
; 6
```

Custom streams

This is a very cool solution for a constant problem where you want to check values coming through a stream. Say you want to raise an alert if the temperature is too high from a stream of constantly in coming temperature values. You can define a custom stream that gets values from an upstream and only send values to a downstream if those are higher than 40 degrees Celsius.

You use the `custom-stream` method to read the events coming and use the `accept` function with downstream to pass the values along:

```
(defn toohot-stream [upstream]
  (ms/custom-stream
    (fn [event downstream]
      (if (< 40 event)
        (accept downstream event)))
    upstream))

(def temperature-channel (ms/create))
(ms/consume (toohot-stream temperature-channel) (fn [e] (println e)))

(accept temperature-channel 1)
; doesn't print
(accept channel 45)
; 45
```

Let's see how we can apply this custom stream to IoT.

There's more…

This will make us of Mosquitto (and Mosquitto spy to send message) as we have done previously. What the following code does is that it takes all the messages coming from a Mosquitto connection, redirects the messages to a meltdown reactor, and then lets it do the magic!

```
(ns melting.withmqtt
  (:require
   [clojurewerkz.machine-head.client :as mh]
   [clojurewerkz.meltdown.reactor :as mr]
   [clojurewerkz.meltdown.selectors :as sel]))

; connect to mqtt
; as a reminder, binaries for mosquitto are here
; http://mosquitto.org/download/
; start server with
; mosquitto
(def conn
  (mh/connect "tcp://127.0.0.1:1883"
    (mh/generate-id)))

; create a reactive point
(def reactor
  (mr/create))

; function to proxy messages from mqtt to
; the above created reactive point
(defn proxy-to-meltdown
  [^String topic _ ^bytes payload]
  (mr/notify reactor topic (String. payload)))

; subcribe to mqtt messages and proxy
; all message to the function defined
(mh/subscribe
  conn
  ["#"]
  proxy-to-meltdown)

; lastly, when the reactor receives any message
; print the event
(mr/on reactor
  (sel/match-all)
  (fn [event]
```

```
(println (:data event))))
```

Bridging core.async

Clojure's `core.async` is one of those Clojure features that makes you love asynchronous programming. While not included in Clojure core, it is straight and easy to put into use and makes Clojure's STM a breeze to use. Unfortunately, most of the examples that can be found on `core.async` make it a bit hard to see how to connect it and plug things together with the rest of your current code and other frameworks.

This recipe wants to close the gap and help you bring out more `core.async` code out there.

Getting ready

This recipe is largely based on `core.async`, but we will use a few other libraries. Here's a sample dependencies section for your `project.clj` file:

```
:dependencies [
[org.clojure/clojure "1.8.0"]
[org.clojure/core.async "0.2.374"]

[com.hellonico.gearswithingears/async-sockets "0.1.0"]
[jarohen/chime "0.1.9"]

; there's more
[com.keminglabs/jetty7-websockets-async "0.1.0"]
[ring "1.2.0"]

]
```

The core async library is obviously required. Other samples will also show a synchronicity integrated with other libraries, so async sockets will help us create channels from socket messages, and chime will give us a timer channel that can be used with `core.async`.

Note that `com.hellonico.gearswithingears` is just a custom version of the `async-sockets` library with a small code fix.

Memories – reviewing core.async basics

First, we will start by remembering how `core.async` works in a short example. This example will read temperature values in Celsius asynchronously from a `core.async` channel and will convert those values to Fahrenheit.

You can think of this as some Clojure code reading values from a sensor, and you need to convert values from the sensor in pseudo real-time:

```
(ns asyncing.simple
    (:require [clojure.core.async :refer :all]))

; convert Celsius to Fahrenheit
(defn c-to-f [c]
  (+ (* 1.8 c) 32))

; create an out channel that reads Celsius values from a channel
; and convert them to Fahrenheit asynchronously.
; remember that >! And <! can only be called within a go block,
; which is, simply said, an asynchronous block of code.
(defn c-to-fer
  [in]
  (let [out (chan)]
    (go (while true (>! out (c-to-f (<! in)))))
    out))

; the in channel that reads Celsius values
(def in-chan (chan))

; the out channel that output Fahrenheit values
(def c-to-fer-out (c-to-fer in-chan))

; a helper method that will print out values coming from the in
; channel.
; This is a simple go loop that reads value forever from the
; channel and prints them.
(defn printer
  [in]
  (go (while true (println (<! in)))))

; start the printer go loop on the Fahrenheit channel
(printer c-to-fer-out)

; put some Celsius values in the original channel
 (>!! in-chan 30)
; 86
```

```
; remember that >!! runs on the main thread, and so if you want to
; make the code async as well, you can use go and >! As above.
(go (>! in-chan 10))
```

Pub/sub

While we are looking at known stuff, a less famous pattern of core async is the included, easy-to-use pub/sub mechanism.

Let's have a look at some sushis and burgers. Create a publisher from a channel using pub, the channel, and a message key:

```
; publish
(def input-chan (chan))
(def our-pub (pub input-chan :food))
```

You can then define subscribers to this publisher using sub, the pub just defined, and an output channel:

```
; subscribe
(def burger-chan (chan))
(sub our-pub :burger burger-chan)

(def sushi-chan (chan))
(sub our-pub :sushi sushi-chan)
```

Finally, with some glue code to print the values from subscribers from different channels:

```
(defn print-loop [channel prefix]
  (go-loop []
    (let [{:keys [option]} (<! channel)]
      (println prefix " " option)
      (recur))))
(print-loop sushi-chan :sushi)
(print-loop burger-chan :burger)
```

You can know dispatch food at will and have a great lunch:

```
(>!! input-chan {:food :burger :option "with cheese"})
(>!! input-chan {:food :burger :option "with avocado"})
```

Also remember that thread can be used to spawn a separate thread and run its own inline code block:

```
(thread
  (>!! input-chan {:food :sushi :option "salmon"}))
```

Now that we have all this async code in mind, let's see how to integrate it nicely with other tools.

How to do it...

Let's get back to the simple Celsius to Fahrenheit example and see how we can enhance things a bit using regular sockets, combined with core async channels. Remember you included the `com.gearswithingears.async-sockets` library in the project; we will make use of that just now.

Async socket server

The idea here is to delegate the handling of connections to a channel, which itself will handle values coming to it through another channel.

Let's start with the glue code to include the library in the namespace, and the Celsius to Fahrenheit conversion code:

```
(ns asyncing.withsockets
  (:require [com.gearswithingears.async-sockets :refer :all]
            [clojure.core.async :as async]))

(defn c-to-f [c]
(+ (* 1.8 (Integer/parseInt c)) 32))
```

Then, let's go to the connection handling block. On the socket connection, this function creates a new async loop that repeatedly reads lines of input. Each input is supposed to be an integer and the value is then simply converted to Fahrenheit and returned to the client:

```
(defn handle-connection [socket]
  (async/go-loop []
    (when-let [line (async/<! (:in socket))]
(async/>! (:out socket)
(str "FAHRENHEIT: " (c-to-f line)))
(recur))))
```

Finally, the main server loop is just accepting connections and adding them to a regular core async channel:

```
(let [server (socket-server 12345)]
  (async/go-loop []
    (when-let [connection (async/<! (:connections server))]
      (handle-connection connection)
      (recur))))
```

```
[nicolassmacbook% telnet 192.168.1.5 12345
Trying 192.168.1.5...
Connected to raspberrypi.
Escape character is '^]'.
10
FAHRENHEIT: 50.0
30
FAHRENHEIT: 86.0
```

A bit of Telnet to talk to the socket and converts values. Note that for the purpose of this book, the socket server is actually running on a simple Raspberry Pi.

Async socket client

The example would not be complete if there was not a client version of this. Since all this code is asynchronous, you can use the following code in the same REPL you were using until now. This is also using an async channel to put values on the socket connection and reads quite nicely:

```
(def socket (socket-client 12345 "localhost"))
(async/>!! (:out socket) "10")
(println (async/<!! (:in socket)))
; CELCIUS TO FAHRENHEIT: 50.0

; close the socket.
(close-socket-client socket)
```

Chiming

Sockets are nice, but a simple and fun way of showing that async's work is to deal with sound. Chime is a simple timer library that provides a channel around timed events. So, to play a short audio clip after a few seconds, you can pass init values to chime and it will push messages on the async channel, always on time, just like a Japanese train.

This example will do just that by asking chime to send a message to a core async channel after two seconds. The handling block will then, without blocking, play the sample audio clip in the background.

Let's start with the usual namespaces declarations:

```
(ns asyncing.withchime
  (:import [javax.sound.sampled AudioSystem])
  (:require [chime :refer [chime-ch]]
            [clj-time.core :as t]
            [clojure.java.io :as io]
[clojure.core.async :as a :refer [<! go-loop]]))
```

This is nothing more than a simple Java interop code block that will play a sound from a wav file:

```
(defn play-sound [file]
 (let [
  sound (io/as-file file)
  input (AudioSystem/getAudioInputStream sound)
  clip (AudioSystem/getClip)]
  (doto clip
   (.open input)
(.start)))))
```

Finally, the chime channel takes a vector of `clj-time` inputs, here two seconds from now, and creates what can be seen as a simple cron channel:

```
(let [chimes (chime-ch [(-> 2 t/seconds t/from-now)])]
  (a/<!! (go-loop []
   (when-let [msg (<! chimes)]
     (play-sound "resources/pendolino.wav")
     (recur)))))
```

At the REPL, and after two seconds, you can hear the sound of a bullet train passing by and you can still keep on typing code.

There's more...

To close this recipe, we will cover more on sockets, this time using WebSockets, with a bit of a mix with Python code.

Client to Python WebSockets

With `pip`, the Python library manager installed, we will install the `tornado` server that has WebSocket support:

```
sudo pip install tornado
```

Then a simple WebSocket server can be written as follows. Since we do not want to go deep into Python details, it's best to simply copy and paste the following in a file named `websockets.py` for now:

```python
import tornado.httpserver
import tornado.websocket
import tornado.ioloop
import tornado.web
import socket
class WSHandler(tornado.websocket.WebSocketHandler):
    def open(self):
        print 'new connection'
    def on_message(self, message):
        print 'sending back message: %s' % message
        self.write_message(message)
    def on_close(self):
        print 'connection closed'
    def check_origin(self, origin):
        return True
application = tornado.web.Application([
    (r'/ws', WSHandler),
])
if __name__ == "__main__":
    http_server = tornado.httpserver.HTTPServer(application)
    http_server.listen(8888)
    myIP = socket.gethostbyname(socket.gethostname())
    print '*** Websocket Server Started at %s***' % myIP
    tornado.ioloop.IOLoop.instance().start()
```

Basically, we implemented a WebSocket handler at path /ws and we hook this into a simple Tornado application. Running the server is then simply done through:

```
python websockets.py
```

Now that we have this, we can write some WebSocket client code from Clojure using the jetty-websocket-async library:

```
(require '[com.keminglabs.jetty7-websockets-async.core :refer [connect!]]
         '[clojure.core.async :refer [chan go >! <! >!! <!!]])

(def c (chan))
(connect! c "ws://localhost:8888/ws")
```

The core async chan contains the connection and we can then retrieve it to send messages to the Python WebSocket server with:

```
(go
  (loop []
      (when-let [ws-req (<! c)]
      (>! (:in ws-req) "Hello remote websocket server!")
      (recur))))
```

To make it more obvious that we can reuse those WebSockets connections, we confirm that we have two channels, in and out, to the WebSocket server:

```
(def in (atom nil))
(def out (atom nil))
```

Here, notice that both in and out are core async channel, as prepared for us by the Jetty WebSocket library:

```
(go
  (let [ws-req (<! c)]
      (reset! in (:in ws-req))
      (reset! out (:out ws-req))))

(defn printer
  [in]
  (go (while true (println (<! in)))))

(printer @out)
(>!! @in "sushi please")
```

Clojure WebSocket server

This has been covered in other places, so we will quickly glance at this Clojure WebSocket server. You can already see that contrary to the Python code, this feels naturally integrated into our async programming code:

```clojure
(require '[com.keminglabs.jetty7-websockets-async.core :refer
[configurator]]
          '[clojure.core.async :refer [chan go >! <!]]
          '[ring.adapter.jetty :refer [run-jetty]])

(defn http-handler
  [req]
  {:response 200 :body "HTTP hello" :headers {}})

; this is the channel where new connections will be put in
(def c (chan))

(def ws-configurator (configurator c {:path "/ws"}))

(def server
  (run-jetty http-handler {:configurator ws-configurator
                           :port 8888, :join? false}))

; this is the websocket connection handler.
; it reads messages on channel :out and just echo them on core
; async channel :in
(defn websocket-echo-handler [ws-req]
  (println "new websocket connection...")
  (go (loop []
      (when-let [msg (<! (:out ws-req))]
        (println "MSG:" msg)
        (>! (:in ws-req) "ECHO: " msg)
        (recur)))))

; note that this go-loop's lifecycle is separated from the server
lifecycle.
(go (loop []
      (let [ws-req (<! c)]
        (websocket-echo-handler ws-req)
        (recur))))
```

On Quasar/Pulsar

Pulsar is a Clojure wrapper for the Quasar library, which is an actor-based programming toolkit for the JVM. When using actor libraries, actors usually map one on one to a thread, and therefore may take more resources than necessary to handle the sometimes simple code they need to process.

Quasar and Pulsar introduce the concept of fibers, or really lightweight processing units, which can send messages to each other. This results in a simple to read and use set of processing units that facilitate asynchronous programming to a new level.

Getting ready

A new `project.clj` file needs to be slightly updated with dependencies. Also note the `java-agent` directive that adds Quasar core to the set of runtime instrumentation.

Note that the purpose of an agent is to provide instrumentation capabilities to the application, in other words, the capability to redefine the signature of the class files during run-time. The juicy details would need a reading of the Quasar code, but let's just say that Quasar does a bit of byte code manipulation to create and manage its fibers.

The following is the `project.clj` file:

```
(defproject quasarland "0.1.0-SNAPSHOT"
  :java-agents [[co.paralleluniverse/quasar-core "0.7.5"]]
  :dependencies [
    [org.clojure/clojure "1.8.0"]
    [co.paralleluniverse/quasar-core "0.7.5"]
  [co.paralleluniverse/pulsar "0.7.5"]
  ])
```

How to do it...

This short section will have a look at how to define, instantiate, and make those actors communicate with each other.

Our namespace declaration will require Pulsar's core and actor namespaces. Note here the usage of `refer-clojure` to avoid conflicts on `promise` and `await`:

```
(ns quasarland.firststeps
  (:use [co.paralleluniverse.pulsar core actors])
  (:refer-clojure :exclude [promise await]))
```

On to your first actors, which, to be honest, will go on a rest and relax:

```
(defsfn relaxing-afternoon []
(println "I am relaxing ..."))
```

defsfn defines a suspendable function that can be used by a fiber or actor and is used exactly like the usual defn.

Now we mostly just defined a function, which we can call a regular function:

```
(relaxing-afternoon)
;I am relaxing ...
```

What we want though is not a function, but something that acts as a standalone processing unit. This is done through the use of spawn, which instantiates a Pulsar actor:

```
(spawn relaxing-afternoon)
 ; #object[co.paralleluniverse.actors.ActorRef 0x130599b8
"ActorRef@130599b8{PulsarActor@1fac12d3[owner: fiber-10000002]}"]
    ; I am relaxing ...
```

You still get the relaxing message on the console, but you also get a reference to an actor. Our actor is still quite lazy and, apart from being lazy on a Sunday afternoon, is not doing much. To make him wake up after a while, we can use some sleeping code:

```
(defsfn relaxing-afternoon-2 []
(println "I am relaxing ...")
; (Thread/sleep 2000) fails here !
  (sleep 2000)
  (println "I am waking up ...")
  )

(spawn relaxing-afternoon-2)
```

After two seconds, your relaxing afternoon starts to get some action. As noted in the comments, make sure you are not using a call to Thread/sleep, which is something that Quasar cannot instrument and will result in an exception at definition time.

Now let's say you want to be able to send a hint to the actor that he should wake up, instead of waiting for him to do it.

For this purpose, you can use the `receive` function, with a key, and code block to execute asynchronously when the message arrives:

```
(defsfn relaxing-afternoon-3 []
  (println "I am relaxing ...")
  (receive
    :wakeup (println "Hey ! Someone woke me up!")))
```

Spawning this next actor, you are now able to send messages to it through the use of the ! call:

```
(def me
  (spawn relaxing-afternoon-3))

(! me :wakeup)
; Hey ! Someone woke me up!
```

Cool! Message passing. Now something weird is happening, when you want to wake the actor again and send the same message:

```
(! me :wakeup)
```

Nothing is happening. This is because the body of the `defsfn` acts as a loop, and once a message is received, the loop naturally ends unless we tell it not to with `recur`:

```
(defsfn relaxing-afternoon-4 []
  (println "I am relaxing ...")
  (receive
    :bump (do (println "Hey ! Stop bumping me!") (recur))))

(def me
  (spawn relaxing-afternoon-4))

(! me :bump)
  ; Hey ! Stop bumping me!
; I am relaxing ...

(! me :bump)
  ; Hey ! Stop bumping me!
; I am relaxing ...
```

All this recurring bumping around must be quite tiring. `recur` calls for the whole block to get called again so that the actor keeps on relaxing, which may not be a problem on such a sunny day after all!

Our actor is getting a bit masochistic and would like to be able to bump himself. Luckily for him, the `defsfn` macro exposes a self-reference that can be used to point to oneself:

```
(defsfn relaxing-afternoon-5 []
  (println "I am relaxing ...")
  (sleep 5000)
  (! @self :bump)
  (receive
    :bump
    (println "bumping myself!")))

(spawn relaxing-afternoon-5)
```

After five seconds, the relaxing afternoon will start sending a message to itself and react to it. `@self` is very useful and a widely used pattern for exchanging messages between different actors. The following sample code brings this to a better light by enhancing the message receiving part so that you can see who has been sending the message. Note that the receive part now gets a vector instead of a simple message keyword and also note that the message sending part is also sending a vector:

```
(defsfn relaxing-afternoon-6 []
  (println "I am relaxing ...")
  (sleep 1000)
  (! @self [:bump @self])
  (receive
    [:bump who]
    (println who " is bumping!")))

(spawn relaxing-afternoon-6)
; ... ActorRef@32c9c341... is bumping!
```

Now sending, people don't usually bump themselves, so we need to introduce someone to do this hard job.

The next example takes two actors, one that sleeps and one that sends a hint of waking up. Our two actors, sleeping man and someone, can be defined easily as follows:

```
(defsfn sleeping-man []
  (println "I keep on sleeping ...")
  (receive
    [:wakeup who]
    (do
      (println "Someone is telling me to wakeup!")
      (println "but ...")
      (recur))))

(defsfn someone [man]
```

```
(sleep 1000)
(! man [:wakeup @self]))
```

And then we can see the interaction between the two people. Note that someone takes a reference to a man so as to be able to send messages to it.

Spawning the sleeping man is just as usual:

```
(def man-asleep (spawn sleeping-man))
```

Spawning someone is slightly different, as the reference to the sleeping man is added as a second parameter to spawn:

```
(spawn someone man-asleep)
;   Someone is telling me to wakeup!
; but ...
; I keep on sleeping ...
(spawn someone man-asleep)
; ... many people ...
; many more sleeping
```

Now that you have seen how to send messages between actors, you are now more than ready to play ping-pong.

How it works...

This example is mostly a direct copy of the Pulsar samples, and should be a no brainer if you have followed the first part of this recipe.

Here we declare two actors, a ping and a pong, that call each other recursively for a while until ping misses the ball and declares gameover:

```
(ns quasarland.pingpong
  (:use [co.paralleluniverse.pulsar core actors])
  (:refer-clojure :exclude [promise await]))

(defsfn ping [pong]
  (if (>= (rand-int 10) 9)
    (do
      (! pong :gameover)
      (println "Missed the ball. Ping Finished"))
    (do
      (! pong [:ping @self])
      (receive
        :pong (println "Ping"))
      (recur pong))))
```

```
(defsfn pong []
  (receive
    :finished (println "Pong finished")
    [:ping ping] (do
                   (println "Pong")
                   (! ping :pong)
(recur)))))
```

Let's start the game!

```
(let [a1 (spawn pong)
b1 (spawn ping a1)])
  ;Pong
  ;Ping
  ;Pong
  ;Ping
  ;Pong
  ;Ping
  ;Missed the ball. Ping finished
  ;Pong finished
```

This ping-ponging is nice, but agreed, it would be nicer if we could avoid passing the other ponger as a reference when doing a spawn. Yes! This can be done using `register!` and a keyword. Let's rewrite `ping` so that it can send message to using a keyword instead of a reference:

```
(defsfn ping []
  (if (>= (rand-int 10) 9)
    (do
      (! :pong :finished)
      (println "Missed the ball. Ping finished"))
    (do
      (! :pong [:ping @self])
      (receive
        :pong (println "Ping"))
      (recur))))
```

Now, before starting the game, we register `pong` as `:pong` to the Quasar system using `register!` and spawn `ping` and `pong` one after the other. Note that `ping` knows there is, and needs, a `:pong` to be registered:

```
(register! :pong (spawn pong))
(spawn pong)
(spawn ping)
; a new game begins !
```

Watching over other actors lifecycles

Now actors can get automatic notifications from other actor lifecycles, for example, say an actor is about to end its lifecycle. You can use `watch!` to receive a message:

```
(let [actor1 (spawn #(sleep 1000))
      actor2 (spawn
               (fn []
                 (let [w (watch! actor1)]
                   (receive
                     [:exit w actor reason]
                 (println "bye .." actor)))))])
  ; bye .. #object[co.paralleluniverse.actors.ActorRef..
```

State of an actor

Actors also have an internal state that can keep values through its full lifecycle. The following example shows how we can keep a time reference and retrieve a time difference.

The actor will stay alive until it receives one message:

```
(let [actor
      (spawn #(do
        (set-state! (System/currentTimeMillis))
        (set-state! (- (receive) @state))
        @state))]
          (sleep 2000)
          (! actor (System/currentTimeMillis)))
(join actor))
; 2004
```

The join call at the end allows it to retrieve the last value of the block.

There's more...

We talked about them briefly previously and here they are: fibers are also asynchronous blocks of code, but with a more lightweight version of actors. You can think of them as light Clojure promises.

In their most simple form, fibers act in a similar way to actors, and you can spawn them using a `spawn-fiber` call:

```
(spawn-fiber (fn [] (sleep 1000) (println "slept well")))
; slept well
```

Fibers communicate through channels, mostly using the `rcv` and `snd` functions to receive and send messages, respectively. Note that those channels are unfortunately different than core async channels, but are used in a similar way:

```
(let [
    ch (channel)
    fiber (spawn-fiber
            (fn []
                (let [m1 (rcv ch)
                      m2 (rcv ch)]
                  (+ m1 m2))))]
(sleep 200)
(snd ch 10)
(sleep 200)
(snd ch 10)
(join fiber))
; 20
```

Channels can be used and shared between different fibers:

```
(let [ch (channel 0 :block true true)
      f #(rcv ch)
      fiber1 (spawn-fiber f)
      fiber2 (spawn-fiber f)]
(snd ch "m1")
(snd ch "m2")
(close! ch)
#{(join fiber1) (join fiber2)})
; #{"m1" "m2"}))
```

Finally, channels can be used in burst mode with `rcv-into` and `snd-seq`:

```
(let [ch (channel)
      fiber (spawn-fiber #(rcv-into [] ch 1000))]
      (snd-seq ch (range 200))
      (close! ch)
      (join fiber))
; [0 1 2 3 4 ...])
```

Blazar

Things get to the point where you would like to know how to link fibers and a socket server, so here is Blazar, a framework that builds on fibers to create a lightning-fast HTTP server, along WebSocket support. The project does not have recent commits, but works nicely with new version of Pulsar and the core idea is neat.

The `project.clj` file needs a bit of care for that:

```
(defproject blazarland "0.1.0-SNAPSHOT"
  :java-agents [[co.paralleluniverse/quasar-core "0.7.5"]]
  :profiles {
    :dev {
      :resource-paths ["resources" "profiles/dev/resources"]
      :source-paths ["src" "profiles/dev/src"]}}
  :dependencies [[org.clojure/clojure "1.8.0"]
  [blazar "0.1.1"]
  [co.paralleluniverse/pulsar "0.7.5"]])
```

But then your fiber-based server can be written in just a few lines!

```
(ns quasarland.blazar
  (:require
    [co.paralleluniverse.pulsar.core :as pc]
    [blazar.http.server :as bs]))
(pc/join
  (pc/spawn-fiber
    #(bs/start-fiber-ring-adapter
      "0.0.0.0"
      8080
      (fn [req] "Hello fiber world!"))))
```

For the purpose of this book yet again, this scaled quite well on a standard Raspberry Pi.

7
Advanced Tips

In this chapter, we will cover the following topics:

- Hacking the Clojure code
- Using Reader Conditionals, compile to Clojure, and ClojureScript
- Real-time shared development with an REPL
- Declarative data descriptions and validations with plumatic/schema

Introduction

We will learn more advanced tips in this chapter. First we will hack the Clojure code to understand how Clojure code works. We will generate class files from Clojure code and then decompile Java code. Understanding how Clojure code is a lot of fun and useful.

Next, we will look at how to write source code that keeps the compatibility between Clojure and ClojureScript and runs on both environments. As ClojureScript is getting more popular nowadays, single code running on both environments improves maintainability, especially writing libraries.

Then, we will try to share REPL real time from a remote client. Using this mechanism, we will try to control the Raspberry Pi from your PC.

Lastly, we will learn prismatic schema, which enables us to define and validate schemas for data. This library is very useful to define data shapes and validate. We will introduce `core.types` and `clojure.spec`, which are the most major features of Clojure 1.9.

Hacking the Clojure code

Along the great amount of code you have been running, it would be very surprising if you had come along a bug in Clojure itself.

There may be features missing, but the core is impressively robust and stable.

Under the hood, Clojure itself delegates byte code generation to a library named ASM. ASM produces the byte code that the Java machine can execute. This is done in real time when a Clojure program is running or can be done ahead of time, for example, when you want to package your code.

This very short recipe will to look at how to compile the Clojure code and see the generated Java byte code.

Getting ready

The Clojure code is hosted on GitHub, so to retrieve the code, head to `https://github.com/clojure/clojure`. To do a `git` checkout, use the following:

```
git clone https://github.com/clojure/clojure.git
```

To build your own version of Clojure, you will need one of the main Java build tools, called `maven`, which as of this writing is at version 3. Download and put the binary, `mvn`, accessible to your terminal:

```
mvn package -Dmaven.test.skip=true
```

Clojure is surprisingly very contained and fast to compile. The packaging only takes a few seconds. Once finished, you can find in the target folder the following two important files:

```
clojure-1.9.0-master-SNAPSHOT-slim.jar
clojure-1.9.0-master-SNAPSHOT.jar
```

The first JAR contains compiled Java classes and noncompiled Clojure code, while the second also contains the compiled Clojure sources. This makes the slim JAR at around 1 MB and the normal JAR at around 3.5 MB.

The advantage of having the Clojure files compiled is that you wait less time when starting the virtual machine and the Clojure environment.

As a reminder, you can start the Clojure Server REPL as easy as:

```
java -cp \
target/clojure-1.9.0-master-SNAPSHOT-slim.jar \
-Dclojure.server.repl="{:port 5555 :accept clojure.main/repl}" \
clojure.main
```

Or the traditional REPL with:

```
java -cp target/clojure-1.9.0-master-SNAPSHOT-slim.jar clojure.main
```

We will use the preceding generated Clojure JAR in a few minutes, so keep the place it was generated in mind.

Now on to see the generated byte code.

How to do it...

Say we have a very simple Clojure program like the following one:

```
(ns gen3
  (:gen-class [:main true]))

(defn -main[]
  (println "hello world"))
```

The preceding code does nothing but print some greetings, but it will make it easier to see what is generated.

Before explaining all the functions and words used here, let's go through the process first:

- The source file needs to be in the usual source folder in a Clojure project, so with Leiningen, this would be `src/gen3.clj`
- We now start an REPL, again with Leiningen, through:

  ```
  lein repl
  ```

- When the REPL has started, we now use the compile directive:

  ```
  (compile 'gen3)
  ; gen3
  ```

You will see that even though the REPL is pretty silent, class files have been generated:

```
Nicolass-MacBook% ls -l target/classes
total 40
drwxr-xr-x@ 3 niko   staff    102 May 25 11:41 META-INF
-rw-r--r--@ 1 niko   staff    831 May 25 11:41 gen3$_main.class
-rw-r--r--@ 1 niko   staff   1302 May 25 11:41 gen3$fn__1248.class
-rw-r--r--@ 1 niko   staff   1494 May 25 11:41
gen3$loading__5569__auto____1246.class
-rw-r--r--@ 1 niko   staff   1788 May 25 11:41 gen3.class
-rw-r--r--@ 1 niko   staff   2372 May 25 11:41 gen3__init.class
```

That is five classes generated, and probably the easier one to see is the `gen3.class` file. This is the file containing the entry point for the program. Let's use the Clojure JAR we have generated previously and the newly generated classes:

```
java -cp ../clojure/target/clojure-1.9.0-master-SNAPSHOT.jar:target/classes
gen3
```

Executing the preceding command will print out the expected message:

```
hello world
```

Nice. So we can see now that the Clojure code is being compiled to byte code in class files and can be executed as standard Java, through the use of only `clojure.jar` in the classpath.

How it works...

If we look at the files generated from the previous command, we can see five classes, as shown in the following screenshot:

We will use a software called JD GUI, which you can download from `http://jd.benow.ca/`, to examine in detail the Java class files generated by the Clojure compiler.

Each function in Clojure is actually compiled to a separate class file, making it easier for class reloading. For example, the -main function that we defined, just like any other function, is compiled to a class.

See the following:

```
import clojure.lang.AFunction;
import clojure.lang.IFn;
import clojure.lang.RT;
import clojure.lang.Var;

public final class gen3$_main
  extends AFunction
{
  public Object invoke()
  {
    return invokeStatic();
  }
  public static final Var const__0 = (Var)RT.var("clojure.core",
"println");
  public static Object invokeStatic()
  {
    return ((IFn)const__0.getRawRoot()).invoke("hello world");
  }
}
```

The main Java objects being used in Clojure are as follows:

- clojure.lang.IFn: This is Clojure function, something that can be invoked.
- clojure.lang.A: This function is mostly an annotated Clojure function.
- clojure.lang.RT: This is the Clojure runtime.
- clojure.lang.Var: This is a variable, a threaded reference, that is also a IFn and so can be invoked.

With this in mind, we can see that the Clojure println function from clojure.core is being kept as a Var from within the gen3 class:

```
public static final Var const__0 = (Var)RT.var("clojure.core", "println");
```

The Var is retrieved through questioning the runtime for a var through RT.var, a namespace, and a function.

What happens when the -main method is called is simply a static call to invokeStatic. This is rather generic, and calls invoke on an IFn object:

```
((IFn)const__0.getRawRoot()).invoke("hello world")
```

const__0 is here a generated reference to the println function in the namespace clojure.core. Calling -main results in executing the body of invokeStatic, which, in turn, invokes the println function with parameters "hello world".

The class gen3 contains a reference to the -main function in namespace gen3:

```
private static final Var main__var = Var.internPrivate("gen3", "-main");
```

And this is invoked in a similar way as previously. gen3__init is a side class responsible for namespace loading, and registering the function under namespaces. This is what is generated for the namespace definition. This allows for easy namespace redefinition and easy reloading of functions.

In simple worlds, the remaining two classes, gen3$fn and gen3$loading, are a different way of loading the preceding namespace definition and can be bypassed for now.

Back to the Clojure code, you may remember the namespace had some metadata in it:

```
(:gen-class [:main true])
```

This is so that the generated entry point class for this Clojure namespace is customized for easier interaction with Java. In particular, the :main true directive tells the compiler to generate a static Java method. Remember you can also customize constructors, getters, setters, and so on here.

There's more...

Now that you are used to it, you can have a look at some more complex Clojure to byte code generation:

```
(ns gen2)

(defn hello [b]
  (let[ a 1]
    (+ b a)))

(defn -main[]
  (println (hello 1)))
```

The preceding code compiles nicely to a few classes, one for each function. Let's look at the class corresponding to the `hello` function:

```
import clojure.lang.AFunction;
import clojure.lang.Numbers;

public final class gen2$hello
  extends AFunction
{
...

  public static Object invokeStatic(Object b)
  {
    long a = 1L;b = null;
    return Numbers.add(b, a);
  }
}
```

In namespace `gen2`, the `hello` function is a class extendingAFunction, so it can be invoked through `invoke`, and the calling main function:

```
import clojure.lang.AFunction;
import clojure.lang.IFn;
import clojure.lang.RT;
import clojure.lang.Var;

public final class gen2$_main
  extends AFunction
{
...
  public static final Object const__2 = Long.valueOf(1L);
  public static final Var const__1 = (Var)RT.var("gen2", "hello");
  public static final Var const__0 = (Var)RT.var("clojure.core",
"println");
  public static Object invokeStatic()
  {
    return
((IFn)const__0.getRawRoot()).invoke(((IFn)const__1.getRawRoot()).invoke(con
st__2));
  }
}
```

Access `Var` that has been registered (loaded) by the __init class and call it with the proper parameters.

We already saw macro in the previous recipe, so a good exercise for the reader would be to see that the Clojure code compile is actually the code after macro expansion. You should be able to do this!

Using Reader Conditionals, compile to Clojure, and ClojureScript

Codes in Clojure and ClojureScript are almost the same but there are few differences. For instance, libraries provided by Java and JavaScript are quite different. Host environments between JVM and JavaScript runtimes are also different.

Before the version 1.7, we use the `cljx` plugin to keep compatibility between them. However, it requires a tooling and the style is not clean.

For such a situation, Clojure 1.7 introduced Reader Conditionals are introduced. Reader Conditionals have richer semantics than `cljx`, such as default expressions and form splicing and no prepossessing.

Using Reader Conditionals, we can share source code among Clojure, ClojureScript, and ClojureCLR. In this recipe, we will demonstrate how we can share single source files between Clojure and ClojureScript.

Getting ready

We will use the Figwheel template to generate a Clojure and ClojureScript project:

```
$ lein new figwheel cljc-example -- --om
```

```
                              Terminal                          — + ×
$ lein figwheel
Figwheel: Validating the configuration found in project.clj

Figwheel: Configuration Valid. Starting Figwheel ...
Figwheel: Starting server at http://localhost:3449
Figwheel: Watching build - dev
Compiling "resources/public/js/compiled/cljc_example.js" from ["src"]...
Successfully compiled "resources/public/js/compiled/cljc_example.js" in 1.743 seconds.
Figwheel: Starting CSS Watcher for paths  ["resources/public/css"]
Launching ClojureScript REPL for build: dev
Figwheel Controls:
          (stop-autobuild)              ;; stops Figwheel autobuilder
          (start-autobuild [id ...])    ;; starts autobuilder focused on optional ids
          (switch-to-build id ...)      ;; switches autobuilder to different build
          (reset-autobuild)             ;; stops, cleans, and starts autobuilder
          (reload-config)               ;; reloads build config and resets autobuild
          (build-once [id ...])         ;; builds source one time
          (clean-builds [id ..])        ;; deletes compiled cljs target files
          (print-config [id ...])       ;; prints out build configurations
          (fig-status)                  ;; displays current state of system
   Switch REPL build focus:
          :cljs/quit                    ;; allows you to switch REPL to another build
     Docs: (doc function-name-here)
     Exit: Control+C or :cljs/quit
  Results: Stored in vars *1, *2, *3, *e holds last exception object
Prompt will show when Figwheel connects to your application
To quit, type: :cljs/quit
cljs.user=> █
```

The generated directory structure is as follows:

```
                        Terminal            — + ×
$ tree
├── README.md
├── dev
│   └── user.clj
├── project.clj
├── resources
│   └── public
│       ├── css
│       │   └── style.css
│       └── index.html
└── src
    └── cljc_example
        └── core.cljs

6 directories, 6 files
$ █
```

We will move the project directory:

```
$ cd cljc-example
$ lein figwheel
```

We can see the following output to run `lein figwheel`:

Then, open your browser and go to the following URL: `http://localhost:3449`:

You can see the message in the browser. After seeing it, let's test the ClojureScript code in the REPL to show an alert dialog on your browser, as shown in the following screenshot:

```
(js/alert "hello !")
nil
```

How to do it...

First, we will create demo.cljc under the src/cljc_example in the project as follows:

Your first Reader Conditional

Let's start with a simple Reader Conditional expression. Reader Conditional start with `#?` as follows:

```
#?(:clj
   "Hello Clojure !"
   :cljs
   "Hello Clojurescript !")
```

`:clj` is for Clojure code, and `:cljs` is for ClojureScript code. So, the results of REPLs are as follows:

- Clojure REPL

  ```
  ;;=> Hello Clojure !
  ```

- Figwheel REPL

  ```
  ;;=> Hello Clojurescript !
  ```

Using Reader Conditionals in namespaces

You can use `:require` in the namespace in the following way:

```
(ns cljc-example.demo
  #?(:clj
     (:require [quil.core :as q])
     :cljs
     (:require [quil.core :as q :include-macros true])))
;;=> nil
```

We will use the `quil` library for both Clojure and ClojureScript. Using ClojureScript, we need to add `:include-macros true`. There are differences in handling exceptions in Clojure and ClojureScript. We use Reader Conditionals as follows:

```
(try
  (/ 1 0)
  (catch
      #?(
         :clj java.lang.Exception
         :cljs ;default
             ) e
   (.getMessage e)))
```

In JVM, dividing by zero causes an exception, `java.lang.Exception`; however, dividing by zero only returns `Infinity`:

- Clojure REPL

  ```
  "Divide by zero"
  ```

- Figwheel REPL

  ```
  Infinity
  ```

The next code is another example of Reader Conditionals for `try` and `catch`. The check-range checks whether the given value `v` is between the lower `l` and higher `h`. If the value is out of range, this function throws an exception or error:

```
(defn check-range [v l u]
  (if-not (and (>= v l) (<= v u))
    #?(:clj (throw (Exception. "out of range"))
       :cljs (throw (js/Error. "out of range")
       )
    v)))
```

We will use `js/Error` in ClojureScript instead of _Exception in Clojure:

```
(try
  (check-range 0 1 10)
  (catch
      #?(
         :clj Exception
         :cljs js/Error
         ) e
    #?(:clj (println (.getMessage e))
       :cljs (println (.-message e)))))
```

In ClojureScript, `(.-message e)` retrieves the error message. `.-function` calls host JavaScript functions.

How it works...

Here, we will explain the form of Reader Conditionals and Splice macros.

The form of Reader Conditionals and Splice macros

The form of Reader Conditionals is as follows:

```
#?(:clj  (Clojure expression)
   :cljs (ClojureScript expression)
   :clr  (Clojure CLR expression))
```

When the preceding code runs on Clojure, `(Clojure expression)` is evaluated. When the code runs on ClojureScript, `(ClojureScript expression)` is evaluated and vice versa.

Splice Reader Conditional macros are the same as Reader Conditional macros, but an expression must be a vector. The expression will be spliced into the resulting read.

We will write the following code:

```
(defn test-splicing-hello []
  #?@(:clj [(print "hello ")(print "world !")(print "\n")]))
;;=> #'cljc-example.demo/test-splicing-hello
```

The expression for the Splice Reader Conditional macro is a vector, and the result of executing the method is as follows:

```
(test-splicing-hello)
;;=> hello world !
;;=> nil
```

The preceding code is equivalent to the following one:

```
(defn test-hello []
  (print "hello ")(print "world !")(print "\n"))
;;=> #'cljc-example.demo/test-hello
```

Splice Reader Conditional macros cannot be located at top level. If we do that, an exception like the following is thrown:

```
#?@(:clj
    [(print "hello ")(print "world !")(print "\n")])
;;=> RuntimeException Reader conditional splicing not allowed at the top
level.  clojure.lang.Util.runtimeException (Util.java:221)
```

Splice Reader Conditional macros are often used in `require/import`. We will show an example in this recipe.

Macros in ClojureScript

ClojureScript's macros are different from those of Clojure. In ClojureScript, macros are defined in a different compilation stage rather than the one from where they are consumed.

So, we need to use the `:include-macros` or `:require-macros` keyword in namespace declarations for ClojureScript.

The `:include-macros` is a sugar for `:require-macros`:

```
(:require [quil.core :as q :include-macros true])
```

The preceding code is the equivalent to the following one:

```
(:require [quil.core :as q])
(:require-macros [quil.core :as q])
```

There's more…

We will use Quil, which is an interactive library for drawings and animations. Quil supports both Clojure and ClojureScript. We will learn how our single source code runs on two different environments.

Building an application for Clojure and ClojureScript

We will learn a more complex usage of Reader Conditionals. We will develop a graphical demonstration for Clojure and ClojureScript.

So, we will create runtimes for Clojure and ClojureScript with a single source file (`.cljc`). We will use Quil, which is a Clojure/ClojureScript library for interactive graphics. It provides over 200 functions that allows it to draw in 2D, 3D, and even in PDF.

The original demo is in the home page in Quil, so let's see how to run it in both Clojure and ClojureScript.

Although the steps here are rather long, we will not only learn how to write code for Clojure and ClojureScript using Reader Conditionals, but we will also learn steps for building and running the two different environments from single source code.

Adding a cljc file for demonstrating Quil

Let's add the `quil_demo.cljc` file, which shows the Quil demo for Clojure and
ClojureScript. The location of the file is under the `src/cljc_example` directory, as shown
in the following screenshot:

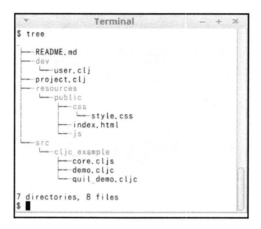

We will modify the generated `project.clj`. We will add the `quil` library as follows:

```
:dependencies [[org.clojure/clojure "1.8.0"]
               [org.clojure/clojurescript "1.8.51"]
               [org.clojure/core.async "0.2.374"
                 :exclusions [org.clojure/tools.reader]]
               [sablono "0.3.6"]
               [org.omcljs/om "0.9.0"]
               [quil "2.4.0"]]
```

In the dependency section, we have added [quil "2.4.0"]. Then we will replace the
main namespace from `cljc-example.core` to `cljc-example.quil-demo` in the
`cljsbuild` section as follows:

```
:cljsbuild {:builds
            [{:id "dev"
              :source-paths ["src"]
              ;; If no code is to be run, set :figwheel true for
continued automagical reloading
              :figwheel {:on-jsload "cljc-example.quil-demo/on-js-
reload"}
              :compiler {:main cljc-example.quil-demo
                         :asset-path "js/compiled/out"
                         :output-to
"resources/public/js/compiled/cljc_example.js"
```

```
                       :output-dir "resources/public/js/compiled/out"
                       :source-map-timestamp true}}
          ;; This next build is an compressed minified build for
          ;; production. You can build this with:
          ;; lein cljsbuild once min
          {:id "min"
           :source-paths ["src"]
           :compiler {:output-to
"resources/public/js/compiled/cljc_example.js"
                      :main cljc-example.quil-demo
                      :optimizations :advanced
                      :pretty-print false}}]}
```

After we finish the preceding modifications, let's restart REPL and Figwheel REPL. We will declare `quil` and `om` libraries for Clojure and ClojureScript:

```
(ns cljc-example.quil-demo
  (:require
   #?@(
       :clj
       [[quil.core :as q]
        [quil.middleware :as m]]
       :cljs
       [[quil.core :as q :include-macros true]
        [quil.middleware :as m]
        [om.core :as om :include-macros true]
        [om.dom :as dom :include-macros true]]
       ))
  #?(:clj (:gen-class)))
```

The following code is for ClojureScript to add the `canvas` tag for drawing graphics used by Quil:

```
#?(
   :cljs
   (defn on-js-reload []
  ;; optionally touch your app-state to force rerendering depending on
  ;; your application
  ;; (swap! app-state update-in [:__figwheel_counter] inc)
     ))
#?(
   :cljs
       (def app-state (atom {:text "Hello quil demo !"})))
#?(
   :cljs
   (enable-console-print!))
#?(:clj
   (println "Using Clojure !")
```

```
   :cljs
   (println "Using Clojurescript !"))
#?(
   :cljs
   (om/root
    (fn [data owner]
      (reify om/IRender
        (render [_] (dom/canvas #js {:id "my-sketch" :height 400 :width
400})))
       ))
    app-state
    {:target (. js/document (getElementById "app"))}))
```

Code here is animating a circle for Clojure and ClojureScript. Fortunately, code is the same in them:

```
(defn setup []
  (q/frame-rate 60)
  (q/color-mode :hsb)
  {:color 0 :angle 0})

(defn update-state [state]
  {:color (mod (+ (:color state) 0.7) 255)
   :angle (+ (:angle state) 0.1)})

(defn draw-state [state]
  (q/background 240)
  (q/fill (:color state) 255 255)
  (let [angle (:angle state)
        x (* 150 (q/cos angle))
        y (* 150 (q/sin angle))]
    (q/with-translation [(/ (q/width) 2)
                         (/ (q/height) 2)]
      (q/ellipse x y 50 50))))

(defn run[]
  (q/defsketch my-sketch
    :host "my-sketch"
    :size [500 500]
    :setup setup
    :update update-state
    :draw draw-state
    :middleware [m/fun-mode]))
```

setup is the initial setup function, and update-state updates the current state.

Testing cljc code in both Clojure and ClojureScript

We will test the preceding code in REPLs in both Clojure and ClojureScript. Let's test it in the Clojure REPL first. Let's type the following:

```
(run)
```

Then, a new window will open and you can see the following:

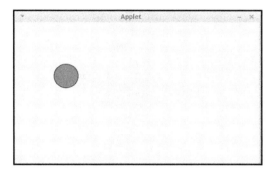

Then we will test it on ClojureScript under Figwheel REPL. Figwheel checks the code updates and refreshes the browser. So, let's save the code, and we can see an animation as follows:

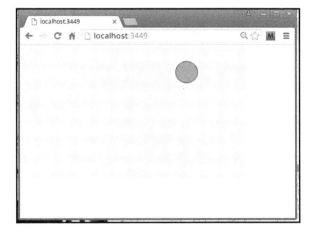

Building and running a demo

Now, let's generate a runtime code for both Clojure and ClojureScript in order to run them without REPL development environments. We will add the following code to run the demo without REPLs:

```
#?(
    :clj
    (defn -main[& args](run)
    )
    :cljs (run))
```

In Clojure, the function name -main is necessary to invoke from the outside of REPL. On the other hand, invoking (run) starts the animation for ClojureScript. The following steps are setting and testing a demo for Clojure outside REPL. To do this, let's add the main section on the project.clj:

```
:main cljc-example.quil-demo
```

Then, type the following:

```
$ lein run
```

lein run invokes the -main function in the namespace declared in the :main section in the project.clj and launches the demo. Now, this is the time to run the demo without REPL. We have to modify the namespace of the main class for uberjar as follows:

```
:profiles {
            :uberjar {
                      :aot [cljc-example.quil-demo]
                      :main cljc-example.quil-demo
                      }
            :dev {:dependencies [[figwheel-sidecar "0.5.3-1"]
                                 [com.cemerick/piggieback "0.2.1"]]
                  ;; need to add dev source path here to get user.clj
loaded
                  :source-paths ["src" "dev"]
                  ;; for CIDER
                  ;; :plugins [[cider/cider-nrepl "0.12.0"]]
                  :repl-options {; for nREPL dev you really need to limit
output
                                 :init (set! *print-length* 50)
                                 :nrepl-middleware
[cemerick.piggieback/wrap-cljs-repl]}}}
```

Then, we will invoke the following command to generate an `uberjar` file:

```
$ lein uberjar
```

```
                              Terminal                            − + ✕
$ lein uberjar
Compiling cljc-example.quil-demo
Compiling cljc-example.quil-demo
Created /home/makoto/clojure/clojure-packt-book/chapter07/cljc-example/target/cljc-example-0.1.0-SNAPSHOT.jar
Created /home/makoto/clojure/clojure-packt-book/chapter07/cljc-example/target/cljc-example-0.1.0-SNAPSHOT-standalone.jar
$ ▮
```

A JAR file generated by `uberjar` contains all classes defined in the dependency section in the `project.clj`. It also contains Clojure core classes. So, the size of the JAR files is large and takes time to generate. Let's run the demo under JVM. The following command line starts the demo:

```
$ java -jar target/cljc-example-0.1.0-SNAPSHOT-standalone.jar
```

We will build the runtime for your browser. To invoke the following command compiles ClojureScript into JavaScript:

```
$ lein cljsbuild once min
```

In the following screenshot, check if the compilation is successful:

```
                              Terminal                            − + ✕
$ lein cljsbuild once min
Compiling ClojureScript...
out of range
Divide by zero
Compiling "resources/public/js/compiled/cljc_example.js" from ["src"]...
Successfully compiled "resources/public/js/compiled/cljc_example.js" in 17.926 seconds.
$ ▮
```

We can specify `dev` or `min` as a build option in the `:cljsbuild` section:

```clojure
:cljsbuild {:builds
            [{:id "dev"
              :source-paths ["src"]
              .......
             {:id "min"
              :source-paths ["src"]
              :compiler {:output-to
"resources/public/js/compiled/cljc_example.js"
                         :main cljc-example.quil-demo
                         :optimizations :advanced
                         :pretty-print false}}]}
```

The `min` option optimizes the highest optimization for the performance and generates the smallest JavaScript code into a single file. It changes names of variables and functions into shorter names. The `min` option generates obfuscated code. On the other hand, the `dev` option does no optimization and is used for developing and debugging; however, it gives slower performance. `resources/public/js/compiled/cljc_example.js` is the single JavaScript code generated from ClojureScript.

The `auto` option automatically generates JavaScript code when ClojureScript code is modified. The following option is useful for debugging:

```
$ lein cljsbuild auto min
```

Now, we will run the demo in your browser. The following command opens a new browser session and launches the demo:

```
$ browser resources/public/index.html
```

Only the following files are necessary to run the ClojureScript demo:

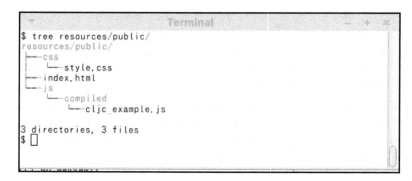

Follow these simple steps to run the demo on your `github.io`:

1. Create your GitHub account if you don't have it.
2. Follow these steps:

```
$ cd (another-directory)
$ git clone
https://github.com/(your-username)/(your-username).github.io
$ cd (your-username).github.io
$ cp -r ($your-cljc-project)/cljc-example/resources/public .
$ git add .
$ git add --all
$ git commit -m "Initial commit"
$ git push -u origin master
```

3. Open your browser:

```
$ browser (your-username).github.io
```

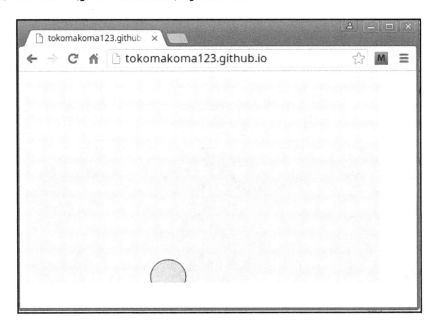

See also

Please see related web sites as follows:

- For differences from Clojure, refer to https://github.com/clojure/clojurescript/wiki/Differences-from-Clojure.
- To try ClojureScript online, refer to http://himera.herokuapp.com/index.html.
- For Quil, refer to http://quil.info/.

Real-time shared development with an REPL

Let's face it, you will spend most of your Clojure time in an REPL, and that satisfaction to get instant feedback from writing code is what will keep you awake at night.

In this recipe, you will see a few REPL *astuce*, tricks, to make your coding easier and help you create a coding workflow that is your own.

We start with basics on how to use a shared REPL and then build on instant feedback and ideas on writing your custom REPL.

Getting ready

The first part of this recipe will show how to connect using the Atom editor. Make sure you have it installed before, if not, go to `https://atom.io`:

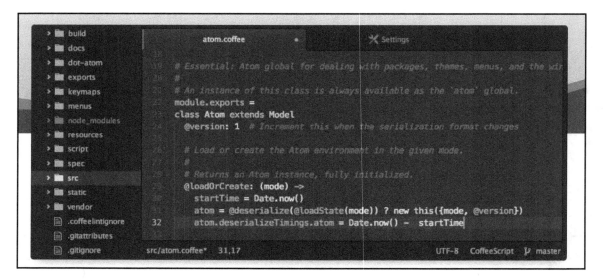

 The default settings do not require any additional settings but you will have to add dependencies to the `project.clj` file as you go reading along.

How to do it...

You will remember how to start a simple REPL with the following:

```
lein repl
```

But let's go slightly beyond that and start an REPL that can be shared nicely with others.

Shared REPLs

For the ultimate DIY sharing experience, it is now time to go and grab your Raspberry Pi (or another machine or a local virtual machine). We will now have a quick look at how to share an REPL on the Raspberry Pi. Note that it could be any computer, but the Raspberry Pi makes it more obvious and the flow easier to understand:

You can start a headless REPL, even outside a Clojure project using the following:

```
lein repl :headless :host 0.0.0.0 :port 9000
```

It is important to bind on `0.0.0.0` or its IPv6 equivalent, otherwise the REPL cannot be accessed remotely. To avoid a random port being chosen, let's force it to be `9000` here as well. Now, connecting to that remote REPL, we will be done using the `:connect` directive. Considering that the Raspberry Pi had an IP of `192.168.1.9`, here is how to connect to it:

```
lein repl :connect 192.168.1.9:9000
```

Now, for the purpose of a small example on the Raspberry Pi, let's try to play with the HDD LED. Let's remove the protection of that LED with the following:

```
sudo "echo none > /sys/class/leds/led0/trigger"
```

While we're at it, let's also change the permission on the brightness:

```
sudo chmod 777 /sys/class/leds/led0/brightness
```

This will allow us to access it using a standard user. Now, with simple shell interaction, let's send the following command to blink it:

```
(use '[clojure.java.shell])
; set this to 0 (off) or 1(on)
(defn set-led [n]
 (sh "sh" "-c"
(str "echo " n " > /sys/class/leds/led0/brightness")))

; now some looping
(dotimes [i 10] (set-led 0) (Thread/sleep 1000) (set-led 1))
```

Christmas already!

Using Atom and proto-repl

Alright, so it was fun to use the REPL, but you would certainly miss a few of the text editor fun. Once in Atom, let's install all the packages needed in one go for some Clojure fun:

Once all three packages shown in the preceding screenshot are installed, let's immediately connect to the already running REPL:

1. Open the Remote Nrepl Connection dialog with:

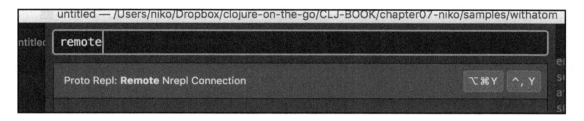

2. And open the connection itself with:

3. In the text editor area, let's type and execute the same code:

And yes, it is still Christmas on the Raspberry Pi (blink, blink)! If you have noticed, some messages are complaining about the lack of a dependency:

```
clojure.tools.namespace.repl not
available. Add as a dependency to allow
refresh.
Refresh Warning: IllegalArgumentException
No such namespace:
clojure.tools.namespace.repl
clojure.lang.Var.find (Var.java:141)
```

Let's add the two following ones in a new Leiningen project:

```
:dependencies [
[proto-repl-charts "0.2.0"]
[org.clojure/tools.namespace "0.2.11"]

[cheshire "5.6.1"]
[org.clojure/clojure "1.8.0"]]
```

Now, after starting a new REPL in this project, with the same command, you now have access to quite a few bonuses. First, you can use something similar to Light Table's instant evaluation. Open the command box and use the following `auto eval` command:

Now back to the text editor section, to see that the code is evaluated instantly in the opened file. This saves a lot of extra key send to REPL shortcuts:

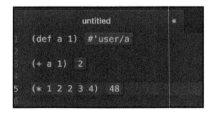

Remember this is still running on the Raspberry Pi, or wherever you started, so anyone else can contribute to the work.

If you remember, we have installed a package named proto REPL graph and added a dependency in the project as well for it. Let's try it out!

The dependency adds a prc namespace that does the integration for you. The default sample graph is already pretty impressive by itself:

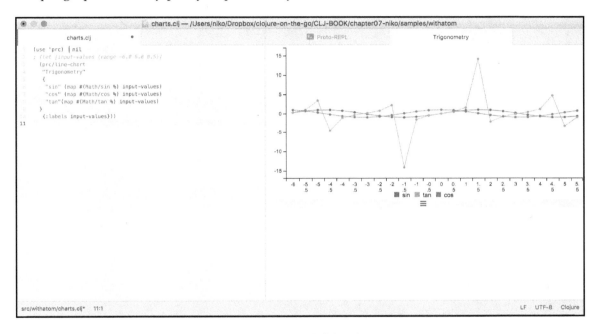

Real-time chart alongside Clojure code

But let's go and do some integration by fetching quotes from Microsoft, and display them in real time in that graph preview:

```
(ns withatom.quotes
  (:require [cheshire.core :refer :all]))

(defn get-quotes
  [label start end]
  (let [query
    (str
      "https://query.yahooapis.com/v1/public/yql"
      "?q=select%20*%20from%20yahoo.finance.historicaldata%20"
      "where%20symbol%20%3D%20%22"
```

```
        label
        "%22%20and%20startDate%20%3D%20%22"
        start
        "%22%20and%20endDate%20%3D%20%22"
        end
   "%22&format=json&env=store%3A%2F%2Fdatatables.org%2Falltableswithkeys")]
      (reverse
        (get-in
        (parse-string
          (slurp query))
         ["query" "results" "quote"])))))

   (let[ result
      (get-quotes "MSFT" "2016-02-10" "2016-03-20")]
      (prc/line-chart
       "MSFT"
       {"quote" (map #(% "Open") result)}
       {:labels (map #(% "Date") result)}))
```

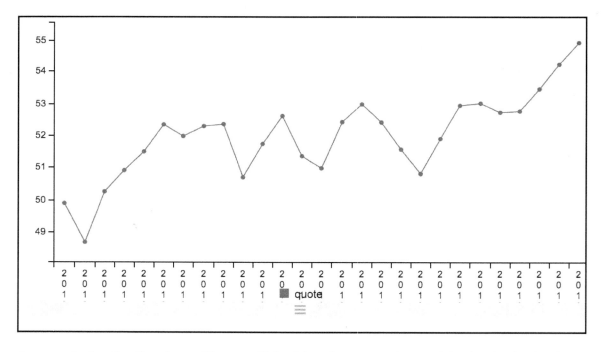

As a reminder, the Raspberry Pi was still fetching the quotes for you! And only the final rendering was done within the Atom editor!

Using an embedded NREPL

You have seen how to use NREPL, which is a very powerful library for REPLing. Let's go one step beyond that and see how to embed your own REPL into your code using that library. First some `project.clj` tweaking:

```
[org.clojure/tools.nrepl "0.2.11"]
```

Then, this is how you start and bind a new REPL server within your code:

```
(use '[clojure.tools.nrepl.server :only
(start-server stop-server)])
(def server (start-server :bind "0.0.0.0" :port 7888))
```

Just for the fun of it, and if you were running this embedded REPL within Atom connected to the Raspberry Pi (!!), then the blinking code would still work!

Keep blinking.

There's more...

Now that we have seen how to connect to a remote shared REPL and have quite a bit of fun with remote berries, let's go beyond and see how to write your own REPL.

Custom REPL using Java interop

Here we will have a look at how to write a simple REPL server and a client, with standard Java interop code and regular socket connections.

Server

The following server will be your point of entry to open a socket, send some Clojure forms for evaluation, `eval` or execute the code on the server, and send the result to the client.

Let's see how this is done:

```
(ns custom-repl.server
    (:import [java.net InetAddress ServerSocket Socket]
        [java.io InputStreamReader OutputStreamWriter]
        [clojure.lang LineNumberingPushbackReader]))

(defn on-thread [f]
  (doto (new Thread f) (.start)))
```

```
(defn create-server
  [accept-socket bind port]
    (let [address (InetAddress/getByName bind)
          ss (new ServerSocket port)]
(on-thread
#(when-not (. ss (isClosed))
                    (try (accept-socket (. ss (accept)))
                         (catch Exception e))
                    (recur)))
      ss))

(defn repl
[ins outs]
    ; set some bindings for the evaluation
    (binding [*ns* (create-ns 'user)
              *warn-on-reflection* false
              *out* (new OutputStreamWriter outs)]
      (let [eof (new Object)
            r (new LineNumberingPushbackReader
(new InputStreamReader ins))]
        (loop [e (read r false eof)]
          (when-not (= e eof)
            (prn (eval e))
            (flush)
            (recur (read r false eof)))))))

(defn socket-repl
[s] (on-thread
#(repl (. s (getInputStream)) (. s (getOutputStream)))))

(def server
    (create-server socket-repl "0.0.0.0" 9001))

; (. server (close))
```

You can see from the previous code, we create a set of local bindings in the repl function. The first binding *ns* create a user namespace to use for evaluation of the different forms. Another binding is *out* which simply pipes the output of the evaluation to the socket used for output.

Finally, each connection creates a thread, with input and output used as bindings in the eval function call.

Client

Writing a simple client that would connect to the preceding server is also quite simple. Say you want to programmatically send code to be evaluated remotely; this is how to do it, again with straightforward Java interop:

```
(ns custom-repl.client
    (:import [java.net  Socket]
        [java.io InputStreamReader OutputStreamWriter]
        [clojure.lang LineNumberingPushbackReader]))

(def client
  (new Socket "localhost" 9001))

(def rdr (new LineNumberingPushbackReader
            (new InputStreamReader (. client (getInputStream)))))
(def wtr (new OutputStreamWriter (. client (getOutputStream))))

(binding [*out* wtr]
  (prn '(+ 1 2 3))
  (flush)
  (read rdr))

(. client (close))
```

This can, of course, be used for regular REPLs as well and eventually any kind of socket connectivity.

The async custom REPL server

Java interop is cool but is also a bit *passe* when you can use core.async. You will need one more dependency in your project.clj file:

```
[com.hellonico.gearswithingears/async-sockets "0.1.0"]
```

A dumb REPL will go on using core.async to handle the request and simply eval the string that has been sent to the server. This is very similar to what we saw in the async chapters applied to something practical!

```
(ns custom-repl.async
  (:require [com.gearswithingears.async-sockets :refer :all]
        [clojure.core.async :as async]))

(defn eval-everything [socket]
  (async/go-loop []
    (when-let [line (async/<! (:in socket))]
```

```
      (async/>! (:out socket) (eval (read-string line)))
      (recur)))))

(let [server (socket-server 12349)]
  (async/go-loop []
    (when-let [connection (async/<! (:connections server))]
      (eval-everything connection)
(recur)))))
```

The async code is nicely shorter and more readable.

Server REPL or more on real-time work on production code

Now, onto one of the good news about the recently released Clojure 1.8! One of the new features that many of us have been waiting for a long time is the ability to just start a server REPL with ease.

Now it just became possible by simply declaring a parameter when starting the virtual machine, being able to connect to it using a simple socket, and having full access to an REPL.

Using the standard JAR file, for example, the one you build in the Clojure source code recipe, we will be using the following JVM parameter when starting `clojure.main`:

```
-Dclojure.server.repl="{:port 5555 :accept clojure.main/repl}"
```

This tells the Clojure runtime to start an `repl` on port `555`, and when a socket connect request is about to be accepted, use the `clojure.main/repl` function to handle the call. Now, for the simplest of cases, this translates into the following command:

```
java \
-cp clojure-1.8.0.jar  \
-Dclojure.server.repl="{:port 5555 :accept clojure.main/repl}" \
clojure.main
```

And effectively, Clojure will simply output the usual feedback message:

```
Clojure 1.8.0
user=>
```

But now, we can connect to it using __telnet__. We define the port to be 5555, so let's telnet to it:

```
niko> telnet 127.0.0.1 5555

Trying 127.0.0.1...
Connected to localhost.
Escape character is '^]'.
clojure.core=>
```

And we have full access to an REPL and the classpath we gave to our running application. So if we reuse the code that we have seen earlier on, say:

```
(def msg "I left a message here")
; #'clojure.core/msg
```

And then disconnect and reconnect to it, we will see that def-ed in the same namespace will still be there and persisted:

```
niko> telnet 127.0.0.1 5555

Trying 127.0.0.1...
Connected to localhost.
Escape character is '^]'.
clojure.core=> msg
"I left a message here"
```

How many sessions are running can be simply seen by using the following global variable:

```
clojure.core=> clojure.core.server/*session*
; {:server "repl", :client "5"}
```

The full map of parameters to start the REPL server is as follows:

```
{:address "localhost" ;; host or dotted name, ipv4 or ipv6
 :port 5555
 :name "repl"
 :accept clojure.main/repl
 :args []
 :bind-err true
 :server-daemon true
 :client-daemon true}
```

And it is also possible to read the configuration from a file.

Declarative data descriptions and validations with plumatic/schema

Clojure is dynamically typed language and often provides productivity when you develop alone or in a small team. However, developments in larger teams sometimes require knowledge about data between members. `prismatic/schema` provides the solution for the aforementioned problems.

In this recipe, we will learn how to add descriptive expressions and validations in Clojure. We will use `prismatic/schema` to define schemas for various data types and validate them with schemas. `prismatic/schema` can define functions that define schemas for input parameters and a return. We will then learn how to coerce one data type to another.

Finally, we will learn other solutions. We will introduce `core/typed` tries to provide a type inferences system similar to Scala. `core/spec` is a new feature and introduced in Clojure 1.9.

Getting ready

Let's create a project using `prismatic/schema`. `prismatic/schema`, which supports both Clojure and ClojureScript. So, let's create a project using Figwheel:

```
$ lein new figwheel schema-example
$ cd schema-example
```

We will add the library dependency for `prismatic/schema` in the `project.clj`:

```
:dependencies [[org.clojure/clojure "1.8.0"]
               [org.clojure/clojurescript "1.8.51"]
               [org.clojure/core.async "0.2.374"
                 :exclusions [org.clojure/tools.reader]]
               [prismatic/schema "1.1.1"]
               [prismatic/schema-generators "0.1.0"]
                ]]
```

Start REPL, and then create `src/schema-example/cljexample.clj` and declare the _`prismatic/schema` library to use:

```
(ns schema-example.clj-example
  (:require [schema.core :as s]))
;;=> nil
```

How to do it...

We will learn basic usages of `prismatic/schema` here. Let's start with a simple schema for books.

My first schema

Let's define a schema for the book. The `Book` is a map and the schema is as follows:

Name	Data type
name	String
author	Array of String
category	Set of keyword
publisher	String

Now, let's define the preceding schema using `prismatic/schema`:

```
(def Book
  {
   :name s/Str
   :author [s/Str]
   :category #{s/Keyword}
   :publisher s/Str})
  ;;=> #'schema-example.clj-example/Book
```

Then, let's check whether a given data is correct by validating with the `Book` schema. `schema.core/validate` validates checks using schema. `validate` returns it's parameter if the data is valid:

```
(s/validate
 Book
  {:name "Clojure Programming CookBook"
   :author ["Makoto Hashimoto" "Nicolas Modrzyk"]
   :category #{:programming :lisp :functional}
   :publisher "Packt Publishing"})
 ;;=> {:name "Clojure Programming CookBook", :author ["Makoto Hashimoto"
 "Nicolas Modrzyk"], :category #{:programming :lisp :functional}, :publisher
 "Packt Publishing"}
```

The following is not a valid schema since the value `:category` is not a set:

```
(s/validate
 Book
```

```
 {:name "Clojure Programming CookBook"
  :author ["Makoto Hashimoto" "Nicolas Modrzyk"]
  :category [:programming :lisp :functional]
  :publisher "Packt Publishing"})
;;=> ExceptionInfo Value does not match schema: {:category (not (set? a-
clojure.lang.PersistentVector))}  schema.core/validator/fn--38164
(core.clj:155)
```

Let's see some validations for some data types:

```
(s/validate s/Str "Makoto")
;;=> Makoto
(s/validate s/Int 100)
;;=> 100
(s/validate s/Num 100.0)
;;=> 100.0
(s/validate s/Bool true)
;;=> true
(s/validate s/Bool nil)
;;=> ExceptionInfo Value does not match schema: (not (instance?
java.lang.Boolean nil))  schema.core/validator/fn--38164 (core.clj:155)
```

Let's check validations for collection types such as array, map, and set:

```
(s/validate [s/Str] ["Makoto Hashimoto" "Nicolas Modrzyk"])
;; => ["Makoto Hashimoto" "Nicolas Modrzyk"]
(s/validate {s/Keyword s/Int} {:year 2016})
;; => {:year 2016}
(s/validate #{s/Keyword} #{:lisp :functional})
;; => #{:lisp :functional}
```

We will validate an any and an enumeration type:

```
(s/validate s/Any "Makoto")
;;=> "Makoto"
(s/validate s/Any 1.0)
;;=> 1.0
(s/validate s/Regex  #".*")
;;=> #".*"
(s/validate (s/enum "01" "02" "03") "01")
;;=> "01"
(s/validate (s/enum "01" "02" "03") "05")
;;=> ExceptionInfo Value does not match schema: (not (#{"03" "02" "01"}
"05"))  schema.core/validator/fn--38164 (core.clj:155)
```

Using schema for records and other types

We can use schema for records. Let's define `Order` type and validate it's instance:

```
(s/defrecord Order
    [name :- s/Str
     price :- s/Num
     qty :- s/Int])
11=> #'schema-example.clj-example/strict-map->Order
(s/explain Order)
;;=> (record schema_example.clj_example.Order {:name Str, :price Num, :qty
Int})
(s/validate Order (map->Order {:name "Clojure Programming Cookbook" :price
32.00 :qty 10}))
;;=> #schema_example.clj_example.Order{:name "Clojure Programming
Cookbook", :price 32.0, :qty 10}
```

The `Order` record has `name`, `price`, and `qty` attributes and their types are string, number, and integer, respectively. `prismatic/schema` provides validations for ranges of values. The next code validates the range of a number:

```
(s/validate (s/pred #(and (< 0 %) (> 10 %))) 5)
;;=> 5
```

`schema.core/maybe` checks whether the value is the specified type or nil:

```
 (s/validate (s/maybe s/Keyword) :price)
;;=> :price
(s/validate (s/maybe s/Keyword) nil)
;;=> nil
(s/validate (s/maybe s/Keyword) 1)
;;=> ExceptionInfo Value does not match schema: (not (keyword? 1))
schema.core/validator/fn--38164 (core.clj:155)
```

In the preceding example, keyword and nil are valid but integer is not valid. The following `NumMapOrSetOrList` validates checked data should be a map with its keys are keywords, set of numbers or array of numbers:

```
(def NumMapOrSetOrList (s/conditional map? {s/Keyword s/Num} set? #{s/Num}
:else [s/Num]))
;;=> #'schema-example.clj-example/NumMapOrSetOrList
(s/validate NumMapOrSetOrList {:qty 1.0})
;;=> {:qty 1.0}
(s/validate NumMapOrSetOrList #{1 2 3})
;;=> #{1 3 2}
(s/validate NumMapOrSetOrList [1 2 3])
;;=> [1 2 3]
```

```
(def SmallInt (s/constrained long #(and (<= -32768 %) (>= 32767 %)))))
;;=> #'schema-example.clj-example/SmallInt
(s/validate SmallInt 10)
;;=> 10
(s/validate SmallInt 500000)
;;=> ExceptionInfo Value does not match schema: (not (schema-example.clj-
example/fn--39713 500000))  schema.core/validator/fn--38164 (core.clj:155)
```

`prismatic/schema` provides recursive data types:

```
(def Recursive {:key s/Int :value s/Str :children [(s/recursive
#'Recursive)]})
;;=> #'schema-example.clj-example/Recursive
(s/validate Recursive
            {:key 1 :value "test", :children
             [{:key 2 :value "test2", :children [] }
              {:key 3 :value "test3", :children [{:key 4 :value "test4"
:children []}]}]})
;;=> {:key 100, :value "test", :children [{:key 2, :value "test2",
:children []} {:key 3, :value "test3", :children [{:key 4, :value "test4",
:children []}]}]}
```

Defining functions with validations

`schema.core/defn` validates input parameters and return types. The following example
defines `int-add` to add integer additions. Let's define `int-add`, whose parameters and
return types are the integer:

```
(s/defn int-add :- s/Int
  [& x :- [s/Int]]
  (reduce + x))
;;=> #'schema-example.clj-example/int-add
```

Let's test the function:

```
(int-add 1 1 2 3)
;;=> 7
(int-add 1 1.0 4)
;;=> 6.0
```

There is no schema check as default. `schema.core/set-fn-validation!` sets the schema
check as follows:

```
(s/set-fn-validation! true)
;;=> nil
(int-add 1 1.0 4)
;;=> ExceptionInfo Input to int-add does not match schema: [nil (not
```

```
(integer? 1.0))]   schema-example.clj-example/eval49222/int-add--49227
(form-init3277965317664434982.clj:262)
(s/set-fn-validation! false)
;;=> nil
(int-add 1 1.0 4)
;;=> 6.0
```

So, let's check if the return type is not valid. The `^:always-validate` always validates schema types:

```
(s/defn ^:always-validate wrong-int-add :- s/Int
    [& x :- [s/Int]]
  (bigdec (reduce + x)))
;;=> #'schema-example.clj-example/wrong-int-add
(wrong-int-add 1 1)
;;=> ExceptionInfo Output of wrong-int-add does not match schema: (not
(integer? 2M))   schema-example.clj-example/eval49476/wrong-int-add--49481
(form-init3277965317664434982.clj:284)
```

In the preceding case, `wrong-int-add` returns `BigDecimal`, and this causes an error.

How it works...

In this recipe, we will check performance of prismatic schema and how we can generate test data using schema.

Performance considerations

Here, we will check performance using `int-add`. Let's compare the performance of `schema.core/with-fn-validation` and `schema.core/without-fn-validation`:

```
(time
 (dotimes [n 100000]
   (s/with-fn-validation
     (int-add 1 2))))
;;"Elapsed time: 587.858912 msecs"
;;=> nil
(time
 (dotimes [n 100000]
   (s/without-fn-validation
     (int-add 1 2))))
;;=> "Elapsed time: 150.847882 msecs"
;;=> nil
```

No schema checking is faster. Then, we will test the performance of (s/set-fn-validation! true) **and** (s/set-fn-validation! false):

```
(s/set-fn-validation! true)
;;=> nil
(time
 (dotimes [n 100000]
   (int-add 1 2)))
;;=> "Elapsed time: 140.624018 msecs"
;;=> nil
(s/set-fn-validation! false)
;;=> nil
(time
 (dotimes [n 100000]
   (int-add 1 2)))
;;=> "Elapsed time: 28.948555 msecs"
;;=> nil
```

In terms of performance, using set-fn-validation is faster than with-fn-validation/without-fn-validation to switch validations. Lastly, we will test the performance of native + function:

```
(time
 (dotimes [n 100000]
   (+ 1 2)))
;;=> "Elapsed time: 7.058001 msecs"
;;=> nil
```

Additions for two numbers are too small to evaluate performance of prismatic/schema. Let's measure performance by calculating additions of a hundred numbers:

```
(time
 (dotimes [n 1000000]
   (apply int-add (range 100))))
"Elapsed time: 3387.52923 msecs"
;;=> nil

(time
 (dotimes [n 1000000]
   (apply + (range 100))))
"Elapsed time: 3681.930561 msecs"
;;=> nil
```

There seems to be no difference between using schema and not using schema.

Generating test data

`prismatic/schema` can be used to generate test data. `prismatic/schema-generators` generates test data from schemas. `prismatic/schema-generators` is still an alpha version, but very useful to generate test data and understand the data structure. So, let's see how it works.

First, we will add `schema-generators.generators` to the `:require` section in the namespace declaration:

```
(ns schema-example.clj-example
  (:require [schema.core :as s]
            [schema.coerce :as coerce :include-macros true]
            [schema-generators.complete :as c :include-macros true]
            [schema-generators.generators :as g  :include-macros true]
               [schema-generators.complete :as gc]
))
;;=> nil
```

Let's add another map key and its value is an `enum` type:

```
(def Book
  {
   :name s/Str
   :author [s/Str]
   :keyword #{s/Keyword}
   :publisher s/Str
   :category (s/enum :it :romance :business-money)})
;;=> #'schema-example.clj-example/Book
```

Then, we will create test data from the `Book`:

```
(g/generate Book)
;;=> {:name "gWTFZ>'", :author ["ECg5Q" " i>Y8z\\2"], :keyword #{},
:publisher "s@", :category :it}
```

The following code will generate 100 data:

```
(g/sample 100 Book)
;;=> ({:name "", :author [], :keyword #{}, :publisher "", :category
:business-money}
;;=>  {:name "", :author [""], :keyword #{:Wt}, :publisher ">", :category
:it}
;;=>  {:name "z", :author [], :keyword #{:j}, :publisher "jK", :category
:business-money}
;;=>     ......
```

It's easy to generate random data:

```
(g/sample 10 s/Str)
;;=> ("" "'" "##" "r8" "" "'Uqn3" "" "F86O2Bl" "AR~2," "")
(g/sample 10 s/Int)
;;=> (-1 -1 -2 1N 0N -9 -1N 23 2 -6)
(g/sample 10 s/Num)
;;=> (0 0.75 0 1 -1 2.0 -4 -2 2.0 0.5)
```

`schema-generators.complete` creates complete data for defined schemas:

```
(gc/complete {:name "foo" :keyword #{:bar}} Book)
;;=> {:name "foo", :author ["ft?" "yY31"], :keyword #{:bar}, :publisher
"kw", :category :romance}
```

There's more...

`prismatic/schema` runs on ClojureScript. We will run Figwheel to test it.

Data coercion with prismatic/schema

Before we learn about this section, let's run Figwheel REPL:

```
$ lein figwheel
```

Then, define `schema-example.cljs-example` namespace and declare schema libraries as
follows:

```
(ns schema-example.cljs-example
  (:require [schema.core :as s :include-macros true]
            [schema.coerce :as coerce :include-macros true]
            [schema-generators.complete :as c :include-macros true]
            [schema-generators.generators :as g :include-macros true]
            [schema-generators.complete :as gc :include-macros true]
            ))
;;=> nil
```

Using ClojureScript, the `:include-macros` option is necessary. Let's assume an order has
two products. `defschema` is a macro for defining schemas and recording the name of the
schema in the metadata:

```
(s/defschema RequestOrder
  { :id s/Str
   :product s/Str
   :qty s/Int
```

```
    :unit-price s/Num
    :product2 s/Str
    :qty2 s/Int
    :unit-price2 s/Num})
;;=> #'schema-example.cljs-example/RequestOrder
```

We will define RequestOrder, whose format is slightly different from RequestOrder:

```
(s/defschema ReplyOrder
  { :order-id s/Str
   :ordered-product [[(s/one s/Str "s")(s/one s/Int "s")(s/one s/Num "s")]]
   })
;;=> #'schema-example.cljs-example/ReplyOrder
```

Two orders are grouped into :order-product and the data type of value is arrays of array. prismatic/schema/one restricts the orders of the sequences of arrays. The previous schema restricts each product is [String, Integer, Number].

We will write a mapping between RequestOrder and ReplyOrder as follows:

```
(defn RequestOrder->ReplyOrder
  [{:keys [id product qty unit-price product2 qty2 unit-price2]  :as
request-params}]
  {:order-id id :ordered-product [[product qty unit-price][product2 qty2
unit-price2]]})
;;=> #'schema-example.cljs-example/RequestOrder->ReplyOrder
```

Then, let's define order-coercer and test it:

```
(def crder-coercer
  (coerce/coercer ReplyOrder
                  {ReplyOrder RequestOrder->ReplyOrder}))
;;=> #'schema-example.cljs-example/order-coercer
(order-coercer
 {:id "10" :product "pencil" :qty 5 :unit-price 1.0 :product2 "note" :qty2
5 :unit-price2 3.0})
 ;;=> {:order-id "10", :ordered-product [["pencil" 5 1] ["note" 5 3]]}
```

We can see that an input map is transformed into an array of arrays. Next, we will try another coercer. The following coercer transforms products into an array of maps:

```
(s/defschema ReplyOrder2
  { :order-id s/Str
   :ordered-product
   [{ (s/required-key :product-name) s/Str
      (s/required-key :qty) s/Int
      (s/required-key :unit-price) s/Num}]})
;;=> #'schema-example.cljs-example/RequestOrder
```

```
(defn RequestOrder->ReplyOrder2
  [{:keys [id product qty unit-price product2 qty2 unit-price2]  :as
request-params}]
  {:order-id id
   :ordered-product [
                       {:product-name product :qty qty :unit-price unit-
price}
                       {:product-name product2 :qty qty2 :unit-price unit-
price2}]})
;;=> #'schema-example.cljs-example/RequestOrder->ReplyOrder2
```

Then, let's test it:

```
(def order-coercer2
  (coerce/coercer ReplyOrder2
                  {ReplyOrder2 RequestOrder->ReplyOrder2}))
;;=> #'schema-example.clj-example/order-coercer2
(order-coercer2
 {:id "10" :product "pencil" :qty 5 :unit-price 1.0 :product2 "note" :qty2
5 :unit-price2 3.0})
 ;;=> {:order-id "10", :ordered-product [{:product-name "pencil", :qty 5,
:unit-price 1} {:product-name "note", :qty 5, :unit-price 3}]}
```

Using core.typed

Here, we will give a brief introduction to `core.typed`, which is a different approach from `prismatic/schema`. `core.typed` is an optional typed system in Clojure and enables to check types statically for vars, function parameters, and macros at compilation time. It is also possible to annotate protocols and data types.

To start with `core.typed`, let's modify `project.clj` as follows and restart REPL:

```
:dependencies [[org.clojure/clojure "1.8.0"]
               [org.clojure/core.typed "0.3.21"]]
  :repositories {"sonatype-oss-public"
"https://oss.sonatype.org/content/groups/public/"}
  :injections [(require 'clojure.core.typed)
               (clojure.core.typed/install)]
```

Create `src/typed_example/core.clj` and declare the namespace as follows:

```
(ns typed-example.core
  {:lang :core.typed}
  (:require [clojure.core.typed :as t]))
```

Then, let's define the annotation of my-add using clojure.core.typed/ann:

```
(t/ann my-add [Number Number -> Number])
;;=> nil
```

We will define my-add using clojure.core/defn and test it:

```
(defn my-add [a b] (+ a b))
;;=> #'typed-example.core/my-add
(my-add 1 2)
;;=> 3
```

It works! Now, we will test a failure case to give a string parameter:

```
(my-add 1 "a")
;;=> Type Error (*cider-repl typed-example:49585*:459:20) Function add
could not be applied to arguments:
;;=> Domains:
;;=>      Number Number
;;=> Arguments:
;;=>      (t/Val 1) (t/Val "a")
;;=> Ranges:
;;=>      Number
;;=> in: (my-add 1 "a")
;;=> ExceptionInfo Type Checker: Found 1 error  clojure.core/ex-info
(core.clj:4617)
```

We can define types in vars as follows:

```
(t/ann d-value BigDecimal)
;;=> nil
```

And let's test the preceding as follows:.

```
(def d-value 10.0M)
;;=> #'typed-example.core/d-value
(def d-value 1)
;;=> Type Error (*cider-repl typed-example:49585*:584:20) Type mismatch:
;;=> Expected:    BigDecimal
;;=> Actual:      (t/Val 1)
;;=> in: 1
;;=> ExceptionInfo Type Checker: Found 1 error  clojure.core/ex-info
(core.clj:4617)
```

It fails to assign 1 to d-value.

core.spec

Clojure 1.9 supports spec library to support structures of data, validations, and generations by specifications by spec_. It's similar to `prismatic/schema__`, but it is included in Clojure, and there is no need to load additional libraries.

Let's create a new project named `spec-example`:

```
$ lein new spec-example
```

Then replace the version of Clojure:

```
:dependencies [[org.clojure/clojure "1.9.0-alpha7"]]
```

We will declare to use `clojure.spec` as follows:

```
(ns spec-example.core
  (:require [clojure.spec :as s])
  )
```

We define a sequence of string using `core.spec` as follows:

```
(s/def ::seq-of-names (s/* string?))
;;=> :spec-example.core/seq-of-names
```

To see the definition, use `core.spec/describe`:

```
(s/describe ::seq-of-names)
;;=> (* string?)
```

Let's test it:

```
(s/conform ::seq-of-names ["Makoto Hashimoto" "Nicolas Modrzyk"])
;;=> ["Makoto Hashimoto" "Nicolas Modrzyk"]
```

It works fine, but the following check fails:

```
(s/conform ::seq-of-names [:Makoto-Hashimoto "Nicolas Modrzyk"])
;;=> :clojure.spec/invalid
```

The following codes are the same as those in the `prismatic/schema` section in this recipe:

```
(s/def ::date (s/map-of keyword? integer?))
;;=> :spec-example.core/date
(s/conform ::date {:year 2016})
;;=> {:year 2016}
(s/conform ::date {:year 2016 :date 10 :month 7})
;;=> {:year 2016, :date 10, :month 7}
```

```
(s/valid? #{"01" "02" "03"} "01")
;;=> true
(s/valid? #{"01" "02" "03"} "04")
;;=> false
(s/valid? (s/nilable string?) "test")
;;=> true
(s/valid? (s/nilable string?) nil)
;;=> true
(s/valid? (s/nilable string?) 1)
;;=> false
(s/def ::small-int #(<= -32768 % 32767))
;;=> :spec-example.core/small-int
(s/conform ::small-int 10)
;;=> 10
(s/conform ::small-int 50000)
;;=> :clojure.spec/invalid
```

To define function specs for the function, use `core.spec/fdef`. We will define a very simple function that restricts values of arguments that are integer and positive. First, we will define `positive-int-add` by `defn`:

```
(defn positive-int-add [x  y]
  (+ x y))
;;=> #'spec-example.core/positive-int-add
```

Then, we will use `core.spec/fdef` to check two arguments that are integer and larger than 0:

```
(s/fdef positive-int-add
        :args (s/and (s/cat :x integer? :y integer?)
                     #(and (< 0 (:x %) ) (< 0 (:y %) )))
        :ret integer?)
;;=> spec-example.core/positive-int-add
```

Let's check the `positive-int-add` function:

```
(positive-int-add 1 10)
;;=> 11
(positive-int-add 1 -20)
;;=> -19
```

Oops, the function didn't check the argument -20. To be `core.spec/fdef` enable, we have to do as follows:

```
(s/instrument #'positive-int-add)
;;=> #'spec-example.core/positive-int-add
```

Let's do it again!

```
(positive-int-add 1 -20)
;;=> ExceptionInfo Call to #'spec-example.core/positive-int-add did not
conform to spec:
;;=> val: {:x 1, :y -20} fails at: [:args] predicate: (and (< 0 (:x %)) (<
0 (:y %)))
;;=> :clojure.spec/args  (1 -20)
;;=>    clojure.core/ex-info (core.clj:4703)
```

Here, `fdef` for `positive-int-add` worked correctly and that's it!

8
Web Applications

In this chapter, we will cover:

- Clojure with Vaadin – easy web widgets
- Quickly create a REST API with Liberator
- Working with Immutant – reusing infrastructure
- Developing with om.next, the next-generation ClojureScript library

Introduction

In this chapter, we will learn web application developments using Clojure. First, we will learn how to develop widget-based developments using Vaadin. We will learn how easy widget-based development is, using Vaadin through Clojure.

Then, we will take a look at Liberator. Liberator is a library for developing resources in REST. We will develop a simple REST API with Liberator at the beginning but we will learn more advanced usages using Liberator.

Next, we will learn about Immutant, a suite of Clojure libraries based on Undertow for web, HornetQ for messaging, Infinispan for caching, Quartz for scheduling and Narayama for transactions. Using Immutant for application developments, we can deploy to a WildFly or JBoss EAP cluster for enhanced features. In this recipe, we will learn to develop advanced web applications using Immutant. We will also learn to how to package and deploy our application.

Finally, we take a look at David Nolen's om.next. Om.next is a successor of om inspired by Facebook's Relay, Netflix's Falcor, and Cognitect's Datomic. It's still alpha but has new concepts for developing applications. In the recipe, we will learn the basic features of om.next.

Clojure with Vaadin – easy web widgets

Vaadin has been around for quite some time and is known to be an all coding-based UI framework for web applications. There are many frameworks out there for just doing web work of course, and even in this chapter we introduce some of the famous ones based on JavaScript libraries.

Vaadin proposes to have a consistent set of easy-to-use widgets, that usually would be Java written. With a bit of Clojure magic, but mostly some ways of bridging the gap between compiled code and scripting, you can now use your favorite language to script the UI using those widgets and see updates in real time. In this recipe, you will also be introduced again to some reactive programming concepts in the scope of Vaadin with Clojure. Enjoy!

Getting ready

To begin with programming in Clojure/Vaadin, you will start by setting up the `project.clj` file with some easy but specific settings. Let's see what is inside.

Project settings

To use the Vaadin classes, we will import the necessary libraries into our project. The Vaadin libraries will be included as regular dependencies. The `project.clj` file is also introducing the `lein-servlet` plugin, which is a plugin that plugs the usual Java-based server-side programming environment named `servlet`. The plugin also embeds a lightweight application server named Jetty.

Finally, the `project.clj` file helps plug things together by starting the Jetty server, with the specified arguments, namely a web application that is bounded to the root path `"/"` and will be configured with the content of a `web.xml` file, which used to be the usual way of configuring a Java web application through an XML file.

Let's start by putting the dependencies together in a `project.clj` file:

```
(defproject vaadin2 "0.1.0-SNAPSHOT"
  :dependencies [
    [org.clojure/clojure "1.8.0"]
    [com.vaadin/vaadin-server "7.6.6"]
    [com.vaadin/vaadin-client-compiled "7.6.6"]
    [com.vaadin/vaadin-themes "7.6.6"]
    [javax.servlet/javax.servlet-api "3.1.0"]]
  :resource-paths ["example00"]
```

```
:plugins [[lein-servlet "0.4.1"]]
  :servlet {:deps [[lein-servlet/adapter-jetty8 "0.4.1"]]
            :config {:engine :jetty :host "localhost"}
            :webapps
{"/"
 {:public "resources"
  :web-xml "src/main/webapp/WEB-INF/web.xml"}}})
```

The Clojure/Vaadin flow

The last part of the configuration may be a bit obscure still, so let's decompose those steps a bit:

1. The Vaadin framework starts with a generic Vaadin servlet, which is basically a Java request handler for server-side web programming.
2. This Vaadin servlet needs mostly one parameter to be started, and that is a call that extends the `com.vaadin.ui.UI` Java class.
3. That Java class has one method, `init`, that will receive a one-time request parameter and the application UI object.
4. The previous UI class will be responsible for writing or delegating all the Java code describing the application.
5. Finally, in the context of this recipe, the UI Java class will make use of the usual way of plugging Clojure scripts in a Java app, making the processing dynamic, and refreshing on each request.

What does that give in Clojure then? You want here to have Clojure code implementing the `init` method of the UI class, where that `init` method loads a Clojure script, and executes a given method; here, we will call the namespace `ex1`, and the method `main`:

```
(ns vaadin2.vaadin2ui
   (:gen-class
    :name vaadin2.vaadin2ui
    :extends com.vaadin.ui.UI))
(defn -init
  [main-ui request]
  (clojure.lang.RT/loadResourceScript "ex1.clj")
  (.setContent
    main-ui
    (.invoke (clojure.lang.RT/var "ex1" "main") main-ui)))
```

Finally, you need to write the `ex1/main` function, where the main function sets the content of the main placeholder.

Here, you can make use of the Vaadin classes at will; this is where it starts. An application usually needs a layout, and our first label will say something like hello in French:

```
(ns ex1
  (:import [com.vaadin.ui VerticalLayout Label]))
(defn main[ui]
  (let [
    layout  (VerticalLayout.)
    label   (Label. "Bonjour le monde!")]
    (.addComponent layout label)))
```

All the elements are in place; the Leiningen servlet plugin will give you a servlet subcommand, including a `run` command to start the server:

lein servlet run

In the default development mode, that command will also open a browser page with the right URL, and here you go, some hello world in French!

The interesting part, as you may already have noticed, is that the Vaadin servlet is calling a script, which means changing the code of that script will make the changes being used straight up on the next request. Try it. Let's change the text of the `ext1.clj` file:

```
(defn main[ui]
  (let [
    layout  (VerticalLayout.)
    label   (Label. "Hello World!")]
    (.addComponent layout label)))
```

Refreshing the browser page, it now nicely translates to English:

With all those greetings possibilities now in your pocket, let's see some more examples of how to use Vaadin in the next section.

How to do it...

In this section, you will be introduced to new widgets, and gradually learn how to interact with widgets using Vaadin events.

Using the Calendar widget

Using the `Calendar` widget is done through standard Java interop. The official Vaadin documentation for the calendar can be found at the following URL: `https://vaadin.com/docs/-/part/framework/components/components-calendar.html`.

Translating the example in the previous link to Clojure gives you:

```
(defn calendar []
  (let[ cal (Calendar. "Today Calendar")]
    (doto cal
      (.setWidth "600px")
      (.setHeight "500px")
      (.setStartDate (Date.))
      (.setEndDate (Date.)) )))
```

You can mount the `Calendar` to the application using what was presented in the first section:

```
(defn main [app]
    (let [layout  (VerticalLayout.)
    calendar (calendar)]
      (doto layout
        (.addComponent calendar))))
```

In the `project.clj` file, for each example, we will change the path of the Clojure resources; so, for example, for the calendar example, add this:

```
:resource-paths ["example01-calendar"]
```

This will make the `loadResourceScript` function look for files in the proper folder. Start the application with `lein servlet run` and:

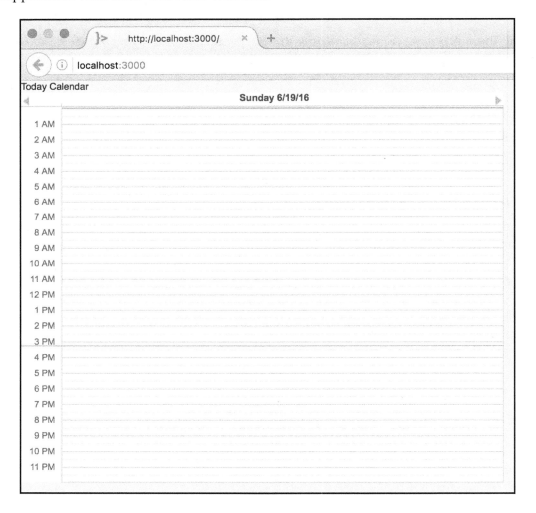

It seems you do not have much to do today, so let's add a bit of fun. You probably forgot about that birthday party, so let's add it now:

```
(def sample-event
  (let [
  start (GregorianCalendar.)
  end (GregorianCalendar.)]
  (.add end java.util.Calendar/HOUR 2)
  (doto
    (BasicEvent.
      "Birthday Part7"
      "At Ren's place"
      (.getTime start)
(.getTime end)) )))
```

And in the `calendar` method, you will need one more line to add the event with:

```
(defn calendar []
  (let[ cal (Calendar. "Today Calendar")]
    (doto cal
...
    (.addEvent sample-event))))
```

Refreshing the page makes the event show immediately:

The calendar event reacts to interaction from the UI, for example, a drag and drop.

Reacting to events

A lot of UI event programming with Vaadin is done in a similar fashion, namely implementing an event listener. The UI event that will be triggered when you move the Calendar event is: `CalendarEvent$EventChangeListener`.

You can do the interface implementation using either `proxy` or `reify`:

```
; using proxy
(def event-change-fn
  (proxy [CalendarEvent$EventChangeListener] []
    (eventChange [eventChangeEvent]
      (println eventChangeEvent))))

; using reify
(def event-change-fn
  (reify CalendarEvent$EventChangeListener
    (eventChange [this eventChangeEvent]
      (println eventChangeEvent))))
```

The choice is up to you, but do not forget to add the handler in the calendar construction function:

```
(.addEventChangeListener event-change-fn))
```

After refreshing the page, dragging the calendar event up or down will trigger the handler, and prints some information for the updated event on the command line.

This way of using `proxy` or `reify` will be widely used in this recipe so make sure to play around a bit to master it before moving on. It's a very important building block, so let's go through one more example with a button handler.

Clicking a button

Clicking a button is about implementing the `ClickListener` interface. Let's go through this together:

```
(defn main [ui]
  (let [layout (VerticalLayout.)
        first-name (TextField.)
        submit-button (Button. "Submit")]
    (.addComponent layout (Label. "First Name"))
    (.addComponent layout first-name)
    (.addComponent layout submit-button)
    (.addListener submit-button
      (proxy [Button$ClickListener] []
        (buttonClick [event]
          (println (.getValue first-name)))))
    layout))
```

The preceding snippet adds a label, a field, and a button to a vertical layout. The button then gets an event handler to react to a click event, and so will print the value of the text field when it is clicked:

With the basics in, it is about time to start organizing the code just a bit; let's see how to organize code into a different namespace, and still see the updates after a refresh.

Using and reloading namespaces

In this example, you will see how to separate Vaadin-related code into different namespaces. Let's say you have a basic layout, with a label and a button:

```
(defn- main-layout []
  (doto (VerticalLayout.)
    (.addComponent (Label. "Hello Clojure!"))
    (.addComponent (button "Press me" show-message))))
(defn main [ui]
(main-layout))
```

You now want to have the code related to buttons in a separate file, buttons.clj:

```
(ns buttons
    (:import [com.vaadin.ui
Button
Button$ClickListener
Notification]))

(defn button-click-listener
  [action]
  (reify Button$ClickListener
          (buttonClick [_ evt] (action))))

(defn listener [button action]
  (.addListener button (button-click-listener action)))

(defn show-message []
```

```
(Notification/show "clicked"))

(defn button
(doto (Button. caption) (listener action)))
```

The first file will reference the buttons namespace with:

```
(ns ex1
  (:require [buttons :as b])
  (:import...))
```

Loading the server, you can see the application and the button showing:

And even nice Vaadin notifications entering the scene, through calls to
Notification/show:

Now if you try to change the code in buttons.clj, and update the function that shows a
Vaadin notification to:

```
(defn show-message []
    (Notification/show "clicked again!"))
```

Refreshing the page and clicking the button again sadly shows the previous message. In
fact, none of the code of the namespace seems to have been updated in the running
container.

To get back to a friendlier development workflow, you can use the `reload-all` directive in the namespace `require` directive, as follows:

```
(:require :reload-all [buttons :as b])
```

And now refreshing the page will get you the original reloading behavior, as if everything was in one file.

Server-side push

Up to now, the UI you have been working on was directly coded in Vaadin code, or was updated through interaction from the user, and reactive code with listeners. To send messages asynchronously, not reacting to user interaction, you will use something named server-side push. Server-side push requires you to do a few things:

- Set up an additional specific Vaadin library
- Set up the application to support push, and start the push WebSocket framework
- Add some asynchronous UI update code

Let's go through an example by looking at how to send a message to the client a few seconds after the application has started.

First, the additional library, unsurprisingly, is named `vaadin-push` and goes into your `project.clj` file:

```
[com.vaadin/vaadin-push "7.6.6"]
```

Second, the first line of Clojure code in the application will set up the push mechanism:

```
(.setPushMode
 (.getPushConfiguration ui)
 (com.vaadin.shared.communication.PushMode/AUTOMATIC))
```

This is a bit cryptic, but basically this just sets the push mechanism to start. Third, or actually before third, let's try to write an async update of the UI:

```
(defn runme []
  (reify Runnable
    (run [_]
      (Thread/sleep 3000)
      ; (Notification/show "Does not work"))))
              (-> (UI/getCurrent) (.access async-ui-update)))))

(defn main[ui]
```

```
(.setPushMode
  (.getPushConfiguration ui)
  (com.vaadin.shared.communication.PushMode/AUTOMATIC))

(let [layout  (VerticalLayout.)]
  (.addComponent layout (Label. "I am getting sleepy ~~~"))
  (.start (Thread. (runme)))
  layout
  ))
```

The code reads by doing a simple layout, starting a thread, and, after 3 seconds, displaying the notification. Running the code by yourself... You will notice very quickly that...the thread starts, waits for 3 seconds and...does nothing. As you read it properly, it doesn't work. What's wrong?

The reason behind the lack of visual update is that the thread that was spawned is not the UI thread anymore, so the refresh does not link to existing UI objects and the update fails.

To perform an async update, we will implement a new `Runnable`, and ask the UI thread to perform the async update. This is done with `UI/getCurrent` to retrieve the UI thread, and `.access` to perform the async update.

So, with those few updates, you now have the following code:

```
(def async-ui-update
    (reify Runnable
      (run [_]
        (Notification/show "Let's sleep"))))

(defn runme []
  (reify Runnable
    (run [_]
      (Thread/sleep 3000)
      ; (Notification/show "Does not work"))))
      (-> (UI/getCurrent) (.access async-ui-update)))))
```

And finally, the notification shows the following:

There's more...

The bricks are laid to do a bit of reactive programming with Vaadin. Let's look at some cases.

Reactive Vaadin – ideas

We will add a standard Clojure atom here to be the reactive point, plus a listener on that atom to perform the async UI updates.

This example adds a reactive text field that shows a notification when its value has been updated:

```
(def last-value
  (atom ""))

(defn runme [msg]
  (let [async-ui-update
    (proxy [Runnable] [] (run [] (Notification/show msg)))]
      (-> (UI/getCurrent) (.access async-ui-update)))))

(defn my-layout [layout]
  (.addComponent layout (Label. "Write something"))
  (let [first-name (TextField. )]
    (.addComponent layout first-name)

    (.addValueChangeListener first-name
      (proxy [Property$ValueChangeListener] []
```

```
            (valueChange [event]
              (dosync (reset! last-value
            (-> event (.getSource) (.getValue)))))))))))

(defn main [ui]
  (.setPushMode
      (.getPushConfiguration ui)
      (com.vaadin.shared.communication.PushMode/AUTOMATIC))
    (let [base (VerticalLayout.)]
      (my-layout base)

      (add-watch last-value :listener
        (fn [key atom old-state new-state]
          (runme new-state)))
    base))
```

You already saw the async UI update mechanism. Here, the new event that will be listened to is `Property$ValueChangeListener`, which is fired when the text field gets a different value after user input. The atom will then hold the last and current value of the text field. Finally, a listener on the atom will fire the async UI update on the atom value being updated:

Reactive Vaadin – CPU monitoring

One of the obvious advantages of Vaadin-ing is that you write server-side code, and some of it gets translated to the browser side.

So we could monitor the CPU usage of a Raspberry Pi, and display its CPU usage. We will use a convenient scheduling library, `hara.ui`, to achieve the CPU polling on the server side, and then reuse the technique of the atom + atom listener to display the updates on the client side.

To add `hara.io` to the project, let's add a line to `project.clj`:

```
[im.chit/hara.io.scheduler "2.3.6"]
```

Then expand on the example code:

```
(ns ex1
  (:use [clojure.java.shell :only [sh]])
  (:use [hara.io.scheduler])
  ...)
(def last-value
  (atom ""))

(defn collect-cpu-fn[t params]
  (let [
    ; linux
    command "grep 'cpu ' /proc/stat | awk '{usage=($2+$4)*100/($2+$4+$5)}
END {print usage "%"}'"
    ; macos
    ; command "top -l 1 | head -n 10 | grep CPU | awk '{print $2}'"
    cpu (:out (sh "bash" "-c" command))]
  (dosync (reset! last-value cpu))))

(def cpu-task
{:handler collect-cpu-fn
 :schedule "/3 * * * * *"
 :params {}})

(def sch1 (scheduler {:print-task cpu-task}))
(start! sch1)
```

The atom value will be updated every 3 seconds, with the latest polled value for CPU usage. The command to monitor the raw CPU usage is slightly different from platform to platform; unfortunately, this is hardly accessible from Java. Fortunately, we can revert to shell to get the information we want.

Following is a screenshot of the application, running on a Raspberry Pi:

Finally, the Vaadin application is accessed from a local browser accessing the Raspberry Pi.

Security Notice: none.

Reactive Vaadin – Telegram on Raspberry Pi

The last example of this recipe brings Telegram bots to your local Raspberry Pi.

The library morse, a wrapper around the Telegram API, is used to register an event coming through your registered bot, meaning the Vaadin-based application will be running on the Raspberry Pi, and will be listening to bot messages caught by the morse polling engine.

In your project.clj, add the following line:

```
[morse "0.1.1"]
```

And then the Vaadin/Clojure code is basically the same as we have seen so far, updating the Clojure atom when a new message is sent to the bot:

```
(ns ex1
  (:use [clojure.java.shell :only [sh]])
  (:require [morse.polling :as p])
  (:require [morse.handlers :refer :all])
  ...)

(def token "<your bot token here ...>")
```

```
(def last-value
  (atom ""))

; telegram bot handler: update the atom when a message is received
(defhandler bot-api
  (message
    message
    (dosync (reset! last-value (:text message)))))

; for this example, simply start a polling method to get events
(def channel
  (p/start token bot-api))
...
```

From there, messages sent to the bot will be picked up by the Raspberry Pi and shown on browsers connecting to the Vaadin application:

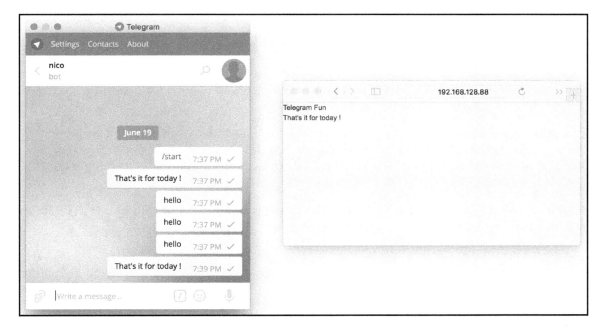

Obviously, things do not end here, and this recipe should have fired your imagination and made you want more. That's good!

Deployment bonus

The `lein servlet` plugin adds the extra bonus of allowing the creation of web Java archives, or WAR files. The command has two patterns:

```
lein servlet war
lein servlet uberwar
```

The first version will only include code related directly to your application, while the second one will also include all the dependencies, depending on your deployment strategy. Obviously, the second one, `uberwar`, is easier but takes more disk space, while the first one, `war`, takes a bit of thinking.

Both ways, though, allow you to deploy to Java web servers at will, and if the requirements are to run in a Java context, this is also a nice way to cover your Clojure usage!

Quickly create a REST API with Liberator

Liberator is a Clojure library for developing resources for REST web services. REST is an abbreviation for **Representational State Transfer** and it's an architectural style for designing web network applications.

Liberator was inspired by Erlang's Webmachine. Webmachine was developed by Justin Sheehy, who is the CTO of Basho Technologies, has developed Riak. Webmachine is a RESTful toolkit for writing well-behaved HTTP applications and helping developers to handle the complexities of an HTTP-based application.

Similarly, using Liberator makes web API developments simpler but provides HTTP rich features such as content negotiation and caching.

Getting ready

Before we learn Liberator, we will create a new project named `liberator-example`. To do this, use `lein new` to create a new Clojure project:

```
$ lein new liberator-example
```

Then, we will modify the generated `project.clj` to make use of Liberator. In addition to a Liberator library, we need the `ring` and `compojure` libraries. We will also need `clj-http` and `cheshire` for the HTTP client to make REST API calls:

```
:dependencies [[org.clojure/clojure "1.8.0"]
               [liberator "0.14.1"]
               [compojure "1.3.4"]
               [ring "1.5.0-RC1"]
               [ring/ring-core "1.5.0-RC1"]
               [buddy "0.13.0"]
               [ring/ring-jetty-adapter "1.4.0"]
               [clj-http "2.2.0"]
               [cheshire "5.6.1"]]
```

Ring server provides a simple web server and it makes testing easier. We will add a ring plugin in the `project.clj` as follows:

```
:ring {:handler liberator-example.example/handler}
:plugins [[lein-ring "0.9.7"]]
```

How to do it...

It's time to try Liberator. Here, we will learn how to implement GET, POST, PUT, and DELETE using Liberator. But let's start with making a simple hello Clojure server using Liberator!

Your first Liberator

First, we will declare the required libraries. We also will use ring server and Compojure. Ring server is a famous web server written in Clojure. Compojure is a router for dispatching web requests to target resources.

`clj.http` and `cheshire.core` enable clients to make requests to REST API services provided by Liberator:

```
(ns liberator-example.example
  (:require
  [liberator.core :refer [resource defresource]]
  [ring.adapter.jetty :refer [run-jetty]]
  [ring.middleware.params :refer [wrap-params]]
  [compojure.core :refer
   [defroutes ANY GET PUT POST DELETE OPTIONS]]
  [clj-http.client :as client]
  [cheshire.core :refer [parse-string generate-string]]))
;;=> nil
```

The following code generates a static HTML content for clients:

```
(defroutes app
  (ANY "/hello" []
       (resource :available-media-types ["text/html"]
                 :handle-ok "<html><h1>Hello Clojure !</h1></html>"))
  (route/not-found "Not Found !"))
;;=> #'liberator-example.example/app
```

In the previous code, we used `compojure.core/defroutes` to define a context as `/hello` and `liberator.core/resource` defines a resource.

Then, let's define a handler and run it. `ring.middleware.params/wrap-params` parses query strings for requests and form bodies:

```
(def handler
  (-> app
      wrap-params))
;;=> #'liberator-example.example/handler
```

Then, start the server and make requests from your browser:

```
(def server (run-jetty handler {:port 3000 :join? false}))
;;=> #'liberator-example.example/server
```

Open your browser with `http://localhost:3000/hello`. You can see the following string in your browser:

To make requests from the command line, use the `curl` command:

```
$ curl -X GET http://localhost:3000/hello
```

The next image shows you how the `curl` command works:

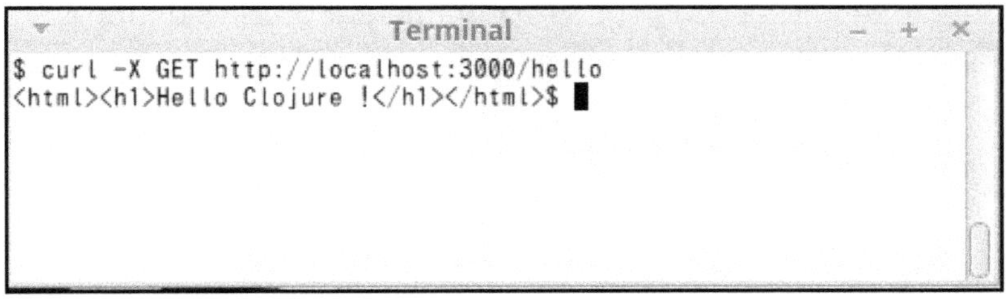

If you test successfully, let's stop the server for further topics in the recipe:

```
(.stop server)
;;=> nil
```

Using defresource

Here, we will use `defresource` macro to define resources:

```
(defresource hello :available-media-types ["text/html"]
         :handle-ok "<html><h1>Hello Clojure from defresource
!</h1></html>")
;;=> #'liberator-example.example/hello
```

Using `defresource`, you can reuse resources with any routes as follows:

```
(defroutes app
  (ANY "/hello" [] hello)
  (route/not-found "Not Found !"))
;;=> #'liberator-example.example/app
```

Let's define a handler and start your server as follows:

```
(def handler
  (-> app
      wrap-params))
;;=> #'liberator-example.example/handler
(def server (run-jetty handler {:port 3000 :join? false}))
;;=> #'liberator-example.example/server
```

You will see a similar result to the first Liberator example. After finishing testing `defresource`, let's stop the server:

```
(.stop server)
;;=> nil
```

Parameterized resources

We will learn how to define a REST API with parameters. So, let's define a `parameterized-hello` resource that has a parameter x as follows:

```
(defresource parameterized-hello [x]
  :available-media-types ["text/html"]
  :handle-ok (format "<html><h1>Hello Clojure from %s !</h1></html>" x)
  )
;;=> #'liberator-example.example/parameterized-hello
```

The previous example enables us to set an arbitrary string to the HTML content.

`defroutes` also has a parameter x and passes to `parameterized-hello`:

```
(defroutes parameterized-hello-app
  (ANY "/hello/:x" [x] (parameterized-hello x))
  (route/not-found "Not Found !"))
;;=> #'liberator-example.example/parameterized-hello-app
```

Define your handler and start your server:

```
(def handler
  (-> parameterized-hello-app
      wrap-params))
;;=> #'liberator-example.example/handler
(def server (run-jetty handler {:port 3000 :join? false}))
;;=> #'liberator-example.example/server
```

Now, open your browser with the following URL:
`http://localhost:3000/hello/your-name`:

```
(.stop server)
;;=> nil
```

Defining GET/POST/PUT/DELETE methods for REST APIs

Here, we will define HTTP methods for a resource. We will define a resource for a customer and define five methods for it in the following table:

Method	Action	Parameter	URL
GET	Returns a list of customers	—	`http://localhost:3000/customer`
POST	Creates a new customer	—	`http://localhost:3000/customer`
GET	Gets a customer	Customer ID	`http://localhost:3000/customer/id`
PUT	Updates a customer	Customer ID	`http://localhost:3000/customer/id`
DELETE	Deletes a customer	Customer ID	`http://localhost:3000/customer/id`

So, let's define a `ref` for a customer whose attributes are name and country:

```
(def customer-ref
  (ref
  {:makoto {:name "Makoto Hashimoto" :country "Japan"}
   :nico {:name "Nicolas Modrzyk" :country "France"}}))
;;=> #'liberator-example.example/customer-ref
```

The resource `customer-list` does not have a parameter. We will define GET and POST methods:

```
(defresource customer-list
  :allowed-methods [:get :post]
  :available-media-types ["application/json"]
  :exists? (fn [_]
             (let [result @customer-ref]
               (if-not (nil? result)
                 {::entry result})))
  :post! (fn [ctx]
           (let [body (parse-string (slurp (get-in ctx [:request :body]))
true)]
             (dosync
               (alter customer-ref assoc (keyword (:id body)) (dissoc body
:id)))))
  :handle-ok ::entry
  :handle-not-found {:error "id is not found"})
;;=> #'liberator-example.example/customer-list
```

The `get` method returns the value of `customer-ref`. The reply of the `get` is handled by the anonymous function of the `:exists?` entry and returns a map with the `::entry` key if the value of the `customer-ref` is not nil. In this case, the entry of `:handle-ok?` is applied and returns the result with a `200` status code. Otherwise, the function of `:handle-not-found` is applied and returns with a `404` status code.

The `post` requests are processed with the function associates with `:post?` that adds the body of the post to the `customer-ref`. The format of the requested body of the `post` is as follows:

```
{"id":"some-id","name":"some-name","country":"country-name"}
```

The next resource, named `customer-entity`, is for parameterized requests. This resource has GET, PUT, and DELETE methods:

```
(defresource customer-entity [id]
  :allowed-methods [:get :put :delete]
  :available-media-types ["application/json"]
  :exists? (fn [_]
              (let [result (get @customer-ref (keyword id))]
                (if-not (nil? result)
                  {::entry result})))
  :put!  (fn [ctx]
              (let [body (parse-string (slurp (get-in ctx [:request :body]))
true)]
                (dosync
                 (alter customer-ref assoc (keyword id) (dissoc body :id)))))
  :delete!  (fn [_]
                (dosync
                 (alter customer-ref dissoc (keyword id))))
  :existed? (fn [_] (nil? (get @customer-ref id ::sentinel)))
  :new? (fn [_] (nil? (get @customer-ref id ::sentinel)))
  :handle-ok ::entry
  :handle-not-found {:error "id is not found"})
;;=> #'liberator-example.example/customer-entity
```

Then, let's define paths for `/customer` and `/customer/id` using `defroutes` as follows:

```
(defroutes customer
  (ANY "/customer" [] customer-list)
  (ANY "/customer/:id" [id] (customer-entity id)))
;;=> #'liberator-example.example/app
```

We will define a handler and start a Jetty server:

```
(def handler
  (-> customer
      wrap-params))
;;=> #'liberator-example.example/handler
(def server (run-jetty handler {:port 3000 :join? false}))
;;=> #'liberator-example.example/server
```

Here, we will use a Clojure-based HTTP client to test the customer REST service. `clj-http.client` makes calls for GET, POST, PUT, and DELETE.

The method `get` with `http://localhost:3000/customer` retrieves all customers in `customer-ref`:

```
(client/get "http://localhost:3000/customer")
;;=> {:status 200, :headers {"Date" "Sun, 26 Jun 2016 20:14:34 GMT",
;;=> "Content-Type" "application/json;charset=UTF-8", "Vary" "Accept",
;;=> "Connection" "close", "Server" "Jetty(9.2.10.v20150310)"},
;;=> :body "{"makoto":{"name":"Makoto Hashimoto","country":"Japan"},
;;=> "nico":{"name":"Nicolas Modrzyk","country":"France"}}",
;;=> :request-time 6, :trace-redirects ["http://localhost:3000/customer"],
;;=> :orig-content-encoding nil}
```

Then, we will test the POST:

```
(client/post "http://localhost:3000/customer"
             {:body (generate-string {:id "rh" :name "Rich Hickey" :country
"United States"})})
;;=> {:status 201, :headers {"Date" "Sun, 26 Jun 2016 14:33:28 GMT",
;;=> "Content-Type" "application/json", "Vary" "Accept", "Connection"
"close",
;;=> "Server" "Jetty(9.2.10.v20150310)"}, :body "", :request-time 8,
;;=> :trace-redirects ["http://localhost:3000/customer"], :orig-content-
encoding nil}
```

Let's check whether the previous entry exists. We only need the body of the response:

```
(->
 (client/get "http://localhost:3000/customer/rh" ) :body (parse-string
true))
;;=> {:name "Rich Hickey", :country "United States"}
```

We will check whether the `PUT` method works:

```
(client/put "http://localhost:3000/customer/rh"
            {:body (generate-string {:name "Rich Hickey" :country
"USA"})})
;;=> {:status 204, :headers {"Date" "Sun, 26 Jun 2016 22:04:35 GMT",
;;=> "Content-Type" "application/json", "Vary" "Accept", "Connection"
"close",
;;=> "Server" "Jetty(9.2.10.v20150310)"}, :body nil, :request-time 9,
;;=> :trace-redirects ["http://localhost:3000/customer/rh"], :orig-content-
encoding nil}
```

So, let's verify whether the update is successful:

```
(->
 (client/get "http://localhost:3000/customer/rh")
   :body
     (parse-string true))
;;=> {:name "Rich Hickey", :country "USA"}
```

Lastly, we will test the `DELETE` method:

```
(client/delete "http://localhost:3000/customer/rh")
;;=> {:status 204, :headers {"Date" "Sun, 26 Jun 2016 14:38:58 GMT",
;;=> "Content-Type" "application/json", "Vary" "Accept", "Connection"
"close",
;;=> "Server" "Jetty(9.2.10.v20150310)"}, :body nil, :request-time 8,
;;=> :trace-redirects ["http://localhost:3000/customer/rh"], :orig-content-
encoding nil}
(.stop server)
;;=> nil
```

How it works...

Here, we will review the major HTTP response codes and then we will learn how to debug and trace applications using Liberator.

Methods and status codes of HTTP

The following table shows the major methods, and their descriptions and actions in Liberator:

Method	Description	
GET	Reads only access to a resource	exists?
PUT	Creates a new resource	put!
DELETE	Used for a removal of a resource	delete!
POST	Updates an existing resource or creates a new resource	post!
PATCH	Is similar to PUT but it sends only differences	patch!

The major HTTP status codes are as follows:

Handle key	Status code
handle-ok	200
handle-created	201
handle-no-content	204
handle-moved-permanently	301
handle-malformed	400
handle-unauthorized	401
handle-forbidden	403
handle-not-found	404
handle-method-not-allowed	405
handle-not-acceptable	406
handle-exception	500
handle-not-implemented	501
handle-unknown-method	501
handle-service-not-available	503

Tracing requests

Liberator has tracing and debugging features. In the following code, we will redefine a handler using `liberator.dev/wrap-trace` to show a trace text and a trace graph:

```
(def handler
  (-> customer
      wrap-params
      (wrap-trace :header :ui)))
;;=> #'liberator-example.example/handler
```

Let's start the server again:

```
(def server (run-jetty handler {:port 3000 :join? false}))
;;=> #'liberator-example.example/server
```

Now let's make a call and see the decision traces in the `X-Liberator-Trace` header as follows:

```
(client/get "http://localhost:3000/customer")
{:status 200,
 :headers
 {"Date" "Mon, 27 Jun 2016 01:52:09 GMT",
  "Content-Type" "application/json;charset=UTF-8",
  "Vary" "Accept",
  "X-Liberator-Trace-Id" "uren6",
  "Link" "<//x-liberator/requests/uren6>; rel=x-liberator-trace",
  "X-Liberator-Trace"
  [":decision (:initialize-context {})"
   ":decision (:service-available? true)"
   ":decision (:known-method? :get)"
   ":decision (:uri-too-long? false)"
   ":decision (:method-allowed? :get)"
   ":decision (:malformed? false)"
   ":decision (:authorized? true)"
   ":decision (:allowed? true)"
   ":decision (:valid-content-header? true)"
   ":decision (:known-content-type? true)"
   ":decision (:valid-entity-length? true)"
   ":decision (:is-options? false)"
   ":decision (:accept-exists? [false {:representation {:media-type
"application/json"}}])"
   ":decision (:accept-language-exists? nil)"
   ":decision (:accept-charset-exists? nil)"
   ":decision (:accept-encoding-exists? "gzip, deflate")"
   ":decision (:encoding-available? {:representation {:encoding
"identity"}})"
   ":decision (:processable? true)"
```

```
    ":decision (:exists? {:liberator-example.example/entry {:makoto {:name
"Makoto Hashimoto", :country "Japan"}, :nico {:name "Nicolas Modrzyk",
:country "France"}, :rh {:name "Rich Hickey", :country "USA"}}})"
    ":decision (:if-match-exists? nil)"
    ":decision (:if-unmodified-since-exists? nil)"
    ":decision (:if-none-match-exists? nil)"
    ":decision (:if-modified-since-exists? nil)"
    ":decision (:method-delete? false)"
    ":decision (:method-patch? false)"
    ":decision (:post-to-existing? false)"
    ":decision (:put-to-existing? false)"
    ":decision (:multiple-representations? false)"
    ":handler (:handle-ok)"],
  "Connection" "close",
  "Server" "Jetty(9.2.10.v20150310)"},
 :body
 "{"makoto":{"name":"Makoto
Hashimoto","country":"Japan"},"nico":{"name":"Nicolas
Modrzyk","country":"France"},"rh":{"name":"Rich Hickey","country":"USA"}}",
 :request-time 8,
 :trace-redirects ["http://localhost:3000/customer"],
 :orig-content-encoding nil,
 :links {:x-liberator-trace {:href "//x-liberator/requests/uren6"}}}
```

We can see the trace of executing flows in the following URL:
`http://localhost:3000/x-liberator/requests/`.

You can see the history of requests you have requested in your browser as in the following screenshot:

Let's open one of the request entries. There are headers, trace, and graph:

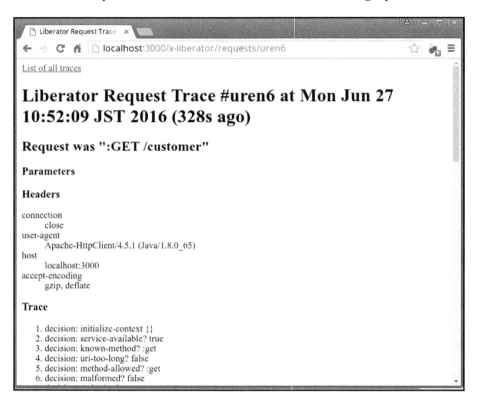

The generated graph is too large to view as a whole. The following is one part of the graph to help you understand the structure. You can generate your own graph in reference to the one created here:

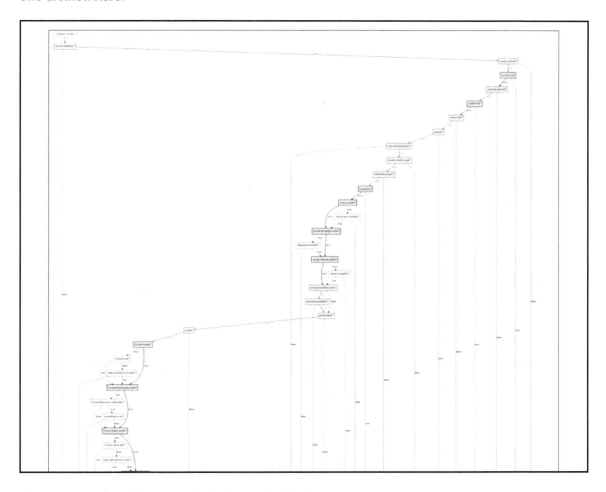

The green and red lines are decision paths for the request.

There's more...

Here, we will show you how to persist resources in your application using `clojure.java.jdbc`. In our example, we will use Apache Derby.

Persistent REST resources using clojure.java.jdbc

In this section, we will use the derby database to store product information and access via REST calls.

Preparing for jdbc

We will use `apache/derby` and `org.clojure/java.jdbc` to access a derby which is a small rdb library. So, we will add these libraries in the `project.clj`:

```
:dependencies [[org.clojure/clojure "1.8.0"]
               [liberator "0.14.1"]
               [compojure "1.3.4"]
               [ring "1.5.0-RC1"]
               [ring/ring-core "1.5.0-RC1"]
               [buddy "0.13.0"]
               [ring/ring-jetty-adapter "1.4.0"]
               [clj-http "2.2.0"]
               [cheshire "5.6.1"]
               [org.clojure/java.jdbc "0.6.1"]
               [org.apache.derby/derby "10.12.1.1"]]])
```

After adding entries, restart your REPL.

Our service spec

We will create a small application to handle product info as follows:

Product	Name	Description	Clock	RAM	Price
macbook air 11.6	Apple	Apple MacBook Air MJVM2LL/A 11.6-Inch laptop	1.6	4	797.00
thinkpad x260	Levovo	Lenovo ThinkPad X260 20F6005HUS 12.5" Ultrabook	2.3	8	1,009.00
ASUS VivoBook	AUSUS	ASUS VivoBook E200HA-US01-GD Portable 11.6	1.8	2	199.99
Dell Inspiron	DELL	Dell Inspiron 11.6-Inch 2 in 1 Convertible Touchscreen Laptop	2.16	4	279.99

To store the previous entries in your database, we will create the following table in Apache Derby:

id	name	maker	description	clock	ram	price
int	varchar(20)	varchar(10)	varchar(100)	float	Integer	BigDecimal

Creating a product table and defining access functions

Let's create a file named using_db.clj under src/liberator_example and define the namespace and declare the libraries to use in it:

```
(ns liberator-example.using-db
  (:require
  [ring.adapter.jetty :refer [run-jetty]]
  [liberator.core :refer [resource defresource]]
  [ liberator.dev :refer [wrap-trace]]
  [ring.middleware.params :refer [wrap-params]]
  [compojure.route :as route]
  [compojure.core :refer
    [defroutes ANY GET PUT POST DELETE OPTIONS]]
  [clj-http.client :as client]
  [cheshire.core :refer [parse-string generate-string]]
  [clojure.java.jdbc :as j]))
```

Here, we will create a derby table named product. We will use java.jdbc/create-table-ddl to create a table:

```
(def db-path "/tmp/db/products")
;;=> #'liberator-example.using-db/db-path
(def db {
        :classname "org.apache.derby.jdbc.EmbeddedDriver"
        :subprotocol "derby"
        :subname db-path
        :create true})
;;=> #'liberator-example.using-db/db
(j/db-do-commands db
                (j/create-table-ddl
                  :product
                  [[:id :int "primary key"
                    "generated always as identity
                (start with 1, increment by 1)"]
                    [:name "varchar(20)" "not null"]
                    [:maker "varchar(10)" "not null"]
                    [:description "varchar(100)" ]
                    [:clock :float]
                    [:ram :int]
```

```
                          [:price "decimal(7,2)"]]))
;;=> (0)
```

Now we will define `insert-product!`, `update-product!`, and `delete-product!` in the following code:

```
(defn insert-product! [db product]
  (j/insert! db :product product))
;;=> #'liberator-example.using-db/insert-product!
(defn update-product! [db id product]
  (j/update! db :product product ["id = ?" id]))
;;=> #'liberator-example.using-db/update-product!
(defn delete-product! [db id]
  (j/delete! db :product  ["id = ?" id]))
;;=> #'liberator-example.using-db/delete-product!
(defn select-product-by-id [db id]
  (first (j/query db ["select * from product where id = ?" id])))
;;=> #'liberator-example.using-db/select-product-by-id
```

We will also define select functions `select-product-by-id` and `select-products`. `select-product-by-id` returns single map associates with id. `select-products` returns all products by an array of maps:

```
(defn make-query-string [m]
  (str (apply str
              (interpose " like ? and "
                         (map name (keys m)))) " like ? "))
;;=> #'liberator-example.using-db/make-query-string
(make-query-string {:var-1 "a" :var-2 "b" :var-3 "c"})
;;=> "var-1 like ? and var-2 like ? and var-3 like ? "
(defn select-products [db & params]
  (let [qs
        (if-not params
          "select * from product"
          (str "select * from product where " (make-query-string (first
params))))
        v (vals (first params))]
    (println (vec (cons qs v)))
    (j/query db (vec (cons qs v)))))
;;=> #'liberator-example.using-db/select-products
```

We will test `insert-product!` to add two products for mac and thinkpad:

```
(insert-product! db
                 {:name "macbook air 11.6" :maker "Apple"
                  :description "Apple MacBook Air MJVM2LL/A 11.6-Inch
laptop"
                  :clock 1.6 :ram 4 :price 797.00})
```

```
;;=> ({:1 1M})
(insert-product! db
                {:name "thinkpad x260" :maker "Lenovo"
                 :description "Lenovo ThinkPad X260 20F6005HUS 12.5
Ultrabook"
                 :clock 2.3 :ram 8 :price 1009.00})
;;=> ({:1 2M})
```

Then we will test `select-product-by-id` and `select-products`:

```
(select-product-by-id db 1)
;;=> {:id 1, :name "macbook air 11.6", :maker "Apple", :description "Apple
MacBook Air MJVM2LL/A 11.6-Inch laptop", :clock 1.6, :ram 4, :price
797.00M}
(select-products db)
;;=> ({:id 11, :name "macbook air 11.6", :maker "Apple", :description
"Apple MacBook Air MJVM2LL/A 11.6-Inch laptop", :clock 1.6, :ram 4, :price
797.00M} {:id 12, :name "thinkpad x260", :maker "Lenovo", :description
"Lenovo ThinkPad X260 20F6005HUS 12.5 Ultrabook", :clock 2.3, :ram 8,
:price 1009.00M})
(select-products db {:name "%a%" :description "%M%"})
;;=> ({:id 11, :name "macbook air 11.6", :maker "Apple", :description
"Apple MacBook Air MJVM2LL/A 11.6-Inch laptop", :clock 1.6, :ram 4, :price
797.00M})
(select-products db {:maker "Apple"})
;;=> ({:id 11, :name "macbook air 11.6", :maker "Apple", :description
"Apple MacBook Air MJVM2LL/A 11.6-Inch laptop", :clock 1.6, :ram 4, :price
797.00M})
```

Defining resources and starting a server

We will define two resources. They are `product-list` and `product-entity`:

```
(defn to-keyword-map [m]
  (into {} (map #(vector (keyword (first %)) (str "%" (second %) "%"))
m)))
;;=> #'liberator-example.using-db/to-keyword-map
(defresource product-list
  :allowed-methods [:get :post]
  :available-media-types ["application/json"]
  :exists? (fn [ctx]
             (let [params (-> ctx
                              (get-in [:request :params])
                              to-keyword-map)
                   result (if (empty? params) (select-products db) (select-
products db params))]
               (if-not (empty? result)
                 {::entry result}))))
```

```
      :post!  (fn [ctx]
              (let [body (parse-string (slurp (get-in ctx [:request :body]))
true)]
                (insert-product! db body)))
    :handle-ok ::entry
    :handle-not-found {:error "no product is not found"})
;;=> #'liberator-example.using-db/product-list
(defresource product-entity [id]
    :allowed-methods [:get :put :delete]
    :available-media-types ["application/json"]
    :exists? (fn [_]
              (let [result (select-product-by-id id)]
                (if-not (empty? result)
                  {::entry result})))
    :put!  (fn [ctx]
            (let [body (parse-string (slurp (get-in ctx [:request :body]))
true)]
                (insert-product! db body)))
    :delete!  (fn [_]
              (delete-product! db id))
    :existed? (fn [_] (empty? (select-product-by-id id)))
    :new? (fn [_] (empty? (select-product-by-id id)))
    :handle-ok ::entry
    :handle-not-found {:error "id is not found"})
#'liberator-example.using-db/product-entity
```

Now it's time to start the server as follows:

```
(defroutes product
  (ANY "/product" [] product-list)
  (ANY "/customer/:id" [id] (product-entity id)))
#'liberator-example.using-db/product
(def handler
  (-> product
      wrap-params))
;;=> #'liberator-example.using-db/handler
(def server (run-jetty handler {:port 3000 :join? false}))
;;=> #'liberator-example.using-db/server
```

Accessing from an HTTP client

We will access the product API service via an HTTP client. So we will create two products. They are ASUS and Dell:

```
(client/post "http://localhost:3000/product"
              {:body
                (generate-string
                  {:name "ASUS VivoBook" :maker "ASUS"
```

```
                     :description "ASUS VivoBook E200HA-US01-GD Portable 11.6"
                     :clock 1.8 :ram 2 :price 199.99})})
;;=> {:status 201, :headers {"Date" "Fri, 01 Jul 2016 00:38:27 GMT",
"Content-Type" "application/json",
;;=> "Vary" "Accept", "Connection" "close", "Server"
"Jetty(9.2.10.v20150310)"}, :body "",
;;=> :request-time 34, :trace-redirects ["http://localhost:3000/product"],
:orig-content-encoding nil}
(client/post "http://localhost:3000/product"
                 {:body
                  (generate-string
                   {:name "Dell Inspiron" :maker "DELL"
                    :description "Dell Inspiron 11.6-Inch 2 in 1 Convertible
Touchscreen Laptop"
                    :clock 2.16 :ram 4 :price 279.99})})
;;=> {:status 201, :headers {"Date" "Fri, 01 Jul 2016 00:38:36 GMT",
"Content-Type" "application/json",
;;=> "Vary" "Accept", "Connection" "close", "Server"
"Jetty(9.2.10.v20150310)"}, :body "",
;;=> :request-time 25, :trace-redirects ["http://localhost:3000/product"],
:orig-content-encoding nil}
```

The requests received HTTP 201 status. Then, check whether there are four products:

```
(-> (client/get "http://localhost:3000/product") :body (parse-string true)
count)
;;=> 4
```

That's fine. We will retrieve the product whose id is 1:

```
(-> (client/get "http://localhost:3000/product/1") :body (parse-string
true))
;;=> {:id 1, :name "macbook air 11.6", :maker "Apple",
;;=>  :description "Apple MacBook Air MJVM2LL/A 11.6-Inch laptop", :clock
1.6, :ram 4, :price 797.0}
```

Let's discount the price of a Dell notebook using HTTP put:

```
(client/put "http://localhost:3000/product/4"
                 {:body
                  (generate-string
                   {:price 259.99})})
;;=> {:status 204, :headers {"Date" "Fri, 01 Jul 2016 12:52:01 GMT",
"Content-Type" "application/json", "Vary" "Accept", "Connection" "close",
"Server" "Jetty(9.2.10.v20150310)"}, :body nil, :request-time 33, :trace-
redirects ["http://localhost:3000/product/4"], :orig-content-encoding nil}
```

And let's make sure the price has changed:

```
(-> (client/get "http://localhost:3000/product/4") :body (parse-string
true) :price )
;;=> 259.99
```

We will delete the Dell notebook from the product database:

```
(client/delete "http://localhost:3000/product/4")
;;=> {:status 204, :headers {"Date" "Fri, 01 Jul 2016 12:52:19 GMT",
"Content-Type" "application/json", "Vary" "Accept", "Connection" "close",
"Server" "Jetty(9.2.10.v20150310)"}, :body nil, :request-time 26, :trace-
redirects ["http://localhost:3000/product/4"], :orig-content-encoding nil}
```

And make sure of it:

```
(-> (client/get "http://localhost:3000/product") :body (parse-string true)
count)
;;=> 3
```

We can see the products in our browser:

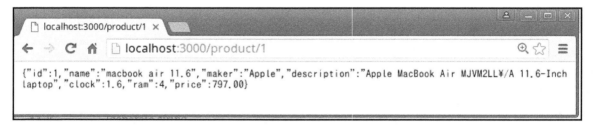

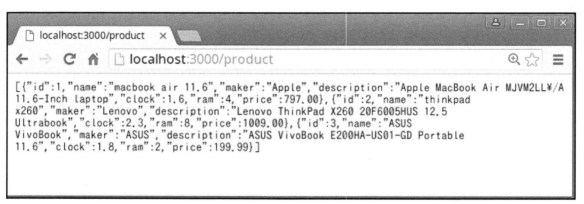

Working with Immutant – reusing infrastructure

Immutant is not your usual Clojure web framework. Immutant allows you to build into existing and robust middleware, WildFly, aka JBoss, and deploy your software in an elegant fashion. In this recipe, you will see how to enhance your ring application with the wide range of services available through the Immutant framework.

While Immutant makes it easy to deploy to WildFly, the development environment is entirely contained and can be done without extra download or installation. Let's have a look!

Getting ready

This first section will probably be totally disappointing; at this stage, we are fully in the domain of Clojure and things work out of the box. Terrible, huh?

Here is the `project.clj` file, with the full list of libraries required:

```
(defproject mutant1 "0.1.0-SNAPSHOT"
  :dependencies [
    [org.clojure/clojure "1.8.0"]
    [org.immutant/immutant "2.1.4"]
    [ring/ring-devel "1.5.0"]]])
```

`ring-devel` is added to the mix to allow for development mode and a refresh on reload workflow.

The code to build the web app follows the ring routing patterns, so most of the following is pretty standard:

```
(ns mutant1.core
  (:require [immutant.web :as web]))

(defn app [request]
  {:status 200
   :body "Hello world"})

(defn -main []
(web/run-dmc app))
```

The `web/run-dmc` method is used for development mode, while `web/run` would be used for production.

On the command line, the standard: `lein run -m mutant1.core` is enough to get you started, and to see the beautiful page coming to you:

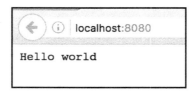

How to do it...

We have seen the basics, and how to get ready; now let's see how to interact with the different middleware frameworks available when using Immutant.

Simple messaging with Artemis

This example will show how to spawn a messaging server, and create a messaging context and a queue, as well as sending and listening to that queue through Clojure code.

What is presented here is actually wildly unofficial, not because it is of alpha quality, but because some parts and namespaces that make things easy have been changed recently.

So instead of using the `hornetq` framework as noted in a lot of documentation around the Interweb, we will use the new library messaging framework Artemis, included in the latest releases of WildFly.

The `project.clj` file gets just a bit complicated, due to the fact we want to avoid including the `hornetq` library, but this should be fixed soon:

```
(defproject mutant2 "0.1.0-SNAPSHOT"
  :dependencies [
  [org.clojure/clojure "1.8.0"]
  [org.immutant/immutant "2.1.4"
    :exclusions [org.projectodd.wunderboss/wunderboss-messaging-hornetq]]
  [org.projectodd.wunderboss/wunderboss-artemis "0.2.0"]
  [ring/ring-devel "1.5.0"]
[compojure "1.5.0"]])
```

You can also note the (re-)introduction of Compojure and you are ready to go!

The following snippet actually asks the framework to create a new messaging server, through the slightly misleading `msg/context` function:

```
(require '[immutant.web :as web] '[immutant.messaging :as msg])
(def messaging-server
  (msg/context :remote-type :hornetq-standalone))
```

Once the messaging server has been programmatically started, we can create a context that will be used to look up queues and topics.

Here, we connect to the messaging server just started, and look up the `hello` queue. This will actually create the queue if it does not exist, or simply connect to it if another service has already registered it:

```
(def mycontext
  (msg/context :host "localhost"))

(def queue
  (msg/queue "hello" :context mycontext))
```

Most of the new function calls are done using the `immutant.messaging` namespace, labelled as `msg`.

Now that you have the queue, it is time to listen to it, and send messages. The `listen` function takes a queue or a topic as well as a callback, as a simple Clojure function:

```
(msg/listen queue
  (fn[msg]
    (println msg)))
```

Then some regular Compojure routing will allow you to send messages to the same queue:

```
(require '[compojure.core :refer :all]
         '[compojure.route :as route])
(defroutes app
  (GET "/" [] "<h1>Hello Compojure World</h1><br/><a href="/msg">Send a
message</a>")
  (GET "/msg" [] (msg/publish queue "world") "OK")
(route/not-found "<h1>Page not found</h1>"))
```

Here we go:

```
(defn -main []
(web/run-dmc app :host "0.0.0.0" :port 8080))
```

Now we can open the page served by the server on port 8080:

Anyway, where in your application you can now use this messaging mechanism? By registering to messages coming from the messaging system.

It would not be a proper messaging system if it could only talk to itself, so let's see how to set up to connect remotely!

Remote messaging

Now we want to set up two servers talking to each other using WildFly messaging queues.

The first server setup is almost identical to the previous example, except that to connect remotely, we need to bind to a different IP address, externally accessible. This is done by adding JVM settings to the Leiningen JVM option, so in `project.clj`, we will add the following:

```
:jvm-opts ["-Dactivemq.netty.host=0.0.0.0"]
```

And if you look carefully in the console logs, you will notice that indeed the messaging system is bound using the preceding settings:

```
22:46:55.000 INFO  [org.apache.activemq.artemis.core.server] (main)
AMQ221020: Started Acceptor at 0.0.0.0:5445 for protocols [CORE]
22:46:55.003 INFO  [org.apache.activemq.artemis.core.server] (main)
AMQ221007: Server is now live
```

Wonderful. Now on to setting up the second server. In the context of this book, the second server is actually running on a Raspberry Pi again, and the most difficult thing is actually to get the IP addresses in the proper order.

This second server uses Clojure code similar to what you have seen up to now. Queue lookup and ring handler routing are basically the same. What changes is the way to retrieve the queue from a remote location.

The first serer was on IP 192.168.1.3, so the following example will make use of that. We also give a number of reconnects up to 30, so that if the first server goes down, this will still wait and try to get a connection. (Try it!!)

Off you go:

```
(def mycontext
  (msg/context
    :host "192.168.1.3" :port 5445 :reconnect-attempts 30))

(def queue
  (msg/queue "hello" :context mycontext))

(defroutes app
(GET "/" [] (msg/publish queue "world") "OK"))
```

The second server is started with the same command:

```
lein run -m mutant3.core
```

The Raspberry Pi here has IP address 192.168.1.7, so let's connect to it:

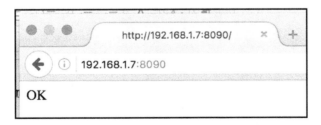

Not very talkative for a web application, but the first server would have received a love message accordingly, and hello world would show up in the console logs. Yeah! Remoting.

Remote procedure call with queues

Extending the previous example, Immutant also provides a way to easily do **remote procedure calls** (**RPCs**) via the queuing system.

This can be a great way to distribute the load to different Raspberry Pis!

Let's go through a distributed hello world using this RPC framework.

The first setup needs to be set up just as in the previous recipe. We will make use of a new queue, queue2 (creative naming is all the rage these days...). This queue2 will then be used from a respond handler, which is the entrance of the procedure call as seen here:

```
(def queue2 (msg/queue "hello2" :context mycontext))

(msg/respond
  queue2
(fn[msg] (str "hello "  msg)))
```

Here, the handler receives one parameter, and sends some polite greeting message.

Note that each respond handler needs a dedicated queue.

On the second server, we will look up queue2, and create a Compojure route to send the RPC request. The msg/request function call actually returns a future, so if we want to do a synchronous answer, we will use the @ symbol to wait until the result of the execution.

This translates into:

```
(def queue2
  (msg/queue "hello2" :context mycontext))

(defroutes app
  (GET "/req" [] @(msg/request queue2 "world")))
```

This second server is again running on the Raspberry Pi. A request to it will post a message to the queue, that message will be picked up by the first server, the callback will be executed, and the result sent back to the second server:

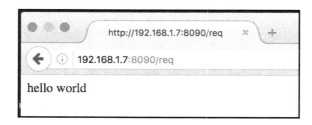

Scheduling code execution

As a bonus, an extensive scheduling framework is also integrated in the Immutant framework.

The following snippet will send dated messages to the queue:

```
(:require ..
   '[immutant.scheduling :as sh])
(sh/schedule #(msg/publish queue (java.util.Date.))
  (->
    (sh/limit 5)
    (sh/in 5 :seconds)
    (sh/every 3 :seconds)))
```

And on the server you set up before, still listening for connections you could see those messages coming:

```
#inst "2016-06-19T14:19:49.932-00:00"
```

Piping and defining data transformation pipelines

Pipes in Immutant allow for multithreaded processing of pipelines, through the use of the queue system.

A pipeline is made of transformative steps, where each step is a standard Clojure function applied to the passing data structure:

```
(ns mutant4.pipes
  (:require [immutant.messaging.pipeline :as pl]))
(defn barme [m]
  (map inc m))

(defonce bar-pipeline
 (pl/pipeline "bar"
   (pl/step barme)
   (pl/step barme)
:concurrency 4))
```

The pipeline uses a specific queue and can only be defined once. Getting the result of the pipeline on a data structure is just like calling a regular function. The result is again a future, so to get the result directly you need to use deref here again:

```
(deref
  (bar-pipeline (take 1000 (repeat 1))))
```

Woohoo…multithreads for your many cores.

Using WebSockets made easy

Immutant would not be a framework if it did not have at least some WebSocket support.

For plain and pure WebSocket support, Immutant provides a `wrap-websocket` support that will take the request and callback definitions to create an async channel.

This small demo will wait for WebSocket connections, send a message to the queue when a client connects, and send some async simple messages to the client:

```
      (require '[immutant.web.async :as async])
(def callbacks
  { :on-open (fn [ch] (println "open!"))
    :on-message (fn [ch msg]
        (dotimes [msg 10]
          (async/send! ch (str msg) {:close? (= msg 9)})
(Thread/sleep 100)))})
```

The main app just waits for requests:

```
(defn app [request]
  (async/as-channel request callbacks))
```

The usual main code adds an extra wrapper for the socket connections:

```
      (require '[immutant.web.middleware :as me])
(defn -main []
  (web/run-dmc (-> app
    (me/wrap-websocket callbacks))
    :host "0.0.0.0"
    :port 8000))
```

For testing, you can write your own client, or use the Chrome Simple Web Socket Client plugin:

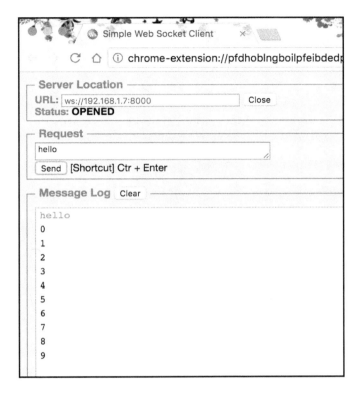

Again, this is running on the Raspberry Pi without any different setup or effort.

There's more...

So you have seen all this coding framework, and it was nice to develop with, but how to distribute your app now? It sounds complicated... Let's see if something can be done about it...

Packaging as standalone

Well, there's good news: to create a distributable JAR file, you have nothing to do! That's right. Nothing out of the ordinary.

Provided you use the `gen-class` directive to your main namespace, and define your main namespace in `project.clj`, you can package all this in a single JAR file using:

```
lein uberjar
```

Any of the examples presented in this recipe will make it smoothly. So, after calling `uberjar`, the WebSocket server can be started with:

```
java -jar target/mutant7-0.1.0-SNAPSHOT-standalone.jar
```

And the Chrome WebSocket client will work all the same.

Packaging as a deployable web archive (WAR file)

For deployment, the `lein immutant` plugin allows you to take the Immutant code and package it as a WAR, and deploy it directly into the WildFly server, using a simple command. WAR is a web archive, and is essentially the Java way of packaging a web application for deployment:

```
NicolassMacBook% lein immutant war
Created
/Users/niko/Downloads/wildfly-10.0.0.Final/standalone/deployments/mutant7-
dev.war
```

This is useful to verify the code runs as expected, and to automate deployment. The plugin and the plugin configuration are added directly to the `project.clj` file. You control where the WAR file is created, as well as the context path:

```
:main mutant7.core
  :plugins [[lein-immutant "2.1.0"]]
  :immutant {
    :war {
      :dev? true
      :destination
"/Users/niko/Downloads/wildfly-10.0.0.Final/standalone/deployments"
      :context-path "/mutant7"}}
```

Suppose you have downloaded WildFly (or another open source Java server such as Tomcat or Jetty); the copied WAR file should trigger a live redeployment of your application if the server is running...as seen in the server logs:

```
00:17:17,688 INFO  [org.wildfly.extension.undertow] (ServerService Thread
Pool -- 65) WFLYUT0021: Registered web context: /mutant7
00:17:17,748 INFO  [org.jboss.as.server] (DeploymentScanner-threads - 2)
WFLYSRV0016: Replaced deployment "mutant7-dev.war" with deployment
"mutant7-dev.war"
00:17:17,761 INFO  [org.jboss.as.repository] (DeploymentScanner-threads -
2) WFLYDR0002: Content removed from location
/Users/niko/Downloads/wildfly-10.0.0.Final/standalone/data/content/30/26210
44f4972384dc11214cf376f3525ffe9ec/content
```

Your Immutant-based web application can now virtually be running everywhere!

Developing with om.next, the next-generation ClojureScript library

In this recipe, we will learn David Nolen's om to build a ClojureScript application. Om is a ClojureScript library to interact with React. React is a very famous JavaScript library developed by Facebook. React enables developments of user interfaces simpler and reusable UI components.

Recently, Nolen started to develop om.next. It's a successor of om and inspired by Facebook's Relay, Netflix's Falcor, and Cognitect's Datomic. It is still alpha but it is worth digging it. The project.clj of om.next is as follows:

https://github.com/omcljs/om/blob/master/project.clj

Getting ready

Before learning om.next, we will create and set up a new project named om-next-example.

Creating a new project for om.next

To create a new project for om.next, issue the following command:

```
$ lein new figwheel om-next-example -- --om
```

Updating the om version

Go to the `om-next-example` directory and update the `om` version in your `project.clj` to enable `om.next` as follows:

```
:dependencies [[org.clojure/clojure "1.8.0"]
               [org.clojure/clojurescript "1.8.51"]
               [org.clojure/core.async "0.2.374"
                 :exclusions [org.clojure/tools.reader]]
                [sablono "0.3.6"
                 :exclusions [cljsjs/react]]
               [org.omcljs/om "1.0.0-alpha37"]]
```

Tips for dependencies

In this recipe, we will use version `1.0.0-alpha37` of `om`, which supports `om.next`. However, using the `figwheel` template generates version 0.3.6 of the `sablono` dependency and it uses the older version of `react`, which causes a runtime problem of `om.next`.

To solve this problem, we have checked the dependencies of libraries. The \ command finds confusing dependencies as follows:

```
Possibly confusing dependencies found:
[sablono "0.3.6"] -> [cljsjs/react "0.13.3-0"]
 overrides
[org.omcljs/om "1.0.0-alpha37"] -> [cljsjs/react-dom "15.0.1-1"] ->
[cljsjs/react "15.0.1-1"]
 and
[org.omcljs/om "1.0.0-alpha37"] -> [cljsjs/react "15.0.1-1"]
  . . . . .
 [org.omcljs/om "1.0.0-alpha37"]
   [cljsjs/react-dom "15.0.1-1"]
  . . . . .
[sablono "0.3.6"]
  [cljsjs/react "0.13.3-0"]
  . . . . .
```

That is the reason why we have excluded `cljsjs/react` from the `sablono` dependency as follows:

```
[sablono "0.3.6"
       :exclusions [cljsjs/react]]
```

Starting figwheel

Start the following command and wait for a prompt for ClojureScript code:

```
$ lein figwheel
```

How to do it...

Let's start with very simple om.next code.

Getting started with om.next

Let's open src/om_next_example/core.cljs and modify as follows:

```
(ns om-next-example.core
  (:require [goog.dom :as gdom]
            [om.next :as om :refer-macros [defui]]
            [om.dom :as dom]))
(enable-console-print!)
(defui HelloClojure
  Object
  (render [this]
    (dom/h1 nil "Hello Clojure !")))

(def hello (om/factory HelloClojure))
(js/ReactDOM.render (hello) (gdom/getElement "app"))
```

Let's save the file and open your browser with http://localhost:3449. You can see
Hello Clojure ! as in the following screenshot:

Then let's modify it as follows and save it:

```
(defui HelloClojure
  Object
  (render [this]
    (dom/h1 nil "Hello Clojurescript !")))
```

You can see the following change in your browser:

Using states

We will learn to handle states in om.next. We will use REPL to develop the ClojureScript application more interactive like live coding. Let's define the namespace and libraries to use:

```
(ns om-next-example.core
  (:require [goog.dom :as gdom]
            [om.next :as om :refer-macros [defui]]
            [om.dom :as dom]
            [cljs-time.core :as t]
            [cljs-time.local :as l]
            [cljs-time.format :as f]))
;;=> nil
(enable-console-print!)
;;=> nil
```

Let's define get-local-now-string to generate a local time string:

```
(defn get-local-now-string []
  (f/unparse
   ;;(f/formatters :date-hour-minute-second-ms)
   (f/formatters :date-time-no-ms)
   (l/local-now)))
;;=> #'om-next-example.core/get-local-now-string
```

It returns a local date and time:

```
(get-local-now-string)
;;=> "2016-07-04T00:25:31+09:00"
```

Now we will define an atom which is a string of local date:

```
(def app-state-date (atom {:date (get-local-now-string)}))
;;=> #'om-next-example.core/app-state-date
```

defui is a macro to define components. It creates a js class, inheriting from
React.Component. The next DateDisplay defines an HTML page for rendering a button
and a current date/time:

```
(defui DateDisplay
  Object
  (render [this]
    (let [{:keys [date]} (om/props this)]
      (dom/div nil
               (dom/button
                #js {:onClick
                     (fn [e]
                       (swap! app-state-date update-in [:date] get-local-
now-string))}
                "Get current time ")
               (dom/h2 nil (str "Date : " date))
               ))))
;;=> #object[Function "function ....
```

Let's define a reconciler that holds app-state-date as a state:

```
(def reconciler-date
  (om/reconciler {:state app-state-date}))
;;=> #'om-next-example.core/reconciler-date
```

Let's add a DOM root for the reconciler to control. The first parameter is a reconciler, the
second one is a component, and the last is a target DOM node:

```
(om/add-root! reconciler-date
              DateDisplay (gdom/getElement "app"))
;;=> #object[om-next-example.core.DateDisplay]
```

To open the `http://localhost:3449`, we can see the following screen:

The preceding code is quite straightforward; we will learn a more sophisticated way. First, we will define an atom for the current date and time in the following code:

```
(def app-state-date2 (atom {:date (get-local-now-string)}))
;;=> #'om-next-example.core/app-state-date
```

Then, we will write a code using readers and mutators in `om.next`. Readers are functions for reading data from states:

```
(defn read-date [{:keys [state] :as env} key params]
  (let [st @state]
    (if-let [[_ value] (find st key)]
      {:value value}
      {:value :not-found})))
;;=> #'om-next-example.core/read-date
```

On the other hand, mutators are functions for updating data in states as follows:

```
(defn mutate-date [{:keys [state] :as env} key params]
  (if (= 'get-current-time key)
    {:value {:keys [:date]}
     :action #(swap! state update-in [:date] get-local-now-string)}
    {:value :not-found}))
;;=> #'om-next-example.core/mutate-date
```

We will create a UI component. We will implement `om/IQuery` to get elements from attributes obtained by the `read` function in `defui`. The function of `:onClick` calls `om/transact!` that updates the state via the mutator rather than directly updates it:

```
(defui DateDisplay2
  static om/IQuery
  (query [this] [:date])
  Object
```

```
(render [this]
        (let [{:keys [date]} (om/props this)]
          (dom/div nil
            (dom/button
              #js {:onClick
                    (fn [e] (om/transact! this '[(get-current-time)]))
                    } "Get current time")
            (dom/h2 nil (str "Date: " date))))))
;;=> #object[Function "function
(this__41642__auto__,writer__41643__auto__,opt__41644__auto__)
;;=> {return cljs.core._write.call(null,writer__41643__auto__,"om-next-
example.core/DateDisplay2";}"]
```

We will specify read and mutate functions when we create the reconciler as follows:

```
(def date-reconciler2
  (om/reconciler
    {:state app-state-date-2
     :parser (om/parser {:read read-date :mutate mutate-date})}))
;;=> #'om-next-example.core/date-reconciler2
```

Now it's time to show it on your browser:

```
(om/add-root! date-reconciler2
  DateDisplay2 (gdom/getElement "app"))
```

How it works...

We will show you a very simple HTML and JavaScript using Facebook's React. Then, we will review the fundamental functions of om.next.

React fundamentals

To understand om and om.next, we will see some simple om code. The following HTML. The first HTML is to show a message of "Hello Clojure !". ReactDOM.render simply sets the string to the element:

```
<!DOCTYPE HTML>
<html>
  <head>
    <meta charset="utf-8">
    <title>Hello Clojure</title>
  </head>
  <body>
    <div id='app'></div>
```

```
        <script src="https://fb.me/react-15.0.1.js"></script>
        <script src="https://fb.me/react-dom-15.0.1.js"></script>
        <script
src="https://cdnjs.cloudflare.com/ajax/libs/babel-core/5.8.23/browser.min.j
s"></script>
        <script type="text/babel">
          ReactDOM.render(<h1>Hello Clojure !</h1>,
                                        document.getElementById('app'));
        </script>
      </body>
</html>
```

The second HTML is the parameterized version. It defines the `Message` function and sets a message in `ReactDOM.render` as follows:

```
<!DOCTYPE HTML>
<html>
  <head>
    <meta charset="utf-8">
    <title>Hello Clojure</title>
  </head>
  <body>
    <div id='app'></div>
    <script src="https://fb.me/react-15.0.1.js"></script>
    <script src="https://fb.me/react-dom-15.0.1.js"></script>
    <script
src="https://cdnjs.cloudflare.com/ajax/libs/babel-core/5.8.23/browser.min.j
s"></script>
    <script type="text/babel">
      var Message = React.createClass({
        render: function () {
        return <h1>Hello {this.props.message} !</h1>;}});
      ReactDOM.render(<Message message="Clojure" />,
                                    document.getElementById('app'));
    </script>
  </body>
</html>
```

defui

What is `defui`? `defui` is a macro for defining components of `om.next`. `defui` has the following syntax:

```
(defui component-name & forms)
```

Typically, `defui` uses the parameters as shown here:

```
(defui component-name
  static om/IQueryParams
  (params [this]    .....)
  static om/Ident
    (ident [this {:keys [name]}] .....)
  static om/IQuery
  (query [this] ....)
  Object
  (render [this] .....))
```

reconciler

What is `reconciler`? It manages states in `om.next` application. `reconciler` takes an application state and parser as follows:

```
(def reconciler
  (om/reconciler
    {:state app-state
     :parser (om/parser {:read read :mutate mutate})}))
;;=> nil

(om/add-root! reconciler
  root-component (gdom/getElement element-id))
;;=> nil
```

Life cycle of components

In addition to defining the `render` function in `defui`, we will add `componentWillMount` and `componentDidMount`:

```
(defui HelloClojure
  Object
  (render [this]
          (dom/h1 nil "Hello Clojure !"))
  (componentWillMount [this]
                      (js/alert  "Will mount !")
                      )
  (componentDidMount [this]
                      (js/alert  "Did mount !")))
;;=> nil
(def hello (om/factory HelloClojure))
;;=> #'om-next-example.core/hello
(js/ReactDOM.render (hello) (gdom/getElement "app"))
;;=> #object[om-next-example.core.HelloClojure]
```

The preceding code shows you a dialog before and after displaying the `"Hello Clojure !"` string in your browser. We summarize methods for the life cycle of components in the following table:

Lifecycle method	Life cycle	Description
componentWillMount	Mounting	Invoked once, both on the client and server, immediately before the initial rendering occurs.
componentDidMount	Mounting	Invoked once, only on the client (not on the server), immediately after the initial rendering occurs.
componentWillReceiveProps	Updating	Invoked when a component is receiving new props. This method is not called for the initial render.
shouldComponentUpdate	Updating	Invoked before rendering when new props or state are being received. This method is not called for the initial render or when `forceUpdate` is used.
componentWillUpdate	Updating	Invoked immediately before rendering when new props or state are being received. This method is not called for the initial render.
componentDidUpdate	Updating	Invoked immediately after the component's updates are flushed to the DOM. This method is not called for the initial render.
componentWillUnmount	Unmounting	Invoked immediately before a component is unmounted from the DOM.

There's more...

We will make a more realistic application using `om.next`.

Task list using om.next

We will create a simple task list to see your tasks and due dates. A screenshot of the application is as follows:

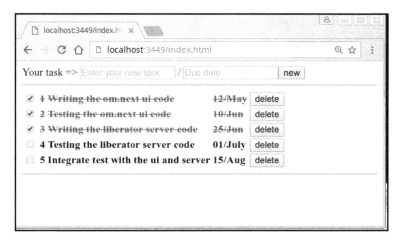

To create a new task, you will add a task description and due date. If you click a checkbox for the specific task, it means the task is finished. The **delete** buttons are to cancel tasks you have entered.

Defining the namespace and libraries to use

Let's define the namespace and libraries to use:

```
(ns om-next-example.task
  (:require [goog.dom :as gdom]
            [om.next :as om :refer-macros [defui]]
            [om.dom :as dom]))
;;=> nil
(enable-console-print!)
;;=> nil
```

The following list is the task list your application manages.

Defining state

In the following code, we will define tasks as an atom of a map:

```
(def task-state
  (atom {:task
         [{:id 1 :task "Writing the om.next  ui code" :due-date "12/May"
:finished false}
          {:id 2 :task "Testing the om.next  ui code" :due-date "10/Jun"
:finished false}
          {:id 3 :task "Writing the liberator server code"  :due-date
"25/Jun" :finished false}
          {:id 4 :task "Testing the liberator server code" :due-date
"01/July" :finished false}
          {:id 5 :task "Integrate test with the ui and server" :due-date
"15/Aug" :finished false}]}))
;;=> #'om-next-example.task/task-state
```

Defining read

Then, we will define a read which is multimethod:

```
(defmulti read-task om/dispatch)
;;=> nil
(defmethod read-task :task
  [env key params]
  (let [state (:state env)]
    {:value (:task @state)}))
;;=> #object[cljs.core.MultiFn]
```

In the previous code, env is like the following:

```
{:query-root :om.next/root,
   ...........
  :children
  [{:type :prop, :dispatch-key :id, :key :id}
   {:type :prop, :dispatch-key :task, :key :task}
   {:type :prop, :dispatch-key :finished, :key :finished}
   {:type :prop, :dispatch-key :due-date, :key :due-date}]},
  :state
 #object [cljs.core.Atom {:val {:task [{:id 1, :task "Writing the om.next
ui code", :due-date "12/May", :finished true} {:id 2, :task "Testing the
om.next  ui code", :due-date "10/Jun", :finished true} ....]}}}],
  :parser
 #object[om$next$impl$parser$parser_$_self "function (env,query,target){
   ...........
```

And `read-task` returns the array of tasks:

```
{:value [{:id 1, :task "Writing the om.next  ui code", :due-date "12/May",
:finished true}
            {:id 2, :task "Testing the om.next  ui code", :due-date
"10/Jun", :finished true}....]}
```

Defining mutate

We will define multimethod named `mutate-task` in the following:

```
(defmulti mutate-task om/dispatch)
;;=> nil
```

There are three methods for mutate, as in the following table:

Operation	Description
task/new	mutate for new tasks
task/toggle	mutate for toggle finished and not finished tasks
task/delete	mutate for delete tasks

Let's define a mutate for `task/new`. Before defining the mutate, we will define a utility function `get-next-id` which generates new IDs for new tasks:

```
(defn get-next-id [task]
  (->>
    (map :id task) (apply max)  inc))
;;=> #'om-next-example.task/get-next--id
(get-next-id (@task-state :task))
;;=> 6
```

The following method is for creating a map for a new task and inserting it into the `task-state`:

```
(defmethod mutate-task 'task/new [env key params]
  (let [
        state (:state env)
        id (get-next-id (:task @state))
        new-task (assoc params :id id)]
    {:action
     (fn []
       (swap! state update :task conj new-task))}))
;;=> #object[cljs.core.MultiFn]
```

Then, we will define a method for toggling the state between finished/not finished for tasks. The `get-index-for-id` is to get an array position for `id`:

```
(defn get-index-for-id
  [id task]
  (-> (for [[index task] (map-indexed vector task)
           :when (= id (:id task))]  index)  first))
;;=> #'om-next-example.task/get-index
```

The following method toggles the state of tasks between finished/not finished:

```
(defmethod mutate-task 'task/toggle
  [env key params]
  (let [state (:state env)
        id (:id params)
        index (get-index-for-id id (:task @state))]
    {:action
     (fn []
       (swap! state update-in [:task index :finished] not))}))
;;=> #object[cljs.core.bMultiFn]
```

Finally, we will define a method for deleting tasks:

```
(defn delete-task
  [task id]
  (-> (remove #(= id (:id %)) task) vec))
;;=> #'om-next-example.task/delete-task
(defmethod mutate-task 'task/delete
  [env key params]
  (let [state (:state env)
        id (:id params)
        task (delete-task (:task @state) id)]
    {:action
     (fn []
       (swap! state assoc :task task))}))
;;=> #object[cljs.core.MultiFn]
```

Defining UIs

We will define two UIs for the task application. They are `ListView` and `TopView`. The `ListView` works with individual tasks and shows them as rows of a table. The elements of a row are checkbox, ID of task, task description, due date, and button for deletion. `TopView` shows tasks as a table and handles new tasks.

Let's see `ListView` first:

```
(defui ListView
  static om/IQuery
  (query [this]
         [:id :task :finished :due-date])
  Object
  (render [this]
          (let [{:keys [id task finished due-date]} (om/props this)
            (dom/tr nil
                    (dom/th nil
                            (dom/input #js
                                       {:type "checkbox"
                                        :className "toggle"
                                        :checked (and finished "checked")
                                        :onChange #(om/transact! this
`[(task/toggle {:id ~id})])}))
                    (dom/th nil
                            (dom/span  #js
                             {:className "id" :style #js {:color (if
finished "red" "black")}}
                             (if finished (dom/s  nil id)  id)))
                    (dom/th nil
                            (dom/span  #js
                             {:className "task" :style #js {:color (if
finished "red" "black")}}
                                       (if finished (dom/s  nil task)
task)))
                    (dom/th nil
                            (dom/span  #js
                             {:className "due-date" :style #js {:color (if
finished "red" "black")}}
                                       (if finished (dom/s  nil due-date)
due-date)))
                    (dom/th nil
                            (dom/button #js
                                        {:onClick #(om/transact! this
`[(task/delete {:id ~id})])}
                                        "delete"))))))
;;=> #object[Function "function (this__47196__auto__,writer__47197__...
```

We have defined a query for the state. The query gets values of id, task, due-date, and finished.

`om/factory` creates functions from UI components to be invoked by parent components:

```
(def list-view (om/factory ListView))
;;=> #'om-next-example.task/list-view
```

So, let's move on to defining `RootView`. We will define `get-element-value-by-id?` and `_set-element-value-by-id!`. `_get-element-value-by-id` gets a value from a specific input field by `id`:

```
(defn get-element-value-by-id [id]
  (.-value (. js/document (getElementById id))))
;;=> #'om-next-example.task/get-element-value-id
```

However, `set-element-value-by-id!` sets a value to an input field:

```
(defn set-element-value-by-id!  [id  value]
  (set! (.-value (. js/document (getElementById id))) value))
;;=> #'om-next-example.task/set-element-value-by-id!
```

We will also define `not-white-space?` to check input fields are not white space:

```
(defn not-white-space? [s]
  (not (= (clojure.string/trim s) "")))
;;=> #'om-next-example.task/not-white-space?
(defn handle-new-task!  [component _]
  (let [new-task (get-element-value-by-id "new-task")
        due-date (get-element-value-by-id "due-date")]
    (when (and (not-white-space? new-task) (not-white-space? due-date))
      (om/transact! component
                    `[(task/new ~{:task new-task :due-date due-date})])
      (set-element-value-by-id! "due-date" "")
      (set-element-value-by-id! "new-task" ""))))
;;=> #'om-next-example.task/handle-new-task!
```

Now we will define `RootView` as follows:

```
(defui RootView
  static om/IQuery
  (query [this]
         (let [subquery (om/get-query ListView)]
           [{:task subquery}]))
  Object
  (render [this]
          (let [props (om/props this)
                task (:task props)]
            (dom/div nil
                     (dom/label nil "Your task =>  ")
                     (dom/input #js {:className "new-task" :id "new-task"
```

```
                                         :placeholder "Enter your new task"})
                     " / "
                     (dom/input #js {:className "due-date" :id "due-date"
                                          :placeholder "Due date"})
                     (dom/button #js
                                 {:onClick #(handle-new-task! this %)}
                                 "new")
                     (dom/hr nil)
                     (apply dom/table #js {:style #js {:text-align "left"}}
                            (map list-view task))
                     (dom/hr nil)))))
;;=> #object[Function "function (this__47196__auto__,)...
```

We have defined `ListView` and `RootView`. It's time to run our application. Let's define the reconciler and set `_RootView` to your browser:

```
(def task-reconciler
  (om/reconciler {:state task-state
                  :parser (om/parser {:read read-task :mutate mutate-
task})}))
;;=> #'om-next-example.task/task-reconciler
(om/add-root! task-reconciler
              RootView
              (gdom/getElement "app"))
;;=> #object[om-next-example.task.RootView]
```

The initial page is as follows:

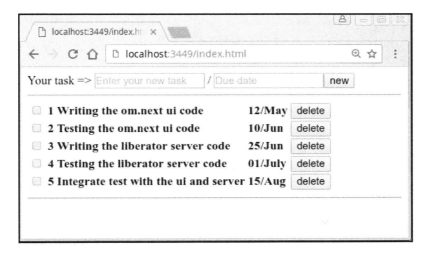

When you click a checkbox, the text's color will turn red and be struck out:

Let's enter a new task as follows:

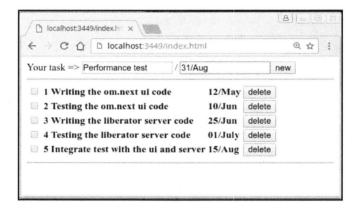

Enter a new task with date and click the **new** button; you will see the new task is in your task list:

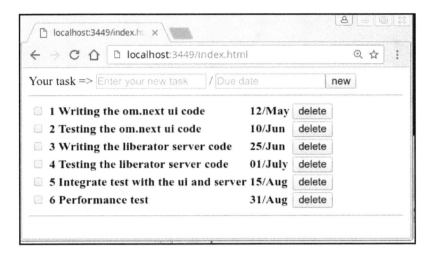

That is it! With this chapter, you've learnt how to develop web applications using Clojure's libraries. Next, we will learn how to test Clojure applications. Let's enjoy testing!

9
Testing

In this chapter, we will cover:

- Behavior-driven development
- Testing with random inputs and pattern-based testing
- Benchmarking with Criterium, performance tips, and other tools

Introduction

In this chapter, we will learn about testing for Clojure applications. With our first recipe, we will introduce behavior-driven development. Making use of Cucumber for behavior-driven development, the recipe implements some interesting BDD applications, including Spark and OpenCV.

The next recipe, on pattern-based testing, shows you the famous Haskell's QuickCheck in Clojure. In this recipe, you will learn to generate test patterns automatically.

With our final recipe for this chapter, *Benchmarking with Criterium, performance tips, and other tools*, we will show you tests for performance. Criterium is the de facto benchmark tool in Clojure. You will learn how to test your performance using Criterium.

You will also learn some performance tips in Clojure. Last but not least, you will also learn how to profile your application from the performance point of view.

Behavior-driven development

Behavior-driven development (BDD) is not a new technique, and there are quite a few blog entries written to present the advantages of some specific library.

This recipe is about using the Cucumber framework in new ways that make the language talk. The primary language you will be using for this recipe will not be Clojure, it will be simple English!!!!!!

You will start by reviewing the basics, and building along some highly interactive patterns to work with Spark, virtual machines, and OpenCV. Let the fun begin…

Getting ready

This Clojure project needs very little to get started. As usual, we add the default dependencies and a Leiningen plugin.

Dependencies

Updating the `project.clj` file for this recipe will be done while you progress along so, here, let's just get the basics in:

```
:plugins [[org.clojars.punkisdead/lein-cucumber "1.0.5"]]
:dependencies [
    [org.clojure/clojure "1.9.0-alpha7"]
]
```

Clojure 1.9 is not required, but it may just be the right time to try new things out. So basically you just need the Cucumber plugin for Leiningen.

The first feature

So with Cucumber and BDD in general, you write features in plain simple English. The file is saved with a filename that ends in `.feature` and will be picked up by the plugin later on.

The first feature will be to assert two values that are equal. That is not the most exciting feature you will read, but it will put the basics in.

So in this first feature, `My First Cucumber`, you want a test case, called a scenario here, that validates that when you add two numbers, you get…well, the expected result. Here is the full feature in plain English:

```
Feature: My First Cucumber
   Simple Example to add two numbers and assert the result

   Scenario: Add two numbers
      Given I add 50 and 100
      Then the result is 150
```

Some words are actually more important than others: `Feature`, `Scenario`, `Give`, and `Then` create the structure of the behavior document.

There is only one feature per document, with a possible description, and one feature gathers many scenarios in the same feature document. Features gather scenarios with similar and compatible points of concern.

A scenario is the equivalent of a test case, and can have one or multiple assumptions and one or multiple assertions.

Assumptions are given through the `Given` word and assertions through the `Then` word.

Designing a folder structure to organize features

To make this feature runnable, we need a bit of folder structure as shown here:

The feature file is at the root of a folder in the Leiningen project, and contains the feature file, a `step_definitions` folder, and a Clojure file within that `step_definitions` folder.

After being sure the folder structure is the same as shown previously, the `first_steps.clj` file is still empty at this stage. You can run this feature with the following command, calling the Cucumber plugin with the folder as a parameter:

```
lein cucumber features00
```

The first output should be similar to the following:

```
Running cucumber...
Looking for features in:  [features00]
Looking for glue in:  [features00/step_definitions]
UU
1 Scenarios (1 undefined)
2 Steps (2 undefined)
0m0.000s
You can implement missing steps with the snippets below:

(Given #"^I add (\d+) and (\d+)$" [arg1 arg2]
  (comment  Write code here that turns the phrase above into concrete
actions  )
  (throw (cucumber.api.PendingException.)))

(Then #"^the result is (\d+)$" [arg1]
  (comment  Write code here that turns the phrase above into concrete
actions  )
(throw (cucumber.api.PendingException.)))
```

What does this mean? As seen, there was indeed one scenario in our file, and two steps, one `Given` step and one `Then` step. Each step in a scenario works with `regexp` to be able to bind the English to some proper Clojure code in the back.

As the output suggests, let's add the missing snippets in `first_steps.clj`. The whole file will be evaluated using regular `eval` calls, so you will not use namespaces here, but just code as if at the REPL.

`Given` takes a `regexp`, bindings, and a body. This will set the assumptions; here, we gather two bindings, a and b, through pattern matching in the `Given` sentence:

- a will eventually be bound to the value 50
- b will eventually be bound to the value 100

The body of `Given` sets the result atom to the addition of a and b. `Then` will be where to put the `clojure.test` assertions (or any other test framework for that matter). Here, `assert` validates the value given in the sentence, with the addition previously:

```
(use 'clojure.test)
(def result (atom 0))
(Given #"^I add (\d+) and (\d+)$" [a b]
      (reset! result (+ (bigdec a) (bigdec b))))
(Then #"^the result is (\d+)$" [expected]
      (assert (= (bigdec expected) @result)))
```

Let's run this `features00` again, with the updated Clojure file:

```
Running cucumber...
Looking for features in:  [features00]
Looking for glue in:  [features00/step_definitions]
..
1 Scenarios (1 passed)
2 Steps (2 passed)
0m0.192s
```

As 100 + 50 still equals 150, we're safe! We can move on to more interesting scenarios.

How to do it...

This section will add a few more feature patterns to the basics.

Many assumptions with tables

It was indeed nice to do additions with two integers, and maybe we can stretch it to a few more values, but eventually having a table to add the values would make more sense. The following is an example of how to use a table within a `Scenario`:

```
Feature: Cuking
  Working with tables
  Scenario: Reading a table
  Given the following cukes:
    | Niko        | 50  |
    | Makoto-san  | 100 |
    | Ikemoto-san | 100 |
    Then the total should be 250.
```

Nothing very surprising at the language level; some cukes here and there. What is interesting to see is obviously how to bind the table to values in the Clojure code of the step definitions.

The Java object that is sent to the `Given` method parameter is a DataTable: `https://cucumber.github.io/api/cucumber/jvm/javadoc/cucumber/api/DataTable.html`.

And, basically, the main methods to access the data would be:

- raw
- cells
- asList
- asMap

In this first example with a table, you notice that a simple call to `raw` on that table followed by a simple `reduce` does the trick. The rest should be easy enough to follow:

```
(use 'clojure.test)
(def total (atom (long 0)))
(defn sum-table[table]
  (reduce + (map #(bigdec (second %)) table)))
(Given #"^the following cukes:$" [table]
    (reset! total (sum-table (.raw table))))
(Then #"^the total should be (\d+).$" [result]
  (assert (= (bigdec result) @total)))
```

The result is indeed 250.

Reading assumptions from a CSV file

Alright, so tables were great but here, again, you eventually reach a wall when you need to share that amount of data between people. At this stage, it looks more straightforward to use a separate file for the data. Let's welcome the new feature, cuking with CSV:

```
Feature: Cuking with csv
  I want to see how to cuke around with csv
  Scenario: Reading a table
  Given data from file "set1.csv":
    Then the total should be 350.
```

The content of the CSV file is straightforward, and contains a similar kind of data:

```
Niko,50
Abe-san,200
Makoto-san,100
```

The steps file does not do anything surprising either; we're just plugging in the `data.csv` library to slurp some data for a given CSV file. The following example needs an extra library, to be added to `project.clj` before running:

```
[org.clojure/data.csv "0.1.3"]
```

Then to the coding section:

```
(require '[clojure.data.csv :as csv]
         '[clojure.java.io :as io])
(defn load-table [file]
 (with-open [in-file (io/reader (str "fixtures/" file))]
   (doall
     (csv/read-csv in-file))))

(defn load-table-from-env []
   (load-table (env :fixtures)))

(Given #"^data from file "(.*?)":$" [file]
  (reset! total (sum-table (load-table file))))
(Given #"^data from environment$" []
  (reset! total (sum-table (load-table-from-env))))
```

So now the scenario loads some data from a given file and validates some rules. If you have not tried environ yet, the book samples also show a way to plug the filename of the CSV file at runtime using environment variables, so that the following will then tell the scenario which file to load at runtime:

```
export FIXTURES=set1.csv ; lein cucumber features02%
```

This is left as a small exercise to the reader, so we can move on to…

Doing it with Excel

From the previous example, you will remember that the expected result was in the feature file while the data for the test was in a CSV file, meaning you'd have to keep the two in sync somehow.

If both the data and the results were in the CSV file, then someone else could be working on inserting the data, while you just run this test using features written in plain English. So here is an example of what the feature text could be:

```
Feature: My First Cucumber
  Working with excel

  Scenario: Expenses Report Example
    Given I use sheet "List1"
    Then the result is validated
```

The Excel spreadsheet will contain sheets of tables as you have been previously dealing with them, then a result sheet that contains the expected result:

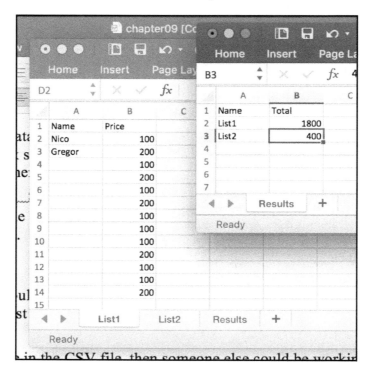

Using docjure, a wrapper around Apache POI, to read the Excel spreadsheet, you would then open the spreadsheet, read in the table data from a worksheet, and the expected result:

```
(use 'dk.ative.docjure.spreadsheet)
(def result (atom 0))
(def expected (atom 0))
(defn load-list [sheet]
  (let [
      book (load-workbook "fixtures/data.xlsx")
    mm
    (map  #(:price %) (rest
        (->> book
            (select-sheet sheet)
            (select-columns {:A :name, :B :price}))))
    results (->> book (select-sheet "Results") (select-columns {:A :Name,
:B :Total}))
    _expected (:Total (first (filter #(= sheet (:Name %)) results)))]
  (reset! result (apply + mm))
```

```
(reset! expected _expected)))
```

This now makes it even easier to interact with external data.

Doing it with web APIs and MongoDB

Yes, Cucumber with remote web APIs. Because data may not always be available locally, you may be wanting to retrieve the data at test time, and assert things on the available data.

The following feature gives you an idea:

```
Feature: My First Cucumber
  Retrieve weather info from HTTP, compute average using MongoDB

  Scenario: Storing Data For Cities
  When I load weather data for the following cities:
    | Tokyo     |
    | Osaka     |
    | Kobe      |
  Then I expect the average temperature to be lower than 30
```

The feature is easy to read, and the underlying code for the steps is not very complicated either.

Basically, the following code does the following:

1. Grabs the next city name from the list.
2. Sends a request to openweathermap.
3. Gets the result as JSON.
4. Stores the JSON directly in MongoDB.
5. Finally, uses the MongoDB aggregation framework to compute the average.

The following snippet follows the previous bullet points:

```
(require  '[monger.core :as mg]
          '[monger.collection :as mc]
          '[monger.operators :refer :all])

(defn endpoint [city]
  (str
    "http://api.openweathermap.org/data/2.5/weather?q="
    city
    "&APPID=<KEY>&units=metric"))

(defn load-weather-data [city]
```

```
(-> (get cl (endpoint city) {:as :json})
    <!!
    :body
    <!!))

(defn store-data-to-mongo [city]
  (mc/insert
    db
    "weather"
    (load-weather-data city)))

(When #"I load weather data for the following cities:$" [table]
  (mc/drop db "weather")
  (doseq [city (.raw table)]
    (store-data-to-mongo (first city))))

(Then #"^I expect the average to be lower than (\d+)$" [maximum]
  (let [
    coll "weather"
    average
      (:avg (first (mc/aggregate db coll [
        {$group {:_id "total" :avg {$avg "$main.temp"}}}])))
    ]
    (assert (< average (bigdec maximum) ))))
```

The BDD framework now helps you go beyond just testing your own code, but also makes interacting with the environment, and the goals of the feature, clear to everyone. It communicates the intention, and allows any other average user to understand the goal, and also be able to change parameters and understand the effect on the testing.

The coming examples in the next section expand vastly on that point to bring BDD to more domains and ideas.

There's more...

The final section of the recipe shows an example of Cucumber interacting with VirtualBox, Flambo, OpenCV, and other frameworks. There is a lot of similar code in all those examples, so the code will be kept to the minimum, and only code that is standing out will be presented in the book (you can of course see the full code in the examples).

The intention of this small section is to show you some ideas and bring the spark in you.

VirtualBox

When playing with VirtualBox, and other VMs, it is nice to be able to validate properties on the VM after boot. Some provisioning frameworks offer the feature; others don't. The fact that you provision the VM with `start sshd at boot` does not always mean that the `sshd` daemon is indeed started at boot.

Here is a feature to put this into context:

```
Feature: VirtualBox Cucumber
  Example on using VirtualBox with Cucumber

  Scenario: Simple VirtualBox Interaction
  When I start the VM "debian"
  And Wait 10 seconds
  Then IP "172.16.2.204" has port "22" opened
  Then I can stop the VM "debian"
```

Obviously, this does not work so well if you retrieve a dynamic IP, but that still gives an idea. The different parts of the Scenario are implemented through bash calls. Basically, start the vm, stop the vm, and check the port is opened with nc:

```
(defn start-the-machine [vm-name]
  (sh/sh "bash" "-c"
    (str "VBoxManage startvm " vm-name " --type headless" )))
(defn stop-the-machine [vm-name]
  (sh/sh "bash" "-c"
    (str "VBoxManage controlvm " vm-name " poweroff" )))
(defn check-port [IP port]
  (sh/sh "bash" "-c"
    (str "nc -z " IP " " port)))
```

You could obviously also give a list of VMs to start…

Freactive

Freactive makes it freac-ing easy to work with atoms…and to have stateful testing. With atoms, you can record the different steps, and validate inputs throughout the journey:

```
Feature: My First Freacting Cucumber
  Meeting people and counting ...

  Scenario: Meeting people
    Given It is a new day
    Given I met Niko
    Given I met Dave
```

```
Then I have met 2 people and the last person was Dave
```

One of the interesting parts of Freactive is cursors, and the ability to create lenses of atoms, and to also have things similar to listeners when the atoms are updated or read.

See below; the `my-lens` atom is *looking at* `people`, plus adding some actions when it is updated. So if `my-lens` is updated, `people` will be updated too, but after the call to the `setter` function:

```
(def people (atom 0))
(def total (atom 0))

(def getter identity)

(defn setter
  [my-atom-state new-cursor-state]
  (swap! total inc)
  new-cursor-state)

(def my-lens
  (lens-cursor people getter setter))
```

Freactive makes it easy to track history in your Scenarios, and also to be able to look back at what kind of data has been transformed or accessed during the test.

Flambo, or BDD meets Apache Spark

There may be some times when, obviously, you want to do pure Apache Spark work, but sometimes that Apache Spark use may simply be a side effect of the test.

Say you want to confirm the number of lines in a file or set of files:

```
Feature: Flambing
  This is a great way to put some notes about Flambing

  Scenario: Word analysis in from a text file
    Given the following text file: "fixtures/sherlock.txt"
    Given we count the number of lines using shell
    Then we wanna check the number of lines is the same
```

Given a file, this `Scenario` just computes the number of lines, but you get the message: this is where you can plug in data analysis on the content of the text itself.

You will remember how easy it is to just start Apache Spark and count the lines with:

```
(def c (-> (conf/spark-conf)
           (conf/master "local")
           (conf/app-name "flame_princess")))
(def sc (f/spark-context c))

(defn word-frequencies [text-file]
  (-> (f/text-file sc text-file)
    f/count))
```

This means that, obviously, what counts in this `Scenario` is the content of the text and what to express to the user. Using a sentiment analysis library, you could validate that your algorithm finds the right sentiment for the text files, but also that your assumptions on the text are correct; then I think this recipe would be a good mood document. It is obviously another example too!

EEP for BDD

You may have heard of the EEP library for BDD. **EEP** stands for **Embedded Event Processing**. This is obviously a very useful library on its own, but how to use it in the context of Cucumber and BDD is also pretty interesting too.

Basically, you start by creating an emitter, which is the centralized place that receives events. Then you register a listener on that emitter, here `:accumulator`, and assign a function that is being called whenever some new event is being sent to the emitter, along with data:

```
(def emitter
  (eem/create {}))

(When #"^the emitter is created$" [])

(When #"^the aggregator is created$" []
  (eem/defaggregator
  emitter
  :accumulator ;; the event type to attach to
  (fn [acc i] (+ acc i)) ;; the function to apply to the stream
  0) ;; the initial state
)
```

Definitions are in the bag, so during your test, you can send data to the aggregator at given times, using `notify`:

```
(When #"^some data is emitted to the aggregator$" []
    ;; send 0-9 down the stream
  (doseq [i (range 10)]
    (eem/notify emitter :accumulator i)))
```

Finally, whenever you need data, you can use `eem/get-handler` that will finalize the event stream and return the computed current result:

```
(Then #"^the state of the aggregator should be (\d+)$" [arg1]
    ;; state is 0 + 1 + 2 + 3 + 4 + 5 + 6 + 7 + 8 + 9
  (assert (= 45
    (eem/state (eem/get-handler emitter :accumulator)))))
```

Where this is good to use is, for example, to retrieve some statistics such as averages, on the data passing by the features of the scenario.

OpenCV

Alright, this is going to be somehow a bit of a bonus! This is a great way to get excited and try new things though. The coming feature writes in easy-to-understand English "features" you expect to find in media content, say, pictures.

For example, the following is simply just adapting the standard face recognition `opencv lena` example, but you do have to agree that this is easier to read than the usual OpenCV code.

Now here, again, the context of this is not about the OpenCV library itself, it is about the content of the image, and how to express it to other people in simple language:

```
Feature: OpenCV Face Recognition
  Playing around with face recognition and cucumber

Scenario: Looking for faces in an image
  When I load the image "fixtures/lena.png"
  And setup the classifier for frontal face recognition
  Then I can find 1 face in the loaded image
```

The whole code includes everything, from reading the image as an object, setting the face detector, starting the face recognition, down to drawing the rectangles:

```
(import '[org.opencv.core Core Mat MatOfRect Point Rect Scalar])
(import '[org.opencv.objdetect CascadeClassifier]
        '[org.opencv.highgui Highgui])
(def image
  (atom nil))
(def faceDetector
  (atom nil))

(When #"^I load the image "(.*?)"$" [_image]
  (reset! image
    (Highgui/imread _image)))

(When #"^setup the classifier for frontal face recognition$" []
  (reset! faceDetector
    (CascadeClassifier. "opencv-data/lbpcascade_frontalface.xml")))

(Then #"^I can find (\d+) face in the loaded image$" [arg1]
  (let [faceDetections      (MatOfRect.)]
    (.detectMultiScale @faceDetector @image faceDetections)
    (let [
      rect-array (.toArray faceDetections)
      len (alength rect-array)]
      ; output for the fun of it
      (doseq [^Rect rect rect-array]
        (Core/rectangle @image
          (Point. (.-x rect) (.-y rect))
          (Point. (+ (.-x rect) (.width rect)) (+ (.-y rect) (.height
rect)))
          (Scalar. 0 255 0)))

      (Highgui/imwrite "target/last-detection.png" @image)

      (assert (= (Integer/parseInt arg1) len )))))
```

Finally, this is putting OpenCV to the use of media analysis in the context of testing and works quite nicely with simply running Cucumber's scenarios and features.

Testing with random inputs and pattern-based testing

It often seems like reinventing the wheel while writing test cases. Always trying to use some handwritten random inputs and trying a few of those inputs on the newly written functions. In this recipe, you will be presented with the Clojure equivalent of QuickCheck patterns, which is a famous testing framework for the Haskell programming language. No need to learn Haskell today, but let's review some cool testing patterns!

Getting ready

In this recipe, one of the main goals is to generate various kinds of data. To achieve that, we will have a mix of handmade data generators and some others will come through libraries. Let's go through the libraries setup.

Libraries

The `project.clj` file is a bit dense today. We will use the `midje` library not for testing but for its `autotest` feature. The `autotest` feature lets you rerun the tests automatically while writing code, and get test reports.

Compojure is not to present anymore. We will use it a bit to generate randomly generated routes, and compare routing results.

The three main libraries – `test.check`, `test.chuck`, and `herbert` – are composing the main course of this recipe.

`test.check` is the base of the Clojure version of QuickCheck, the testing framework. `test.chuck` brings some more utilities and methods to `test.check`, and finally `herbert` brings schema-based random value generation.

That gives the following:

```
(defproject quickchecks "0.1.0-SNAPSHOT"
  :profiles {:dev {:dependencies [
  [midje "1.8.3"]
  :plugins [[lein-midje "3.2"]]}}
  :dependencies [
  [org.clojure/clojure "1.8.0"]
  [compojure "1.5.1"]

  [org.clojure/test.check "0.9.0"]
  [com.velisco/herbert "0.7.0"]
  [com.gfredericks/test.chuck "0.2.6"]
  ])
```

Let's put all this into practice!

Generating random values or groups of values

To understand property-based testing, we will start by having a look at some methods to generate random inputs.

Random inputs are generated using…generators. No, seriously. This is the name the `test.check` library is using.

You can see the output of a generator using another simple generator, named `sample`. `sample` takes a generator, and by default generates 10 values taken from the input generator.

In the following first example, the sample generator takes a generator that always returns the same value, 1.

Let's start an REPL:

```
(require '[clojure.test.check.generators :as gen])

(gen/sample (gen/return 1))
; (1 1 1 1 1 1 1 1 1 1)
```

As expected, `sample` returns 10 times the same value, here 1. The default size for the sample is 10, but you can also set a given size:

```
(gen/sample (gen/return 1) 5)
; (1 1 1 1 1)
```

Obviously, you are not going to be able to test much if the random testing always involves the same value, so let's move to a bit more variety. The `elements` generator takes a sequence, and takes random elements from it:

```
(gen/sample (gen/elements (range 10)))
; (6 2 6 1 0 0 0 5 2 7)
```

Running the same generator twice does return different random sequences. You can also generate a sequence of sequences, by using either the list or the vector generators. Here is how you would do it:

```
(gen/sample (gen/not-empty (gen/vector gen/int)) 5)
; ([-2 -2] [1] [-1 2 0] [2 0] [5 -5])
```

The vector generator takes a generator as parameter, and generates a vector of random size.

You can ask both the sample and the vector to be of size 3, and the sample generator will then generates three samples of size 3 as seen here:

```
(gen/sample (gen/not-empty (gen/vector gen/int 3)) 3)
; ([0 0 0] [0 1 0] [0 2 2])
```

Let's raise the bar a bit. To generate a group of values of different types, you can use tuples. The tuples generator takes as many generators as you want; here, one for random integers and one for random non-empty strings:

```
(gen/sample (gen/tuple gen/int (gen/not-empty gen/string)) 3)
; ([0 "1"] [0 "Â©"] [1 "8"])
```

The `test.chuck` utility brings some fun `regexp` based string generation to you:

```
(require '[com.gfredericks.test.chuck.generators :as gen'])

(gen/sample
(gen/not-empty (gen'/string-from-regex #"(B(A|O)M)+")) 1)
 ; ("BOM")
; try it !
(gen/sample
(gen/not-empty (gen'/string-from-regex #"B(A|O){2}M")) 1)
```

Now, when generating tuples, usually the different values of a set have a co-relation, and this is where the Herbert library comes in.

Random values based on schema

The `Herbert` generator brings both grammars and generators to the utility belt of random generators.

> Beware, the namespaces used are different! But their use is similar and will be used in the same testing context later on.

To generate a sequence of `int` using Herbert, you will use the `hg/sample` method that you can use in the same way as the `test.check` one we have seen up to now.

The `hg/sample` generator then takes a grammar, and the generator will then generate values based on that grammar.

That gives the following:

```
(require '[miner.herbert.generators :as hg])
(hg/sample '[int*] 5)
; ([] () [2 0] () (-4 -2))
```

Sweet world randomness.

You probably have had enough integer randomness for some time, so let's look at tuples now:

```
(hg/sample '{:a int :b [sym+] :c str} 3)
```

The grammar, which is quoted, is a map of three key-value pairs, with keys in :a:b:c, and the values are:

- A random integer for :a
- A vector of symbols for :b
- A string for :c

Running the previous Herbert generators gives you:

```
; ({:c "", :b (*mt), :a 0}
; {:c "", :b [_... !.Z _B3.], :a 0}
; {:c "}", :b (.14 .), :a 9223372036854775807})
```

And obviously running it twice gives different values, but all the values are according to the grammar.

Another example, this time generating one map with more details:

```
(hg/sample '{:a num :b pos :c neg :d (vec int+ zero+)} 1)
; ({:c -2.0, :b 1, :d [9223372036854775807 0], :a 1.5E-5})
```

You now have reviewed how to use generators and how to create random values according to specific patterns. Let's put this into action.

How to do it...

QuickCheck, random-based testing takes the random generator we have seen and uses it for testing.

To achieve this, you will:

- Write a specification, with a name
- Write the size of the number of sampling iterations
- Define random patterns for inputs to the specification
- Define a set of properties to check for each random value

Your first test.check specification

Keeping this in mind, let's go through a first specification and a first example. Let's import some namespaces for properties, generators, and a test helper named `defspec`:

```
(ns quickchecks.core
  (:require    [clojure.test.check.properties :as prop])
  (:require    [clojure.test.check.generators :as gen])
  (:require    [clojure.test.check.clojure-test :refer [defspec]]))
```

Your first specification will be as follows:

- Given a name, `some-ones`
- Will be set how many times to call the generators, here 5
- Validate a property for all values of the generator using `prop/for-all`
- Always generate the value 1, using the `gen/return` you have seen before

The validation is an assertion on the value of the generator, here 1:

```
(defspec some-ones
  5
  (prop/for-all [v (gen/return 1)]
    (= v 1)))
```

We should be pretty safe with that one and this is a test that should pass pretty often.

Auto-running tests

To run the test automatically, a good option is to use `autotest` of `midje`, using:

```
lein midje :autotest
```

This reloads and reruns the needed test namespaces and the dependent code. A sample output would be:

```
================================================================
Loading (quickchecks.core0)
{:result true, :num-tests 5, :seed 1466917660382, :test-var "some-ones"}
>>> Output from clojure.test tests:

0 failures, 0 errors.
>>> Midje summary:
No facts were checked. Is that what you wanted?
[Completed at 14:07:40]
```

Note that the previous test will obviously fail if the generated values are not always 1. The second example will fail unless you specify a smaller iteration size, say, 1:

```
(defspec some-ones-and-twos
  2
  (prop/for-all [v (gen/elements [1 2])]
    (= v 1)))
; fails ...
```

Usually, it is always good to give a size big enough to have a big sampling pool, but not too big, so as to not slow down the test iterations.

More specifications and generators

The following code will generate a list from a pool size of three elements making sure the generated list is either empty, or its first value is lower than 5:

```
(defspec some-g
  5
  (prop/for-all [v (gen/list (gen/elements [1 2 3]))]
    (or (empty? v)
      (< (first v) 5))))
```

Coupling things together a bit more, you can have the generators outside the `defspec` block, as well as the tested functions.

This new example shows how to generate a tuple of parameters and use the generated input as parameters to the tested function `my-f`:

```
(def my-g
(gen/elements [1 2 3 4 5]))
(defn my-f[a b c]
   ; (println a " " b " " c)
  (+ a b c))
(defspec tuppling
  1000
  (prop/for-all [v (gen/tuple my-g my-g my-g)]
    (>= 20 (apply my-f v))))
```

Note that it is pretty useful to at least show some sample output through `println`, and also note that you have just generated randomized inputs of 1,000 entries, with quite a simple random definition.

The last example here checks that the arithmetic still works:

```
(defn my-eq [a b]
  (> 1e10 (- b a)))
(defn my-tan [v]
  (/ (Math/sin v) (Math/cos v)))

(defspec cosintan
  1000
  (prop/for-all [v (gen/elements (range 1 10000))]
     (my-eq (Math/tan v) (my-tan v) )))
```

Obviously, you could perform something similar using tests, but you have to admit the previous version is nicely readable.

Generators and de-structuring

You have seen before the `gen'` namespace. Here, we will see another useful utility from `test.chuck`, de-structuring of the generators.

One of the previous examples was showing how to use `apply` for parameters, but this is making it easier:

```
...
; in the namespace definition
(:require    [com.gfredericks.test.chuck.properties :as prop'])
...
(defn my-len [n]
  (count (str n)))
```

```
(defspec split-n-spec
  10
  (prop'/for-all [ [ele ele2] (gen/tuple gen/int gen/int)]
        (< 0 (my-len (+ ele ele2)))))
```

See how `ele` and `ele2` are assigned to each value of the tuple. Be careful, we use `prop'/for-all` from the `test.chuck` namespace, which is different from the usual prop from `test.check`.

Herbert

From the first part of the recipe, you remember Herbert, which allows random inputs to be generated using a grammar.

To use Herbert's property with `defspec`, you have to do a bit of parameter gymnastics from what you have seen up to now.

Here the checks come first, and the template for generation comes second.

The example generates a map of two key-value pairs, `:a` and `:b`, and checks that the first value of `:a` contains a map integer of value 0 in its second parameter:

```
(defspec hello-again
  10
  (hg/property
    (fn [m] (== (get-in m [:a 1 :int]) 0))
        '{:a (vec kw {:int 0}) :b str}))
```

This technique is very useful when you want to have and generate large maps or large vectors of inputs according to some data structure coming from the outside world.

There's more...

The last part of this recipe would like to show briefly how to apply the concepts introduced to API testing, and in this context, compojure routing.

Say you have a set of routes in an API; it would be great to generate random inputs and make sure the logic is well contained, and at least does not break the fundamentals of your application.

We will consider the very simple routing, where a request with an ID reaches the application, and the application always returns `"Hello Foo"`.

Obviously, this is not a great application to generate millions of dollars, but there might be something in there:

```
(def my-routes
  (routes
(GET "/:id" [] "Hello Foo")))
```

The route is simple, but you would like to generate random inputs and send requests to those compojure apps to verify the returned results.

Here is a simple utility method that shows the map sent to the routing function. As you will have noticed, this simply sends a map with the request type, the uri, headers and some parameters:

```
(defn request [uri app & params]
  (app      {:request-method :get
             :headers {"content-type" "text/plain"}
             :uri uri
             :params params}))
```

With this in your toolkit, let's use the application my-routes, and the utility method to write a spec that tests our application:

```
(defspec ringing
  10
  (prop/for-all [a gen/int]
    (= "Hello Foo"
(:body (request (str "/" a) my-routes [])))))
```

The generator gives you a random int, that is then used to create the uri for the request. Finally, we make sure the returned result from the application is pretty rock solid, always returning some nice Foo greetings.

The first example is pretty static, so what if you want to actually have dynamically generated routing?

It works pretty much all the same, and the only new thing is using a let block to bind the routing within the test scope:

```
(defspec ringing-2
  100
  (prop'/for-all [a gen/int]
    (let [local-routes
          (routes  (GET "/:id" [] (str "Hello Foo" a)))]
      (= (str "Hello Foo" a) (:body (request (str "/" a) local-routes
[]))))))
```

With this recipe, you are all set! Enjoy large sets of random testing!

Benchmarking with Criterium, performance tips, and other tools

In this recipe, we will learn how to test, measure, and improve the performance of your application. We will show you a Clojure-based benchmark tool.

Getting ready

To use Criterium, we need to add the `criterium` library in your `project.clj` as follows:

```
(defproject performance-example "0.1.0-SNAPSHOT"
  :description "FIXME: write description"
  :url "http://example.com/FIXME"
  :license {:name "Eclipse Public License"
            :url "http://www.eclipse.org/legal/epl-v10.html"}
  :dependencies [[org.clojure/clojure "1.8.0"]
                 [criterium "0.4.4"]])
```

Then, restart your REPL.

How to do it...

Here, we will show you how to test the performance of your code using Criterium.

Using Criterium

Criterium is a micro benchmark tool for measuring the computation time of Clojure expressions.

It performs given expressions multiple times and reports statistical information including means and std-deviations of execution time. Criterium also considers JVM characteristics such as the optimization of JIT compiler and effects of GC.

Let's assume we will measure performances for `apply`, `reduce`, and `reducers`.

In the recipe, we will measure performances with a small benchmark that calculates the sum of the square from 1 to 1 million:

```
1^2 + 2 ^2 + 3 ^3 + ..... + 1,000,000 ^2
```

First of all, let's declare the namespace and library to use as follows:

```
(ns performance-example.criterium-example
  (:require [criterium.core :refer
              [bench with-progress-reporting report-result quick-bench
benchmark quick-benchmark]]
            [clojure.core.reducers :as r]
            [criterium.stats :as stats]
            ))
```

We will measure execution time for benchmark for `apply`, `reduce`, and `reducers`. We will run each three times as follows:

```
(dotimes [_x 3]
  (time (apply + (map #(* % %) (range 1 1000001)))))
;;=> "Elapsed time: 158.034419 msecs"
;;=> "Elapsed time: 98.81966 msecs"
;;=> "Elapsed time: 92.167793 msecs"
(dotimes [_x 3]
  (time (reduce + (map #(* % %) (range 1 1000001)))))
;;=> "Elapsed time: 165.243023 msecs"
;;=> "Elapsed time: 103.53534 msecs"
;;=> "Elapsed time: 157.971972 msecs"
(dotimes [_x 3]
  (time (r/fold + (r/map #(* % %) (range 1 1000001)))))
;;=> "Elapsed time: 144.123838 msecs"
;;=> "Elapsed time: 89.670486 msecs"
;;=> "Elapsed time: 81.810268 msecs"
```

In the preceding tests, the results of performance tests varies in the same expression. We'd like to know the performance more accurately. Criterium is used for such a requirement. Now we will run benchmarks using Criterium for `apply`, `map`, and `reducers`:

```
(bench (apply + (map #(* % %) (range 1 1000001))))
Evaluation count : 660 in 60 samples of 11 calls.
            Execution time mean : 92.660075 ms
     Execution time std-deviation : 1.823143 ms
    Execution time lower quantile : 91.480376 ms ( 2.5%)
    Execution time upper quantile : 98.511451 ms (97.5%)
                    Overhead used : 9.581787 ns
Found 5 outliers in 60 samples (8.3333 %)
    low-severe    5 (8.3333 %)
 Variance from outliers : 7.8662 % Variance is slightly inflated by
```

```
outliers
(bench (reduce + (map #(* % %) (range 1 1000001)))))
Evaluation count : 660 in 60 samples of 11 calls.
            Execution time mean : 91.840883 ms
   Execution time std-deviation : 1.425659 ms
  Execution time lower quantile : 90.996427 ms ( 2.5%)
  Execution time upper quantile : 95.662824 ms (97.5%)
                Overhead used : 9.581787 ns
Found 2 outliers in 60 samples (3.3333 %)
    low-severe      2 (3.3333 %)
 Variance from outliers : 1.6389 % Variance is slightly inflated by
outliers
(bench (r/fold + (r/map #(* % %) (range 1 1000001)))))
Evaluation count : 840 in 60 samples of 14 calls.
            Execution time mean : 76.441841 ms
   Execution time std-deviation : 1.431449 ms
  Execution time lower quantile : 75.755372 ms ( 2.5%)
  Execution time upper quantile : 82.202533 ms (97.5%)
                Overhead used : 9.581787 ns
Found 10 outliers in 60 samples (16.6667 %)
    low-severe      6 (10.0000 %)
    low-mild        4 (6.6667 %)
 Variance from outliers : 7.8176 % Variance is slightly inflated by
outliers
```

To compare execution time means, `reducers` are the fastest.

By default, `bench` is quiet when your benchmarks in progress. To avoid this, use `with-progress-reporting` to get progress information. `with-progress-reporting` reports the intermediate status of your benchmarks:

```
(with-progress-reporting
  (bench (Thread/sleep 1000) :verbose))
Estimating sampling overhead
Warming up for JIT optimisations 10000000000 ...
   compilation occurred before 275187 iterations
   compilation occurred before 35488371 iterations
   compilation occurred before 69326040 iterations
   compilation occurred before 70151349 iterations
   compilation occurred before 105364533 iterations
   compilation occurred before 140577717 iterations
Estimating execution count ...
Sampling ...
Final GC...
Checking GC...
Finding outliers ...
Bootstrapping ...
Checking outlier significance
```

```
Warming up for JIT optimisations 10000000000 ...
   compilation occurred before 1 iterations
Estimating execution count ...
Sampling ...
Final GC...
Checking GC...
Finding outliers ...
Bootstrapping ...
Checking outlier significance
amd64 Linux 3.16.0-38-generic 4 cpu(s)
Java HotSpot(TM) 64-Bit Server VM 25.65-b01
Runtime arguments: -Dfile.encoding=UTF-8 -XX:+TieredCompilation -
XX:TieredStopAtLevel=1 -XX:-OmitStackTraceInFastThrow -
Dclojure.compile.path=/home/makoto/clojure/clojure-packt-
book/chapter09/criterium-example/target/classes -Dcriterium-
example.version=0.1.0-SNAPSHOT -Dclojure.debug=false
Evaluation count : 780 in 60 samples of 13 calls.
        Execution time sample mean : 77.498879 ms
              Execution time mean : 77.517145 ms
Execution time sample std-deviation : 1.418071 ms
    Execution time std-deviation : 1.441261 ms
    Execution time lower quantile : 76.678226 ms ( 2.5%)
    Execution time upper quantile : 82.447959 ms (97.5%)
                Overhead used : 9.491795 ns

Found 6 outliers in 60 samples (10.0000 %)
    low-severe    1 (1.6667 %)
    low-mild     5 (8.3333 %)
 Variance from outliers : 7.8102 % Variance is slightly inflated by
outliers
```

How it works...

In this section, we will show you some fundamental performance tips to improve your application.

Type hints

Type hints are there to assist the compiler in avoiding reflections that decrease the performance. Type hints are Clojure's metadata tags placed on symbols for function parameters, `let`-bound names, var names, or expressions, and they are used by the compiler.

Let's show some examples to reduce overheads of reflections. The following code returns the length of the string using the length method in the String class:

```
(def str "This is a String")
;;=> #'performance-example.performance-tips/str
(time (dotimes [_ 100000]
         (.length str)))
;;=> "Elapsed time: 660.444886 msecs"
;;=> nil
```

To improve the performance, add a type hint ^String for str:

```
(def ^String str "This is a String")
;;=> #'performance-example.performance-tips/s
(time (dotimes [_ 100000]
         (.length str)))
;;=> "Elapsed time: 14.516152 msecs"
;;=> nil
```

The next example shows type hinting for the function parameters and how it improves the performance:

```
(defn my-concat [s1 s2]
  (.concat s1 s2))
;;=> #'performance-example.performance-tips/my-concat
(time
 (dotimes [_ 100000]
   (my-concat "Hello " "World !")))
;;=> "Elapsed time: 653.67418 msecs"
;;=> nil
(defn my-concat2 [^String s1 ^String s2]
  (.concat s1 s2))
;;=> #'performance-example.performance-tips/my-concat2
(time
 (dotimes [_ 100000]
   (my-concat2 "Hello " "World !")))
;;=> "Elapsed time: 20.369515 msecs"
;;=> nil
```

From the performance aspect, the reflection is not desirable for your application. To check reflections in your application, set *warn-on-reflection* to be true. It warns when reflection occurs:

```
(set! *warn-on-reflection* true)
;;=> true
(def str "This is a String")
;;=> #'performance-example.performance-tips/str
(-> str .toString .toLowerCase)
```

```
;;=> Reflection warning, /home/makoto/clojure/clojure-packt-
book/chapter09/performance-
example/src/performance_example/performance_tips.clj:59:0 - reference to
field toString can't be resolved.
;;=> Reflection warning, /home/makoto/clojure/clojure-packt-
book/chapter09/performance-
example/src/performance_example/performance_tips.clj:59:0 - reference to
field toLowerCase can't be resolved.
;;=> "This is a String"
```

In the previous situation, add ^String for str to avoid the warning:

```
(-> ^String str .toUpperCase .toLowerCase)
;;=> "this is a string"
```

Sometimes, setting *warn-on-reflection* always to be true is useful. To do this, add the following to your ~/.lein/profiles.clj_ file:

```
:warn-on-reflection true
```

Using appropriate data types

Let's compare vector and list. First, we will measure the performance of accessing vectors:

```
(def x (into [] (repeat 1000000 "Clojure Programming Cookbook")))
;;=> #'performance-example.performance-tips/x
(time (first x))
"Elapsed time: 0.093379 msecs"
;;=> "Clojure Programming Cookbook"
(time (nth x 999999))
;;=> "Elapsed time: 0.157437 msecs"
;;=> "Clojure Programming Cookbook"
(time (x 999999))
;;=> "Elapsed time: 0.134643 msecs"
;;=> "Clojure Programming Cookbook"
(time (last x))
"Clojure Programming Cookbook"
;;=> "Elapsed time: 59.058957 msecs"
;;=> 999999
```

Then, let's test with list:

```
(def y (range 1000000))
;;=> #'performance-example.performance-tips/y
(time (nth y 999999))
;;=> "Elapsed time: 23.200696 msecs"
;;=> "Clojure Programming Cookbook"
```

```
(time (last y))
;;=> "Elapsed time: 48.545212 msecs"
;;=> "Clojure Programming Cookbook"
```

Index accesses for vector are faster than those of list. However, both performances of `last` are not good. So we will define a new `last` named `my-last`:

```
(defn my-last [s]
  (nth s (dec (count s))))
;;=> #'performance-example.performance-tips/my-last
(time (my-last x))
;;=> "Elapsed time: 0.210762 msecs"
;;=> "Clojure Programming Cookbook"
(time (my-last y))
;;=> "Elapsed time: 23.701789 msecs"
;;=> "Clojure Programming Cookbook"
```

The previous is better for vector and list.

Maps versus records versus types

We will test the performance of `maps`, `records`, and `types`. We will define `RecordLocation` and `TypeLocation`; those are the records and types as follows:

```
(defrecord RecordLocation [x y z])
;;=> performance_example.performance_tips.RecordLocation
(deftype TypeLocation [x y z])
;;=> performance_example.performance_tips.TypeLocation
```

Then, we will define `map-location`, `record-location`, and `type-location`:

```
(def map-location {:x 0.0 :y 0.0 :z 0.0})
;;=> #'performance-example.performance-tips/map-location
(def record-location (->RecordLocation 0.0 0.0 0.0))
;;=> #'performance-example.performance-tips/record-location
(def type-location (->TypeLocation 0.0 0.0 0.0))
;;=> #'performance-example.performance-tips/type-location
```

Let's define the `ILocation` protocol and extend the protocols for `map`, `record`, and `type` in the following:

```
(defprotocol ILocation
  (move [self x y z]))
;;=> ILocation
(extend-protocol ILocation
  clojure.lang.PersistentArrayMap
  (move [self x y z]
```

```
     {:x (+ (map-location :x) x)
      :y (+ (map-location :y) y)
      :z (+ (map-location :z) z)})
     RecordLocation
         (move [self x y z]
         (->RecordLocation
          (+ (:x self) x)(+ (:y self) y)(+ (:z self) z)))
     TypeLocation
     (move [self x y z]
         (->TypeLocation
          (+ (.-x self) x)(+ (.-y self) y)(+ (.-z self) z))))
 ;=> nil
```

Now, let's measure the performances for them. First, we will test the move method for map:

```
(with-progress-reporting
   (bench   (move map-location 2.0 3.0 2.0)))
```

The result is as follows:

```
Evaluation count : 386864340 in 60 samples of 6447739 calls.
            Execution time mean : 147.959163 ns
   Execution time std-deviation : 6.447521 ns
   Execution time lower quantile : 139.499802 ns ( 2.5%)
   Execution time upper quantile : 162.371977 ns (97.5%)
              Overhead used : 9.727097 ns
```

Then, we will test for record:

```
(with-progress-reporting
   (bench (move record-location 2.0 3.0 2.0)))
```

We got the better result:

```
Evaluation count : 455571960 in 60 samples of 7592866 calls.
            Execution time mean : 121.687435 ns
   Execution time std-deviation : 3.484611 ns
   Execution time lower quantile : 117.866370 ns ( 2.5%)
   Execution time upper quantile : 128.063522 ns (97.5%)
              Overhead used : 9.727097 ns
```

Lastly, we will test the type:

```
(with-progress-reporting
   (bench (move type-location 2.0 3.0 2.0)))
```

This is better than the previous two:

```
Evaluation count : 590518980 in 60 samples of 9841983 calls.
             Execution time mean : 93.307679 ns
    Execution time std-deviation : 2.608460 ns
   Execution time lower quantile : 90.346986 ns ( 2.5%)
   Execution time upper quantile : 99.742274 ns (97.5%)
                   Overhead used : 9.727097 ns
```

The following table is the summary of benchmarks:

Data type	Time (ns)
Map	147
Record	121
Type	93

Primitive arrays

Let's consider using primitive arrays in Clojure. The following code is to calculate $2 + 2^2 + 3^2 + \ldots + n^2$ using vector:

```
(def array1 (into [] (repeatedly 1000 #(rand 10))))
;;=> #'performance-example.performance-tips/array1
(defn my-calc1[ar]
  (reduce +
          (map (fn [x] (* x x))
               ar)))
;;=> #'performance-example.performance-tips/my-calc1
```

We will define `array2` that is a primitive array of `double`:

```
(def array2 (double-array (repeatedly 1000 #(rand 10))))
;;=> #'performance-example.performance-tips/array2
```

This is equivalent to the following:

```
double[] array2;
```

Let's check the array is created correctly:

```
(alength ^doubles array2)
;;=> 1000
Try to get the first element.
(aget ^doubles array2 0)
```

```
;;=> 7.069889039765091
```

We will define my-calc2 using amap and areduce:

```
(defn my-calc2[ar]
  (let [xs
        (amap ^doubles ar
              idx ret
              (let [x (aget ^doubles ar idx)]
                (* x x)))]
    (areduce xs i ret (double 0)
             (+ ret (aget ^doubles xs i)))))
#'performance-example.performance-tips/my-calc2
```

Let's test the performance of both cases:

```
(bench (my-calc1 array1))
(bench (my-calc2 array2))
Using a primitive type is faster.
Execution time mean : 69.387426 Âµs
Execution time mean : 54.874642 Âµs
```

Working with transient data structures

Clojure's transient is a data structure which allows mutable updates. We will learn how we use it and compare the performance with Clojure's persistent data structure.

The following code is using transient:

```
(defn rand-seq1 [n m]
  (loop [i 0 s (transient [])]
    (if (< i n)
      (recur (inc i) (conj! s (rand m)))
      (persistent! s))))
```

The transient data structure allows mutable functions such as conj!, disj!, pop!, assoc!, and dissoc!. We cannot use these functions for persistent data structures. To get persistent data, use persistent!.

We will define the same function not using transient:

```
(defn rand-seq2 [n m]
  (loop [i 0 s []]
    (if (< i n)
      (recur (inc i) (conj s (rand m)))
      s)))
```

Then, let's run benchmarks:

```
(bench (rand-seq1 1000000 10))
(bench (rand-seq2 1000000 10))
```

We got the following results and using a primitive array was faster:

```
transient => Execution time mean : 86.779352 ms
non-transient => Execution time mean : 128.905613 ms
```

Memoize functions

We introduce you to memoize, which caches the arguments and results of function calls. Memoize improves performance if a function calls with the same arguments repeatedly; on the other hand, the use of memoize consumes memory.

We will define a `factorial` function in the following:

```
(defn factorial [num]
  (if (= num 1)
    num
    (* num (factorial (dec num)))))
```

Then, we will define the memoize version of factorial:

```
(def memoize-factorial (memoize factorial))
```

Now, let's measure the performance of the non-memoize version and the memoize version:

```
(time (factorial 3000N))
;;=> "Elapsed time: 11.111595 msecs"
;;=> 4149359603......
(time (factorial 3000N))
"Elapsed time: 11.260317 msecs"
;;=> 4149359603......
```

We ran the non-memoize version of factorial twice. The execution times are almost the same. Next, we will test the memoize version of factorial:

```
(time (memoize-factorial 3000N))
"Elapsed time: 11.258368 msecs"
;;=> 4149359603......
(time (memoize-factorial 3000N))
"Elapsed time: 0.084887 msecs"
;;=> 4149359603......
```

The first execution is almost the same as the non-memoize version. But the second call is quite fast.

There's more...

Here, we will show you other tools for profiling performance.

Logging with timbre and profiling with tufte

ptaoussanis/timbre is a logging API for Clojure/Script. timbre is fast, flexible, and easy to configure with map. ptaoussanis/tufte is a simple profiling and performance monitoring tool for Clojure/Clojurescript.

To enable timbre and tufte, we will add their libraries to your project.clj and restart your REPL:

```
(defproject performance-example "0.1.0-SNAPSHOT"
  :description "FIXME: write description"
  :url "http://example.com/FIXME"
  :license {:name "Eclipse Public License"
            :url "http://www.eclipse.org/legal/epl-v10.html"}
  :dependencies [[org.clojure/clojure "1.8.0"]
                 [criterium "0.4.4"]
                 [com.taoensso/timbre "4.6.0"]
                 [com.taoensso/tufte "1.0.0-RC1"]])
```

Then, let's create src/performance_example/timbreexample.clj_. We will add the namespace and library to use:

```
(ns performance-example.timble-example
  (:require
   [clojure.core.reducers :as r]
    [taoensso.timbre :as timbre
      :refer (log  trace  debug  info  warn  error  fatal  report
              logf tracef debugf infof warnf errorf fatalf reportf
              spy get-env log-env)]
    [taoensso.tufte :as tufte :refer (defnp p profiled profile)]))
;;=> nil
```

Now, let's test logs:

```
(error "timbre error")
;;=> 16-07-18 14:40:12 phenix ERROR [performance-example.timble-example:15]
- timbre error
;;=> nil
(info "timble info")
;;=> 16-07-18 14:40:49 phenix INFO [performance-example.timble-example:18]
- timble info
;;=> nil
```

We have tested two log levels. The next example is to see the expression and the result using `spy`:

```
(def x 10)
;;=> #'performance-example.timble-example/x
(spy (* x 10) )
16-07-15 00:06:50 phenix DEBUG [performance-example.timble-example:16] - (*
x 10) => 100
;;=> nil
```

It prints the expression and the value of evaluation. `set-level!` changes the current log level:

```
(timbre/set-level! :info)
;;=> {:level :info}
(debug "this is a debug message")
;;=> nil
```

The previous example sets the log level to `info`. So the debug log is not printed. Let's set the level back to `debug`:

```
(timbre/set-level! :debug)
;;=> {:level :debug}
(debug "this is a debug message")
;;=> 16-07-18 13:28:03 phenix DEBUG [performance-example.timble-example:30]
- this is a debug message
;;=> nil
```

The debug log is printed. We will define a macro that prints how long an expression takes in milliseconds in the log. We will define `ms-time` to convert nanoseconds to milliseconds:

```
(defn ms-time[s]
  (double (/ (- (System/nanoTime) s) 1000000)))
;;=> #'performance-example.timble-example/ms-time
```

Then, we will define a macro for printing time in the log:

```
(defmacro with-perf-log [f s]
  `(let [st# (System/nanoTime)]
     ~s
     (~f (format "%s -> %10.3fms" '~s (ms-time st#)))))
;;=> #'performance-example.timble-example/with-perf-log
```

Let's test the macro:

```
(with-perf-log info (Thread/sleep 1000))
;;=> 16-07-18 13:38:19 phenix INFO [performance-example.timble-example:?] -
(Thread/sleep 1000) ->    1002.858ms
;;=> nil
(with-perf-log debug (Thread/sleep 1000))
;;=> 16-07-18 13:38:41 phenix DEBUG [performance-example.timble-example:?]
- (Thread/sleep 1000) ->    1002.345ms
;;=> nil
```

We will set logging to output to a file. We will use merge-config and set up a log file there:

```
(timbre/merge-config!
 {:appenders {:spit (appenders/spit-appender {:fname "/tmp/my-
file.log"})}})
;;=> {:level :debug, :ns-whitelist [], :ns-blacklist [], :middleware [],
;;=> :timestamp-opts {:pattern "yy-MM-dd HH:mm:ss", :locale :jvm-default,
;;=> :timezone :utc}, :output-fn #function[taoensso.timbre/default-output-
fn],
;;=> :appenders {:println {:enabled? true, :async? false, :min-level nil,
:rate-limit nil,
;;=> :output-fn :inherit, :fn
#function[taoensso.timbre.appenders.core/println-appender/fn--22162]},
;;=> :spit {:enabled? true, :async? false, :min-level nil, :rate-limit nil,
:output-fn :inherit,
;;=> :fn #function[taoensso.timbre.appenders.core/spit-appender/self-
-22170]}}}
(debug "this is a debug message")
;;=> 16-07-18 14:38:37 phenix DEBUG [performance-example.timble-example:47]
- this is a debug message
;;=> nil
```

We will try to use `ptaoussanis/tufte`. The results of Criterium benchmarks are accurate, however they take time to measure.

`tufte` is much simpler and no warm-up is necessary. Additionally, it measures multiple expressions at a time and generates comparison reports.

We will use `taoensso.tufte/profile` and `taoensso.tufte/p` to run benchmarks and get reports of them. The following is how we make use of `profile`. Let's assume we'd like to compare three expressions:

```
(tufte/add-basic-println-handler! {})
;;=> #{:basic-println}
(profile {}
 (dotimes [_ 10]
   (p :apply  (apply + (map #(* % %) (range 1 1000001))))
   (p :map  (reduce + (map #(* % %) (range 1 1000001))))
   (p :reducers (r/fold + (r/map #(* % %) (range 1 1000001))))))
;;=>          pId    nCalls    Min      Max      MAD      Mean
Time% Time
;;=>          :map    10     97.0ms   148.02ms  17.27ms  113.45ms
37 1.13s
;;=>          :apply  10     95.26ms  149.86ms  13.86ms  106.6ms
35 1.07s
;;=>    :reducers    10     75.67ms  106.29ms  9.25ms   84.31ms
28 843.07ms
;;=>    Clock Time
100 3.05s
;;=>Accounted Time
100 3.04s
;;=> nil
```

Using jvisualvm

`jvisualvm` is included in Oracle's JDK. Using `jvisualvm`, you can see a lot of JVM activities which Clojure is running. Let's run `jvisualvm` and connect to your Clojure REPL.

To run `jvisualvm`, you need to install Oracle's JDK. `jvisualvm` exists in the `$JAVA_HOME/bin`. You need to add that path to `$PATH` and start `jvisualvm` as follows:

```
$ jvisualvm
```

Then, you can see the following:

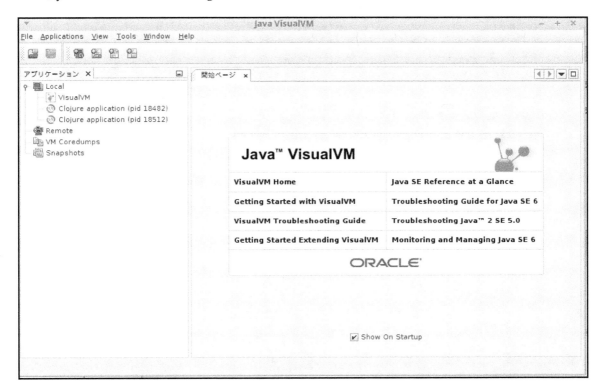

Running REPL starts two JVM processes. One is for a client and the other is for a server. To identify JVM for an REPL server, click **Overview** | **System properties** and check `sun.java.command`.

`sun.java.command` has the following properties:

```
sun.java.command=clojure.main -m leiningen.core.main repl
sun.java.command=clojure.main -i /tmp/form-init800242616981374350.clj
```

Choose the latter one:

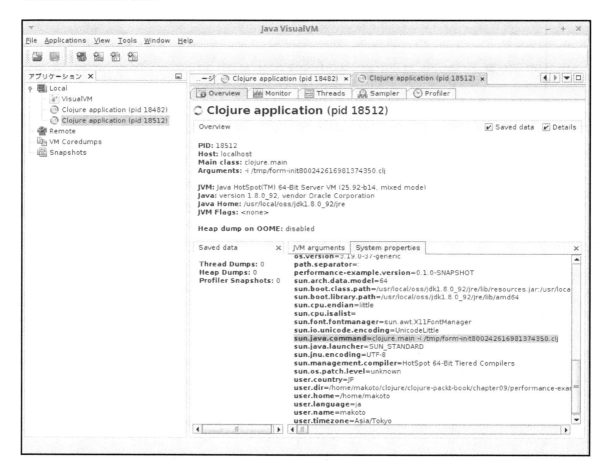

To see which functions are consuming CPU, click on the **Sampler** tab and push the **CPU** button. Then, let's run the following expression in your REPL and check which function consumes the maximum CPU resources:

```
(time (reduce + (range 100000000)))
```

Clicking **Self Time[%]** shows the functions consuming the highest CPU percentage:

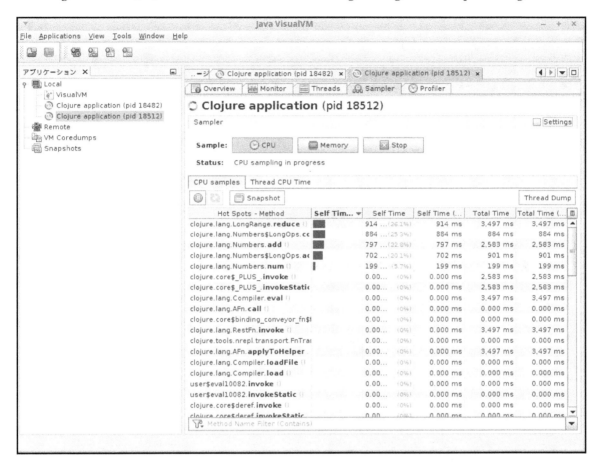

The following code is to calculate the `pi` using the Leibniz formula:

```
(defn calculate-pi
  [iter]
  (let [n (filter odd? (iterate inc 1))]
    (* 4.0
      (apply + (map / (cycle [1 -1]) (take iter n))))))
```

We will see which functions are consuming more CPU resources in `jvisualvm`:

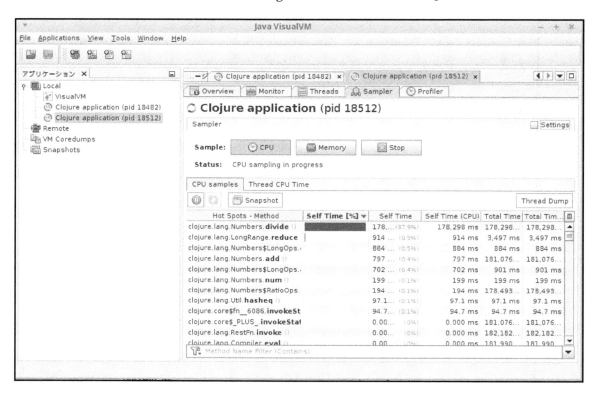

To see the graph of the functions consuming the most memory, click the **Memory** button. You can see the following:

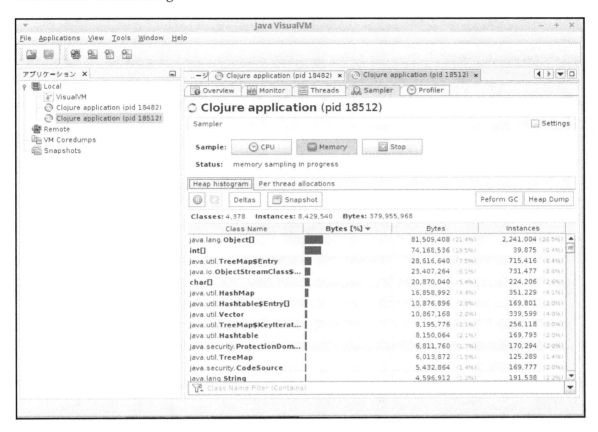

Let's select the **Threads** tab. We can see the activities of threads here. Put in the following code and see what happens:

```
(.start (Thread. (fn [] (Thread/sleep 10000))))
```

You can see a new thread was generated:

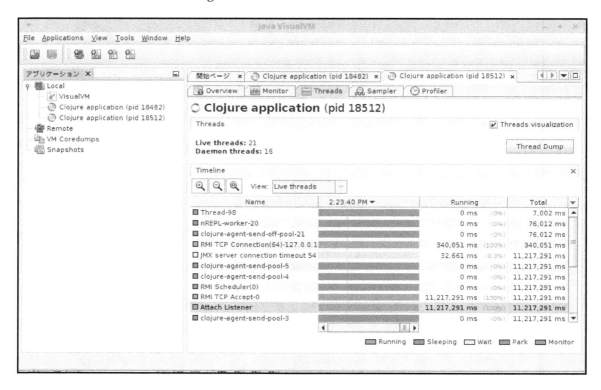

In the preceding screenshot, `Thread-98` was generated and running. That is it! In this chapter, we have learned about tests. In the next chapter, we will learn about DevOps and using AWS with Clojure.

10
Deployment and DevOps

In this chapter we will cover the following topics:

- Riemann - monitoring deliverance and slacking
- Deploying Clojure with Docker
- Clojure on Amazon Web Services

Introduction

This chapter will focus on deploying and monitoring your Clojure code. The first part will delve into deploying Clojure code with Docker containers, locally, remotely, and then to a platform as a service. Then you will have a look at how to monitor your application and, by extension, the servers where your code is running, using a Clojure-written monitoring tool named Riemann.

Lastly, we will look at how we can make use of AWS services, including EC2, S3, and Lambda.

Riemann - monitoring deliverance and slacking

It always seems like a real pain to use monitoring in production. The only thing that should be important is to get the information you want when you want it, in the same way that you can pick up this book when you need to take your daily Clojure shot.

In this recipe, we will look at Riemann, `http://riemann.io`, a stream-based monitoring framework. Riemann comes with easy client APIs, simple setup, an interactive dashboard, and simple interaction with other notification frameworks, such as the new kid on the block and Slack.

The Riemann service, at its core, is written in Clojure and configured in Clojure. Event handling through streams concepts feels and acts very functional.

Eventually, it should also become a breeze to set this up for your cluster of Raspberry Pi's, and collect IoT knowledge in real time.

Getting ready

This recipe is a bit different from the other ones as the main point of interaction is a service, so we will quickly go through installing the daemon, configuring it, preparing the client, and reviewing the dashboard.

Installing the Riemann service

The package comes as an installer for a variety of platforms. The default installer for Raspberry Raspian and a few other Linux distributions is a deb file, which can be downloaded from the Riemann website, `http://riemann.io`:

```
dpkg -I riemann_0.2.11_all.deb
```

Once Riemann is installed, you can start it with the following:

```
sudo systemctl start riemann
```

You can also control the daemon with the usual `systemd` commands.

Getting the daemon started is half the battle, so we will also have a quick look at steps to configure the daemon for remote access.

Configuring the Riemann daemon

While many crustier configuration details will be coming later on in this recipe, let's review the basics of configuring the daemon.

The default configuration file is located at /etc/riemann/riemann.config, and, in its original form, is pretty short. This places the daemon logs in the /var/log folder, and instructs them to listen to TCP, UDP, and WebSocket connection (yes! Websockets...):

```
(logging/init {:file "/var/log/riemann/riemann.log"})

; Listen over TCP (5555), UDP (5555), and websockets
; (5556)
(let [host "0.0.0.0"]
  (tcp-server {:host host})
  (udp-server {:host host})
  (ws-server  {:host host}))
```

Note that the default host is not 0.0.0.0, but localhost, so make sure you change it before going ahead so that you can send events from remote machines.

The Riemann dashboard

The dashboard itself has been developed in the Ruby language, using the Sinatra framework, but I am sure that you'll go and implement a Riemann dashboard in Clojure and ClojureScript in no time.

Now, on to installing the dashboard, packaged as a Ruby gem:

```
sudo gem install riemann-dash --no-ri --no-rdoc
```

Then start the dashboard itself:

```
riemann-dash
```

It can now be accessed at `http://localhost:4567/`:

We will look at how to populate this in a few minutes, but first let's send some events to the Riemann daemon.

Riemann-health

The default dashboard feels a bit empty by default, and it feels a bit sad to look at all this whiteness, so let's quickly see how to add details for a single host.

Riemann has a simple script that can be started to send vital info about the host. The install is done through `gem install` with the following command:

```
sudo gem install riemann-tools
```

The script can then be started with the following:

```
riemann-health --host riemann-host
```

In the preceding command, `riemann-host` is either the hostname or the IP of the machine running the Riemann daemon.

Alright, now we have the daemon sending events to the Riemann host, but now you would eventually like to visualize them.

Just enough dashboard configuration

The dashboard can be seen as a set of tags with widgets in each tab.

In each tab, to enter the selection mode, you press *Control/Meta* + click to select a widget, or *Option* + *Command* + click on a Mac.

If you do that properly, the view changes color. In the following screenshot, the bottom widget is selected and has turned dark gray:

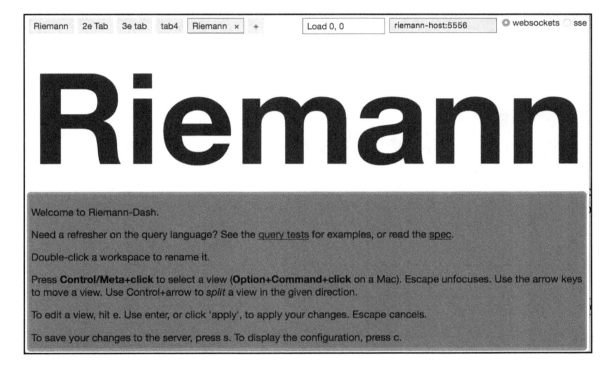

You can then move that widget around by using the arrow keys:

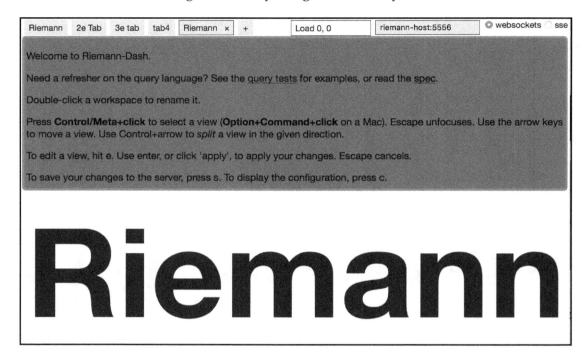

Eventually, you can edit its content by pressing the *e* key. Here, we will just want to see the health of the main server, in this case, the machine running Riemann-health.

We will use the flot widget, and avoid monitoring the machine where the Riemann daemon is working, in this sample, `Debian-jessie-amd64-netboot`:

 Note: It seems the query cannot be empty, so if you get no data showing on the dashboard later, make sure you have a query.

You can then escape widget editing by pressing *Esc* twice, the second time to escape widget selection mode. You should get something like the following:

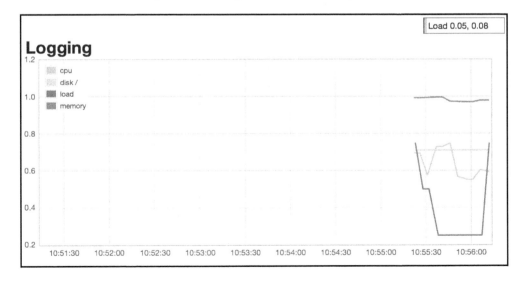

With almost no effort, you already have live data coming from your system.

If you want to limit the amount of data coming from it, update the query to show only, say, the CPU usage:

```
host != "Debian-jessie-amd64-netboot"  and service = "cpu"
```

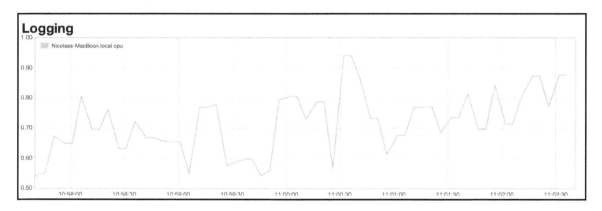

When you are happy with the layout of your dashboard, press the *s* key to persist the configuration to disk.

Make sure you have a bit of fun with the widget before moving on!

Preparing to send events

Finally, to get ready to send some events, we will use the Riemann client for Clojure. Therefore, we'll have to add the Riemann client to the `project.clj` file of a new Clojure project. You will also play with some Slack integration later, so let's add a library to help us do that. Here is how the dependencies should look:

```
:dependencies [
  [riemann-clojure-client "0.4.2"]
  [slack-rtm "0.1.3"]
  [org.clojure/clojure "1.8.0"]]
```

Now, let's fly to monitoring Island!

How to do it...

Now that we have all this set up and ready, you will start by sending some reporting event.

Basic event reporting for a service

The snippet is the usual, deceptively short Clojure snippet, and you will only get three lines of code at this stage:

```
(require '[riemann.client :as r])
(def c (r/tcp-client {:host "riemann-host"}))
(-> c (r/send-event {:service "first-service" :state "ok"}))
```

Let's break down the preceding code snippet:

- The first line is a simple namespace `require`
- The second line gets a `tcp-client` (you could also use UDP here)
- The TCP client reconnects to the Riemann daemon by itself
- The last line does the event sending

The event is simply composed of a `:service` and a `:state` here. Back to the dashboard we used earlier. Let's add something to see how the new service looks:

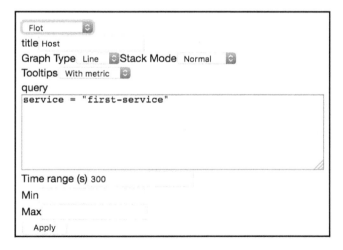

And…it's pretty empty:

So what's missing? Maybe…yes! Let's give a value to this event. This is done through the metric parameter:

```
(-> c (r/send-event
    {:service "first-service" :state "ok" :metric 10}))
```

With a bit of variation in the metric itself, you may eventually get some nice drawing, and with luck it will look the same as the following:

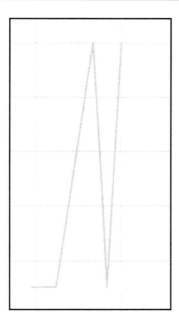

The following are two important keys to include in the event map:

- :description, which will be shown in the log view
- :tag, which will be useful in any searches

Switch to a log widget, as shown next:

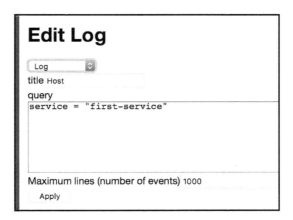

Switching and sending a description will take you to the following:

Host				
host	**service**	**state**	**metric**	**description**
Nicolass-MacBook.local	first-service	ok	100	first description

This method is very useful in helping you track your different services. That's it. Just make sure you play around with the tags and search before moving on.

Expiring events

If you sent a few events before reading this (and I'm certain you did) you may have noticed the value tends to disappear. This is because the default Riemann daemon configuration expires events on a regular basis, as seen here.

Have a quick look at the Riemann configuration file at `/etc/riemann/riemann.config`, shown at the bottom:

```
(periodically-expire 5)

(let [index (index)]
  ; Inbound events will be passed to these streams:
  (streams
    (default :ttl 60
      ; Index all events immediately.
      index

      ; Log expired events.
      (expired
        (fn [event] (info "expired" event))))))
```

What this does is expire the event after a 60 second `ttl`, and send a new `expired` event derived from the event that has expired. If you still have the log widget running, it will show up as in the following screenshot:

Host				
host	**service**	**state**	**metric**	**description**
Nicolass-MacBook.local	first-service	ok	100	first description
Nicolass-MacBook.local	first-service	expired		

This is your first encounter with the concept of Riemann streams, so let's see how they work.

How it works...

As shown in the Riemann documentation, streams typically do one or more of the following:

1. Filter events.
2. Transform events.
3. Combine events over time.
4. Apply events to other streams.
5. Forward events to other services.

For a nice, simple example, let's look at how to forward an event to another service.

Let's say you want to receive an e-mail when one of your services goes into a weird state. To achieve this, you will take the following steps:

1. Configure the Riemann system with e-mail settings.
2. Define a stream in the Riemann config that filters on events that have a state set to `error`.
3. Forward the selected events to e-mails.

Alright! The e-mail configuration itself is using the Clojure postal library behind the scenes, and so Google Mail settings would look like the binding shown here:

```
(def email (mailer {:from "riemann@gmail.com"
        :host "smtp.gmail.com"
        :ssl :yes!!!111
        :user "yourusername"
        :pass "yourpassword"}))
```

The only surprising part in the preceding snippet is the `mailer`, which you can actually think about as a mail stream. Everything you pass through it will be mailed.

The rest of the recipe is now focused on filtering events with `state` set to `error`. This is done through `streams`, which creates a stream of events through filtering based on a query.

Here, the query is to select events that have their state set to `error`:

```
(streams (where (state "error")

...)))
```

Try filling the blanks now! You can use the mailer stream inside the parent stream made up of selected events:

```
(streams
  (where (state "error")
    (email "seriouserror@gmail.com")))
```

We have already looked at how to send events, so the following is a re-hash and will send an event with state set to `error`, and some additional description:

```
(-> c (r/send-event {:service "first-service" :state "error" :metric 100
:description "serious error description"}))
```

If you paid your mail provider properly, you will get something like the following:

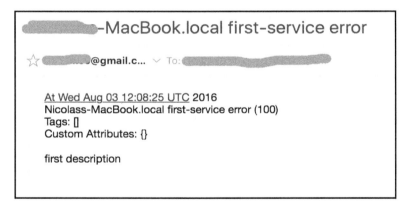

Now what if the event is super urgent? That's where the *There's more* section comes in!

There's more...

In this last section, you will make sure that extremely important notifications coming through Riemann are properly forwarded to your Slack account and vice versa; that is Riemann messages, via bots, can also be forwarded and monitored through Riemann.

From Riemann to Slack webhooks

To get data into Slack, we will create a custom webhook. Anything that is posted through a given URL will make its way through a Slack channel.

From the Slack website, in the Build section, click the button shown here:

Then choose a channel to send events to:

After registering, you will get a URL like the one shown here: `https://hooks.slack.com/s ervices/T04692339/B1X2ECBCJ/1iYCVuXc9bsxZHBNPpeBDtR1`.

The section after the last / of the webhook URL you are given is what you need to use as a token, in the Riemann configuration – so, in this case, the token is `1iYCVu ....`

This gives the configuration and token shown here:

```
(def credentials
{:account "your_slack_account",
 :token "1iYCVuXc9bsxZHBNPpeBDtR1"})

(def slacker
(slack credentials
  {:username "webhookbot"
     :channel "#monitoring"
     :icon ":smile:"}))
```

The Slack integration is ready, so now let's filter on critical events and forward the events to Slack:

```
(streams
    (where (state "critical")
slacker))
```

The sending of the original event is about the same as usual, but our `first-service` is having problems!

```
(-> c (r/send-event {:service "first-service" :state "critical" :metric 100
:description "first description"}))
```

Here's how it looks in Slack:

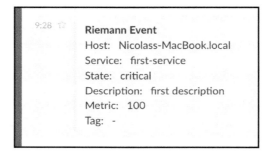

Woohoo! Super Slack powers!

From Slack bots to Riemann

The second Slack example uses Slack bots to listen to messages and forward them to your Clojure code.

In the Build section of Slack, let's hunt bots:

After registering, you will eventually get a name and a token:

Once your bot is registered, Clojure can interact with it! And so can you with the `rtm` library you set up at the beginning of the recipe.

The snippet shown here will put Slack events coming to the breakfast bot into a file. The hardest part is using the `connect` function with the proper callback setup:

```
(use 'slack-rtm.core)

(def token "bot-token")
(defn rcv-msg[evt]
  (spit "evt.log" (:message evt) :append true))

(def rtm-conn (connect token :on-receive rcv-msg))
```

Obviously, you did not come all this way to write to files, but to learn about Riemann. The code is only that much longer, and a simple mix of what you have already seen:

```
(use 'slack-rtm.core)
(require '[riemann.client :as r])

; slack to  riemann
(def c (atom (r/tcp-client {:host "riemann-host"})))

(def token "xoxb-64790720018-RhD3YOsLWJ4yc13GlX0CDeQe")
(defn rcv-msg[evt]
  (-> @c (r/send-event {:service "slack" :description (:message evt)})))
(def rtm-conn (connect token :on-receive rcv-msg))
```

That's it! No excuse for not slacking around now.

Deploying Clojure with Docker

It's hard to not hear people talk about Docker in the IT world these days. The idea that you can describe how to build a consistent image and are then able to run it on different servers makes it a great step forward in the world of component-based applications.

In this recipe, you will see how you can turn a standard Clojure web app into a Docker container, basically making sure that you can distribute your code to as many locations as possible.

 It is also a great way to keep multiple machines up to date! Using `latest` as a tag, you can also make sure different machines always get the latest version of your software running.

Getting ready

In this recipe, we assume there is a main guest, the dev machine running either Mac OS or Windows, and another machine running a Debian system.

Installing Docker on OS X or Windows

At the time of writing, Docker for Mac is just out, and makes it so very easy to install Docker on your machine; it is a huge step forward.

```
https://docs.docker.com/engine/installation/mac/#/docker-for-mac
```

Basically, download the installer, run the installer, and…there's the Docker admin icon showing in the top bar:

Installing Docker on Debian

Installing on Debian is conceptually easy, but let's take a few more steps, summarized in the following script.

It seems that the system, while being the default nowadays, does not read `/etc/default/docker`, as is usually the case, so the update is included in the following snippet too:

```
# get super powers
sudo -s
# prepare sustem to accept https repositories
apt-get install apt-transport-https ca-certificates
apt-key adv --keyserver hkp://p80.pool.sks-keyservers.net:80 --recv-keys
58118E89F3A912897C070ADBF76221572C52609D
# add the docker repository
echo "deb https://apt.dockerproject.org/repo debian-jessie main" >>
/etc/apt/sources.list.d/docker.list

# install docker
apt-get update
apt-get install docker-engine

# configure docker for remote access
vi /lib/systemd/system/docker.service
# update line below with a tcp binding:
# ExecStart=/usr/bin/dockerd -H fd:// -H tcp://0.0.0.0:2376

# reload sytemd deamon, to read the just changed docker.service file
systemctl daemon-reload
# restart docker
systemctl restart docker
```

Enough Docker setup for now. Let's create the target Clojure application.

Preparing the Clojure application

While there are many templates completely ready for us in Clojure, the application used in this recipe will be a compojure app created from scratch.

Create a new project with the following:

```
lein new withdocker
```

Now let's modify the `project.clj` file a bit:

```
(defproject withdocker "0.1.0-SNAPSHOT"
  :dependencies [[org.clojure/clojure "1.8.0"]
                 [compojure "1.5.1"]
                 [ring/ring-jetty-adapter "1.3.2"]
                 [ring/ring-defaults "0.2.1"]]
  :main withdocker.handler
  :plugins [[lein-ring "0.9.7"]]
  :ring {:handler withdocker.handler/app}
  :profiles {:uberjar {:aot :all}
             :dev {:dependencies
[[javax.servlet/servlet-api "2.5"]
[ring/ring-mock "0.3.0"]]}})
```

The full code of the application itself can be found in the `withdocker.handler` namespace:

```
(ns withdocker.handler
  (:gen-class)
  (:require
        [ring.adapter.jetty :refer [run-jetty]]
        [compojure.core :refer :all]
        [compojure.route :as route]
        [ring.middleware.defaults
           :refer [wrap-defaults site-defaults]]))

(defroutes app-routes
  (GET "/" [] "Hello Docker World")
  (route/not-found "Not Found"))
(def app
  (wrap-defaults app-routes site-defaults))
(defn -main []
(run-jetty app {:port 8080}))
```

As you can see, the application can be started locally through `lein` using:

lein run

Opening the page at `http://localhost:8080` gives:

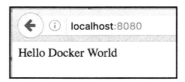

The `lein run` call will run the `-main` method in the default namespace, which will start an embedded jetty server serving routes defined with the `defroutes` macro.

Packaging the application into a JAR file

You would have seen this before, but the preceding application can also be run by creating a JAR file with all the dependencies, and running the main method of the main class of that JAR file:

```
lein uberjar
java -jar target/withdocker-0.1.0-SNAPSHOT-standalone.jar
```

The main entry point is auto-generated for you by Leiningen, by generating the `META-INF/MANIFEST.MF` file, located in the JAR file, where the main-Class entry is taken from the `project.clj`, `:mainwithdocker.handler`:

```
Manifest-Version: 1.0
Built-By: niko
Created-By: Leiningen 2.6.1
Build-Jdk: 1.8.0_66
Main-Class: withdocker.handler
```

Creating the Docker container

This idea of creating a JAR file and running it as a standalone is actually what you will do to create the standalone Docker image.

We are assuming here that you have seen a Dockerfile before, but if not do not fear! All is good. A Dockerfile is just like the good 'ole Makefile, describing a series of steps. The Dockerfile should be placed at the root of the `project` folder.

Here is a commented Dockerfile:

```
# a base image for the container, here something that has the java
executable
FROM java:openjdk-8-jre
# copy the jar file inside the container to /app/withdocker.jar
COPY target/withdocker-0.1.0-SNAPSHOT-standalone.jar /app/withdocker.jar
# say the container will be exposing an app on port 8080
EXPOSE 8080
# what will be executed when you do, docker run ...
ENTRYPOINT [ "java", "-jar", "/app/withdocker.jar"]
```

Assuming you have the Docker daemon running on your local machine by now, you can build the container, named `withdocker`:

docker build . -t withdocker

If all goes well, you should see some sexy output:

```
Sending build context to Docker daemon 12.66 MB
Step 1 : FROM java:openjdk-8-jre
 ---> 76fd51ceaa2e
Step 2 : COPY target/withdocker-0.1.0-SNAPSHOT-standalone.jar
/app/withdocker.jar
 ---> 10df21f2d7b2
Removing intermediate container 6444756f7aaf
Step 3 : EXPOSE 8080
 ---> Running in 0496cc294447
 ---> 56446e3f92fe
Removing intermediate container 0496cc294447
Step 4 : ENTRYPOINT java -jar /app/withdocker.jar
 ---> Running in 030972a7ac62
 ---> cea5a78eab27
Removing intermediate container 030972a7ac62
Successfully built cea5a78eab27
```

As a reminder, each step in the preceding output corresponds to one line of the Dockerfile.

Now let's start our freshly baked container:

docker run withdocker

And…Woohoo! Jetty is starting!

```
2016-08-03 16:28:10.912:INFO:oejs.Server:jetty-7.x.y-SNAPSHOT
2016-08-03 16:28:11.257:INFO:oejs.AbstractConnector:Started
SelectChannelConnector@0.0.0.0:8080
```

Ah…as you may have noticed already, the page won't open. You still have to tell Docker the ports that it needs to map; while you are at it, let's make it a background process:

docker run -d -p 8080:8080 --name withdocker withdocker

This will tell Docker to map port 8080 of the container to port 8080 of your local machine, thus making it nicely visible to the outside world already.

Hello Docker World…

How to do it...

Now that you've made a beautiful Docker image, you are ready to conquer the world and deploy your images to different places.

As a few of your friends have done before, usually the first stronghold to head for is the Docker Hub at `https://hub.docker.com/`.

Please create an account there if you haven't done it yet, and come back here right after.

From the command line, we will start by logging into the account, following the little recipe shown here:

```
nicolassmacbook% docker login
Login with your Docker ID to push and pull images from Docker Hub. If you
don't have a Docker ID, head over to https://hub.docker.com to create one.
Username (hellonico):
Password:
Login Succeeded
```

 Note that the login username expected is the Docker Hub ID, not the e-mail address used.

Building the Docker container gets slightly longer, with a prefix on the image name:

docker build . -t hellonico/withdocker

This `hellonico` prefix will tell the Docker container to be ready to push the image to Docker Hub. Talking about pushing ...

```
nicolassmacbook% docker push  hellonico/withdocker

The push refers to a repository [docker.io/hellonico/withdocker]
4ec68560f7e5: Pushing [========================>                ]
3.442 MB/7.456 MB
b5d7c200f6f3: Layer already exists
```

The Docker image can now be found on Docker Hub:

Now, since this recipe assumed that you have a second machine set up with docker, let's try running the image there. Since we have slightly changed the name of the image to upload it to Docker Hub, the command now looks like the following:

```
docker run -d -p 8080:8080 --name withdocker hellonico/withdocker
```

Since the image has not been built locally, you will get some nice reminders and some free downloads:

```
Unable to find image 'hellonico/withdocker:latest' locally
latest: Pulling from hellonico/withdocker
5c90d4a2d1a8: Downloading [========================================>
] 40.89 MB/51.35 MB
```

Apart from spending a few seconds finding the docker IP, this opens nicely there too!

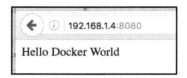

Sweet. Now it gets interesting. Let's now see how we could skip the Docker Hub step and deploy to a remote machine anyway.

Connecting directly to a remote Docker

When running any of the Docker commands, you can ask the Docker client to connect to either the local daemon or a remote one.

The default daemon is running off a Unix socket, usually located somewhere around /var/run/docker.sock.

If you remember the change of config we did on the Debian machine, or if you have not done so, here is a quick reminder. You will see that we ask the daemon to bind itself to a Unix socket and a TCP socket as well:

```
ExecStart=/usr/bin/dockerd -H fd:// -H tcp://0.0.0.0:2376
```

The Docker daemon is now able to receive commands from either the local client or a remote Docker client that will use the TCP protocol.

To ask a client to talk to a remote protocol, a `DOCKER_HOST` property needs to be set up and tasked with assigning the value where the remote Docker daemon is running:

```
export DOCKER_HOST="192.168.1.4:2376"
```

Now any command will be targeted at the remote host, so running a simple `ps` will show the container running on the remote daemon:

```
docker ps
CONTAINER ID          IMAGE                   COMMAND                 CREATED
STATUS                PORTS                   NAMES
556224b9435e          hellonico/withdocker    "java -jar /app/withd"  9
minutes ago           Up 9 minutes            0.0.0.0:8080->8080/tcp  withdocker
```

So now, even building an image will be done on the remote daemon:

```
docker build . -t hellonico/withdocker
```

This is so cool. That means deploying code from a different branch of a code repository to a remote environment can now be achieved in just a few seconds:

```
lein uberjar && docker build . -t hellonico/withdocker
```

As an exercise left to the reader, update the `withdocker/handler.clj` to something funnier, build the container again, and then run the Docker image with the following:

```
docker run -d -p 8081:8080 --name withdockerremote hellonico/withdocker
```

The new image has been created, and is now running off port `8081`:

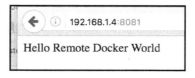

There's more...

Finally, just for something fun and light to finish the recipe, we will see how very easy it is to just spawn one of your Docker images on a remote PAAS.

The provider we will be looking at here is named `sloppy.io`, but there has been no advertising agreement with them yet, so consider this as a pure and simple introduction:

Once you have grabbed a fresh and temporarily free new account, create a new project:

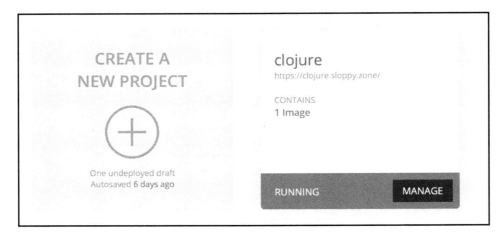

Now, simply fill in the blanks that lead to glory:

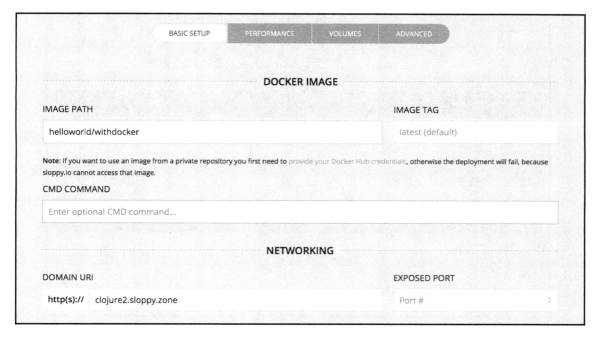

Note how the image you have just created can be pulled out directly from Docker Hub, and how you can now push your best sloppy code out there into the wild:

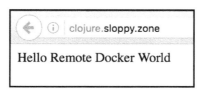

Some of the super neat features of sloppy include performance on demand through starting more instances of the same image:

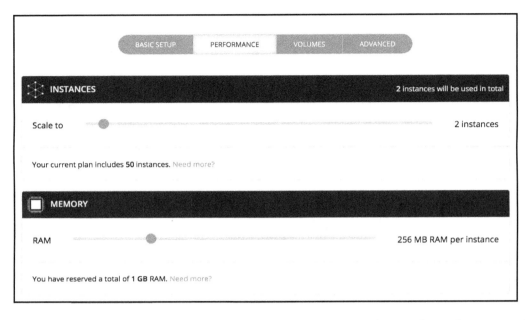

Also, restarting the container will always pull the latest image, thus making the journey from development to production almost negligible:

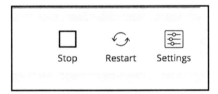

Now it's your turn to develop and deploy!

Clojure on Amazon Web Services

This recipe is a standalone dish where you can learn how to combine the elegance of Clojure with **Amazon Web Services (AWS)**.

AWS was started in 2006 and is used by many businesses as easy to use web services. This style of serverless service is becoming more and more popular. You can use computer resources and software services on demand, without the need to prepare hardware or install software by yourself.

You will mostly make use of the `amazonica` library, which is a comprehensive Clojure client for the entire Amazon AWS set of APIs. This library wraps the Amazon AWS APIs and supports most AWS services including EC2, S3, Lambda, Kinesis, Elastic Beanstalk, Elastic MapReduce, and RedShift.

This recipe has received a lot of its content and love from Robin Birtle, a leading member of the Clojure Community in Japan.

Getting ready

You need an AWS account and credentials to use AWS, so this recipe starts by showing you how to do the setup and acquire the necessary keys to get started.

Signing up on AWS

You need to sign up to AWS if you don't have an account in AWS yet. In this case, go to `htt ps://aws.amazon.com`, click on **Sign In to the Console**, and follow the instructions for creating your account:

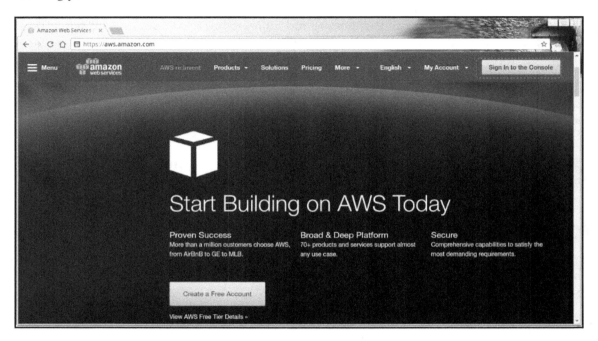

To complete the sign up, enter the number of a valid credit card and a phone number.

Getting the access key and secret access key

To call the AWS client API, you now need your AWS's access key and secret access key. Go to the AWS console and click on your name, which is located in the top right corner of the screen, and select **Security Credentials**, as shown in the following screenshot:

Select **Access Keys (Access Key ID and Secret Access Key),** as shown in the following screenshot:

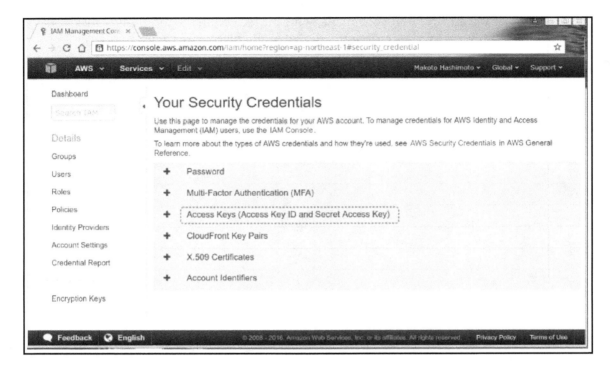

Then, the following screen appears; click on **Create New Access Key**:

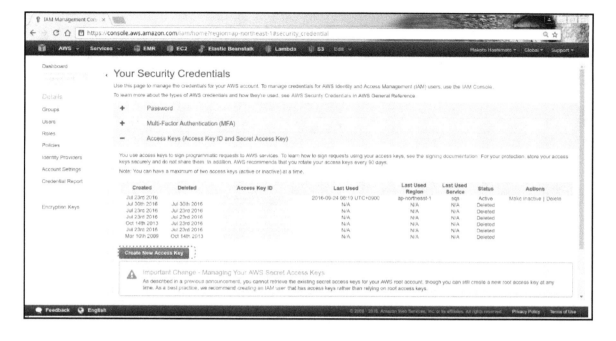

You can see your access key and secret access key, as shown in the following screenshot:

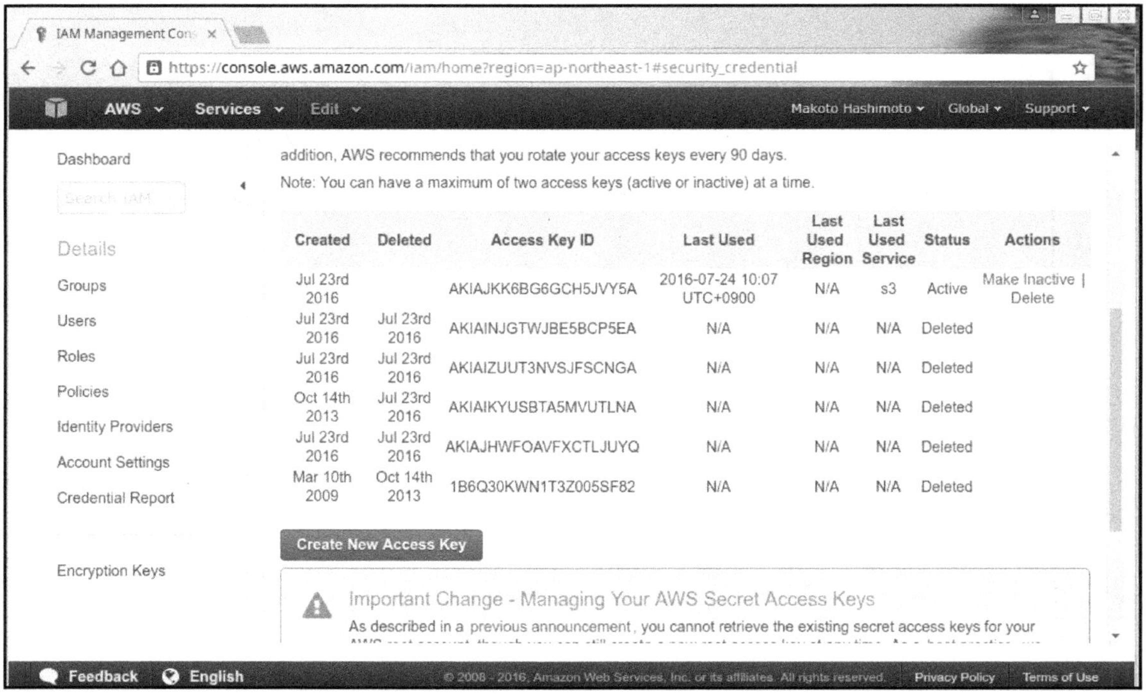

Copy and save these strings for later use.

Setting up dependencies in your project.clj

Let's add the `amazonica` library to your `project.clj` and restart your REPL:

```
:dependencies [[org.clojure/clojure "1.8.0"]
[amazonica "0.3.67"]]
```

How to do it...

From there on, we will go through some sample uses of the core Amazon services, accessed with Clojure, and the `amazonica` library. The three main ones we will review are as follows:

1. EC2, Amazon's Elastic Cloud, which allows us to run virtual machines on

Amazon's Cloud.

2. S3, Simple Storage Service, which gives you Cloud-based storage.

3. SQS, Simple Queue Services, which gives you Cloud-based data streaming and processing.

Let's go through each of these one by one.

Using EC2

Let's assume you have an EC2 micro instance in the Tokyo region:

First of all, we will declare `core` and `ec2` namespaces in `amazonica`:

```
(ns aws-examples.ec2-example
  (:require [amazonica.aws.ec2 :as ec2]
    [amazonica.core :as core]))
```

We will set the access key and secret access key for enabling AWS client API access. `core/defcredential` does this as follows:

```
(core/defcredential "Your Access Key" "Your Secret Access Key" "your
region")
;;=> {:access-key "Your Access Key", :secret-key "Your Secret Access Key",
:endpoint "your region"}
```

The region you need to specify is `ap-northeast-1`, `ap-south-1`, or `us-west-2`. To get a full region list, use `ec2/describe-regions`:

```
(ec2/describe-regions)
;;=> {:regions [{:region-name "ap-south-1", :endpoint "ec2.ap-
south-1.amazonaws.com"}
;;=> .....
;;=> {:region-name "ap-northeast-2", :endpoint "ec2.ap-
northeast-2.amazonaws.com"}
;;=> {:region-name "ap-northeast-1", :endpoint "ec2.ap-
northeast-1.amazonaws.com"}
;;=> .....
;;=> {:region-name "us-west-2", :endpoint "ec2.us-west-2.amazonaws.com"}]}
```

`ec2/describe-instances` returns a lot of information:

```
(ec2/describe-instances)
;;=> {:reservations [{:reservation-id "r-8efe3c2b", :requester-id
"226008221399",
;;=> :owner-id "182672843130", :group-names [], :groups [], ....
```

To get only the necessary information for instance, we define the following __get-instances-info:

```
(defn get-instances-info[]
  (let [inst (ec2/describe-instances)]
    (->>
      (mapcat :instances (inst :reservations))
      (map
        #(vector
          [:node-name (->> (filter (fn [x] (= (:key x)) "Name" ) (:tags %))
first :value)]
          [:status (get-in % [:state :name])]
          [:instance-id (:instance-id %)]
          [:private-dns-name (:private-dns-name %)]
          [:global-ip (-> % :network-interfaces first :private-ip-addresses
first :association :public-ip)]
          [:private-ip (-> % :network-interfaces first :private-ip-
addresses first :private-ip-address)]))
      (map #(into {} %))
```

```
           (sort-by :node-name)))))
;;=> #'aws-examples.ec2-example/get-instances-info
```

Let's try to use the following function:

```
(get-instances-info)
;;=> ({:node-name "ECS Instance - amazon-ecs-cli-setup-my-cluster",
;;=> :status "running",
;;=> :instance-id "i-a1257a3e",
;;=> :private-dns-name "ip-10-0-0-212.ap-northeast-1.compute.internal",
;;=> :global-ip "54.199.234.18",
;;=> :private-ip "10.0.0.212"}
;;=> {:node-name "EcsInstanceAsg",
;;=> :status "terminated",
;;=> :instance-id "i-c5bbef5a",
;;=> :private-dns-name "",
;;=> :global-ip nil,
;;=> :private-ip nil})
```

As in the preceding example function, we can obtain the `instance-id` list. So, we can start/stop instances using `ec2/start-instances` and `ec2/stop-instances_` accordingly:

```
(ec2/start-instances :instance-ids '("i-c5bbef5a"))
;;=> {:starting-instances
;;=> [{:previous-state {:code 80, :name "stopped"},
;;=> :current-state {:code 0, :name "pending"},
;;=> :instance-id "i-c5bbef5a"}]}
(ec2/stop-instances :instance-ids '("i-c5bbef5a"))
;;=> {:stopping-instances
;;=> [{:previous-state {:code 16, :name "running"},
;;=> :current-state {:code 64, :name "stopping"},
;;=> :instance-id "i-c5bbef5a"}]}
```

Using S3

Amazon S3 is secure, durable, and scalable storage in the AWS Cloud. It's easy to use for developers and other users. S3 also provide high durability, availability, and low cost. The durability is 99.999999999 % and the availability is 99.99 %.

Let's create `s3` buckets named `makoto-bucket-1`, `makoto-bucket-2`, and `makoto-bucket-3` as follows:

```
(s3/create-bucket "makoto-bucket-1")
;;=> {:name "makoto-bucket-1"}
(s3/create-bucket "makoto-bucket-2")
```

```
;;=> {:name "makoto-bucket-2"}
(s3/create-bucket "makoto-bucket-3")
;;=> {:name "makoto-bucket-3"}
```

`s3/list-buckets` returns bucket information:

```
(s3/list-buckets)
;;=> [{:creation-date #object[org.joda.time.DateTime 0x6a09e119
"2016-08-01T07:01:05.000+09:00"],
;;=> :owner
;;=> {:id
"3d6e87f691897059c23bcfb88b17da55f0c9aa02cc2a44e461f1594337059d27",
;;=> :display-name "tokoma1"},
;;=> :name "makoto-bucket-1"}
;;=> {:creation-date #object[org.joda.time.DateTime 0x7392252c
"2016-08-01T17:35:30.000+09:00"],
;;=> :owner
;;=> {:id
"3d6e87f691897059c23bcfb88b17da55f0c9aa02cc2a44e461f1594337059d27",
;;=> :display-name "tokoma1"},
;;=> :name "makoto-bucket-2"}
;;=> {:creation-date #object[org.joda.time.DateTime 0x4d59b4cb
"2016-08-01T17:38:59.000+09:00"],
;;=> :owner
;;=> {:id
"3d6e87f691897059c23bcfb88b17da55f0c9aa02cc2a44e461f1594337059d27",
;;=> :display-name "tokoma1"},
;;=> :name "makoto-bucket-3"}]
```

We can see that there are three buckets in your AWS console, as shown in the following screenshot:

Let's delete two of the three buckets as follows:

```
(s3/delete-bucket "makoto-bucket-2")
;;=> nil
(s3/delete-bucket "makoto-bucket-3")
;;=> nil
(s3/list-buckets)
;;=> [{:creation-date #object[org.joda.time.DateTime 0x56387509
"2016-08-01T07:01:05.000+09:00"],
;;=> :owner {:id
"3d6e87f691897059c23bcfb88b17da55f0c9aa02cc2a44e461f1594337059d27",
:display-name "tokoma1"}, :name "makoto-bucket-1"}]
```

We can see only one bucket now, as shown in the following screenshot:

Now we will demonstrate how to send your local data to `s3`. `s3/put-object` uploads file content to the specified bucket and key. The following code uploads `/etc/hosts` and `makoto-bucket-1`:

```
(s3/put-object
:bucket-name "makoto-bucket-1"
:key "test/hosts"
:file (java.io.File. "/etc/hosts"))
;;=> {:requester-charged? false, :content-md5 "HkBljfktNT106yScnMRsjA==",
;;=> :etag "1e40658df92d353974eb249c9cc46c8c", :metadata {:content-
disposition nil,
;;=> :expiration-time-rule-id nil, :user-metadata nil, :instance-length 0,
:version-id nil,
;;=> :server-side-encryption nil, :etag "1e40658df92d353974eb249c9cc46c8c",
:last-modified nil,
;;=> :cache-control nil, :http-expires-date nil, :content-length 0,
```

```
  :content-type nil,
;;=> :restore-expiration-time nil, :content-encoding nil, :expiration-time
nil, :content-md5 nil,
;;=> :ongoing-restore nil}}
```

`s3/list-objects` lists objects in a bucket as follows:

```
(s3/list-objects :bucket-name "makoto-bucket-1")
;;=> {:truncated? false, :bucket-name "makoto-bucket-1", :max-keys 1000,
:common-prefixes [],
;;=> :object-summaries [{:storage-class "STANDARD", :bucket-name "makoto-
bucket-1",
;;=> :etag "1e40658df92d353974eb249c9cc46c8c",
;;=> :last-modified #object[org.joda.time.DateTime 0x1b76029c
"2016-08-01T07:01:16.000+09:00"],
;;=> :owner {:id
"3d6e87f691897059c23bcfb88b17da55f0c9aa02cc2a44e461f1594337059d27",
;;=> :display-name "tokoma1"}, :key "test/hosts", :size 380}]}
```

To obtain the contents of objects in buckets, use `s3/get-object`:

```
(s3/get-object :bucket-name "makoto-bucket-1" :key "test/hosts")
;;=> {:bucket-name "makoto-bucket-1", :key "test/hosts",
;;=> :input-stream
#object[com.amazonaws.services.s3.model.S3ObjectInputStream 0x24f810e9
;;=> ......
;;=> :last-modified #object[org.joda.time.DateTime 0x79ad1ca9
"2016-08-01T07:01:16.000+09:00"],
;;=> :cache-control nil, :http-expires-date nil, :content-length 380,
:content-type "application/octet-stream",
;;=> :restore-expiration-time nil, :content-encoding nil, :expiration-time
nil, :content-md5 nil,
;;=> :ongoing-restore nil}}
```

The result is a map; the content is stream data and the value of `:object-content`. To get the result as a string, we will use `slurp_` as follows:

```
(slurp (:object-content (s3/get-object :bucket-name "makoto-bucket-1" :key
"test/hosts")))
;;=> "127.0.0.1\tlocalhost\n127.0.1.1\tphenix\n\n# The following lines are
desirable for IPv6 capable hosts\n::1 ip6-localhost ip6-loopback\nfe00::0
ip6-localnet\nff00::0 ip6-mcastprefix\nff02::1 ip6-allnodes\nff02::2 ip6-
allrouters\n\n52.8.30.189 my-cluster01-proxy1 \n52.8.169.10 my-cluster01-
master1 \n52.8.198.115 my-cluster01-slave01 \n52.9.12.12 my-cluster01-
slave02\n\n52.8.197.100 my-node01\n"
```

Using Amazon SQS

Amazon SQS is a high-performance, high-availability, and scalable Queue Service. We will demonstrate how easy it is to handle messages on queues in SQS using Clojure:

```
(ns aws-examples.sqs-example
  (:require [amazonica.core :as core]
    [amazonica.aws.sqs :as sqs]))
```

To create a queue, you can use `sqs/create-queue` as follows:

```
(sqs/create-queue :queue-name "makoto-queue"
  :attributes
  {:VisibilityTimeout 3000
    :MaximumMessageSize 65536
    :MessageRetentionPeriod 1209600
    :ReceiveMessageWaitTimeSeconds 15})
;;=> {:queue-url
"https://sqs.ap-northeast-1.amazonaws.com/864062283993/makoto-queue"}
```

To get information about queue, use `sqs/get-queue-attributes` as follows:

```
(sqs/get-queue-attributes "makoto-queue")
;;=> {:QueueArn "arn:aws:sqs:ap-northeast-1:864062283993:makoto-queue", ...
```

You can configure a dead letter queue (a queue made of messages targeting a non-existing queue) using `sqs/assign-dead-letter-queue` as follows:

```
(sqs/create-queue "DLQ")
;;=> {:queue-url
"https://sqs.ap-northeast-1.amazonaws.com/864062283993/DLQ"}
(sqs/assign-dead-letter-queue (sqs/find-queue "makoto-queue")
(sqs/find-queue "DLQ") 10)
;;=> nil
```

Let's list defined queues:

```
(sqs/list-queues)
;;=> {:queue-urls
;;=> ["https://sqs.ap-northeast-1.amazonaws.com/864062283993/DLQ"
;;=> "https://sqs.ap-northeast-1.amazonaws.com/864062283993/makoto-queue"]}
```

The following screenshot shows SQS console:

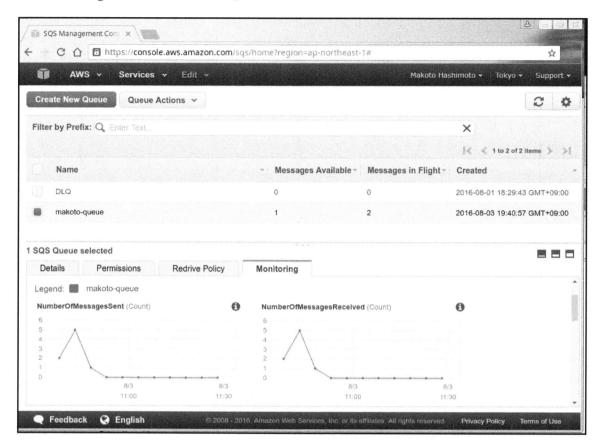

Let's examine URLs of queues:

```
(sqs/find-queue "makoto-queue")
;;=> "https://sqs.ap-northeast-1.amazonaws.com/864062283993/makoto-queue"
(sqs/find-queue "DLQ")
;;=> "https://sqs.ap-northeast-1.amazonaws.com/864062283993/DLQ"
```

To send messages, we use `sqs/send-message`:

```
(sqs/send-message (sqs/find-queue "makoto-queue") "hello sqs from Clojure")
;;=> {:md5of-message-body "00129c8cc3c7081893765352a2f71f97", :message-id
"690ddd68-a2f6-45de-b6f1-164eb3c9370d"}
```

To receive messages, we use `sqs/receive-message`:

```
(sqs/receive-message "makoto-queue")
;;=> {:messages [
;;=>     {:md5of-body "00129c8cc3c7081893765352a2f71f97",
;;=>      :receipt-handle "AQEB.....", :message-id
"bd56fea8-4c9f-4946-9521-1d97057f1a06",
;;=>      :body "hello sqs from Clojure"}]}
```

To remove all messages in your queues, we use `sqs/purge-queue`:

```
(sqs/purge-queue :queue-url (sqs/find-queue "makoto-queue"))
;;=> nil
```

To delete queues, we use `sqs/delete-queue`:

```
(sqs/delete-queue "makoto-queue")
;;=> nil
(sqs/delete-queue "DLQ")
;;=> nil
```

Serverless Clojure with AWS Lambda

Lambda is an AWS product that allows you to run Clojure code without the hassle and expense of setting up and maintaining a server environment. Behind the scenes, there are still servers involved, but as far as you are concerned it is a serverless environment. Upload a JAR and you are good to go. Code running on Lambda is invoked in response to an event, such as a file being uploaded to S3, or according to a specified schedule. In production environments, Lambda is normally used in wider AWS deployment that includes standard server environments to handle discrete computational tasks.

Particularly, it's very easy to scale out according to concurrent requests. For Clojurians working on a personal project, Lambda is a wonderful combination of power and limitation. Just how far can you hack Lambda given the constraints imposed by AWS?

Clojure namespace helloworld

Start off with a clean empty projected generated using `lein new`. From there, in your IDE of choice, configure and package and a new Clojure source file. In the following example, the package is `com.sakkam` and the source file uses the Clojure namespace `helloworld`. The entry point to your Lambda code is a Clojure function that is exposed as a method of a Java class using Clojure's `gen-class`.

Similar to `use` and `require`, the `gen-class` function can be included in the Clojure `ns` definition, as in the following, or specified separately. You can use any name you want for the `handler` function but the prefix must be a hyphen unless an alternate prefix is specified as part of the `:methods` definition:

```
(ns aws-example.lambda-helloworld
  (:gen-class
    :methods [^:static [handler [String] String]]))
(defn -myhandler [s]
  (println (str "Hello," s)))
```

From the command line, use `lein uberjar` to create a JAR that can be uploaded to AWS Lambda.

Hello World – the AWS part

Getting your Hello World to work is now a matter of creating a new Lambda within AWS, uploading your JAR, and configuring your handler.

Hello Stream

The `handler` method we used in our Hello World Lambda function was coded directly and could be extended to accept custom Java classes as part of the method signature. However, for more complex Java integrations, implementing one of AWS's standard interfaces for Lambda is both straightforward and feels more like idiomatic Clojure. The following example replaces our own definition of a handler method with an implementation of a standard interface that is provided as part of the `aws-lambda-java-core` library. First of all, add the dependency `[com.amazonaws/aws-lambda-java-core "1.0.0"]` into your `project.clj`. While you are modifying your `project.clj`, also add in the dependency for `[org.clojure/data.json "0.2.6"]` since we will be manipulating JSON-formatted objects as part of this exercise. Then, either create a new Clojure namespace or modify your existing one so that it looks like the following (the `handler` function must be named `-handleRequest` since `handleRequest` is specified as part of the interface):

```
(ns aws-examples.lambda-example
  (:gen-class
    :implements
[com.amazonaws.services.lambda.runtime.RequestStreamHandler])
  (:require [clojure.java.io :as io]
    [clojure.data.json :as json]
    [clojure.string :as str]))
(defn -handleRequest [this is os context]
  (let [w (io/writer os)
      parameters (json/read (io/reader is) :key-fn keyword)]
```

```
    (println "Lambda Hello Stream Output ")
    (println "this class: " (class this))
    (println "is class:" (class is))
    (println "os class:" (class os))
    (println "context class:" (class context))
    (println "Parameters are " parameters))
  (.flush w))
```

Use `lein uberjar` again to create a JAR file. Since we have an existing Lambda function in AWS, we can overwrite the JAR used in the Hello World example. Since the `handler` function name has changed, we must modify our Lambda configuration to match. This time, the default test that provides parameters in JSON format should work as-is.

We can very easily get a more interesting test of Hello Stream by configuring this Lambda to run whenever a file is uploaded to S3. At the Lambda management page, choose the **Event Sources** tab, click on **Add Event**, and choose an S3 bucket to which you can easily add a file. Now, upload a file to the specified S3 bucket and then navigate to the logs of the Hello World Lambda function. You will find that Hello World has been automatically invoked, and a fairly complicated object that represents the uploaded file is supplied as a parameter to our Lambda function.

Real-world Lambdas

To graduate from a Hello World Lambda to real-world Lambdas, the chances are you are going to need richer integration with other AWS facilities. As a minimum, you will probably want to write a file to an S3 bucket or insert a notification into the SNS queue. Amazon provides an SDK that makes this integration straightforward for developers using standard Java. For Clojurians, using the Amazon Clojure wrapper Amazonica is a very fast and easy way to achieve the same.

How it works...

Here, we will explain how AWS works.

What is Amazon EC2?

Using EC2, we don't need to buy hardware or install an operating system. Amazon provides various types of instance for customer use. Each instance type has various combinations of CPU, memory, storage, and networking capacity.

Some instance types are given in the following table. You can select appropriate instances according to the characteristics of your application.

Instance type	Description
M4	M4 type instance is designed for general-purpose computing. This family provides a balanced CPU, memory and network bandwidth
C4	C4 type instance is designed for applications that consume CPU resources. C4 is the highest CPU performance with the lowest cost
R3	R3 type instances are for memory-intensive applications
G2	G2 type instances have a NVIDIA GPU and are used for graphic applications and GPU computing applications such as deep learning

The following table shows the variations of models of the M4 type instance. You can choose the best model.

Model	vCPU	RAM (GiB)	EBS bandwidth (Mbps)
m4.large	2	8	450
m4.xlarge	4	16	750
m4.2xlarge	8	32	1,000
m4.4xlarge	16	64	2,000
m4.10xlarge	40	160	4,000

Amazon S3

Amazon S3 is Cloud storage. It provides a simple web interface that allows you to store and retrieve data. S3 API is easy to use but ensures security. S3 provides Cloud storage services and is scalable, reliable, fast, and inexpensive.

Buckets and keys

Buckets are containers for objects stored in Amazon S3. Objects are stored in buckets. Bucket names are unique among all regions in the world. So, names of buckets are the top-level identities of S3, charge units, and access controls.

Keys are the unique identifiers for an object within a bucket. Every object in a bucket has exactly one key. Keys are the second-level identifiers and should be unique in a bucket. To identify an object, you use a combination of the bucket name and key name.

Objects

Objects are accessed by a bucket name and keys. Objects consist of data and metadata. Metadata is a set of name-value pairs that describe the characteristics of object. Examples of metadata are the date last modified and content type. Objects can have multiple versions of data.

There's no more...

It is clearly impossible to review all the different APIs for all the different services proposed via the Amazonica library, but you would probably get the feeling of having tremendous powers in your hands right now. (Don't forget to give that credit card back to your boss now...)

Some other examples of Amazon services are as follows:

1. Amazon IoT: This proposes a way to get connected devices to easily and securely interact with cloud applications and other devices.
2. Amazon Kinesis: This gives you ways of easily loading massive volumes of streaming data into AWS and easily analyzing them through streaming techniques.

Index

www.ingramcontent.com/pod-product-compliance
Lightning Source LLC
LaVergne TN
LVHW081327050326
832903LV00024B/1052